# International Studies in Entrepreneurship

Volume 54

This series highlights cutting-edge research in entrepreneurship, small business/SMEs, economic development, and policy. Volumes in the series feature empirical studies, theoretical analyses, practical applications, and policy recommendations in regional and global contexts, and explore a wide variety of topics with regard to entrepreneurship, including demographics, new venture financing, research & development, business creation, labor dynamics, technology management, and education. Springer and Series Editors welcome proposals for research monographs, edited volumes and reference works in all areas of entrepreneurship research.

David B. Audretsch • Iris A. M. Kunadt
Editors

# The COVID-19 Crisis and Entrepreneurship

## Perspectives and Experiences of Researchers, Thought Leaders, and Policymakers

Springer

*Editors*
David B. Audretsch
Institute for Development Strategies
Indiana University
Bloomington, IN, USA

Iris A. M. Kunadt
Institute for Development Strategies
Indiana University
Bloomington, IN, USA

ISSN 1572-1922 ISSN 2197-5884 (electronic)
International Studies in Entrepreneurship
ISBN 978-3-031-04654-4 ISBN 978-3-031-04655-1 (eBook)
https://doi.org/10.1007/978-3-031-04655-1



This Springer imprint is published by the registered company Springer Nature Switzerland AG
The registered company address is: Gewerbestrasse 11, 6330 Cham, Switzerland

# Contents

# About the Editors

**David B. Audretsch** is a Distinguished Professor and the Ameritech Chair of Economic Development at Indiana University, where he also serves as Director of the Institute for Development Strategies. He is an Honorary Professor of Industrial Economics and Entrepreneurship at the WHU-Otto Beisheim School of Management in Germany and a part-time professor of entrepreneurship at the University of Klagenfurt in Austria. Audretsch's research has focused on the links between entrepreneurship, government policy, innovation, economic development, and global competitiveness.

**Iris A. M. Kunadt** holds a Ph.D. from Max Planck Institute of Economics/University of Hamburg. Her research focuses on entrepreneurship, public policy, and strategic management of places. Before starting social and civic entrepreneurship initiatives she worked at Fraunhofer IMW and as a consultant on applied research projects.

# The Journey: Navigating the COVID-19 Crisis

**Iris A. M. Kunadt and David B. Audretsch**

**Abstract** When the COVID-19 disease became a pandemic in Winter/Spring 2020 and one country after the other installed far-reaching lockdowns, it soon became clear that this was a crisis never experienced so far for all parts of our life. This was the starting point of this book. The authors of this chapter and editors of the book point to the unprecedented challenges regarding the economy, democracy, (mental) health, and social life and outline what happened in the years 2020–2022 till the publication of the book. The most fundamental perception that emerged during the COVID-19 pandemic and that is reflected in other chapters is that we live in an era of predictable unpredictability. The most important challenge for the future is how to make societies and the economies resilient to crisis yet to come. This chapter points to entrepreneurs as solution leaders. In a time of great uncertainty entrepreneurs are the ones who are used to live with great uncertainty and take the challenge to look for solutions.

**Keywords** COVID-19 · Entrepreneurs · Uncertainty · Economic shock · Historical event · Democracy · Crisis management

At first reflection, it surely seems like it was, to paraphrase Charles Dickens, "the worst of times." However, upon closer inspection, the great author found in his *Tale of Two Cities* (Dickens, 1859) glimmers of hope and optimism, even where others succumbed to despair and gloom, "It was the best of times, it was the worst of times, it was the age of wisdom, it was the age of foolishness, it was the epoch of belief, it

I. A. M. Kunadt (✉)
Institute for Development Strategies, Indiana University, Bloomington, IN, USA
e-mail: iriskunadt@gmx.net

D. B. Audretsch
Ameritech Chair of Economic Development, Institute for Development Strategies, Indiana University, Bloomington, IN, USA
e-mail: daudrets@indiana.edu



D. B. Audretsch, I. A. M. Kunadt (eds.), *The COVID-19 Crisis and Entrepreneurship*, International Studies in Entrepreneurship 54,
https://doi.org/10.1007/978-3-031-04655-1_1

was the epoch of incredulity, it was the season of light, it was the season of darkness, it was the spring of hope, it was the winter of despair."

And so it was during the Great Pandemic starting in 2020. There was much to morn. As of May 2021, 170 million cases resulting in 3.54 million deaths had been registered globally. And there was more to come. In an extraordinary gesture of unification, the International Labor Organization (ILO), Food and Agricultural Organization (FAO) of the United Nations, International Fund for Agricultural Development (IFAD), and the World Health Organization (WHO) warned. The COVID-19 pandemic has led to a dramatic loss of human life worldwide and presents an unprecedented challenge to public health, food systems, and the world of work. The economic and social disruption caused by the pandemic is devastating: tens of millions of people are at risk of falling into extreme poverty, while the number of undernourished people, currently estimated at nearly 690 million, could increase by up to 132 million by the end of the year".[1]

There was also a plethora of subtle and not so subtle changes that left virtually no one on the planet untouched, ranging from social distancing to mental health, remote work and job insecurity, and at-home schooling. On March 11, 2020, the director general of the World Health Organization (WHO), Dr. Tedros Adhanom Ghebreyesus declared that the spread of the global COVID-19 epidemics had become so prevalent that it constituted a pandemic: "The WHO has been assessing this outbreak around the clock, and we are deeply concerned, both by the alarming levels of spread and severity and by the alarming levels of inaction. We have therefore made the assessment that COVID-19 can be characterized as a pandemic."[2] As *Medical News Today* reflected, "With these few words, Dr. Tedros made clear that the way in which we lived was going to change imminently—and it did."[3]

In fact, the impact on world GDP growth rates is massive and most likely long-lasting and it triggered a health and fiscal response unprecedented in terms of speed and magnitude (Yeyati, 2021). The World Economic Outlook October 2021 states, "The global economy is projected to grow 5.9% in 2021 and 4.9 percent in 2022, 0.1 percentage point lower for 2021 than in the July forecast. The downward revision for 2021 reflects a downgrade for advanced economies—in part due to supply disruptions—and for low-income developing countries, largely due to worsening

[1]" Impact of COVID-19 on people's livelihoods, their health, and our food systems," joint statement by the International Labor Organization (ILO), Food and Agricultural Organization (FAO) of the United Nations, International Fund for Agricultural Development (IFAD), and the World Health Organization (WHO), October 13, 2020, accessed on May 31, 2021 at https://www.who.int/news/item/13-10-2020-impact-of-covid-19-on-people's-livelihoods-their-health-and-our-food-systems.

[2]Maria Cohut, "Global impact of the COVID-19 pandemic: 1 year on," *Medical News Today*, March 12, 2021, accessed on May 31, 2021 at https://www.medicalnewstoday.com/articles/global-impact-of-the-covid-19-pandemic-1-year-on.

[3]Maria Cohut, "Global impact of the COVID-19 pandemic: 1 year on," *Medical News Today*, March 12, 2021, accessed on May 31, 2021 at https://www.medicalnewstoday.com/articles/global-impact-of-the-covid-19-pandemic-1-year-on.

pandemic dynamics. This is partially offset by stronger near-term prospects among some commodity-exporting emerging market and developing economies. Rapid spread of Delta and the threat of new variants have increased uncertainty about how quickly the pandemic can be overcome. Policy choices have become more difficult, with limited room to maneuver."[4]

The impact of the pandemic extended beyond health and economic concerns. As governments responded to the pandemic with draconian policy measures, alarm spread across the globe about a new threat to democracy. As *Forbes* warned, "The COVID-19 pandemic doesn't just threaten people's health. It is also threatening people's civil liberties across the globe. Even before this crisis, democracy was on the decline worldwide."[5]

Some governments used the pandemic as a legitimization for a totalitarian grab for power. "The coronavirus has proved a great boon to the world's authoritarians. From the imposition of border closures to the utilization of mass digital surveillance, moves that may have once been classed as dangerous expansions of state power are now being lauded as necessary steps in the global effort to curb a pandemic. Extraordinary times, it has been collectively agreed, call for extraordinary measures."[6] It seemed that democracy was not well suited for dealing with a global crisis, such as the pandemic. Empirical evidence pointed to a higher incidence of death from COVID-19 exhibited by countries with a greater degree of democracy than by their less democratic counterparts (Cepaluni et al., 2020).

Across the globe, the policy response to the pandemic was through the imposition of suffocating regulations, which greatly curtailed social and private freedoms. These same policy interventions have concomitantly entrenched the powerful and the dominant (Kuckertz et al., 2020). By contrast, civil liberties and individual freedom were sacrificed, as panicked citizens turned to strong governments imposing authoritarian measures for reassurance (Amat et al., 2020).

The extent of human carnage was daunting. The deaths piled up and hospitalizations soared, as families were irrevocably disrupted and traumatized. No price could ever be put on the misery and suffering from social isolation and loss of human contacts. Still, every coin has two sides, and so it was during the pandemic. Babies were born, unions celebrated, and milestones reached. As airports, restaurants, and clubs closed, the gift of a much-needed respite from what had widely been the overwhelming task, and concomitant *Fauda*, or chaos, of juggling work, family,

---

[4] World Economic Outlook October 2021, https://www.imf.org/en/Publications/WEO/Issues/2021/10/12/world-economic-outlook-october-2021.

[5] Evan Gerstmann, "How The COVID-19 Crisis Is Threatening Freedom and Democracy Across the Globe," *Forbes*, April 12, 2020, accessed on April 20, 2020, at https://www.forbes.com/sites/evangerstmann/2020/04/12/how-the-covid-19-crisis-is-threatening-freedom-and-democracy-across-the-globe/#187f4ccc4f16

[6] "The EU Watches as Hungary Kills Democracy," *The Atlantic*, April 2, 2020, accessed on April 11, 2020, at https://www.theatlantic.com/international/archive/2020/04/europe-hungary-viktor-orban-coronavirus-covid19-democracy/609313/

friends, and technology in a globalized era, was silently welcomed by more than a few.

As the world went quiet, reflection and introspection were rediscovered. The pandemic, with all its attendant horrors and tragedies, also imposed such a change of pace in daily living that it was hard not to reflect on what exactly had been lost. Core values and beliefs re-emerged having been lost in the impossible schedules of modern life.

It is exactly such reflections and insights that we aspire to capture and articulate in this book. We had the idea to record the assessments and (personal) impressions of researchers, experts, and policymakers regarding this unique time in all our lives in a book. The challenge was how to provide both focus and scope at the same time. Thanks to guidance from Dr. Prashanth Mahagaonkar, who serves as the Senior Editor of Books for Business, Management & Finance at Springer Nature Publishers, we found our answer. The resulting book includes perspectives spanning a broad spectrum of countries from around the globe. All authors have a background in economics or entrepreneurship. By taking an economic perspective and specifically looking at entrepreneurship, we gain important insights regarding the impact of the pandemic on economic activity apart from statistics. The authors' informed views are a great seismograph indicating future challenges and solutions that are induced by the pandemic. While we can kind of real-time observe the course of the pandemic through indicators like the incidence and hospitalization rate, as well as the vaccination rate, the economic and social impact of the pandemic will become only visible in years to come.

For such a book, we have a role model. As Tolstoy (1887) famously noted, "Happy families are all alike; every unhappy family is unhappy in its own way," so too it is with crises. While being unique, the pandemic was surely not the first such challenge. After the twin devastations of the Great Depression and the Second World War, the world was back at work. But more subtly, that work did not seem to provide the fulfillment and sense of purpose as it had for earlier generations. A sense of alienation and unease permeated what had been a source of fulfillment for previous generations—work. Sociologists, such as William H. Whyte (1956), found the root of this alienation and social debilitation in the new plight of work as *The Corporation Man*. With the unprecedented automization and productivity, much had been gained, but something had been lost. Studs Terkel (1974), the great oral historical and radio broadcasting personality, set out to identify, or at least articulate, what exactly was happening to the lives of people in their work, through his book, aptly titled, *Working*. For his methodology, he relied on what he knew best—oral history. Let people record the historical moment through their own voices and reflections. Thus, his now classic book came with a telling subtitle, *Working: People Talk About What They Do All Day and How They Feel About What They Do*. As to which voices reflecting which people, Terkel's guiding star was diversity and heterogeneity.

When the first lockdown took place in March 2020, we had the feeling of being part of a never experienced societal calamity that would have an impact on all of us and all parts of life. We all experienced great uncertainty not knowing how the next month would turn out. Although back then, we did not expect the corona pandemic to last that long, the enormity of this unprecedented challenge confronting society was very clear. The longer we live in times of the pandemic (2022 is the third year), more and more people reckon that this will not be the last crisis we will have to cope with. The economist's double Christmas issue's lead article, published December 2021, is titled "The new normal: the era of predictable unpredictability is not going away".[7] This has become sort of common knowledge, with the COVID-19 pandemic lasting longer than expected and storms, floods, and fires across the globe reminding us of climate change as the biggest challenge to come.

The COVID-19 pandemic has put economies and entrepreneurial ecosystems under severe pressure, on the one hand. On the other, it has accelerated change in an unexpected speed. An amazing thing to observe is how fundamentally strong this crisis was in order to stimulate change. Forced through the pandemic people, enterprises, institutions, and states had to move forward to cope with the challenges they were confronted with. This is especially true for digitization in all parts of society with home office, home schooling, and online shopping as the new normal.

Before March 2020, one could hardly imagine that global markets could be affected as fundamentally as we experienced from one month to the other. The pandemic with all its different national answers and political strategies has had an enormous impact on production processes, supply chains, just-in-time supply, and production around the world with production stops or short work in major industries. Lockdowns led to the close down of whole industries like tourism, culture, and retail. The impact on local communities and regions is not yet foreseeable.

While reflecting on the pandemic we still live in, the chapters in this book point to future challenges and solutions likewise. Although entrepreneurship and entrepreneurial ecosystems got under pressure, we see that with digitization and the invention of vaccines entrepreneurship and innovation are a central key to overcoming crisis.

However, the state of crisis that emerged in the course of the pandemic leaves entrepreneurship at risk. State intervention, state financing, and regulation put pressure on entrepreneurship. The old issues of the right balance of market and state intervention become urgently relevant. Other than, for example, employees and public servants, entrepreneurs lack a social safety net. The risks businesses will face in the future stay high.[8]

When the pandemic hit us hart, most countries worldwide chose severe lockdowns as the only possible measure to remain viable.[9] As a consequence, political leaders accepted the interruption of connectedness on a professional and private level. Although thanks to technology this unprecedented disconnection and interruption of real-life meetings, conferences, discussions, exchange of ideas, and

[7]The Economist, Christmas Double Issue, Dec 18–31, 2021, "The new normal. The era of predictable unpredictability is not going away".

[8]https://www.weforum.org/agenda/2021/01/building-resilience-in-the-face-of-dynamic-disruption/, accessed Jan 4, 2022.

[9]https://ourworldindata.org/covid-stay-home-restrictions, accessed Jan 4, 2022.

knowledge spillovers could be switched into the digital sphere. This, however, did not make up for anything. Chapters in this book point to the fact that, hence, major channels of entrepreneurial ecosystems were on hold or slowed down. The pandemic overwhelmed people with new challenges so they were kept from original tasks. The lack of routines required additional energy. Research should, therefore, take a closer look at what happened to such knowledge spillovers during crisis.

Never in recent history, so many individuals have been confronted with such great uncertainty in daily life. The pandemic forced individuals in private as well as professional life to leave routines and take on change. All experienced what it means to act under uncertainty. Everyone engaged in a process of adapting and coping, creating new routines and changing them on a daily basis. However, the pandemic also showed that not everyone feels comfortable with uncertainty. Mental health problems increased massively. Some feel better and are more used to act under uncertainty than others. Some like uncertainty and take the challenge in order to handle the crisis mode; some are totally swamp and hate the situation.

People who like to act under uncertainty are entrepreneurs. They embrace uncertainty and envision the future. They have something in mind and try to create. They focus on challenges and look for solutions always in respond to demand and preferences in the market. They are agile.

In an era of "predictable unpredictability," uncertainty is the new normal and an overarching challenge for societies. In order to cope with the "new normal unpredictability," we need entrepreneurial people. We can find them on all levels, in all organizations and in all fields of society and in all regions. Entrepreneurship is needed not only in the high-tech or platform or digital context. It is also needed in all other parts of society. Agents of change can be found in every institution, organization, industry, and region.

The entrepreneurial ecosystem needs people in organizations, companies, and political institutions who understand the importance of an entrepreneurial culture and support and push entrepreneurial ways of change. Not everyone, however, has to become an entrepreneur. It is likewise important to support entrepreneurs who prefer to go beyond the horizon.

In searching for voices to remember and reflect on the *Zeitalter*, or era of the Pandemic, we follow the path paved a generation earlier by Terkel. We have carefully searched out and selected a diverse and broad group of disparate voices to tell their own story in their own way. We purposefully eschewed imposing a common style and format on the resulting team of authors, instead emphasizing the authenticity inherent in each chapter constating a unique voice. All chapters point to future challenges as well as promising solutions and help us understand what keeps economic activity and entrepreneurial ecosystems functioning in times of crisis. They are all special because they combine personal experiences with academic expertise.

The book takes five different angles. Part 1 "The future is uncertain and entrepreneurial" directs our view to the pandemic as a learning incidence and points to the solving power of entrepreneurship and entrepreneurial ecosystems in future crises. Papers in the second part "Economies under pressure: challenges for the future after the Coronavirus crisis" examine actors under pressure and point to future economic challenges that can be identified from today's standpoint in the ongoing pandemic. Part 3 "Reflecting on the future: entrepreneurship research and policy-making after the Coronavirus crisis" provides insights to how the pandemic affects knowledge creation and knowledge transfer, specifically the impact on researchers and transfer of research. Part 4 "Acting under uncertainty: Personal Perspectives from Sweden, Egypt and Germany" gives us some insights into personal experiences in Sweden, Egypt, and Germany. They help us keep in mind that although the pandemic was a fundamental disruption for all of us, policy responses differed and were experienced in very different individual ways. Part 5 "The educational ecosystem for entrepreneurship: moving the digital way forward after the Coronavirus crisis" focuses on international education environments and the entrepreneurial action generated by universities. The chapters in this part provide great examples of creative change based on digitization and induced through the pandemic. All in all, the articles in this book provide a broad and multidisciplinary view on how people reflect and react to the pandemic across the globe and how positive changes can be initiated.

As the subsequent contents of this book will confirm, this has resulted in an extraordinary collection of authentic and thoughtful essays giving voice to what is an unprecedented challenge. As Sir Winston Churchill once observed, "Everyone can recognize history when it happens. Everyone can recognize history after is has happened; but only the wise man knows at the moment what is vital and permanent, what is lasting and memorable." The ensuing pages are replete with exactly such wise voices.

## References


Amat, F., Arenas, A., Falcó-Gimeno A., & Muñoz, J. (2020, April 6). Pandemics meet democracy: Experimental evidence from the COVID-19 Crisis in Spain. *SocArXiv*. https://osf.io/preprints/socarxiv/dkusw/.

Cepaluni, G., Dorsch, M., & Branyiczki, R. (2020). *Political regimes and deaths in the early stages of the COVID-19 pandemic*. SSRN. https://papers.ssrn.com/sol3/papers.cfm?abstract_id=3586767

Dickens, C. (1859). *A tale of two cities*. Chapman & Hall.

Kuckertz, A., Brandle, L., Gaudig, A., & Hinderer, S. (2020, June 15). Startups in times of crisis – a rapid response to the COVID-19 pandemic. *Journal of Business Venturing Insights, 13*(June), e00169.

Terkel, S. (1974). *Working: People talk about what they do all day and how they feel about what they do*. Pantheon/Random House.

The Economist. *Christmas double issue, Dec 18th–31st 2021, leaders: The new normal*. The era of predictable unpredictability is not going away.

Tolstoy, L. (1887). *Anna Karénina*. Thomas Y. Crowell &.

Whyte, W. H. (1956). *The corporation man*. Simon and Schuster.

Yeyati, F. (2021). *Social and economic impact of COVID-19*. Brookings Global Working Paper#158, https://www.brookings.edu/research/social-and-economic-impact-of-COVID-19/

**Iris A.M. Kunadt** holds a Ph.D. from Max Planck Institute of Economics/University of Hamburg. Her research focuses on entrepreneurship, public policy, and strategic management of places. Before starting social and civic entrepreneurship initiatives she worked at Fraunhofer IMW and as a consultant on applied research projects.

**David B. Audretsch** is a Distinguished Professor and the Ameritech Chair of Economic Development at Indiana University, where he also serves as Director of the Institute for Development Strategies. He is an Honorary Professor of Industrial Economics and Entrepreneurship at the WHU-Otto Beisheim School of Management in Germany and a part-time professor of entrepreneurship at the University of Klagenfurt in Austria. Audretsch's research has focused on the links between entrepreneurship, government policy, innovation, economic development, and global competitiveness.

# Part I
# The Future is Risky and Entrepreneurial

# Resilience Is the New Competitive

**Mark Sanders**

**Abstract** In this chapter, I argue that the COVID pandemic brings home the message that economies need to be prepared for shocks. But preparing for shocks is not the same as preparing for the last shock. Instead, it means we also need to prepare for unknown unknowns. I then argue that the transition to an entrepreneurial society is a no-regret strategy to do so. Entrepreneurs, defined here as people willing and able to challenge the status quo, deal with the unexpected daily. The same skills, talent, resources, and institutions that make them successful in doing so also help us handle a rapidly changing status quo. I then argue that traditional entrepreneurship policies will not suffice. Instead, institutions need to be reformed to ensure challengers of the status quo gain and maintain access to resources such as capital, labor, and knowledge. I conclude the chapter by briefly outlining three such reforms that would help build a more resilient, entrepreneurial economy.

**Keywords** Resilience · Competitiveness · Entrepreneurial society · Institutional reforms · Banking system

## 1 Introduction

The COVID pandemic of 2020–2021 is likely to go down in history as one of those pivotal moments that define a person's life in *before* and *after*.[1] In this chapter, I would like to propose that the pandemic also represents a structural break for entrepreneurship researchers and policy makers. Not because so many have suffered and died, but because the pandemic caused an unprecedented set of restrictions to be imposed almost overnight in many parts of the world. Governments have shut down

[1] Or not. After all, we have thought so when Lehman Brothers crashed in 2008, when the two airliners hit the Twin Towers in 2001 and when the Berlin Wall fell in 1989. Time will tell.

M. Sanders (✉)
Maastricht University School of Business and Economics, Maastricht, The Netherlands
e-mail: m.sanders@maastrichtuniversity.nl



D. B. Audretsch, I. A. M. Kunadt (eds.), *The COVID-19 Crisis and Entrepreneurship*, International Studies in Entrepreneurship 54,
https://doi.org/10.1007/978-3-031-04655-1_2

schools, universities, international travel and tourism, festivals, and museums. Many things that we believed to be unthinkable in peacetime before the spring of 2020 were realities only months later. As the worst of the pandemic seems to be behind us at the time of writing, we can start to make sense of what happened. And if we look at the COVID pandemic of 2020–2021 through the lens of an entrepreneurship scholar, what do we see?

One can of course investigate how the pandemic and the lockdowns have affected entrepreneurs and how entrepreneurship may have helped or hindered the adjustment of our economies to these exogenous shocks. And many have begun to do so, as recent special issues in entrepreneurship field journals prove (e.g., Brown & Rocha, 2020; Brown & Cowling, 2021; Clampit et al., 2021). I follow that debate with interest, but I do not consider myself particularly well-positioned to make big contributions to that discussion here. Instead, I would like to argue that the pandemic has taught us another important lesson: All economies must be prepared to deal with shocks.

Most of these shocks are so-called known unknowns. We have always known that a global pandemic was a serious risk and in fact have experienced them before. A larger global population that lives in closer proximity to more animals in densely populated cities that are more connected across the world makes smaller and bigger outbreaks more probable, frequent, and serious (Morse et al., 2012; Dodds, 2019; Tollefson, 2020). Similarly, we know that climate change is destabilizing the weather and we should anticipate that more extreme weather events to affect our economies in the future (Seneviratne et al., 2012), potentially causing migration flows (Brown, 2008; Perch-Nielsen et al., 2008) and disruptions in food production (Ray et al., 2019; Parry et al., 2004). And although I am much less of an expert on global politics, there too it seems to me that the emerging multipolar global order is rather a source of more, not less instability (Kegley & Raymond, 1992; Goldstone et al., 2010). Fortunately, social distancing, mouth masks, and curfew are not "the new normal," but this environment that is increasingly unstable and will confront us with more and more intense shocks, is.

Preparing for these known unknowns, one can take two approaches. We can prepare for the shocks by stocking up on medical supplies, creating elaborate contingency plans and investing large sums in our emergency response and healthcare systems. But such an approach is very costly and brings no benefits if the shocks do not happen. Or more likely, it happens in different ways than one has planned for. Moreover, that approach leaves us vulnerable for all shocks we do not anticipate. Instead, I would argue that the known unknowns make it desirable to build a more resilient economy. And the fact that there are also unknown unknowns makes this transition urgent.

I propose in this chapter that the Entrepreneurial Society (Audretsch, 2007, 2009) is a no-regret strategy to build such resilience. But I also note that COVID has not brought us closer to such an entrepreneurial society. Our "risk regulation reflex" (Helsloot & Schmidt, 2012; Trappenburg & Schiffelers, 2012) is stronger than ever and (consequently) state bureaucracies have (re)asserted a central position in many developed economies during the pandemic. If anything, the pandemic has brought us closer to a managed society (Audretsch & Thurik, 2000). And entrepreneurship scholars should rally to reverse that trend. In the remainder of this chapter, I will first sketch **what makes an entrepreneurial society** and argue **how it helps build economic resilience**. Then, I discuss how the **"naive" entrepreneurship policies**, such as throwing COVID recovery funds at cheap credit, venture capitalists, or startups or keeping armies of zombie SMEs afloat with wage and turnover subsidies, **will not get us there**. Then, I will show how **current policy developments tend to take us away from a more entrepreneurial society**, and finally, I **elaborate some proposals to prevent or reverse that trend.**

## 2 An Entrepreneurial Society Is Resilient...

Audretsch (2007, 2009) argued that entrepreneurship became an important source of innovation and economic growth in the USA over the twentieth century and competition from efficient, managed economies abroad, notably Japan and Germany, pushed the USA into this direction. When you read Audretsch' work and that of other authors on the topic (Audretsch & Thurik, 2000), they describe this shift more as the result of external forces and evolution, not as the result of a deliberate strategy. Since, several authors (Audretsch et al., 2018; Economidou et al., 2018) have argued that Europe now faces the same pressures with the rise of East Asian economies and scholars have started thinking how to proactively bring about a more entrepreneurial society in Europe (Elert et al., 2019; Sanders et al., 2020).

It is important to note that an entrepreneurial society is not merely a society with a high level of self-employment or new firm formation (e.g., GEM's Reynolds et al. (1999) TEA measures). By those metrics, developing countries like Uganda would do a lot better than the USA or Europe. For that reason, scholars have developed more sophisticated, multidimensional metrics, such as the Global Entrepreneurship and Development Index (GEDI) (Acs et al., 2017), the Collaborative Innovation Bloc (Elert & Henrekson, 2019), the National and Regional Innovation System (Nelson, 1993; Freeman, 1995; Braczyk et al., 1998), and the Entrepreneurial Ecosystem (EES) framework (Stam, 2015; O'Connor et al., 2018; Wurth et al., 2021). I will not go into the details of these different methods, but I will say that what all have in common is the idea that it is the quality, not quantity of entrepreneurial activity that counts and that it is the institutional environment that determines the quality of entrepreneurial activity.

It was the late William Baumol who argued that the supply of entrepreneurial talent in society is exogenously given (which is not the same as assuming it to be constant) and it is the institutions, the "manmade rules of the game" (North, 1991), that determine where this talent flows and what it can achieve.[2] Baumol distinguished between productive, unproductive, and destructive entrepreneurial activities

[2] See Henrekson and Stenkula (2021) for a detailed account of the work of William Baumol.

(Baumol, 1996) and argued that it is the prevalent set of institutions that determines which activities are and which are not likely to gain a person status, power, and wealth. Importantly, Baumol assumed it was the self-interested quest for private gains that drives entrepreneurial talent into profitable activities and the trick would be to align what is privately (most) profitable with what is socially most desirable. With this "correct" set of institutions, entrepreneurship becomes a force of good.

Despite the intuitive appeal of Baumol's ideas, it has proven difficult to theoretically model or empirically test his intuition. Except for the collapse of the Soviet bloc in the late 1980s, institutions typically change only very gradually and co-evolve with their environment under the influence of a complex web of factors (North, 1993; Seo & Creed, 2002). Importantly, the same factors that drive institutional change also impact the relative attractiveness of productive, unproductive, and destructive entrepreneurial activities, so it becomes impossible to disentangle cause and effect. Moreover, we cannot directly observe entrepreneurial talent and must therefore somehow proxy for it. And as Baumol hypothesized that it is institutions that determine in what activities entrepreneurial talent manifests itself, one cannot measure entrepreneurial talent by looking at a limited set of manifestations across very diverse institutional arrangements.

The abovementioned measures, all trying to capture the interplay between institutions and entrepreneurship, thus had to rely on theory and trial and error to identify what combinations of observed institutions and observed entrepreneurial activities generate innovation and growth. That approach, unfortunately, becomes tautological, as it leads us to include only those activities and those institutions that together seem to correlate with growth and innovation, whereas it is not clear if the observed institutions indeed cause entrepreneurial talent to manifest itself in the observed activities and therefore cause the observed growth.

The COVID pandemic has now shown us that this approach is indeed incomplete. "Socially desirable outcomes" are broader than the "innovation and growth" that Schumpeterian entrepreneurs bring. It includes, importantly, also the ability of our economy to absorb and adapt to external shocks. And this aspect of the Entrepreneurial Society has received little attention to date.

In my humble opinion, we should understand Baumol's "entrepreneurial talent" as the ability and willingness of people to challenge a status quo. In that definition, entrepreneurship is an approach to challenges and problems, much more than it is a job title or an activity that we can observe. It manifests itself in self-employment, firm owners, startups, lawyers, lobbyists, and criminals alike, but there are also many that do not have or show entrepreneurial talent in undertaking these activities. And the reverse is also true. Entrepreneurial talent can manifest itself in the actions of categories of people we typically do not consider entrepreneurial, productive, or otherwise, such as university professors, teachers, politicians, civil servants, and healthcare workers. I would argue these groups have shown that there too a considerable amount of entrepreneurial talent is present. This "definition" of entrepreneurial talent defies clean empirical measurement, but for my purposes here, I can follow the Potter Steward doctrine, who, in concurring in Jacobellis vs Ohio, wrote: "I shall not today attempt further to define the kinds of material I understand to be embraced within that shorthand description ["i.e. hard-core pornography"], and perhaps I could never succeed in intelligibly doing so. But *I know it when I see it* (...)."[3]

The COVID pandemic and the many drastic and arguably exogenous changes in the "rules of the game" it entailed, present us with an opportunity to see the interplay between the allocation of entrepreneurial talent and the exogenous, rapidly changing "manmade rules of the game" the pandemic inspired. If Baumol's theory holds, we would expect entrepreneurial talent to reallocate and manifest itself according to where new profitable opportunities arose.

And we did see such effects. The global hunt for face masks and respirator equipment brought out the worst in people, but also illustrated how savvy entrepreneurs indeed directed their talent to new opportunities for personal gain. In the absence of clear rules and institutional arrangements, not all this activity was socially beneficial. But that only reinforces Baumol's point.

I would argue, however, that the most impressive manifestations of entrepreneurial talent during the pandemic were not found in cases where suddenly new profit opportunities arose in a regulatory vacuum. The ability and willingness of people to adjust to the new situation and experiment with new approaches in a rapidly changing environment were prominently visible in teachers, adopting digital technology to homeschool pupils and students almost overnight; in nurses and doctors suspending old and developing new protocols to handle the influx of highly contagious COVID patients; in artists, who moved their artistic expressions online in a myriad of ways; and in restaurateurs, who switched to delivery services and developed other creative ways to tap into new markets. The rapid changes in the manmade rules of the game that all these people faced forced them to tap into their entrepreneurial talent. And what we have seen suggests that such talent can really be found everywhere.

This observation sits a little uncomfortably with Baumol's theory. It seems that only a small fraction of the total entrepreneurial talent in society ends up in manifestations we would traditionally label as "entrepreneurial activity." The bulk of it lies dormant and only awakens when large shocks make it "profitable" to mobilize it. If entrepreneurial talent is distributed normally in society (and why would it not), then it is only the right tail that, under normal circumstances, engages in creating the diversity and challenging the status quo in a stable selection environment. In crisis times, when the selection environment itself changes and all are facing the need to adapt, the entire distribution springs to life. And the degree to which an economy can successfully handle a shock then depends crucially on its institutions channeling resources to those creating the diversity of approaches that the new selection environment can start working on.

This corresponds well with the view that the Entrepreneurial Society is the economic equivalent of Karl Popper's (1945) "Open Society" (Sanders, 2019). In such a society, institutions not only shape the selection environment in which ideas can compete, but they also support and promote the creation of diversity. Popper

[3] https://mtsu.edu/first-amendment/article/392/jacobellis-v-ohio

described this dynamic for the political and scientific spheres. Important institutions to promote diversity in politics and science include the freedom of speech and anonymous peer review, respectively. Schumpeter described this dynamic for the economy as the process of "creative destruction," where new entrants challenge incumbents and replace them if successful in the market. Under normal circumstances, evolutionary change is a slow and painstaking process, and change comes from the steady creation of diversity under a stable selection environment. Both Schumpeter (1943) and Popper (1945) worried most about the process of creative destruction stalling as incumbents and vested interests would block challengers' access to vital resources. The challenge to build (or maintain) an Entrepreneurial Society is therefore to design institutions that increase and maintain the flow of resources to challengers of the status quo, to keep the creation of diversity and the selection process going.

In times of crisis, such as in the COVID pandemic, the evolutionary process turns on its head. The normal process where new varieties challenge the old stops. Instead, the selection environment changes rapidly and abruptly, such that previously dominant routines lose their fitness. This means that all economic agents need to start experimenting and learning. If a society can quickly mobilize the resources to generate variety under these circumstances, it can choose from more options to handle the new situation and thus limit the impact and speed up the recovery after the shock. Societies that can limit the impact and recover fast are said to be resilient (Martin et al., 2016). Where evolution is normally a slow and painstaking process, in a crisis like the global COVID pandemic, evolution is on steroids. And it is not the institutions that drive the allocation of talent in normal times that matter, but those that ensure access to resources for entrepreneurial talent.

This shifts the focus from the institutions Baumol (1996) focused on, to the institutions that determine access to resources for entrepreneurial talent. In normal times, this entrepreneurial talent is manifest in challenging the status quo ante. In times of crisis, it is manifest in adjusting to the status quo post. I would hypothesize that an institutional arrangement that routinely channels resources to challengers, an Entrepreneurial Society, can also generate more diversity faster in a time of crisis. This, if nothing else, requires us to rethink entrepreneurial policy making.

## 2.1 . . .*But Cannot Be Achieved with Traditional Entrepreneurship Policies*. . .

Under traditional entrepreneurship policies, I understand the policies we have designed to support what, under normal circumstances, we define as productive entrepreneurial activity. Entrepreneurship policy differs per country and region and has many nuances and shades of gray. But in the end, most packages will contain a mix of government subsidies to incubators, startups and venture capitalists, preferential tax treatment and regulatory exemptions for small- and medium-sized (young) firms, and public support for educational programs that teach (or preach to) the young to start a business.

More sophisticated policy makers will look at the multidimensional measures discussed earlier and try to improve the institutional foundations that support a high-quality entrepreneurial ecosystem. And let me start by saying that such policy interventions do not hurt. But to build and maintain an Entrepreneurial Society they are insufficient (Economidou et al., 2018). The COVID crisis has shown that the entrepreneurial talent such policies reach is only a very small (be it important) part of the entrepreneurial talent distribution in society. A truly Entrepreneurial Society would mobilize and enable its entire potential. Moreover, a lot of the resources and efforts in these policies end up supporting ventures that are not very or not at all entrepreneurial. Preferential tax treatments for (young) SMEs benefit a lot of firms that do not wish to challenge the status quo in their business. And teaching young people how to start and run a business is in no way a guarantee that such businesses will be of the challenging kind. Consequently, policies and institutions should aim to empower an entrepreneurial approach to problems and challenges anywhere.

## 2.2 . . .and the Closed Society and Managed Economy Have a Strong Appeal in Times of Crisis. . .

The policy responses in the COVID crisis, however, go in the opposite direction. The governments that could afford to do so have channeled massive amounts of resources to their "entrepreneurs" in ways that discourage rather than stimulate entrepreneurial talent. In my own country, the Netherlands, tens of billions of euro's have been spent on supporting firms that lost turnover and subsidizing the wage bill of millions of workers at risk of losing their jobs due to the lockdowns. Ironically, however, these support measures were often conditional on the business owners *not* finding solutions to the changed circumstances. The government would compensate for *lost* turnover, so finding new ways to compensate for such losses yourself was discouraged. All solutions found would reduce your support one for one. The wage bill subsidies were also conditional on *not* firing redundant workers, keeping them locked out of the labor market, where demand in other sectors (e.g., health, supermarkets, delivery services) soared. These policies did not support entrepreneurial talent, but instead moved the economy into hibernation. The patient was kept in his coma, so to speak, while the doctors were trying to find a cure.

On first sight, this approach was successful. In the Netherlands, business failure rates have never been lower than in the COVID years 2020–2021. But coming out of the COVID coma, there is now a large pool of support-addicted firms keeping underemployed workers on their payroll, while the Dutch labor market has tightened to the point that there have never in history been so many vacancies per unemployed. Combined with the European Central Bank keeping interest rates at record lows, already since 2008, there is still no need for the patients' own immune systems to do anything about the virus. And one might be worried that the "cures" are now getting worse than the disease.

If fear is bad counsel, panic is worse. Yet it is well documented that in our response to disaster and crisis, we tend to overreact and try to reestablish order by trying to regulate in a volatile situation. The Dutch Risk and Responsibility Program defined the dynamic of regulatory responses to crisis events as the Risk Regulation Reflex:

> the pitfall of a hasty response following an incident leading to disproportionate measures. Disproportionality is a danger not only in legislation but also in regulation, norm setting, implementation and in the responsibility attributed to government. (von Tol, 2012, p. 281)

This reflex has also guided (the Dutch) governments in their response to the COVID pandemic. When GPs in the Netherlands realized that their vaccines were not being used and risked going to waste, they quickly (and entrepreneurially) set up a system to get the vaccines to people that wanted them. But the Ministry of Health blocked the initiative with new rules or the rigid application of old ones, unfit for the situation. The managed society prevailed. Vaccines went to waste, but proper procedure was reestablished. When after a brief relaxation of lockdown rules in June, infections among young people spiked (entirely predictable and not causing any serious disease or stress in hospitals), the government again panicked and re-introduced rules that blocked creative entrepreneurs that had carefully redesigned their activities to be COVID proof. Current debates on the introduction of a vaccination passport to create "safe" spaces for the vulnerable are equally misguided, as vaccination helps people stay out of hospital, but will not prevent them from carrying and transmitting the virus and its more recent and contagious mutations.

I do not want to begrudge all those that benefitted the support they have received in dire times. On the contrary, after all, the pandemic cannot be considered a normal business risk and the government imposed many restrictions that made continuation of a lot of activities impossible. So, it is only natural that the government also support the people affected. But the challenge the Dutch government now faces, and I suspect this is familiar to many governments around the world, is how to take their patients off life support without causing an immediate backlash. It would have been better, perhaps, to also try to build up the patients' own immune systems by investing in an Entrepreneurial Society, to make us more resilient.

## 2.3 ...*But Institutional Reforms Can Get Us to a More Resilient, Entrepreneurial Society*

Our Horizon 2020 research project concluded just before the COVID pandemic (www.projectfires.eu) has therefore gained new relevance. In that project, we already concluded that traditional entrepreneurship policy is not enough, and we developed a much broader institutional reform agenda to bring the Entrepreneurial

Society to Europe (e.g., Elert et al., 2019; Sanders et al., 2020). The overarching principles to guide institutional reform for an open, entrepreneurial society include *neutrality, transparency, moderation, contestability, legality, and justifiability* (Elert et al., 2019). Presenting some 50 reform proposals that importantly need to be carefully fitted to local, regional, and national conditions (see Sanders et al., 2020), the aim was to create an open society in which effective contestability is ensured by institutions that "back challengers." Of these 50 proposals, there are many smaller no-regret reforms that would work well in normal and crisis times, and the COVID pandemic has convinced me that also the more fundamental reforms that we discussed are urgent, not to prepare for the next pandemic, but to get our societies in better shape to cope with whatever else lady Fortune has in store for us.

To make this discussion more concrete, I will briefly discuss three such fundamental reforms and argue why they have gained urgency in the COVID pandemic.

In a market economy, participation in society has been largely monetized. This means that everyone must have access to the payment and savings infrastructure. We used to handle our transactions with claims on the central bank in the form of banknotes and coins. That technology now seems outdated, and under the cover of public insurance and guarantees, commercial banks provide the debt that (digitally) circulates in our economy as money (Lawson, 2018). This monetized debt is a cheap source of financing for banks and a justification for the central bank to interfere firmly in the credit policy and risk management of individual banks. Yet all these rules, supervision, and precautionary measures do not remove the fundamental uncertainty about access to the payment system. Our money remains a claim on a private and commercial organization that should, in principle, go bankrupt if it makes the wrong decisions. In addition, all this risk-averse supervision on the asset side of the bank balance sheet limits access to credit and therefore financial resources for borrowers who cannot demonstrate stable collateral, a rock-solid balance sheet and/or a reliable track record. And of course, that description fits all challengers of the status quo, the entrepreneurs.

Entrepreneurs benefit from a stable and reliable payment and savings system, of course. But why does this have to be at the expense of their access to capital? Can't it be otherwise? The answer is yes. To keep people safe from worries about the value of their medium of exchange and store of value, the central bank could introduce a digital form of cash that meets the basic needs for payment and savings: central bank digital currency (CBDC). Your money is then safely in the bank with all the conveniences that this entails, but is ultimately a claim on the central bank, just like cash. As a result, a bankruptcy of a commercial bank must no longer be avoided at all costs and banks are again able to take and manage risks (or if that goes wrong, to go bankrupt in an orderly manner). By putting that alternative into circulation, the central bank is restoring neutrality in lending. Not in the sense that entrepreneurs will get cheap and abundant bank credit, but in the sense that banks can offer them that credit again at a fair, risk-weighted price. This promotes entrepreneurs' access to capital in a transparent and efficient way.

If such a system had been in place at the start of the COVID pandemic, managing effective demand in the economy would have been much simpler, as would the practical implementation of the massive support packages that many countries had to set up overnight. If all firms and consumers hold an account at the central bank, one can quickly credit their accounts in times of crisis, to prevent unnecessary contractions in demand. The indirect route via the balance sheet of commercial banks is much less effective, especially in times of high uncertainty, when demand for new credit is depressed and collateral values fall. Commercial banks are well-positioned to spend money into circulation in normal times, as Schumpeter described, as arbiters of society. But they are ineffective in doing so in times when existing loans turn bad and new ones are not in demand. Moreover, it would greatly reduce the worries over bad credit overhang and the potential impact of writing these off post-COVID.

The same principles and philosophy—the neutral and transparent safeguarding of basic needs and organizing what must be contestable in a truly open and competitive market—lie under the proposal of a "Negative Income Tax (NIT)" (Friedman, 2013). This is in fact a form of universal basic income at a level that is high enough so concerns about basic needs can be put aside while at the same time low enough that sufficient incentives remain to participate in society by wanting to create value for others. For the Entrepreneurial Society, a NIT is of great importance because entrepreneurial venturing will then compete with other forms of labor market participation on a (more) level playing field. But more importantly, also for employees, the choice between working for a small startup and a large multinational is no longer driven by considerations of job security and associated rights and certainties, but by the work itself and the reward offered for it. Here, too, a neutral, because unconditional, basic provision leads to better access to an important production factor for entrepreneurs in a completely transparent way. If people are no longer dependent on their jobs for their livelihood, they will ask for more money for the annoying jobs and less for the nicer ones. Then, challenger and challenged compete for good workers with good work, not on the (supposed) security offered.

An NIT in times of COVID would have the additional benefit of having secured all citizen's basic needs by design. There is no need to protect jobs because people depend on them for their livelihoods. Instead, people can choose themselves what activities to pursue with their talents and time, under the new constraints. There would be no need for employers without work to keep them on the payroll, not for employees without work, to stay. Keeping skilled workers on the payroll even if there is no work due to a lockdown, is still a good idea. But doing so will be less costly when an NIT covers the basic needs of workers, and hence, support packages can be supplementing instead of replacing incomes. In combination with the existence of a CBDC, the NIT or basic income would give governments a powerful direct tool to maintain and support purchasing power among consumers in times of crisis, even if it is organized at a relatively low level in normal times.

Finally, in Elert et al. (2019), we argued in the field of knowledge development for institutional reforms toward open innovation. Knowledge is, in addition to labor and capital, the most important resource for entrepreneurship. It is expensive to produce but with modern technology dirt cheap to reproduce. Most important, the use of knowledge is non-rival. That is, my use of knowledge does not reduce the usefulness of the same knowledge for others. A market organization in which knowledge owners can exclude others from use is not the best arrangement to organize access under such circumstances. Knowledge was, for practical reasons, a free "good" for most of history. Whoever had it could use it, and the idea of ownership rights to knowledge and ideas just did not come to people's mind. Yet even at that time the world certainly did not stand still. Patents have undeniably proved their worth in the past and given innovation a strong boost, but in the current era, intellectual property is so stretched and expanded that it is more of a brake on innovation than a driver of knowledge development. In Elert et al. (2019), we therefore argued for a firm limitation in the scope of patent and intellectual property law. To provide incentives for the promotion of new knowledge and to reward performance in this field, innovation prize systems and publicly funded science and research can complement the system. However, the knowledge that is generated there belongs in the public domain, so that knowledge becomes freely available again and its use enables entrepreneurs to combine new and old knowledge into new challenges for existing practices and positions.

The COVID crisis has illustrated the power of open knowledge systems. The vaccines have been developed quickly and based on knowledge in the public domain, developed with public money and in close global collaborations (e.g., Andreadakis et al., 2020; Corey et al., 2020; Cross et al., 2021; Druedahl et al., 2021). The search for effective vaccines was kick-started with the publication of the virus' genetic code on January 11, 2020. The first clinical tests in humans followed on March 16. But as the pandemic progressed, old institutions reasserted themselves and started to hinder the further development and use of this new knowledge to the benefit of all (Moon et al., 2021). Patent and IP regulations block especially developing countries from accessing and using the publicly funded R & D in the developed world that has been hijacked and appropriated by pharmaceutical firms. They claim that patent and IP protection is essential to incentivize them to develop new cures and treatments in the future. But the COVID pandemic has shown that they fail to do so, even when the demand is urgent and clear. Incumbent pharmaceutical companies use patents and IP to cultivate their cash cows. Treatments ensure lengthy, preferably lifelong use for chronic, rich country diseases. It underlines the views of Baumol once more. Under the current institutional arrangements, that is where these companies can generate most wealth, power, and prestige for their owners. They are more than happy to profit from the global demand for COVID vaccines, and perhaps producing the vaccines in the required volumes is indeed best left to Big Pharma. But they will not prevent the next pandemic and have a vested interest in restricting access to "their" knowledge and products.

The reform agenda to establish a more Entrepreneurial Society in Europe has gained urgency with the COVID pandemic. Not because those institutions prevent pandemics or because a healthy entrepreneurial ecosystem might, but because these open institutions ensure that people, firms, and consequently the economy and society at large are more resilient when disaster strikes. And resilience is the new competitive.

## References

Ács, Z. J., Szerb, L., & Autio, E. (2017). *Global entrepreneurship and development index 2011*. Springer International Publishing.

Andreadakis, Z., Kumar, A., Román, R. G., Tollefsen, S., Saville, M., & Mayhew, S. (2020). The COVID-19 vaccine development landscape. *Nature Reviews. Drug Discovery, 19*(5), 305–306.

Audretsch, D. B. (2007). *The entrepreneurial society*. Oxford University Press on Demand.

Audretsch, D. B. (2009). The entrepreneurial society. *The Journal of Technology Transfer, 34*(3), 245–254.

Audretsch, D. B., Mamtora, A., & Menendez, H. (2018). Creating an entrepreneurial society in Europe. *The Journal of Technology Transfer, 43*(6), 1437–1448.

Audretsch, D. B., & Thurik, A. R. (2000). Capitalism and democracy in the 21st century: From the managed to the entrepreneurial economy. *Journal of Evolutionary Economics, 10*(1), 17–34.

Baumol, W. J. (1996). Entrepreneurship: Productive, unproductive, and destructive. *Journal of Business Venturing, 11*(1), 3–22.

Braczyk, H. J., Cooke, P. N., Heidenreich, M., & Krauss, G. (Eds.). (1998). *Regional innovation systems: The role of governances in a globalized world*. Psychology Press.

Brown, O. (2008). *Migration and climate change*. United Nations.

Brown, R., & Cowling, M. (2021). The geographical impact of the Covid-19 crisis on precautionary savings, firm survival and jobs: Evidence from the United Kingdom's 100 largest towns and cities. *International Small Business Journal, 39*(4), 319–329.

Brown, R., & Rocha, A. (2020). Entrepreneurial uncertainty during the Covid-19 crisis: Mapping the temporal dynamics of entrepreneurial finance. *Journal of Business Venturing Insights, 14*, e00174.

Clampit, J. A., Lorenz, M. P., Gamble, J. E., & Lee, J. (2021). Performance stability among small and medium-sized enterprises during COVID-19: A test of the efficacy of dynamic capabilities. *International Small Business Journal, 40*(3), 403–419. https://doi.org/10.1177/02662426211033270

Corey, L., Mascola, J. R., Fauci, A. S., & Collins, F. S. (2020). A strategic approach to COVID-19 vaccine R & D. *Science, 368*(6494), 948–950.

Cross, S., Rho, Y., Reddy, H., Pepperrell, T., Rodgers, F., Osborne, R., Eni-Olotu, A., Banerjee, R., Wimmer, S., & Keestra, S. (2021). Who funded the research behind the Oxford-AstraZeneca COVID-19 vaccine? Approximating the funding to the University of Oxford for the research and development of the ChAdOx vaccine technology. *BMJ Global Health, 6*(12), e007321.

Dodds, W. (2019). Disease now and potential future pandemics. In *The World's worst problems* (pp. 31–44). Springer.

Druedahl, L. C., Minssen, T., & Price, W. N. (2021). Collaboration in times of crisis: A study on COVID-19 Vaccine R & D Partnerships. *Vaccine, 39*(42), 6291–6295.

Economidou, C., Grilli, L., Henrekson, M., & Sanders, M. (2018). Financial and institutional reforms for an entrepreneurial society. *Small Business Economics, 51*(2), 279–291.

Elert, N., & Henrekson, M. (2019). The collaborative innovation bloc: A new mission for Austrian economics. *The Review of Austrian Economics, 32*(4), 295–320.

Elert, N., Henrekson, M., & Sanders, M. (2019). *The entrepreneurial society: A reform strategy for the European Union* (p. 173). Springer Nature.

Freeman, C. (1995). The 'national innovation system' in historical context. *Cambridge Journal of Economics, 19*(1), 5–24.

Friedman, M. (2013). Negative income tax: The original idea. In *Basic income: An anthology of contemporary research* (pp. 398–401). Wiley Blackwell.

Goldstone, J. A., Bates, R. H., Epstein, D. L., Gurr, T. R., Lustik, M. B., Marshall, M. G., Ulfelder, J., & Woodward, M. (2010). A global model for forecasting political instability. *American Journal of Political Science, 54*(1), 190–208.

Helsloot, I., & Schmidt, A. (2012). The intractable citizen and the single-minded risk expert–mechanisms causing the risk regulation reflex pointed out in the Dutch risk and responsibility programme. *European Journal of Risk Regulation, 3*(3), 305–312.
Henrekson, M., & Stenkula, M. (2021). *William J. Baumol: Innovative contributor to entrepreneurship economics*. IFN working paper 1403.
Kegley, C. W., Jr., & Raymond, G. A. (1992). Must we fear a post-cold war multipolar system? *Journal of Conflict Resolution, 36*(3), 573–585.
Lawson, T. (2018). Debt as money. *Cambridge Journal of Economics, 42*(4), 1165–1181.
Martin, R., Sunley, P., Gardiner, B., & Tyler, P. (2016). How regions react to recessions: Resilience and the role of economic structure. *Regional Studies, 50*(4), 561–585.
Moon, S., Alonso Ruiz, A., & Vieira, M. (2021). Averting future vaccine injustice. *New England Journal of Medicine, 385*(3), 193–196.
Morse, S. S., Mazet, J. A., Woolhouse, M., Parrish, C. R., Carroll, D., Karesh, W. B., Zambrana-Torrelio, C., Lipkin, W. I., & Daszak, P. (2012). Prediction and prevention of the next pandemic zoonosis. *The Lancet, 380*(9857), 1956–1965.
Nelson, R. R. (Ed.). (1993). *National innovation systems: A comparative analysis*. Oxford University Press on Demand.
North, D. C. (1991). Institutions. *Journal of economic perspectives, 5*(1), 97–112.
North, D. C. (1993). *Five propositions about institutional change*. University Library of Munich.
O'Connor, A., Stam, E., Sussan, F., & Audretsch, D. B. (2018). Entrepreneurial ecosystems: The foundations of place-based renewal. In *Entrepreneurial ecosystems* (pp. 1–21). Springer.
Parry, M. L., Rosenzweig, C., Iglesias, A., Livermore, M., & Fischer, G. (2004). Effects of climate change on global food production under SRES emissions and socio-economic scenarios. *Global Environmental Change, 14*(1), 53–67.
Perch-Nielsen, S. L., Bättig, M. B., & Imboden, D. (2008). Exploring the link between climate change and migration. *Climatic Change, 91*(3–4), 375–393.
Popper, K. R. (1945). *The open society and its enemies*. Princeton University Press.
Ray, D. K., West, P. C., Clark, M., Gerber, J. S., Prishchepov, A. V., & Chatterjee, S. (2019). Climate change has likely already affected global food production. *PLoS One, 14*(5), e0217148.
Reynolds, P. D., Hay, M., & Camp, S. M. (1999). *Global entrepreneurship monitor*. Kauffman Center for Entrepreneurial Leadership.
Sanders, M. (2019). De open samenleving is een ondernemende samenleving. In R. Claassen & J. Van Erp (Eds.), *Ondernemen in de open samenleving* (pp. 29–39). Boom Uitgevers Den Haag. isbn:978-94-6236-967-2.
Sanders, M., Marx, A., & Stenkula, M. (2020). *The entrepreneurial society: A reform strategy for Italy, Germany and the UK* (p. 252). Springer Nature.
Schumpeter, J. A. ([1943] 2010). *Capitalism, socialism and democracy*. Routledge.
Seneviratne, S. I., Nicholls, N., Easterling, D., Goodess, C. M., Kanae, S., Kossin, J., Luo, Y., Marengo, J., McInnes, K., Rahimi, M., Reichstein, M., Sorteberg, A., Vera, C., & Zhang, X. (2012). Changes in climate extremes and their impacts on the natural physical environment. In *Managing the risks of extreme events and disasters to advance climate change adaptation* [Field, C. B., V. Barros, T.F. Stocker, D. Qin, D.J. Dokken, K.L. Ebi, M.D. Mastrandrea, K.J. Mach, G.-K. Plattner, S.K. Allen, M. Tignor, & P.M. Midgley (eds.)]. *A Special Report of Working Groups I and II of the Intergovernmental Panel on Climate Change (IPCC)* (pp. 109–230). Cambridge University Press.
Seo, M. G., & Creed, W. D. (2002). Institutional contradictions, praxis, and institutional change: A dialectical perspective. *Academy of Management Review, 27*(2), 222–247.
Stam, E. (2015). Entrepreneurial ecosystems and regional policy: A sympathetic critique. *European Planning Studies, 23*(9), 1759–1769.

Tollefson, J. (2020). Why deforestation and extinctions make pandemics more likely. *Nature, 584*(7820), 175–176.
Trappenburg, M., & Schiffelers, M. J. (2012). How to escape the vicious circle: The challenges of the risk regulation reflex. *European journal of risk regulation, 3*(3), 283–291.
von Tol, J. (2012). Opening editorial to the special issue on the risk regulation reflex. *European journal of risk regulation, 3*(3), 281–282.
Wurth, B., Stam, E., & Spigel, B. (2021). Toward an entrepreneurial ecosystem research program. *Entrepreneurship Theory and Practice*. https://doi.org/10.1177/1042258721998948

**Mark Sanders** is Professor of International Economics at Maastricht University, the Netherlands. His research interests include innovation economics, entrepreneurship, and economic development, with a special focus on the role of entrepreneurial activity and finance in the introduction of renewable energy technologies.

# Depths of Change: Ranging from Clubhouse to Game Changer

## A Reflection on What Changed During the Corona Pandemic and What Will Remain

**Andreas Pinkwart and Anna-Tina Pannes**

**Abstract** The corona crisis pushed a burning glass over the need for modernization in our country and acted as a catalyst for developments that were thus accelerated. The depth and stability of the changes brought about by the pandemic vary. This article addresses these varying depths of change and asks what will remain "post-corona." In particular, the digitalization booster experienced by education, administration, and companies in the context of the lockdowns will have a lasting effect.

**Keywords** Game changer · Public administration · Entrepreneurship · Education · Digitalization

## 1 Introduction: Turning Point

The months of February and March 2020 mark a turning point. A new era was established: "before corona" and "after corona." The cut and changes were soon recognized as being so profound that one expectation seemed to become a certainty: After the crisis, nothing will ever be the same again. With the experience of one and a half years into the pandemic, this can perhaps be objectified as "some things will change." The world after corona will not be a different one. But some focus has changed, some trends have been reinforced, and some awareness has been raised. The corona crisis thus "helped" to recognize and drive—it pushed a burning glass over the need for modernization in our country and acted as a catalyst for developments that were thus accelerated. In particular, it acted as a digitalization booster, because for the vast majority of activities, in times of "lockdown," the rule was: what cannot be done digitally, cannot be done at all.

A. Pinkwart · A.-T. Pannes (✉)
Ministry of Economic Affairs, Innovation, Digitalization and Energy of the State of North Rhine-Westphalia, Düsseldorf, Germany
e-mail: Tina.Pannes@mwide.nrw.de



D. B. Audretsch, I. A. M. Kunadt (eds.), *The COVID-19 Crisis and Entrepreneurship*, International Studies in Entrepreneurship 54,
https://doi.org/10.1007/978-3-031-04655-1_3

In view of the enormous economic, and above all health, consequences caused by the pandemic, it may be advisable to dispense with the simple formula of "the crisis as an opportunity." But recognizing the forces that were mobilized and the changes that were triggered by the pandemic is part of dealing with the crisis in a responsible manner. It is important to reflect on what has proven to be successful during and as a consequence of the pandemic situation and what needs to be pushed further or needs to be readjusted.

Both, depth and stability of the changes caused by the pandemic will vary. Some will remain exceptional—especially the absence of physical contact and personal interaction. Several trends are already proving to be hype, coinciding with progress in controlling the pandemic. The platform "Clubhouse," for example, caused a great furor in the political online community, due to unusual meetings of users with journalists and (top) policy makers—however, after a few months, the group of policy makers had returned to their "normal" agenda, and the enthusiasm for this communication format had vanished. In some areas, change may occur at a medium level of upheaval—such as in terms of diversification of supply chains in response to the experience of interrupted access during the pandemic. However, in some areas, the depth of change will be truly severe. Perhaps, historical reflections will one day describe the peak phase of the pandemic as a breakthrough in digital transformation. This would certainly be possible if the efforts made during the acute crisis can be continued in areas where the pandemic served as a key driver. And if, in addition, not only do sensitivities change, but the mindsets of policymakers, entrepreneurs, and citizens continue to be attuned to the digital age.

The following sections highlight the pressure for change resulting directly from the first lockdown triggered by the pandemic and the subsequent restrictions for the education sector, public administration, and specific sectors of the economy. By considering the world of work and social interaction spaces, two sectors are subject to scrutiny in which the long-term impact of the digital-driven era diverges. A glance at the start-up sector reveals a level of stability arising from digital expertise and two stories that combine economic success with societal hope for the end of the pandemic. Such inspirational stories are also needed in climate protection. Once the task of overcoming the pandemic has been accomplished, the challenge of the century—climate neutrality—will be imminent and requires considerable transformation. Whether the corona pandemic will be a game changer remains open for the time being—in any case, the next innovation boosts must emerge without a crisis.

## 2 Changes (1): The Crisis Becomes a Driver of Innovation

The pandemic has ruthlessly exposed Germany's need for modernization. The country is falling behind in areas that seem almost trivial given the profound changes brought by the digital transformation. Manually maintained Excel spreadsheets and paper-based contact tracking are only two prime examples. At the same time, the pandemic has stimulated digitalization as the usual way of working, purchasing, selling, and learning has simply become impossible. Numerous aspects that were previously considered inconceivable became reality. Numerous developments took place more rapidly than policy timeframes would otherwise allow. For schools and universities, for public administration, and the economy, in March 2020, everything was digital—suddenly, ultimately, and without alternative.

## 2.1 *Education: Suddenly Going Digital*

When the decision was made to close schools in response to the pandemic, digitalization abruptly became mandatory. The need for modernization in education—in terms of equipment as well as practical implementation—was ruthlessly exposed. Most of the German states did not have learning platforms that could be used comprehensively. Essential features for remote teaching, such as cloud or video conferencing systems, were missing. As an alternative and to ensure the supply of virtual teaching, many schools relied on providers that had established in the business world. At the same time, great strength was developed, and immense efforts were made. Today, after many months of the pandemic, we know that especially young people had to accept major restrictions and that the absence of social contact with classmates over long periods put a heavy burden on many of them. Yet we owe young people the best possible conditions for education, which is precisely why we must leverage the potential that became visible during the crisis. The boost in digitalization that was born out of necessity is changing everything.

Two years ago, even digital enthusiasts probably would not have thought that teaching in schools without the physical presence of students and teachers in the classroom would become reality so soon. Neither was the expectation that schools would receive such an immense technological boost within such a short period. The complex sector of education, where ideological positions also weigh heavily, has hitherto been characterized by a gradual pace of reform. The pace of reform and resource commitment mobilized during the pandemic lockdowns must now be sustained. The world had long been more digital than the schools, and the need for digitally supported education in a digital world had long been urgently clear. In this respect, the opportunity arose to boost digital transformation and help schools get connected—metaphorically speaking, as there was also a lack of digital infrastructure.

In North Rhine-Westphalia, the efforts made by the Minister of Education and the state government as a whole to make up for past omissions have been intensified. The funds provided by the state and federal government to help school authorities modernize and equip their school buildings are substantial—well over six billion euros for this legislative period alone. This includes funds from the "DigitalPakt Schule" totaling over one billion euros to improve the digital infrastructure of schools, as well as a further total of almost 400 million euros in federal funding and over 100 million euros in state funding. Funds are used to equip teachers and students with mobile devices and ensure reliable IT administration (MSB NRW, 2022a).

Of course, in addition to the technical aspects, pedagogical and didactic tasks need to be addressed, especially concerning the ideal combination of face-to-face and remote teaching. The resources provided by the Ministry for School and Education, such as the guidelines for remote learning, as well as professional advice and best practices, as well as networking activities, have addressed these issues and supported schools and teachers during the implementation phase. The LOGINEO platform, the NRW Education Media Library (Bildungsmediathek NRW), and other resources facilitate the process of organizing digital teaching (MSB NRW, 2022b).

The universities also moved into full digital operation due to Corona. In the process, they were able to push forward the transformation process that had already been initiated as part of the Digital University NRW (DH.NRW) initiative. With the new state portal for studying and teaching ORCA.nrw (Open Resources Campus NRW), the state, in cooperation with DH.NRW, is building a comprehensive support structure for digitalization in teaching. The objective of this initiative is that by the end of 2022, staff and students of all universities will be able to access free educational resources throughout Germany and beyond. In addition, a state-wide streaming service for recordings of lectures (educast.nrw) as well as services to support university didactics for digital teaching will be available (MKW NRW, 2022).

The investments and forced innovations set a new standard during the corona crisis, anchoring teaching and learning with digital media in a sustainable way. Hence, it is now crucial to move from the "must" of suddenly enforced remote teaching to a "can"—where the benefits of digitally supported education now need to be taken to a new level of application. The enthusiasm expressed not only by the digitally affine but also by newly enthusiastic teachers needs to be encouraged. In the education sector in particular, we would like to see more optimism and less alarm.

Curiosity and a desire to experiment should be the guiding principles behind the new digital opportunities that are offered. Virtual reality applications, for example, can open entirely new worlds of learning and experience. A geography lesson in which students look at green, blue, and brown spots on greasy maps will hardly spark interest. A virtual dive into the rainforest, a visit to the African savannah, or a trip to the fractured edges of melting glaciers can be an exciting, active, and multifaceted learning experience. The often demanded "different point of view" can be technically realized with VR applications.

In addition, the use of artificial intelligence (AI) can be beneficial. The Ruhr Universität Bochum, for example, is investigating the use of AI in digital teaching as part of their "KI:edu.nrw" project (DH.NRW, 2022a). With the project "AliSe—Adaptives Lernen in der Studieneingangsphase" (adaptive learning in the introductory phase of studies) (DH.NRW, 2022b), students at the University of Wuppertal are supported utilizing an adaptive learning environment that facilitates the individual diagnosis and repetition of school knowledge relevant for different courses at university.

The digital world must be opened up in education. To do this, we need to introduce young people to digital tools and techniques. Hence, in collaboration with the zdi network and industry, the state of North Rhine-Westphalia has set up the pilot project "Pakt für Informatik" (Pact for Information Technology) (MWIDE NRW, 2021a). The project is developing a new form of practice-oriented learning for students focusing on the requirements of the digital age and the new demands on skilled workers. In addition, the state has introduced the mandatory study of computer science in grades 5 and 6 at all secondary schools. The training and post-qualification of teachers likewise need to focus on the pedagogical and didactic opportunities of digitalization. To trigger educational innovations, the state is in the process of establishing an EdTech incubator within an international network (MWIDE NRW, 2021b). Start-ups from the EdTech sector, still suffering from limited access to the education sector, can provide valuable impulses for the development and introduction of digital tools and content, including the qualification of teachers.

Moreover, the buzzword "lifelong learning" finally has to become reality. The fact that there was no corresponding boom in the use of further education programs despite the heavy use of short-time work suggests that there is room for improvement in terms of the low-threshold nature, flexibility, and attractiveness of the programs. Education is a lifelong process. The world of work is characterized by constant changes in the respective job requirements. We do not know what tomorrow's jobs will look like in the future. There is a need to prepare people for using technologies that do not exist today to solve problems that we do not yet know of. Cognitive skills, independence, personal responsibility, and the ability to work as a team are gaining importance. What used to be called "switching sides" and still is rare needs to be utilized much more: Teachers visit companies and observe their processes and structures, and company employees provide insights into the business world at schools. Academic education and vocational education are increasingly converging—the transitions in education have to correspond to this in the future. This could resemble the following: Modular degrees from different educational institutions could be bundled into certificates, students could attend virtual courses from different universities, and professionals could participate in academic education. Especially, the combination of working and learning can benefit significantly through digital solutions. The support of such "irregular" careers, through financial assistance by the government, based on the existing concept of the German Education Promotion Act, a midlife BAföG (Bundesausbildungsförderungsgesetz), so to speak, needs to be designed accordingly.

## 2.2 *Public Administration: Finally Digital*

It quickly became clear that the way out of the pandemic would be vaccination, and the way forward in pandemic management would be the use of digital tools and technologies. Digitalization proved to be a crisis diffuser and freedom preserver, because pandemic management was and is closely linked to the politically challenging issue of restrictions on freedom. To prevent serious negative effects on the health of citizens and the stability of the healthcare system, political decisions had to be made that interfered massively and in several waves with personal and economic freedoms. Above all, political responsibility during the crisis was characterized by constantly balancing the extent and appropriateness of these restrictions. Digitalization became the advocate for freedom.

Digital technology not only made various impacts of the pandemic more bearable, but also acted as an enabler. Digitalization successfully helped to enhance the efficiencies of public health departments, to accelerate the search for and licensure of effective vaccines, to develop a nationwide vaccination infrastructure and administration, and to provide electronic vaccination and testing certificates to implement "2G/3G" (vaccinated, recovered, and tested, respectively) rules.

The fact that the "sudden" need for digitalization in digital administration initially revealed the deficits relentlessly was—in the best case—a salutary shock. In fact, to a certain extent the situation is a bit absurd: While Japan is launching a government program for "Society 5.0," the pandemic hit Germany, in terms of the equipment of health departments, in the age of the fax machine.

Within the Ministry of Economy and Digitalization, which is leading the way toward the digitalization of administration as a model ministry, the enormous advantages of the digital edge that had already been gained could be witnessed clearly: Due to the pre-pandemic implementation of electronic administrative processes and the experience with remote work, the entire ministry was prepared and able to work at full capacity when the lockdown started.

Creating a fully digital process for fast and unbureaucratic support for companies in the lockdown was the first pandemic-related task. NRW's Emergency Aid 2020—the largest and fastest funding program in the state's history—approved roughly about 435,000 applications and distributed 4.5 billion euros within a few weeks in March and April (MWIDE NRW, 2021c). This was followed by further interim aid, loan programs, guarantees, and tax relief enacted by the state and federal governments.

Likewise, early in the pandemic, the federal government launched the nationwide contact tracing system via an app. The development of the so-called Corona-Warn-App was accompanied by great controversy. In a nutshell, it may be possible to say in a conciliatory manner: The app is somewhat better than its reputation, and the lessons learned can be used for future optimization. In fact, the app is the first digital application available to the public that is provided by the public health system. This could be a quantum leap in that a new user- and innovation-oriented spirit must take hold in order to bring the entire health sector into the digital age. The fact that the vaccination card was then available digitally in a reasonably short time may be a hopeful start. In any case, more agility has to enter the system—the many dynamic players in the start-up sector could be the key drivers here.

For this reason, a regularly scheduled round table was initiated as part of municipal model projects on digital pandemic management in North Rhine-Westphalia. The objective of this initiative is to provide information on comprehensive approaches to digital pandemic management and to connect experts from the digital and healthcare sectors. In addition, the state government's CIO regularly invites selected representatives from a wide range of disciplines to participate in a "think tank." The focus of this think tank is on reviewing the applicability, availability, and impact of digital tools. As a result, measures for politics, administration, and society will be proposed (IT.NRW, 2002).

In the context of digital pandemic management, a fundamental question of the digital economy also emerged: fair access to the platform economy. Instead of monopolistic providers, gateways must be created that are open to all market actors. In the case of pandemic-related digital contact tracing, for example, North Rhine-Westphalia decided against commissioning an app operator and instead developed an open interface that can be accessed by all providers. In the interest of ensuring plurality in contact tracing systems, the state government has pushed ahead with the implementation of the gateway solution "IRIS connect" to digitally link contact tracing apps and health authorities. Thus, health authorities with access to "IRIS connect" no longer need to request separate queries from the various app operators. Instead, they simply perform a central query via the gateway and receive the relevant information from all connected apps via a secure data transmission path. The gateway solution "IRIS connect" is centrally available for all municipalities and app operators (IT.NRW, 2022a).

The fax age in the health offices mentioned at the beginning will now come to an end. In coping with the pandemic, these health authorities are a central service authority that requires strengthening through digital solutions, especially in times of contact tracing. The nationwide introduction of the software "SORMAS" or the interface "SORMAS eXchange" and its use is a central objective in digitally supported pandemic management. The value that SORMAS adds is based on its unique selling propositions. It enables cross-municipality networking via a secure digital exchange of personal data records between public health authorities as well as the automated visualization of maps and transmission chains to better and more quickly track and contain infection events. Having a uniform solution on one release level has great advantages in this regard. "SORMAS" offers interfaces that allow all software providers to connect (IT.NRW, 2022b).

The issue of access is not only one of fair competition for providers but also one that affects user administration in terms of digital sovereignty. North Rhine-Westphalia has initiated the development of an exchange platform for open-source applications, which is part of an overarching platform network of public administration. The aim is to enable open-source software-based IT applications in various administrations to be initially exchanged within the administration and then to be jointly developed further. Open-source software should be offered to public authorities in a legally secure, transparent, and sustainable manner and therefore become easier for them to use. The platform will comprise a central part as well as compatible, decentralized "satellites." As part of this, North Rhine-Westphalia is developing the first decentralized "satellite" as a joint platform for the state and local authorities (MWIDE NRW, 2021). In addition to strengthening digital sovereignty, this will primarily foster more innovation and competition. Open-source software can revitalize the IT economy in Germany and serve as an instrument for promoting small and medium-sized enterprises (SMEs) and start-ups, especially in the Gov-Tech sector.

## *2.3 Business: Digital or Not at All*

The corona crisis was a stress test for the entire economy. Success in this test under real conditions was closely connected to the level of digitalization and digital enthusiasm for development: It became evident that companies that had already positioned themselves well in terms of digitalization managed the crisis better than the digital latecomers.

From today to tomorrow when the lockdown came, the weighing of whether and how digitalization makes sense or not ended abruptly. Essentially, there was only one alternative that was as unexpected as it was abundantly clear: Entrepreneurs who still wanted to participate in the economy in some form had to go digital and upgrade.

Work from home or remote work was no longer something that characterized particularly "progressive" companies, but the everyday life of thousands of companies and employees. Those who were able had to. And those who had to usually could—the necessity made the opportunity more evident. While maintaining the same level of productivity, more tasks could be performed working from home. This was more than many companies had generally assumed.

The pressure to keep physical distance created a boom in digital technology. Video conferencing tools have replaced analog team meetings across all industries and have become an indispensable part of work processes in the current phase of a gradual return to face-to-face work. Events—from in-house conferences to congresses and trade fairs—have been held digitally. The strong increase in industry demand for remote services such as condition monitoring or remote maintenance will continue in the future.

German grocery retailers, who have so far only shown limited enthusiasm for digital reform given the low margins, were stable but faced competition (some of which they partnered with through investments): Delivery services experienced a boom as many customers shed their previous skepticism about digital grocery shopping during the corona pandemic.

E-commerce—at times the only possible option for keeping retail going—was suddenly the only lifeline for retailers to stay alive on their own. The fact that the shift to online commerce must be well prepared and thought through hit many hard—especially small businesses. The pandemic forced them into a difficult situation: While the shift to digital processes became more necessary than ever, in many cases they were not able to make this digital transition—whether in terms of expertise or funding needed for the software. The fact that the big beneficiary of the crisis is an online giant may be as unsurprising as it is discouraging. After all, many local retailers have shown enormous commitment and creativity—supported by a #supportyourlocals movement—to create interesting offers that can continue to lead the way in combining the analog and digital worlds in the future. It will now be a matter of accepting the trend toward a digital lack of alternatives, which occurred long before corona and facing up to the challenges. There will be no turning back.

All these examples show: The corona pandemic has created a stressful situation across the board, affecting all industries and all types of companies. It has ruthlessly exposed the digital reality of the economy, along with all the other side effects. Many reservations about digital solutions are already beginning to be dispelled—be it attitudes toward remote working, remote services, or online grocery shopping. The learning experiences will be of significant benefit now that face-to-face and digital are alternatives again. It is to be expected that the digitalization push will ensure a permanently different way of doing business.

At the same time, the title of this chapter—digital or not at all—must be qualified. The pandemic has not only clarified what can be done digitally but also what would be better-done hybrid or entirely analog in the future. In any case, the first face-to-face congresses and trade fairs show that both networking and product presentation are seeking a way "back" into the physical sphere.

Likewise, in vocational orientation, there is a lot of reason to reconcile the newly opened-up possibilities of the digital world with the power of personal encouragement. During the corona crisis, analog services in vocational orientation and training were digitalized at full speed. Apprenticeship fairs took place virtually, and online seminars replaced face-to-face learning. Much could be maintained in this way. At the same time, the limits of digitalization were revealed, for example, in vocational orientation, where the direct in-person experience of work is the focal point. Digital offers have not been able to stabilize the training markets everywhere, because addressing young people and accessing offers has become more difficult.

Ultimately, this suggests a future dovetailing of digital and personal/physical solutions. An analysis of digital strengths in the organizational sphere, as well as digital weaknesses in the social sphere, forms the basis for an effective balance of technological, economic, and social requirements within the economy of the future.

## 3 Effects on Start-Ups and Entrepreneurship Processes

An economic downturn on a crisis level does not fail to have an impact on the creation of new ventures. Three trends emerge—partly as a result of the crisis, partly as a continuation of developments that were already occurring before the pandemic: differentiation, resilience to the crisis, and expansion of motives. And it has become obvious that the crisis also produces winners—economically, but especially in research and development.

## 3.1 Start-Up Stability

The overall economic downturn as a result of the lockdown has been significant: According to the Federal Statistical Office, economic output in Germany declined by 4.9% in 2020 (Statistisches Bundesamt, 2021). The number of new businesses has declined as well (Institut für Mittelstandsforschung Bonn, 2021a). However, what is true for the economy as a whole is also true for the start-up sector: Even in such a broadly effective crisis, there are not only numerous losers but also areas that can maintain their position or even profit. The corona crisis has triggered different, sector-specific effects on start-up activity in Germany. While the hospitality and tourism sectors, compared to the previous year, recorded a 25% decline in new businesses in 2020, start-up activity in the mail order and Internet trade, mechanical engineering, software, and games sectors has increased significantly (ZEW, Creditreform, 2021).

For North Rhine-Westphalia, the "startupdetector report 2020" shows an increase in start-up activity despite the corona pandemic: According to this report, in 2020, there were 15.2% more new venture foundations than in the previous year. Compared to the federal level (12.5%), this number is disproportionate (startupdetector UG, 2021).

The resilience of start-ups to crisis has become particularly visible during this period. The rapid adaptability of young start-ups, their flexibility of business models, and their strongly digitally oriented processes have in many cases enabled numerous start-ups to cope with crisis more successfully.

At the same time, new opportunities emerge as a result of the pandemic: According to the "Global Entrepreneurship Monitor," in 2020 an increasing share of start-ups will exploit business opportunities that have only arisen as a consequence of the pandemic (RKW Kompetenzzentrum, 2021). These include young companies in areas that benefit from changing habits created by the pandemic, such as delivery services or online services. In any case, whether corona motivated or coincidentally boosted them, those that launched a digital learning platform in 2020, used an app to improve commodity trading, or created services in telemedicine are on the cutting edge.

It appears that this trend is also emerging in North Rhine-Westphalia. The first half of 2021 shows a recovery in start-up figures after the pandemic-related decline. The number of new businesses has increased not only in North Rhine-Westphalia but in most of the federal states. In comparison to previous years, liquidation figures continue to decline. A positive trend can also be observed in the number of business start-ups as well as commercial takeovers and hybrid entrepreneurship in North Rhine-Westphalia (Institut für Mittelstandsforschung Bonn, 2021b).

Finally, the third trend is continuing: the widening of the range of motives. Even in times of pandemic, an ongoing increase in public welfare-oriented start-up motives is noticeable. For the third year in a row, more start-ups in the German Start-up Monitor study are classifying their products or services as green economy or social entrepreneurship. In 2020, over 40% of the young companies were already considering themselves part of the green economy (43.4%; 2019: 36.6%) or social entrepreneurship (42.6%; 2019: 41.9%) (Bundesverband Deutsche Startups, 2020). This development bears great potential, as the grand challenges of our time need creative and courageous pioneers that are committed toward the common good as well as the future. They renew the principle of the social market economy by combining economic and social opportunities.

## 3.2 *Opportunities in Times of Crisis: Two Cases*

Every crisis also produces winners. The most prominent recent example from Germany is not only a victory in economic terms but also a victory over the virus. The company BioNTech, located in Mainz, Germany, founded in 2008 by Uğur Şahin and Özlem Türeci and listed on Nasdaq since the end of 2019, came to global recognition by developing the corona vaccine. Part of their success was the "piggybacking" with Pfizer in response to the crisis, which allowed the roll-out to take place at the required pace and scale. Such rapid scaling by partnering with established players is particularly suitable in crisis, as well as in times of increasingly short innovation cycles. In such cases, it is essential to be able to act quickly and efficiently.

Another example of a German start-up that succeeded during the crisis by helping to cope with it is the company Ubirch. Based in Cologne, Germany, Ubirch is a good example of the flexibility and crisis resilience of start-ups. Founded in 2014, the company specializes in data backup in an Internet-of-things context. The two CEOs Stephan Noller and Karim H. Attia quickly realized that data was going to play a crucial role in the pandemic response. Starting in mid-2020, the small company focused on digital verification as a new business area. By early August 2020, their pilot solution for the digital mapping of vaccination status was already used in two counties. Ultimately, this real-world application, as well as their overall rapid product adaptation, put Ubirch on the radar of major corporations. In March 2021, the German Federal Ministry of Health commissioned IBM, Ubirch, govdigital, and Bechtle to develop the digital proof of vaccination for Germany (UBIRCH GmbH, 2022). As a result, one of the largest digitalization projects in the medical sector—with over 100 million certificates issued—was realized with the help of this Cologne-based start-up.

The future holds other large fields in which both mRNA technology and cryptographically protected data will play an important role—the first in cancer therapy and the latter in the supply and tracking of solar power or the documentation of supply chains. So BioNTech and Ubirch, but also the many other agile start-ups active in the health sector, can certainly surprise the world with more successful innovations in the future.

# 4 Changes (2): What Will Remain?

After the crisis, not everything will be different than before. Some euphoria, even some concern, will be mitigated by a new normal. However, the developments during the pandemic outlined above will become more solidified in the foreseeable future. The question of what will remain can be taken up by contrasting two examples: The world of work is one area where the digital experience is causing pervasive change. The area of social interaction will be the one where the analog will prevail. Dystopias in which encounters take place only in virtual space simply do not correspond to what makes people human.

## *4.1 Work*

Because humans always strive to use humor to heal, even in dire situations, social media was full of jokes about sweatpants in the home office and the request to mute the microphones. In fact, the corona crisis abruptly and radically changed the world of work—unleashing unexpected flexibility and creativity. Through the high level of commitment shown by everyone involved, many workplace tasks could be quickly digitalized and thus relocated to an off-site work environment.

As a result of almost one and a half years of more flexible work organization, not only the demands of the workforce have changed. Companies have also benefitted from crucial learning experiences. What is clear is that the new flexibility is hardly reversible. In this sense, the pandemic represented a forced experiment, and the results cannot be ignored: The wishes of employees and the requirements of a company can generally be reconciled.

Like in the field of education—where pedagogical–didactic change is necessary in addition to technical progress—the change in the world of work is not just about technical (equipping with mobile technology) and legal (working time legislation) issues, but also about cultural ones. At the same time, there will be a wide variety of solutions: Occupational fields and workplaces are diverse and therefore also offer different possibilities for the use of remote working. Nevertheless, even in cases where work from home would be possible for the entire working time, this will not necessarily be the solution of choice. In many cases, a combination of remote and face-to-face work has proven successful. For teamwork, but also for the social elements that naturally play a role in professional life, face-to-face contact is not completely dispensable. As a digital pioneer, the Ministry of Economics and Digitalization was already prepared for digital and mobile working before the first virus-related lockdown. However, the desire for face-to-face contact can now clearly be recognized, so that the mix of remote work and days of physical presence is proving valuable.

However, the new world of work also demands adjustments from employees and managers alike. The timing of work, virtual conferences, and physical presence, as well as leisure time, must be weighed up. Besides that, life circumstances and living conditions must be considered when planning work from home. On the one hand, a new world of work requires a change in management behavior, and on the other, it places new demands on employees' responsibility and self-organization. Technology alone does not solve all those questions.

With the emergence of the pandemic, aspects of occupational health and safety took on a new significance, which must be continued. In this context, all parties involved in the businesses generally worked together very responsibly and rapidly.

Indeed, it can be foreseen that the world of work is the area where a "before corona" and "after corona" will establish. Lessons learned during the pandemic will help shape the future, which will be more digital, more agile, and more diverse.

## *4.2 Humans*

In one of his novels, science fiction author Isaac Asimov, known as the inventor of "Robot Laws," creates a world where people only "see" each other, not meet (Asimov, 1957). The hologram, sent to every place and meeting, replaces the physical encounter. Human closeness is lost; actual face-to-face contact is considered obscene.

As people began to get used to digital conferences and video contact during the first lockdown, the question of whether such dystopian ideas might be realized loomed in the air. After all, a vast amount of communication worked well online, contact had to be avoided, hugs were becoming somewhat indecent, and the next pandemic would only be a matter of time. Isn't "seeing" by means of screens the great progress for the benefit of mankind? In fact, however, it turns out that the core characteristic of humans, which makes them a social being, seems hardly changeable. In many cases, it is not organizational or productivity-related issues that bring back at least some of those digital conferences to the world of analog face-to-face exchanges. What is becoming evident is that direct contact, communication enriched with facial expressions and gestures, has added value—for social interaction, creativity, and dynamism. Whether it is brainstorming in a team, building trust with colleagues, or motivating effects within a team—certainly no argument—can be made for completely replacing these special features of personal communication, and there is no reason to believe such a development will occur. Rather, it will be a matter of both. Some things will take place digitally, some analogously, and many in a hybrid fashion.

Along with the first vaccinations, online platforms were filled with images documenting humans' insatiable need for companionship. Grandmothers holding their grandchildren again, friends reuniting after months, colleagues enjoying the "after-work beer."

And the flood disaster that hit the German states of North Rhine-Westphalia and Rhineland-Palatinate in July of this year brought no doubt about empathy and cohesion. The commitment shown by so many was extraordinary, ranging from the smallest donation in kind to substantial monetary donations, from providing brief relief efforts to days of support in mud, dirt, and garbage. People's willingness to help surpassed every expectation.

Nothing will be lost, though we will gain new opportunities. This is where the policy principle of putting digitalization at the service of people becomes concrete: Digital technology is not an end in itself but is used wherever it is useful and wherever it helps.

It would be encouraging if we could continue to expand the virtuosity by which we operate the digital as well as direct communication channels today. Coming generations will cross borders anyway, equally at home in virtual worlds with avatars or holograms as they are in the living room or on the sports field. The worlds will also merge: Pokémon Go, a game that was popular for a certain time, was only a modest start in this regard. In the future, virtual reality will become a companion in the physical world—navigation commands will be transmitted as an overlay on the glasses of pedestrians, geographically separated people will be able to be "present" as avatars, and tourist attractions will enrich the experience with digitally produced effects. Where, for example, not only ruins can be viewed, but also their original shape can be appreciated. The younger generation will take this for granted. But the prediction that even the most VR-conscious young person will also seek social face-to-face contact with their peers seems likely. The "youth benches" that some cities are investing in for young people to "hang out" instead of traditional park benches should therefore not be hastily eliminated again.

## 5 From Zeroing COVID to Zero $CO_2$

Experiencing the corona pandemic—a disaster coming from nature, but also the human power to counter it—was and is an experience that suggests a reference to climate protection. It is imperative that the determination showed by the economy, society, and government agencies in combating the corona pandemic be preserved and strengthened for the task of the century which is the transformation toward climate neutrality. The forces mobilized for one goal—Zeroing COVID—must be mobilized at an even higher level for enabling the achievement of the other goal—Zero $CO_2$ by 2045.

The lessons learned from the pandemic and its management will provide valuable insights into this regard. Increased use of work from home and virtual conferences can reduce car travel and eliminate the need for some business flights. Remote services will reduce traffic. Digital technology will help to reduce resource consumption, for example, by using AI-driven monitoring to reduce material consumption and support the circular economy or by using intelligent traffic systems—likely involving autonomous vehicles—to manage traffic flows. Likewise, the energy transition is significantly driven by digital advances: Virtual power plants and intelligent interlinking of sectors, including integrated neighborhood concepts for housing, transport, and work, will help reduce greenhouse gas emissions and make more efficient use of volatile renewable energies.

The link between the corona pandemic and the two major transformation tasks lies in the fact that the digital transformation has received a boost as a result of the pandemic. This boost can also be used for the path toward climate neutrality. For both, most important are innovation and determination.

The rapid development and approval of vaccines mark the transition from pandemic management to hope for the end of the pandemic and the withdrawal of restrictions. The underlying research and development are a prime example of the importance of political priority for innovation. And prioritizing innovation simultaneously increases degrees of freedom. Restrictions that were implemented during the corona pandemic may have re-emphasized the importance of freedom, which at times seemed to be blurring into something that was supposedly taken for granted. Leveraging digital technology has given validity to this value by limiting, mitigating, or removing pandemic constraints through digitally supported management. Likewise, the transformation toward zero $CO_2$ also is a freedom issue shaped by the correlation between technology-driven progress and human development opportunities—or simplified: the more innovations, the greater the degrees of freedom. It will have to be a matter of not obstructing development opportunities with politically unimaginative bans (and thus jeopardizing the entire project through a lack of acceptance), but rather one of using creativity and innovation to find ways to enable living, working, and mobility under conditions of freedom—while at the same time ensuring that climate targets are met.

For this purpose, the cooperation and courage mobilized in tackling the pandemic need to be embraced. During the crisis, business, society, politics, and public administration have shown that procedural efficiency and speed of implementation can be increased. This spirit is now urgently required for climate protection.

Following the significant decision of the German Federal Constitutional Court regarding the Federal Climate Protection Act, which highlighted the rights of the younger generation with remarkable clarity, a broad consensus to sharpen the climate targets quickly emerged throughout the country. The state of North Rhine-Westphalia was the first to follow suit with higher targets. By 2030, greenhouse gas emissions are to be reduced by 65% compared to the reference year of 1990. By 2045, Germany—one of the world's largest industrial nations—aims to become climate neutral. From today's perspective, this is a timeframe in which usually bypasses are planned and completed in this country.

In the same way that the outbreak of the corona pandemic boosted the pace of science, business, and government, climate protection now needs to be accelerated by considering the—short—timeframe. In this context, great potential lies among those players that are characterized by high agility and fast development as well as roll-out cycles: Collaboration with start-ups will prove particularly rewarding in matters of climate protection. In line with this expectation, a project has just been launched in one of the transformation hotspots of North Rhine-Westphalia. In particular, the search for solutions to global climate protection and sustainability goals is taking shape in a region, where the economy and jobs previously dominated by lignite: The Global Entrepreneurship Centre is being established in Rheinisches Revier, in Cologne, Germany, which is going to attract top international talents (Zukunftsagentur Rheinisches Revier, 2022). Here, the transformation will become visible in a more concentrated way than in any other place in Germany.

Consequently, the level of ambition must be raised significantly. The small-scale measures that were possible during the pandemic—simpler procedures ranging from the procurement of medical supplies to the use of patios in restaurants—will now have to be applied on a large scale. Specific measures must follow the right mindset: The government needs to become an enabler—shifting from intervening toward enabling.

Measures and projects that are not approved quickly will not contribute to climate protection in the critical phase: To achieve the set goals by 2030, corresponding investments in infrastructure and facilities must be approved and must have started in the construction phase no later than 2025. For this, enabling regulations are needed that establish clear priorities in the sense of permitting procedural priority for the Green Deal. Thus, a special procedural right for permits that contribute to the achievement of climate goals is needed. Achieving the Green Deal requires a political and societal consensus to enable and accelerate industrial transformation through a goal-oriented, efficient, digitized, and planning-safe procedural law. This involves a consensual renunciation of excessive procedures—a piece of pragmatism in the sense of the great human task.

## 6 Outlook: Game Changer

The recent corona crisis is a manifestation of one of the mega-trends of our time—pandemics and natural disasters—and at the same time touches on all other mega-trends: digitalization, climate protection, globalization, and complexity. Within this crisis, all the contemporary trends have become apparent in their interdependency and impact. Whether the pandemic will continue to be seen as the turning point that divides time into "before" and "after" remains an open question. However, it will certainly remain a benchmark experience to which future discussions will repeatedly draw attention, as indeed it is one of the few experiences shared by mankind.

This chapter focused on the depths of change exhibited by the corona pandemic. As to the introductory question of whether and to what extent the crisis will be a game changer, we will only be able to provide the answer in retrospect by leaving the field to historians. But the evidence indicates that some things will remain "stably different." In fact, there is one area where the pandemic experience has changed the "game" for good: digital transformation. There are (at least) three reasons for this: First, companies, citizens, administrators, and policy makers have learned, sometimes in painful, sometimes in inspiring, ways that the "rules of the game"—to stay within the metaphor—are mandatory. It became evident that without digital tools and technology, the system would not function in crises, while in normal times it would function poorly and that digitalization offers opportunities that must (finally) be exploited. During the crisis, digital technology also became an advocate for civil liberties and made it possible to mitigate political dilemmas. Second, it will not be possible to fall behind the experience gained with flexibility, independence of location, low-threshold access, etc.—whatever worked well for a year and a half does not need to be justified as a change but, conversely, calls the previous status quo into question. And third, at the very least, a responsible approach to the crisis must produce a palette of learning experiences and empowerment for the future. How resilient the economy and society are to the challenges and crises ahead will significantly depend on whether we can raise the level of ambition in digitalization.

But whether this will happen, whether the corona crisis will one day be seen as a time full of suffering and restrictions, though also a decisive and, above all, sustainable digitalization booster, is not certain. However, there is no question that this role as a game changer would be desirable.

## References


Asimov, I. (1957). *The naked sun*. Doubleday.

Bundesverband Deutsche Startups. (2020). *Deutscher startup monitor 2020*. http://www.deutscherstartupmonitor.de/wp-content/uploads/2020/09/dsm_2020.pdf. Accessed 26 Jan 2022.

DH.NRW. (2022a). *Kooperationen*. http://www.dh.nrw/kooperationen/KI:edu.nrw-75. Accessed Jan 26, 2022.

DH.NRW. (2022b). *Kooperationen*. http://www.dh.nrw/kooperationen/ALiSe-74. Accessed Jan 26, 2022.

Institut für Mittelstandsforschung Bonn. (2021a). *Existenzgründungen*. http://www.ifm-bonn.org/statistiken/gruendungen-und-unternehmensschliessungen/existenzgruendungen-insgesamt. Accessed Jan 26, 2022.

Institut für Mittelstandsforschung Bonn. (2021b) *Existenzgründungen und Liquidationen*. http://www.ifm-bonn.org/statistiken/gruendungen-und-unternehmensschliessungen/gewerbliche-existenzgruendungen-und-liquidationen. Accessed Jun 26, 2022.

IT.NRW. (2002). *Think-Tank*. http://www.it.nrw/think-tank. Accessed Jan 26, 2022.

IT.NRW. (2022a). *Pandemiemanagement*. http://www.it.nrw/digital-gestuetztes-pandemiemanagement. Accessed Jan 26, 2022.

IT.NRW. (2022b) *Digitale tools*. http://www.it.nrw/kernstuecke-des-digitalen-pandemiemanagements. Accessed Jan 26, 2022.

MKW NRW. (2022). *Vernetzte Hochschulen*. http://www.mkw.nrw/digitalisierung. Accessed Jan 26, 2022.

MSB NRW. (2022a). *DigitalPakt*. http://www.schulministerium.nrw/digitalpakt. Accessed Jan 26, 2022.

MSB NRW. (2022b). *Lehren und Lernen in der digitalen Welt*. http://www.schulministerium.nrw/digitalisierung. Accessed Jan 26, 2022.

MWIDE NRW. (2021a). *Pakt für Informatik*. http://www.wirtschaft.nrw/pressemitteilung/pakt-fuer-informatik. Accessed Jan 26, 2022.

MWIDE NRW. (2021b). *Digitalstrategie 2.0*. http://www.wirtschaft.nrw/pressemitteilung/digitalstrategie-2-0. Accessed Jan 26, 2022.

MWIDE NRW. (2021c). *Corona-Hilfen*. http://www.wirtschaft.nrw/pressemitteilung/groesste-und-schnellste-hilfsaktion-fuer-die-wirtschaft-der-landesgeschichte. Accessed Jan 26, 2022.

MWIDE NRW. (2021). *Open-Source-Software*. http://www.wirtschaft.nrw/pressemitteilung/land-startet-pilotprojekt-fuer-open-source-software. Accessed Jan 26, 2022.

RKW Kompetenzzentrum. (2021). *Global entrepreneurship monitor*. Unternehmensgründungen im weltweiten Vergleich. Länderbericht Deutschland 2020/21. http://www.rkw-kompetenzzentrum.de/publikationen/studie/global-entrepreneurship-monitor-20202021/. Accessed Jun 26, 2022.

startupdetector UG. (2021). *startupdetector report 2020*. http://www.startupdetector.de/reports/startupdetector-report-2020.pdf. Accessed Jan 26, 2022.

Statistisches Bundesamt. (2021). *Folgen Corona-Pandemie*. http://www.destatis.de/DE/Presse/Pressemitteilungen/2021/03/PD21_N023_p001.html. Accessed Jan 26, 2022.

UBIRCH GmbH. (2022). *Digitaler Impfnachweis*. http://www.ubirch.com/de/der-digitale-impfnachweis. Accessed Jan 26, 2022.

ZEW, Creditreform. (2021). *Junge Unternehmen*. http://ftp.zew.de/pub/zew-docs/jungeunternehmen/jungeunternehmen_0821.pdf?v=1629293695. Accessed Jan 26, 2022.

Zukunftsagentur Rheinisches Revier. (2022). *Projekte*. http://www.rheinisches-revier.de/051-gec-global-entrepreneurship-centre. Accessed Jan 26, 2022.

**Andreas Pinkwart** has been Minister for Economic Affairs, Innovation, Digitalization and Energy of the State of North Rhine-Westphalia since 2017. He was previously Rector of the HHL Leipzig Graduate School of Management and Chair for Innovation Management and Entrepreneurship (2011–2017). From 2005 to 2010, he was Minister for Innovation, Science, Research and Technology and Deputy Prime Minister in North Rhine-Westphalia.

**Anna-Tina Pannes** is an advisor at the Ministry of Economic Affairs, Innovation, Digitalization and Energy of the State of North Rhine-Westphalia. She received her doctorate (Dr. rer. pol.) from the University of Duisburg-Essen for developing an analytical approach to informal decision-making processes in government formations.

# Oxygenating Innovation? The Not-So-Brave New World of COVID-19?

**Norris Krueger**

**Abstract** *Scaling value propositions as if stakeholders finally matter.*

Why is it that while COVID has imposed possibly the most VUCA: volatility (V), uncertainty (U), complexity (C) and ambiguity (A) in recent memory, many new and small firms are nonetheless scaling? What has COVID forced us to learn—or **re**-learn?

Everywhere we turn, we hear about "Industry 4.0" where industry players and stakeholders make up a complex, dynamic web of relationships, facilitated by ever-proliferating open innovation models and a recognition that linear relationships have given way to complex, dynamic ecosystems that require multilateral engagement (e.g., Müller et al., *Technological Forecasting & Social Change 132*:2–17, 2018). Alas, the dominant models for innovation systems remain firmly focused on institutional players too often to the exclusion of the innovators themselves. We need to understand that innovation communities **are** an ecosystem. This essay introduces the reader to what we might call the "**ecosystem mindset**."

**Keywords** Entrepreneurial ecosystems · Innovation policy · Entrepreneurial communities · Ecosystem builders

## 1 Designing Viable, Scalable, Sustainable Value Propositions Is a Team Sport

Scalable value propositions get articulated via interactions with multiple stakeholders, usually with partially competing interests (that often are far from static). If any organization seeks to scale its value propositions, its business models and

N. Krueger (✉)
College of Doctoral Studies, UOPX, Boise, ID, USA

University of Management and Technology, Lahore, Pakistan

American University, Washington, DC, USA

Entrepreneurship Northwest, Boise, ID, USA

ISM, Vilnius, Lithuania



D. B. Audretsch, I. A. M. Kunadt (eds.), *The COVID-19 Crisis and Entrepreneurship*, International Studies in Entrepreneurship 54,
https://doi.org/10.1007/978-3-031-04655-1_4

business model innovation must embrace this new reality. To use Carmine Bianchi's fortuitous phrase, communities, industries, and organizations advance best when information operates "outside-in" (Bianchi, 2021, Bianchi & Vignieri, 2021).

The problems and questions facing modern organizations are more than complicated, they are complex: Not just difficult but wicked problems. Strategic action is no longer about risks but about uncertainty; assets and resources need to be deployed very differently under Knightian uncertainty (Lampert et al., 2020). Strategic foresight thus requires rich, diverse information flows that cannot obtain from a top-down, institutions-led bureaucratic approach. In particular, consider that many of these complex problems address many of society's biggest challenges (e.g., the UN's Sustainable Development Goals). Solving for any of them requires embracing a variety of wicked problems and thus embracing a multilateral approach.[1] An ecosystem approach.

That is, innovation largely arises from outside or, perhaps more specifically the information needed to innovate successfully comes from multiple sources external to the organization. For example, would you rather leave entrepreneurship policy to bureaucratic forces and entrenched interests or to entrepreneurs and their champions?

Consider also the rise of visible co-opetition that has also characterized Industry 4.0. Even pre-COVID, supply chains have become more like a relationship chain, better still, a web of relationships (Sanders, 2020; Sanders et al., 2007). Thus, our focus turns profitably to understanding and facilitating connections and thus the connectors.

Innovation is essential to meeting the great challenges of today. At the heart of great innovation is identifying and validating a value proposition that serves customers and/or other stakeholders, often in disruptive (even subversive) fashion. Further, the great challenges of today demand that the viable value proposition must also be scalable and sustainable—no avoiding the absolute demand for impact and for serving multiple stakeholders.

How can we identify scalable, sustainable value propositions? If we must balance the interests of an increasing variety of stakeholders, that add to the complexity of our task. However, it also adds to our entrepreneurial capabilities. Multiple, varied stakeholders bring greater demands but also bring multiple, varied sources of information (and other resources.)[2,3]

COVID has taught us how to be virtual effectively. It has also taught that getting all the right people at the table is even more important on Zoom. If the right people and processes are in place, innovation can accelerate (e.g., Maggioncalda, 2020). If

[1] A powerful video on this point from UNCTAD's Chantal Line Carpentier: https://www.youtube.com/watch?v=Vnidf6hO71M

[2] A recent literature review: Antoniuk et al. (2021).

[3] Even broadening the definition of "competitor" pays off https://ecorner.stanford.edu/articles/how-to-rethink-competition/

the right people are **not** at the table, we are already seeing them create their own tables!

Nonetheless, policymakers and major institutions seem wedded to an intuitively plausible yet practically confounding model with no Antoine Lavoisier in sight but plenty of Joseph Priestlys.

### *1.1 Phlogiston? (Lavoisier v. Priestly)*

What happens when something burns (oxidizes)? Careful experiments showed that when something burns even to ashes, it somehow gains weight. How can that be? Phlogiston was hypothesized as the inherent ingredient for anything that oxidizes; Burn something and it releases phlogiston. Of course, that requires phlogiston to have **negative** mass! However, the math worked. Perfectly. And of course, Antoine Lavoisier and others eventually realized that burning combines the original material with oxygen. Meanwhile, Joseph Priestly had demonstrated the existence of oxygen though even he could not let go of the phlogiston model.

When we look at entrepreneurial ecosystems and models of innovation systems, we are seeing powerful evidence for "oxygen" while policy and practice stay wedded to the "phlogiston" of top-down, institution-driven models.

## 2 It Takes an Ecosystem to Build a Village? Entrepreneurial Ecosystems!

In studying entrepreneurial ecosystems on the ground, it is hard not to see clear implications for constructing and evaluating scalable value propositions. While the open innovation world and others talk "ecosystem", it has become painfully clear that healthy entrepreneurial communities grow often *despite* the institutions and power players that nonetheless claim the high ground. When Feld (2012) articulated this phenomenon, he distinguished between "leaders" and "feeders" where institutional players are the "feeders" who support activities driven by the wishes of entrepreneurs. This "flips the script" from a top-down model to a bottom-up regime. Even in the top-down model, the institutions often intend to not be directive but facilitating the grassroots efforts. Alas, too often the power imbalances intrude, too often the bureaucratic imperative nudges them to feel entitled to be directive.

If we lived in a world of hierarchies, that might even be reasonable. The top-down, institutions-led model assumes that institutions and power players individually and collectively have the requisite knowledge to ensure that any innovation will be implemented. Also, this way the innovative activity is also unlikely to disrupt (let alone subvert) the *status quo*. Think of it as an organizational-level Dunning–Kruger effect (Kruger & Dunning, 1999). Worse, it encourages, even codifies the

HIPPO effect. Thomke has studied the pernicious impacts of deferring to the HIPPO, the **HI**ghest **P**aid **P**erson's **O**pinion (e.g., Ghosh et al., 2020). Instead of soliciting a breadth of information, why not just listen to the Most Important Person in the room[4]?

We live in a world where disruption has become the norm. While COVID has been the genesis of much deep disruption, it has uncovered even more issues. Consider Exhibit A for all this: Supply chains. COVID upended many but it also laid bare even more situations where the organization's supply chain was already vulnerable. In our haste to "optimize" and "lean" our channels, we subtracted much of the resiliency that the Industry 4.0 model offered (Ellram et al., 2020; the prescient Sanders et al., 2007).

## 2.1 *Innovation Operates in Complex, Dynamic Adaptive Systems*

In the entrepreneurial ecosystems world, a favored metaphor is that innovative economies are not tidy, well-ordered farms; they are as messy as a chaotic, ever-evolving rain forest (Hwang & Horowitt, 2012). Behind the metaphor is the important reality that economies, like societies, are complex adaptive systems with remarkable and dynamic connectivity[5] (e.g., Brett, 2019).

In complex systems, it is difficult to predict impacts of even the most powerful entities or the seemingly largest interventions. It is far better to look at cumulative impacts of smaller actions. As early as 2013, the OECD found that most communities sought to grow the entrepreneurial ecosystem by establishing helpful enabling conditions while practitioners demanded bold action (Feld, 2012; Krueger, 2013; Feld & Hathaway, 2020). One fruitful focus is not on "enabling" conditions but instead of removing "disabling" conditions. The Ewing Marion Kauffman Foundation[6] proposed moving toward "zero barriers". In a complex dynamic system, it is exceedingly hard to predict the impact of an enabling condition; it is much more straightforward to remove a barrier.[7]

---

[4]Dunning-Kruger on steroids? www.ideatovalue.com/lead/nickskillicorn/2019/01/hippos-are-killers-of-ideas/

[5]BCG (www.bcg.com/en-in/publications/2020/valuable-productivity-gains-covid-19) notes that increasing social connectivity yields disproportionate increases in successful innovation.

[6]Ewing Marion Kauffman Foundation (2017). "***Zero Barriers***: Three Mega Trends Shaping the Future of Entrepreneurship". www.kauffman.org/what-we-do/resources/state-of-entrepreneurship-addresses/2017-state-of-entrepreneurship-address

[7]Entrepreneurship research pioneer Al Shapero (1975) noted how removing a barrier for a potential entrepreneur could lead to entrepreneurial action.

### 2.2 *Open Innovation*

One area that "walks the walk" in taking advantage of all this is Open Innovation. What happens when we actually listen to the maxim, "Its not the idea, it's the execution", that is does not matter where the idea arose but whether value gets created? While there still are times to assiduously protect your IP, there are many opportunities to identify those who can create the most value. What is the point of keeping IP that you cannot implement? (Bettenmann et al., 2022; Bogers et al., 2020; Scuotto et al., 2020; West & Bogers, 2014).

Consider also the growing need for even SMEs to work with multiple stakeholders and for everyone, the need to address the complexity of sustainability. The more complex the strategic position, the more we need inputs and insights from others in the ecosystem. Yet despite its success, OI remains on the periphery of strategic thinking so we need to embrace how OI both benefits from and drives ecosystem thinking.

## 3 One Ring to Rule Them All?

Why top-down might work? If knowledge spillover is only one way (from institutions to the unwashed masses), innovation absolutely needs visible, credible top-down support—**if** governance mechanisms exist to reduce information asymmetry, enhance network effects, and enforce unselfishness.

One example of a powerful top-down model is Amazon. They are evidences that an effective aggregator can encourage innovation despite near-monopoly power. While powerful institutions can enable and encourage innovation in products but also constrains competition (witness how Amazon creates knockoff products) via a near-irreversible power imbalance that Amazon does not see as unfair.

### 3.1 *The Triple Helix and Its Offspring*

Given the academic world's strong interest in placing institutions at the heart of most management domains and the potential for elegant models. Enter the famed "triple helix" which asserts that all we need for innovation is to have academe, industry, and government in the room... then magic happens! We will have entrepreneurship without entrepreneurs, innovation without innovators—taking the human completely out of the equation.

A few years ago, a prominent country proposed to crowdsource their national innovation policy, invited experts and citizens alike to comment. The draft was "crowdsourced" by a small group of like-minded government officials then posted as a Google doc for comments. However, any suggestion that challenged the

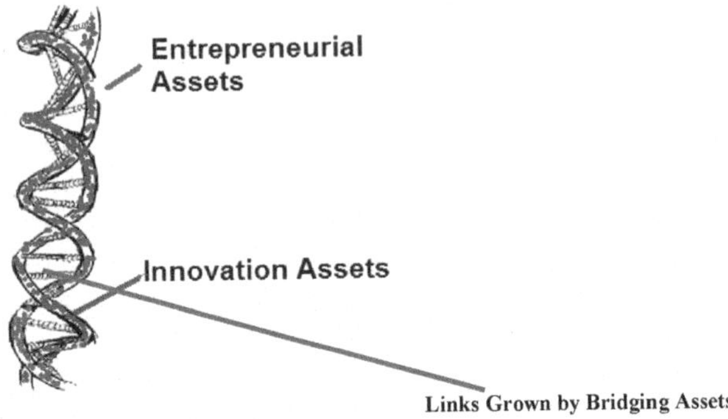


**Fig. 1** Bridging assets model (own drawing from Brännback et al., 2008)

assumptions or conclusions were attacked. I remember one comment sniffing something like "it is absolutely true that XXX does NOT need more entrepreneurs and innovators" and another that "any meaningful innovation came directly from government." Exhibit A for why top-down models always win? Confirmation bias on steroids?

Once an industry or community has achieved a high level of innovativeness, it usually appears to have healthy relationships between academe, industry, and government that accompany an innovative community. The trap is that is **not** how the community **became** innovative.

Consider the DNA molecule that inspired the triple helix metaphor. The triple helix model proposes that the DNA of an economy has three strands: academe, industry, and government. For simplicity, consider the double helix that we are familiar with. Strong, well-defined strands paint a compelling picture. With one small problem: Where is the information in the DNA molecule? Is it in the strands? No!

DNA's information is in the connections, the crosslinks. Any biologist who looked at a helix model that lacked the crosslinks would be unamused at best. So should we. In an economic system, the information in those crosslinks is not carried by amino acids; it is carried by people (Brännback et al., 2008).

Consider here a different helix model. An older model suggests three key elements: innovation assets (knowledge and resources) and entrepreneurial assets plus **bridging assets** that connect the other two. (Here we allow the DNA strands to carry information.) This version places the connecting and thus the connectors at center stage (Fig. 1).

## 3.2 *The* In*tangible Infrastructure of Innovation: Why Connecting (and* Connectors*) Matter*

The community development literature is quite persuasive that economic activity is, in Granovetter's famous words, deeply co-embedded with social activity. This raises another crucial argument for the ecosystem model. So much of the top-down, institutions-led approach focuses on the tangible aspects of the infrastructure (physical resources like capital, etc.) However, what makes an innovative community is driven by its **intangible** infrastructure. Back in the 1980s, Flora and Flora (1993) and Emery and Flora (2006) showed how social and cultural elements of the community could foster or constrain innovative activity. Does your community or organization enhance or attenuate the perception of actionable opportunities (Krueger, 2000)? Entrepreneurial human capital and entrepreneurial social capital are essential yet lay outside the top-down models except indirectly.

Another way to look at this is where and how an ecosystem is nurturing entrepreneurial potential (and where it is not.) The entrepreneurial potential of a community (or industry or organization) is very much a function of the quantity and quality of its potential entrepreneurs (Krueger & Brazeal, 1994). If we look through the lens of intentions, that mean asking where and how an ecosystem makes entrepreneurial/innovation activity desirable both personally and socially and asking where and how it makes it feasible personally and collectively.

One implication is if we are to democratize innovation and entrepreneurship, we need to build the entrepreneurial potential of under-represented groups. That means growing potential entrepreneurs (Krueger, 2021).

One crucial but less-obvious implication is that even the worst ecosystem nonetheless does some things well and even the best have areas for major improvement. Whether if you perceive your community/industry ecosystem as strong or weak, ecosystem builders offer useful insights.

Remember our HIPPOs? In Fig. 2, which of these three types of network do you think they perceive? (Which might they prefer?) Most people think of networks as the centralized form on the left but that paints a picture of an unhealthy ecosystem. The middle one is better and likely the most common but great ecosystems look more like the third.

If an ecosystem looks more like the network on the right, connections and connecting become of great importance. And thus connectors. Institutions do not connect, people do. Quite illuminatingly, Stephenson[8] found in a major USA city that a list of the top connectors had almost **zero** overlap with a list of the city's 100 most influential people. If Bianchi (2021) is right that ecosystems need outside-in governance, which group is more likely to broadly and unselfishly connect? So who **are** these superconnectors? (Fig. 2)

[8] See also www.bit.ly/Karen_S [if any bit.ly link expires, please contact author].

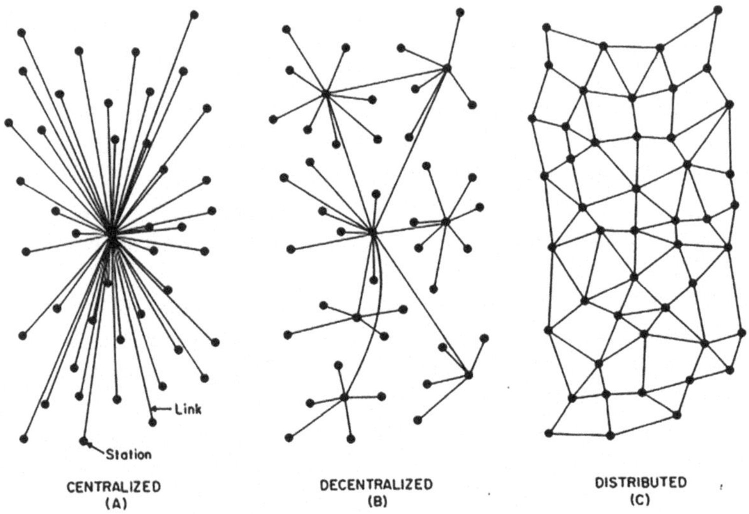


**Fig. 2** Type of networks (Baran, 1964)

## 4 *Liaison-animateurs*

What local economies need are connectors, yes. But the key is having a robust set of proactive, unselfish superconnectors which Sweeney (1987) felicitously dubbed "*liaison-animateurs*"—both brokers **and** energizers. The type of connector does matter. Following Stephenson (2009), are you a gatekeeper zealously guarding access to people and resources or are you unselfishly connecting? The introduction of a single unselfish connector often has immediate, significant impact especially where proactive (Feldman & Zoller, 2012). Even where a community has built a sizable directory of resources, a human "navigator" is a difference-maker as premier ecosystem resource mapper SourceLink[9] has shown repeatedly.

### 4.1 *Ecosystem Building and Ecosystem Builders*

Putting *liaison-animateurs* front and center, the Kauffman Foundation recognized this and launched ESHIP,[10] an immense effort to grow and support bottom-up entrepreneurial champions that they labeled "ecosystem builders". Marshaling the

[9]www.JoinSourceLink.com [Resource Navigator and Rails] https://www.joinsourcelink.com/identify/resource-navigator; https://www.kcsourcelink.com/blog/post/blog/2017/06/13/take-a-ride-on-the-kcsourcelink-resource-rail

[10]ESHIP overview: www.bit.ly/ESHIPgoals; www.bit.ly/ESHIPdashboard

insights and experience of hundreds of active ecosystem builders offers powerful evidence for bottom-up efforts led not by the institutions but the voice of the entrepreneurs they serve.

Around the globe, is it any surprise that the best programs to entrepreneurship and innovation look very much like ecosystem builders and *liaison-animateurs*? Highly collaborative models that are driven by the voice of the entrepreneur include Startup Chile and the Netherlands' Startup Delta. More recent efforts include Finland-based Startup Commons, Lithuania's Creative Shock, and European Startup Heatmap/ Deep Ecosystems.

## 4.2 Mindset: How Do Ecosystem Builders/Liaison-Animateurs Think?

So what makes a *liaison-animateur*, an ecosystem builder? To understand any profession, we need to ask: How do they think? What do they know? What do they know how to do? How do they behave? We already have tools to both assess and nurture mindset and skills and we would welcome additional research allies.

It would seem quite likely that these entrepreneurial champions share multiple facets of the entrepreneurial mindset. Do they exhibit a bias toward action, a facility for connecting the dots, cognitive flexibility, or resilience to adversity (cf. Krueger, 2015; Hattenberg et al., 2021)? We already have tools to test for these and other facets.

Similarly, EntreComp is a robust toolkit for assessing core entrepreneurship skills and for growing them. How does your ecosystem provide opportunities to nurture such skills and to reward their deployment? We also expect to see higher levels of noncognitive skills like metacognition, foresight (Djuricic et al., 2021), dot-connecting, and judgment (Foss & Klein, 2012). How does your ecosystem support individual judgment and action in promoting innovation? Dealing with a highly complex, dynamic, interconnected system, judgment is an essential skill.

The inherent complexity suggests two facets that differentiate the ecosystem builder. First, entrepreneurship is not about risk-taking, it is really about embracing ambiguity (Csonka-Peeren & Cozzarin, 2021) in a complex, fast-changing system. It is about changing the odds, not beating them. Like entrepreneurs, ecosystem builders must cope with ambiguity, i.e., cope with the unknowables (e.g., Csonka-Peeren & Krueger, 2021). Too many bureaucratic support mechanisms strive to exclude the unknowables rather than embrace them. Second, maybe the most promising diagnostic is market orientation—do you mold your activities toward your stakeholders or try to mold them (product orientation)? In a complex, dynamic, multistakeholder, don't we **need** a strong market orientation (Kaffka & Krueger, 2021)?

# 5 What Do Ecosystem Builders/Liaison-Animateurs Know?

What makes ecosystem thinking important? Perhaps we need to think less about the entrepreneurial mindset and more about the **ecosystem** mindset? Circling back to the basics of ecosystems, we touched on the key facets that differentiate them from older, more linear models of innovation systems. The table below shares a set of critical assumptions that guide ecosystem builders—the "old school" thinking versus the ecosystem mindset. Whether we are trying to nurture innovation in an organization or a community, we need to shift our deep anchoring assumptions from those of a bureaucratic mindset to the ecosystem mindset.

| | Moving from... | to.... |
|---|---|---|
| The key drivers operate | **Top-down** | **Bottom-up** |
| Governance | **Inside-out** | **Outside-in** |
| The key leverage points | **Institutions** | **People/*Liaison-animateurs*** |
| How are economies structured? | **Hierarchies** | **Networks** |
| Linear or nonlinear? | **Linear models** | **Nonlinear/complex** |
| Dynamic or static? | **Discrete, static** | **Connected, dynamic** |
| Successful strategies are? | **Intentional** | **Emergent** |

# 6 Other Implications for Innovators

## *6.1 Technology Commercialization*

Universities and other institutions have always underachieved in turning ideas into reality, too often because the bureaucratic imperatives override more bottom-up approaches (Lerner, 2009; OECD, 2013; Kariv, 2019; Theodoraki et al., 2020; Siegel & Guerrero, 2021; Choi et al., 2022). One sterling example of a successful bottom-up, ecosystem-connected program is the Chalmers School of Entrepreneurship, where student teams serve as "surrogate parents" to new ventures (Lundqvist, 2014; Lackéus & Williams-Middleton, 2015).

The US Air Force's SBIR program was recently re-invented and expanded into AFWERX, a potent innovation effort that operated almost obsessively with the bottom-up, outside-in approach to great effect. A recent study of AFWERX concluded "innovation could benefit from more bottom-up, decentralized approaches that reduce barriers to entry, minimize lock-in advantages for incumbents, and attract a wider range of new entrants" (Howell et al., 2021). Isn't this exactly what we are looking for?

## 6.2 *Implications for Innovation Policy*

What might all these mean for policy and legislation to support innovation? We need to take the ecosystem model seriously (e.g., Stam, 2015; Acs et al., 2017; Audretsch & Belitski, 2021; Wurth et al., 2021). Lerner (2009) pointed out the consistent inability of the US federal government to encourage entrepreneurship and innovation, largely for reasons shared above. Another Kauffman-supported effort was the development of "America's New Business Plan", a cavalcade of ideas for policy changes at the local, state, and federal level.[11] The USA's Right To Start[12] effort is building support at the state level for these ideas.

Education and learning need to be at the heart of all these as well. Audretsch showed how to build entrepreneurial capital requires building both entrepreneurial social capital (quality and quantity of connectivity) and entrepreneurial human capital (mindset and skills). Part of the Netherlands' success at innovation derives from finding ways to do both synergistically (OECD, 2018). Ecosystems and ecosystem thinking needs to be at the heart of entrepreneurship education and we are already seeing signs of that (https://bit.ly/2021GWUecosystems; Krueger & Steidle, 2020; Steidle, 2021).

Another vital implication is that we need the very best entrepreneurship and innovation education, especially if we are to truly support under-represented groups.[13] We have learned so much even in the last few years about how to grow entrepreneurial mindsets and skills (Krueger, 2007; Jones, 2019; Penaluna, 2020[14]). One big implication here is this means that we now can rigorously assess impact.[15]

If we are to grow entrepreneurial potential in all of our citizens, it is also important that entrepreneurship and innovation education and learning be co-embedded with ecosystem development. OECD's Entrepreneurship360 project found that this co-embeddedness was central to all of the best primary-secondary entrepreneurship education projects. One powerful example is Aalto University's student-designed, student-led programming (Startup Sauna, Slush, etc.), where their programs co-evolved with the ecosystem itself (Björklund & Krueger, 2016). Another OECD effort has generated reports in multiple countries on how higher education and the ecosystem can (and must) work together productively.[16]

---

[11] Ewing Marion Kauffman Foundation. (2019). "America's New Business Plan". www.kauffman.org/currents/americas-new-business-plan-expands-what-it-means-to-be-pro-business/ See also www.StartUsUpNow.org.

[12] www.RightToStart.org, led by former Kauffman leader (and author of *The Rain Forest*) Victor Hwang.

[13] e.g., "What We Owe Entrepreneurial Learners", in *2021 International Council for Small Business Global Education Report* (www.bit.ly/GlobalEdManifesto).

[14] And the propitiously titled "An Education System Fit for an Entrepreneur" commissioned by the UK.

[15] Some newer tools: HEInnovate.eu's EPIC tools to assess impact of education/training, EntreComp for entrepreneurial skills, and OECD's Better Entrepreneurship Policy tool.

[16] Example of the Netherlands (www.bit.ly/OECDdelta).

*Community Navigators:* A recent example of how a top-down entity like the US Small Business Administration can support bottom-up grassroots entrepreneur support is the new Community Navigator[17] program that identified "hub" entities who will get money and resources to "spokes", ecosystem builders supporting under-represented (and under-funded) populations. For example, Idaho Connect (www.idahoconnect.org) built an alliance of Hispanic, Black, Native American, and veteran entrepreneur support groups. If we wish to increase diverse, inclusive local economic communities, this bottom-up, outside-in model is essential (again Kauffman, fn 6, 10, 11; Krueger, 2021).

## 7 Why the Phlogiston Model Matters Here

The crazy thing about phlogiston is that the math worked. All one had to do was to believe that matter could have negative weight. The math worked equally well for oxidation. Priestly discovered oxygen but stubbornly tried to shoehorn oxygen into the phlogiston model (called oxygen "dephlogistonated air"). It took Lavoisier to point out that oxygen was the simplest and best answer. We in the social sciences are far from immune from canonizing an elegant model, then elaborating and elaborating every time we find an anomaly. Judging by the citation counts, we have no shortage of Priestlys and a dire shortage of Lavoisiers.

Instead of complicating the top-down, institutions-led models to account for the entrepreneurs and innovators themselves and to account for their champions and connectors, why not embrace the connecting and connectors in an ecosystem as the oxygen of innovation?

Swiss innovation guru Paul Hobcraft said it best:

> *"We have entered the new innovation era as we combine in ways not possible until recently. If we take any industry, any societal problem, as we tackle climate challenges it is the power of connected innovation that will make a difference and give us our breakthroughs. We have the tools to tackle big (and stubbornly small) challenges in collective environments. We are not changing everything as we are still searching for the "how and what" but we are pushing ourselves by opening up to the "where and why" in such different connecting ways. We are recognizing that sharing what we know accelerates understanding for all those involved."*

### *7.1 Understanding Ecosystems and How They Work Is Becoming Essential for Us [Author Emphasis]*

*Recognizing ecosystems are vital, combining human, technology, and data allows us to pursue multiple possibilities, explore them faster than before, evaluate them in*

[17] https://www.sba.gov/local-assistance/community-navigators.

*quicker, smarter ways and scale those that show promise for all of us to be more efficient, considerate, and respectful of finite resources to undergo a change from individualism to revaluing community and supporting each other in resourceful ways and respecting all that is around us needs to be more balanced. "We can search not just for entirely new capabilities but we can take real advantage of actively reshaping so much to rejuvenate and value much that is all around us in different ways of behavior and reflection. It is the power of ecosystems that can allow us to innovate differently and more designed for sustaining what we have of this planet we rely upon."* [Hobscraft, 2021].

Hobcraft speaks for many of those leading a quiet (and oft-times less than quiet) revolution in innovation.

Growing innovation post-COVID means a deep embrace of ecosystems and ecosystem thinking, not paying lip service or cherry-picking tiny pieces. That means finding more Lavoisiers. In academic research, in education, and in policy circles, we need them. Will **you** embrace the ecosystem mindset? Will **you** be your ecosystem's Lavoisier?

## References

Acs, Z. J., Stam, E., Audretsch, D. B., & O'Connor, A. (2017). The lineages of the entrepreneurial ecosystem approach. *Small Business Economics, 49*(1), 1–10.

Antoniuk, N. A., Plikus, I. Y., & Jammal, M. (2021). Sustainable business development vision under the covid-19 pandemic. *Health Economics & Management Review, 1*, 37–43. https://doi.org/10.21272/hem.2021.1-04

Audretsch, D. B., & Belitski, M. (2021). Towards an entrepreneurial ecosystem typology for regional economic development: The role of creative class & entrepreneurship. *Regional Studies, 55*(4), 735–756.

Baran, P. (1964). On distributed communications networks. *IEEE transactions on Communications Systems, 12*(1), 1–9.

Bettenmann, D., Giones, F., Brem, A., & Gneiting, P. (2022, Winter). Break out to open innovation. *Sloan Management Review, 63*(2), 39–43.

Bianchi, C. (2021). Fostering sustainable community outcomes through policy networks: A dynamic performance governance approach. In *Handbook of Collaborative Public Management*. Edward Elgar Publishing, forthcoming.

Bianchi, C., & Vignieri, V. (2021). Dealing with "abnormal" business growth by leveraging local area common goods: An outside-in stakeholder collaboration perspective. *International Journal of Productivity & Performance Management, 70*(3), 613–634. https://doi.org/10.1108/IJPPM-07-2019-0318

Björklund, T. A., & Krueger, N. F. (2016). Generating resources through co-evolution of entrepreneurs and ecosystems. *Journal of Enterprising Communities: People & Places in the Global Economy, 10*(4), 477–498.

Bogers, M., Chesbrough, H., & Strand, R. (2020). Sustainable open innovation to address a grand challenge: Lessons from Carlsberg & the green fiber bottle. *British Food Journal, 122*(5), 1505–1517.

Brännback, M., Carsrud, A., Krueger, N., Jr., & Elfving, J. (2008). Challenging the triple helix model of regional innovation systems: A venture-centric model. *International Journal of Technoentrepreneurship, 1*(3), 257–277.

Brett, A. (2019). *Admired disorder*. BabyBooks.
Choi, H., Yoon, H., Siegel, D., Waldman, D. A., & Mitchell, M. S. (2022). Assessing differences between university & federal laboratory postdoctoral scientists in technology transfer. *Research Policy, 51*(3), 104456.
Csonka-Peeren, J., & Cozzarin, B. P. (2021). A conceptual model of ambiguity attitudes for entrepreneurship experiments. *Journal of Behavioral and Applied Management, 21*(2), 62–80.
Csonka-Peeren, J., & Krueger, N. (2021). *Opportunity judgment & management*. Decision Sciences Institute, virtual.
Djuricic, K., Stenholm, P., & Krueger, N. (2021). Entrepreneurial foresight at the Core of entrepreneurial expertise: Between complexity & the future. *Academy of Management* (virtual).
Ellram, L., Flynn, B., Harland, C., Kovács, G., Sarkis, J., & Tate, W. (2020). Report of the online forum action agenda for effective post COVID-19 supply chains. *Technical report*.
Emery, M., & Flora, C. (2006). Spiraling-up: Mapping community transformation with community capitals framework. *Community Development, 37*(1), 19–35.
Feld, B. (2012). *Startup communities: Building an entrepreneurial ecosystem in your city*. John Wiley.
Feld, B., & Hathaway, I. (2020). *The startup community way: Evolving an entrepreneurial ecosystem*. John Wiley.
Feldman, M., & Zoller, T. D. (2012). Dealmakers in place: Social capital connections in regional entrepreneurial economies. *Regional Studies., 46*(1), 23–37.
Flora, C. B., & Flora, J. L. (1993). Entrepreneurial social infrastructure: A necessary ingredient. *The Annals of the American Academy of Political & Social Science, 529*(1), 48–58.
Foss, N. J., & Klein, P. G. (2012). *Organizing entrepreneurial judgment: A new approach to the firm*. Cambridge University Press.
Ghosh, S., Thomke, S., & Pourkhalkhali, H. (2020). The effects of hierarchy on Learning & Performance in business experimentation. *Academy of Management Proceedings, 2020*(1), 20500.
Hattenberg, D. Y., Belousova, O., & Groen, A. J. (2021). Defining the entrepreneurial mindset and discussing its distinctiveness in entrepreneurship research. *International Journal of Entrepreneurship and Small Business, 44*(1), 30–52.
Hobscraft, P. (2021). Accelerating innovation requires ecosystem thinking. *Ecosystems 4 Innovating* (blog). https://ecosystems4innovating.wordpress.com/2021/04/08/accelerating-innovation-comes-from-ecosystem-thinking
Howell, S. T., Rathje, J., Van Reenan, J., & Wong, J. (2021, April). *Opening up military innovation: Causal effects of 'bottom-up' reforms to U.S. defense research*. Centre for Economic Performance Discussion Paper #1760.
Hwang, V. W., & Horowitt, G. (2012). *The rain forest: The secret to building the next Silicon Valley*. Wiley.
Jones, C. (2019). *How to teach entrepreneurship*. Edward Elgar Publishing.
Kaffka, G., & Krueger, N. F. (2021), Sensemaking beyond the customer: An analysis of entrepreneurs' market orientation development. *Academy of Management*, Virtual.
Kariv, D. (2019). *Educating entrepreneurs: Innovative models and new perspectives*. Routledge.
Krueger, N. (2000). The cognitive infrastructure of opportunity emergence. *Entrepreneurship Theory & Practice, 24*(3), 5–24.
Krueger, N. F. (2007). What lies beneath? The experiential essence of entrepreneurial thinking. *Entrepreneurship Theory & Practice, 31*(1), 123–138.
Krueger, N. (2013). Startup communities (emphasis on communities). In OECD. (2013). *Entrepreneurial Ecosystems & Growth-Oriented Entrepreneurship Workshop*.
Krueger, N. (2015). *OECD Thematic paper on entrepreneurial education in practice; Part 1, the entrepreneurial mindset*. Published online, www.oecd.org/cfe/leed/Entrepreneurial-Education-Practice-pt1.pdf
Krueger, N. (2021). Beyond "Getting Asked to Dance": Inclusive entrepreneurial ecosystems. In T. M. Cooney (Ed.), *The palgrave handbook of minority entrepreneurship*. Palgrave Macmillan.

Krueger, N., & Brazeal, D. V. (1994). Entrepreneurial potential & potential entrepreneurs. *Entrepreneurship Theory & Practice, 18*(3), 91–104.

Kruger, J., & Dunning, D. (1999). Unskilled & unaware of it: How difficulties in recognizing One's own incompetence Lead to inflated self-assessments. *Journal of Personality & Social Psychology, 77*(6), 1121–1134.

Krueger, N., & Steidle, S. (2020). *Why healthy entrepreneurial ecosystems matter to entrepreneurship educators and researchers*. CEEC, virtual. Retrieved at https://youtu.be/tqHHo5_ubTI

Lackéus, M., & Williams-Middleton, K. (2015). Venture creation programs: Bridging entrepreneurship education & technology transfer. *Education and Training, 57*(1), 48–73.

Lampert, C. M., Kim, M., & Polidoro, F., Jr. (2020). Branching & Anchoring: Complementary asset configurations in conditions of Knightian uncertainty. *Academy of Management Review, 45*(4), 847–868.

Lerner, J. (2009). *Boulevard of broken dreams: why public efforts to boost entrepreneurship and venture capital have failed--and what to do about it*. Princeton University Press.

Lundqvist, M. A. (2014). The importance of surrogate entrepreneurship for incubated Swedish technology ventures. *Technovation, 34*(2), 93–100.

Maggioncalda, J. (2020, November 27). Calling all entrepreneurs: It's time to build an innovation engine for the virtual era. *Fast Company*. www.fastcompany.com/90568249/calling-all-entrepreneurs-its-time-to-build-an-innovation-engine-for-the-virtual-era, online.

Müller, J. M., Buliga, O., & Voigt, K.-I. (2018). Fortune favors the prepared: How SMEs approach business model innovations in industry 4.0. *Technological Forecasting and Social Change, 132*, 2–17.

OECD. (2013). *Entrepreneurial ecosystems & growth-oriented entrepreneurship workshop*. https://www.oecd.org/cfe/leed/entrepreneurialecosystemsandgrowth-orientedentrepreneurshipworkshop-netherlands.htm

OECD. (2018). *Supporting entrepreneurship & innovation in higher education in the Netherlands*. https://www.bit.ly/OECDdelta.

Penaluna, A. (2020). Designing change: Seeing beyond the obvious and influencing others. In *How to become an entrepreneurship educator*. Edward Elgar Publishing.

Sanders, N. R. (2020). *Supply chain management: A global perspective*. Wiley Global Education.

Steidle, S. (2021) *Exploring the role(s) of community colleges in addressing wicked problems through multi-stakeholder collaboration: An entrepreneurial approach to sustainability*. PhD dissertation, Old Dominion University.

Sanders, N. R., Locke, A., Moore, C. B., & Autry, C. W. (2007). A multidimensional framework for understanding outsourcing arrangements. *Journal of Supply Chain Management, 43*(4), 3–15.

Scuotto, V., Orlando, B., Cilla, V., Nicotra, M., Di Gioia, L., & Briamonte, M. F. (2020). Uncovering the micro-foundations of knowledge sharing in open innovation partnerships: An intention-based perspective of technology transfer. *Technological Forecasting and Social Change, 152*, 119906.

Shapero, A. (1975). The displaced, uncomfortable entrepreneur. *Psychology Today, 8*, 83-88+.

Siegel, D. S., & Guerrero, M. (2021). The impact of quarantines, lockdowns, & 'reopenings' on the commercialization of science: Micro and macro issues. *Journal of Management Studies*, forthcoming.

Stam, E. (2015). Entrepreneurial ecosystems & regional policy: A sympathetic critique. *European Planning Studies, 23*, 1759–1769.

Stephenson, K. (2009). Neither hierarchy nor network: An argument for heterarchy. *People & Strategy., 32*(1), 4–13.

Sweeney, G. (1987). *Innovation, Entrepreneurs & Regional Development*. St. Martin's Press.
Theodoraki, C., Messeghem, K., & Audretsch, D. (2020). The effectiveness of incubator co-opetition strategy in the entrepreneurial ecosystem: Empirical evidence from France. *IEEE Transactions on Engineering Management*, 1–14.
West, J., & Bogers, M. (2014). Leveraging external sources of innovation: A review of research on open innovation. *Journal of Product Innovation Management, 31*(4), 814–831.
Wurth, B., Stam, E., & Spigel, B. (2021). Toward an entrepreneurial ecosystem research program. *Entrepreneurship Theory and Practice*, forthcoming.

**Norris Krueger**, Ph.D., is a professionally trained educator with multiple national and global awards for best practice, emphasizing cutting-edge project-based learning. This helped him become a leading thinker and doer in expert entrepreneurial thinking. Most current work focuses on entrepreneurial ecosystems where he works to drive great research on bottom-up entrepreneur-led development. Norris was a leader in the Kauffman Foundation's ESHIP initiative to promote best-in-class ecosystem building working on metrics and policy.

# Part II
# Economies Under Pressure: Challenges for the Future After the COVID-19 Crisis

# COVID-19, Schumpeter, and the Size of the Market

**Pontus Braunerhjelm and Emma Lappi**

**Abstract** During the first quarter of 2020, the global economy was rapidly hit by a pandemic which led to state-wide lockdowns and the worst economic crisis since the World War II. Both the supply and the demand sides of economies were severely affected, followed by a dramatic dip in global GDP. As a response, policymakers introduced an unprecedented number of interventions to back up employees, firms, and industries to counteract the collapsing markets. Our main objective is to explore how these fundamental policy interventions are likely to influence the future potential and functioning of markets. Historically swings in the pendulum favoring either market-based solutions or more regulated public sectors have coincided with disruptive crises. The overall question is what will happen during post-COVID-19, will governments withdraw their crisis policies and how will a possible retreat be organized? Are we entering an era of permanently increased governmental interventions? More precisely, we identify three specific threats to the market-oriented economy: the extension and development of governmental expenditures, protectionistic measures, and the level of state aid and the degree of competition at markets. We are particularly interested in the effect of the COVID-19 measures, and their possible extension, on Schumpeterian dynamics, both in terms of entry and

This chapter was written before the war between Russia and Ukraine broke out. The challenges and problems addressed in this chapter will all be further aggravated due to this new international crisis.

P. Braunerhjelm (✉)
Department of Industrial Economics and Management, KTH Royal Institute of Technology, Stockholm, Sweden

Swedish Entrepreneurship Forum, Stockholm, Sweden

Blekinge Institute of Technology, Karlskrona, Sweden
e-mail: pontus.braunerhjelm@indek.kth.se

E. Lappi
Department of Strategy and Innovation, Copenhagen Business School, Frederiksberg, Denmark
e-mail: el.si@cbs.dk



D. B. Audretsch, I. A. M. Kunadt (eds.), *The COVID-19 Crisis and Entrepreneurship*, International Studies in Entrepreneurship 54,
https://doi.org/10.1007/978-3-031-04655-1_5

exits (Schumpeter I) and how the position of large firms will be affected (Schumpeter II).

**Keywords** Market economy · Public sector · State intervention · Size of government · Size of market · Fiscal framework · State aid · Competition

# 1 Introduction

At the end of the first quarter of 2020, the global economy was hit by a pandemic which led to state-wide lockdowns and a major economic crisis. Both the supply and the demand sides of economies were severely affected, and global GDP shrank by around 3.5% in 2020 (OECD, 2021). International trade fell, global supply chains were disrupted, followed by a subsequent decrease in real output for both small and large countries. To tackle the crisis, large-scale government interventions followed, targeting both the lack of demand and the supply sides. These comprehensive policy packages were designed and implemented with a short-time perspective to provide instantaneous stimulus to the real economy. Within the EU, this was made possible by abolishing regulations governing fiscal policies and state aid.

During the COVID-19 crisis, governments have increased their expenditures and interventions, paralleled by a decline of the private sector. The crisis also created an impetus for platform firms taking advantage of the transition toward more digital solutions, accentuating the debate of how large tech firms influence competition. More precisely, it has been argued that the dominant position of these firms may over time harm economic dynamism, entry, and innovation.

The economic impact of the pandemic on entrepreneurship has so far varied. Obviously, the initial impact of the lockdowns, the ensuing declining demand, bottle-necks in supply chain etc., meant that businesses could not operate as usual and close downs followed. Other challenges were associated with the regulatory complexities of applying for state support and the ability to retain healthy staff on site or working from home. Yet, after an initial surge in bankruptcies, the massive support measures that were introduced as the crisis aggravated helped firms to survive. In fact, in the US, around 540,000 bankruptcies occurred in 2020 as compared to 770,000 cases in 2019. This somewhat surprising effect is likely to reflect that generous government subsidies implied that a number of "zombie" firms managed to survive, despite miniscule long-term possibilities to remain at the market. Hence, "excessive" firm survival rates are not necessarily a good thing as exits are an important part of creative destruction. Entry has also increased in several countries, e.g., in Sweden, a 10% rise was registered between 2019 and 2020.[1]

Our main objective is to explore how the fundamental changes in the world economy related to the COVID-19 crisis may influence the future size and

[1] This is according to the figures released by the Administrative Office of the U.S. Courts.

functioning of markets. The turning points in this pendulum swing, i.e., markets versus public sectors, typically seem to coincide with disruptive events that test the limits of the market and the state. How will governments' retreat look like? Are we entering an era of permanently increased governmental interventions? The outcome relates to the coming redesign of the Maastricht conditions and whether the temporary abolition of state aid rules will be fully reimposed. But also fiscal policies in general matter, and how the expanding public expenditures can be financed, i.e., through taxes, increased debts or by printing money? Can we expect trade and foreign direct investment to return to previous trajectories or will we see more of protectionism, hidden behind the veil of resilience arguments to guarantee supply chains? Will "buy American" types of campaigns be stepped up and how will trade adjustment mechanisms (tariffs) to limit carbon dioxide emissions be used? To what extent can competition authorities harvest the inherent benefits of digitization without promoting global supremacy to the big tech platform firms? We are particularly interested in the effect of the COVID-19 measures, and their possible extension, on Schumpeterian dynamics, both in terms of entry and exits (Schumpeter I) and how the position of large firms will be affected (Schumpeter II).

The discussion about the size of the market goes far back.[2] Size is defined in several ways in the previous literature, e.g., the numbers of consumers and producers, the regulatory burden, governmental expenditure as share of GDP, or related to economies of scale and trade costs. The political economy literature refers to the night-watchman state as compared to a more comprehensive welfare state, while public interest (Pigou, 1938) proponents stress the role of the state for functioning markets. This was later challenged by the public choice school, emphasizing the inefficiencies of regulated markets, rent-seeking behavior, and nontransparent structures (Buchanan, 1967; Stigler, 1971).

We relate the size of the market and its function to the following factors: the extension and development of governmental expenditures, the openness of markets, and the level of state aid and the degree of competition at markets. Thus, we address the question of COVID-19 and market size by looking at selective variables on the macro- (fiscal policies/governmental expenditure), meso- (international trade and openness), and the micro-levels (state aid and competition). Even though governmental expenditures and state aid are closely interlinked, we prefer to distinguish between them to emphasize that there is a difference between for instance huge infrastructure projects and cash injections to companies.

The rest of the chapter is organized in the following way. In Sect. 2, we firstly discuss how the governments have responded to the crisis, i.e., what type of government interventions were used as the crisis evolved and how these were funded. Section 3 continues by discussing three threats to the market that originates in policies undertaken during the COVID-19 crisis, as well as proposals to extend and continue some of these measures. More precisely, these threats are related to expanding governmental sectors, the influence on openness, and competition and market concentration. In the following Sect. 4, we discuss and evaluate the potential

---

[2] See for instance Beckmann (2017).

strengths and weaknesses with the proposed policies, emphasizing the importance of a balanced redesign of the fiscal framework and state aid rules in the EU. Section 5 concludes and elaborates on how Schumpeterian dynamics has been affected by the COVID-19 crisis.

## 2 Background

During the last two decades, the world economy has experienced three major crises: the 2001 IT-bubble, the 2008-financial crisis, and more recently the COVID-19 crisis. The former two crisis have had their roots in the financial and real estate sectors (Reinhart & Rogoff, 2009) whereas the COVID-19 crisis deviates from this pattern by originating from a pandemic which has impacted basically all parts of the economy. Due to the state-wide lockdowns which restricted the mobility of individuals and good and services, the supply side of the economy was hit first. The distortions of the global production chains were then transmitted to the demand side of the economy (Guerrieri et al., 2020, Fornaro & Wolf, 2020). This is a specific feature of the COVID-19 crisis which makes it unique and also implies considerable challenges for public policy.

The impact of COVID-19 quickly became apparent in terms of declining GDP growth and the strains it imposed on public finances. When a country is exposed to a shock of that magnitude politicians will activate whatever available tools there are to stabilize the economy. During the financial crisis 2008–2009, monetary policies were primarily used, focusing on lowering interest rates. Since monetary policies are close to, or already in, a liquidity trap (interest rates are close to zero), the measures undertaken in the COVID-19 crisis have relied more upon fiscal policy measures as well as a number of other more unconventional policy tools (Braunerhjelm, 2021) in order to uphold demand and facilitate the survival of firms and industries.

### 2.1 *Some Graphic Illustrations*

The COVID-19 crisis evolved rapidly with the spread of the virus leading to large-scale lockdowns of regions and entire nations. Graph 1 shows the evolution of quarterly GDP from 2002 to the first quarter of 2021. In the figure, GDP is indexed to 2015 and the data are obtained from OECD.[3] We plot the GDP for the US, European Union member states (EU27), and the countries within Euro area (EA19).[4]

[3]OECD (2021), Quarterly GDP (indicator). doi: 10.1787/b86d1fc8-en.

[4]The European Union (EU27) countries include 27 member states according to year 2020: Belgium, Bulgaria, Czechia, Denmark, Germany, Estonia, Ireland, Greece, Spain, France, Croatia, Italy, Cyprus, Latvia, Lithuania, Luxembourg, Hungary, Malta, the Netherlands, Austria, Poland, Portugal, Romania, Slovenia, Slovakia, Finland, and Sweden. Euro area (EA19) countries include 19 countries taken from the 2015 definition: Belgium, Germany, Estonia, Ireland, Greece, Spain,

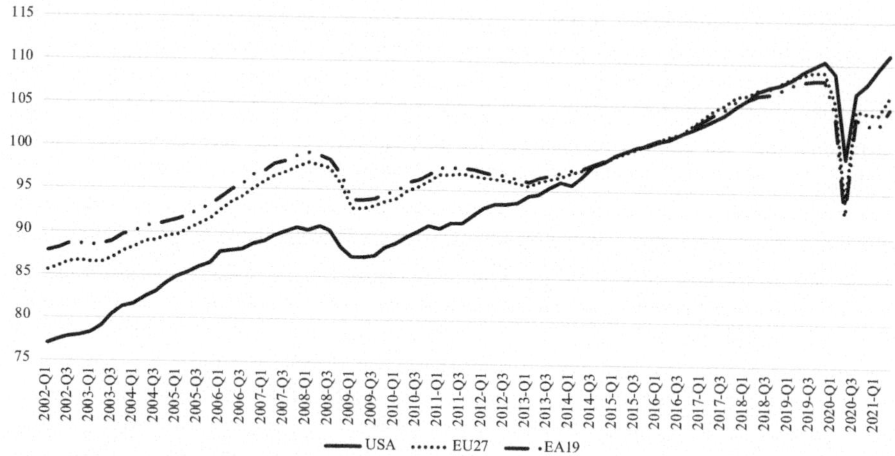


**Graph 1** Gross Domestic Product (Index 2015 = 100). Note: Graph based on authors own imputations. Data provided by OECD

Directly after the first quarter of 2020, the GDP dropped approximately to early 2005 levels in the euro area. The decline in GDP across the board was clearly larger than during the 2008-crisis. However, the recovery has been fast, and the economies have experienced a V-shaped recovery. The recovery has so far been more profound for the US than for the European region, where the US GDP levels have returned to the precrisis levels. Still, the uncertainty about the recovery is high, particularly with regard to the medium- and long-term, as is the impact of the undertaken policy intervention.

During the COVID-19 pandemic, a plethora of policy interventions were embarked upon by governments, e.g., see OECD (2020). Many governments launched short-term stimulus packages such as tax-cuts to individuals and firms and provided state-guaranteed loans. According to the World Bank (2020), approximately 800 different policy instruments have been used to combat the COVID-19-induced recession. The European Union has recently decided on expenditures amounting to 2 trillion euro whereof 1.2 trillion is destined for EU's long-term budget (2021–2027). More than 800 billion euros have been set aside to restore the immediate economic and social damage caused by the pandemic. The main part consists of the 750 billion euros earmarked for the Recovery and Resilience Facility Fund (RRF), targeting reforms and growth-enhancing investments in the EU countries. Around 360 billion are loans and 390 billion direct grants. These expenditures at the EU level are planned to be financed through a mix of revenue at the EU level and contributions from Member States. The European Commission has also already issued bonds to finance the loans to the member states. The EU has also announced that possible future revenues could be linked to a carbon border adjustment

France, Italy, Cyprus, Latvia, Lithuania, Luxembourg, Malta, the Netherlands, Austria, Portugal, Slovenia, Slovakia, and Finland.

mechanism, a digital levy, or the EU Emissions Trading System, and even possibly through a financial transaction tax or a new common corporate tax base.

Similar measures to stabilize the economy have been undertaken in the US. For example, the Paycheck Protection Program (PPP) was introduced to alleviate financial constraints for smaller firms while the CARES Acts allocated loans to firms and cash transfers to households amounting to 2000 billion USD. There were also executive orders to, for example, continue the student loan repayment relief, deferring collections of employee social security payroll taxes, and help households to avoid evictions and foreclosures. The total stimulus packages, including those suggested by the present US administration, are in the range of 20–25% of GDP. The crisis relief packages were largely financed by issuing bonds and borrowing, thus increasing the US debt even further (presently 125% of GDP).

The central banks also had an active role in the COVID-19 short-term recovery interventions. The European Central Bank (ECB) for example introduced the Pandemic Emergency Purchase Program (PEPP) which is a 1.85 trillion Euro asset purchase program of private and public sector securities. The program was founded under the Asset Purchase Program (APP) which is included in the nonstandard monetary policy measures started by the ECB, since interest rates and required reserve ratio were close to (or at) zero. A similar situation prevailed in the US where for example, the federal funds rate was set to a span of 0–0.25%, the cost of discount window lending was lowered, and the FED acquired residential and commercial treasuries and mortgage-backed securities. Thus, central banks did not have access to their standard tools to combat the recession, leading to the experimental asset purchase programs and giving more weight to fiscal policy measures targeting households, firms, state, and local governments.

We have information on the number of state interventions through the Global Trade Alert (GTA) database which collects data on state interventions affecting trade in goods and services, foreign investment, and labor force migration. The data provide indication on whether the intervention are likely to discriminate against foreign commercial interests. In Graph 2, we aggregate the number of such intervention to a quarterly frequency for the period 2009–2020. The number of interventions are separated between the US, the national-level interventions of EU-27 countries, and the European Union-level interventions.[5]

In the earlier period, the US government is shown to intervene more frequently the EU countries which, however, was reversed in the period after 2017. As the COVID-19 crisis struck in the second quarter of 2020, the number of interventions started to increase at the EU level, the US, and at the national level in the EU. This was followed by a clear decrease by the end of 2020. What the graph does not show is the magnitude or severity of the interventions. For example, the EU-level interventions are potentially of larger magnitude and affect several jurisdictions, and can

[5]The European Union-level directives and interventions are those commissioned from the EU and usually multiple jurisdictions, i.e., member states, have to integrate them into national legislations.

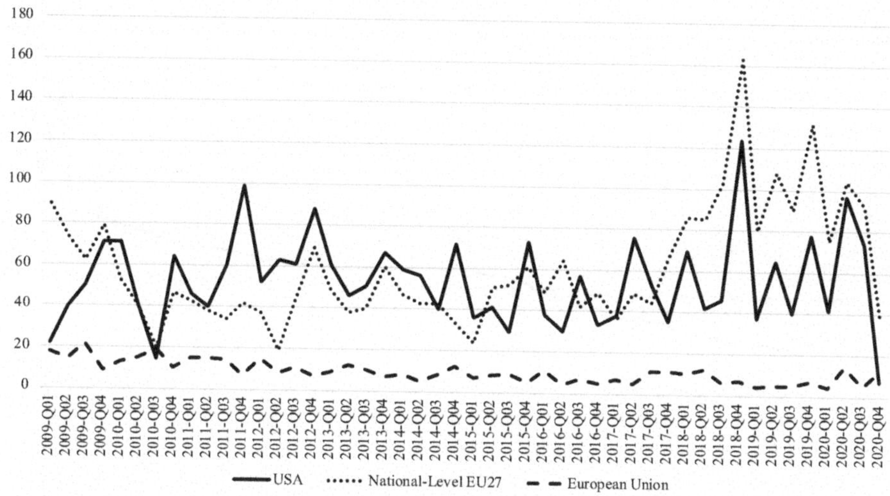


**Graph 2** Interventions likely to discriminate against foreign commercial interests. Note: Graph based on authors own computations. Data provided by Global Trade Alert (DTA) Database

have a larger impact on foreign commercial interest than an intervention set by a single country.

As noted above, governments undertook large-scale expansionary fiscal policies during the crisis, mainly financed through increased governmental debts. We have information on the absolute levels of government expenditures for the US and for the European area (Graph 3a and b).

The total government expenditures throughout the years have been steadily increasing. However, during 2020, government expenditure increased substantially for both the US and Europe. The US experienced a dramatic increase in public spending 2020–2021 due to pandemic-related health costs and the massive interventions the government undertook to fight of the economic downturn. These large increases in the expenditure have been financed through debt during the COVID-19 crisis. Graph 4 plots the consolidated government debt as a share of GDP for the US, the European Union member states (EU27), and the countries within Euro area (EA19) for the period 2018 to early 2021. The data are obtained from Eurostat.

It is well known that the US has had a higher debt-to-GDP ratio than Europe as shown in Graph 4. After and during the second quarter of 2020, there was a large increase in the debt ratio for both the US and the European economies. In that period, real GDP also decreased, paralleled by simultaneous and rapid increases in governmental expenditure and debts. Thus, the pandemic had led to weakened public finances within months in most countries, albeit there are considerable country level differences. As a complement to debt as a share of GDP, we present data on the public net lending or borrowing in absolute terms for the US and Europe where

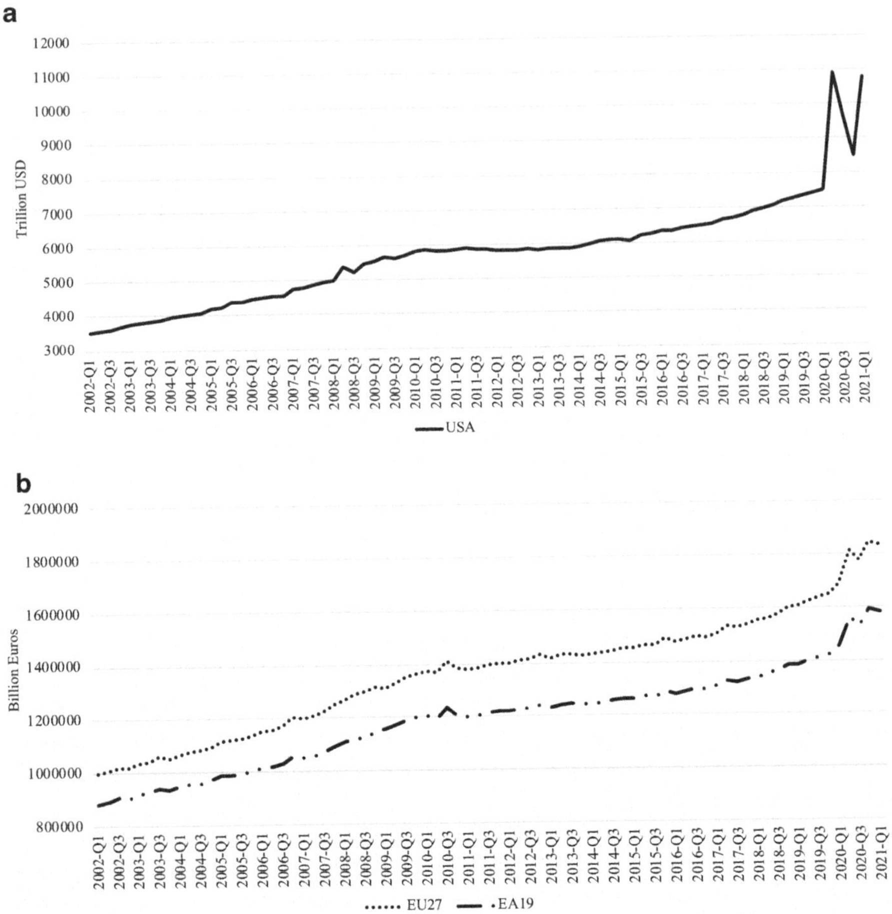


**Graph 3** (**a**) Government expenditure—USA. (**b**) Government expenditure—EU27 and Euro area. Note: Graphs based on authors own computations. Data provided by Federal Reserve Bank of St. Louis and Eurostat

data have been provided by Federal Reserve Bank of St. Louis and Eurostat across the years 2002 to the first quarter of 2021.

As shown in Graph 5a and b during the 2008-crisis, there was a large increase in net borrowing in Europe whereas only a modest increase took place in the US in relative terms. The European figures during the COVID pandemic were twice as high compared to the 2008–2009 financial crisis. The immediate jump in net borrowing decreased in the subsequent months after the initial drop. Exactly the same patterns can be observed for the US during the pandemic, but with even larger dip in the new borrowing immediately when the pandemic hits. Overall, the

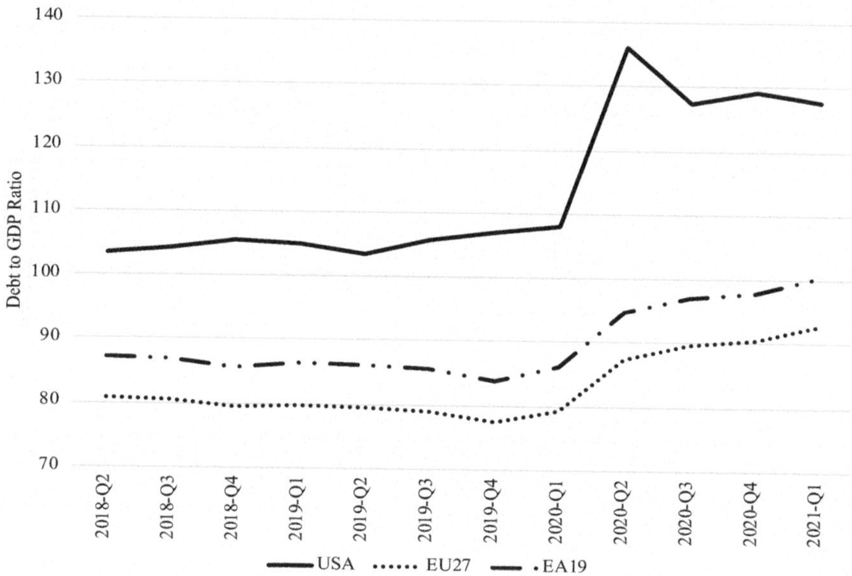


**Graph 4** Government debt as a share of GDP. Note: Graph based on authors own computations. Data provided by Eurostat

magnitude of the impact of pandemic to public spending and borrowing have been considerably larger as compared to the financial crisis 2008–2009.

Hence, the data reveal that the COVID-19 crisis has had a sharp instantaneous effect on the real economy. The severe GDP drop was followed by increased governmental expenditures, rising debt levels in absolute and relative terms. Most economies, particularly the US, have experienced a rather fast rebound of real output which might mirror a more efficient policy design, at least in the short-term.

# 3 Three Threats to the Market Economy

## *3.1 A Perpetuating Increasing Public Sector?*

As described above, public finances have expanded and become under pressure due to the government responses as the COVID-19 crisis evolved. Extending the observations to all OECD countries for which data are available, government expenditures have increased since 2019 while GDP per capita fell.[6] Similarly, the fiscal deficit among OECD countries averaged 3.2% of GDP in 2019 which increased in all countries, exceeding 5% of GDP for 18 countries in 2020. Also, the debt level has

[6]Data from OECD (2021).

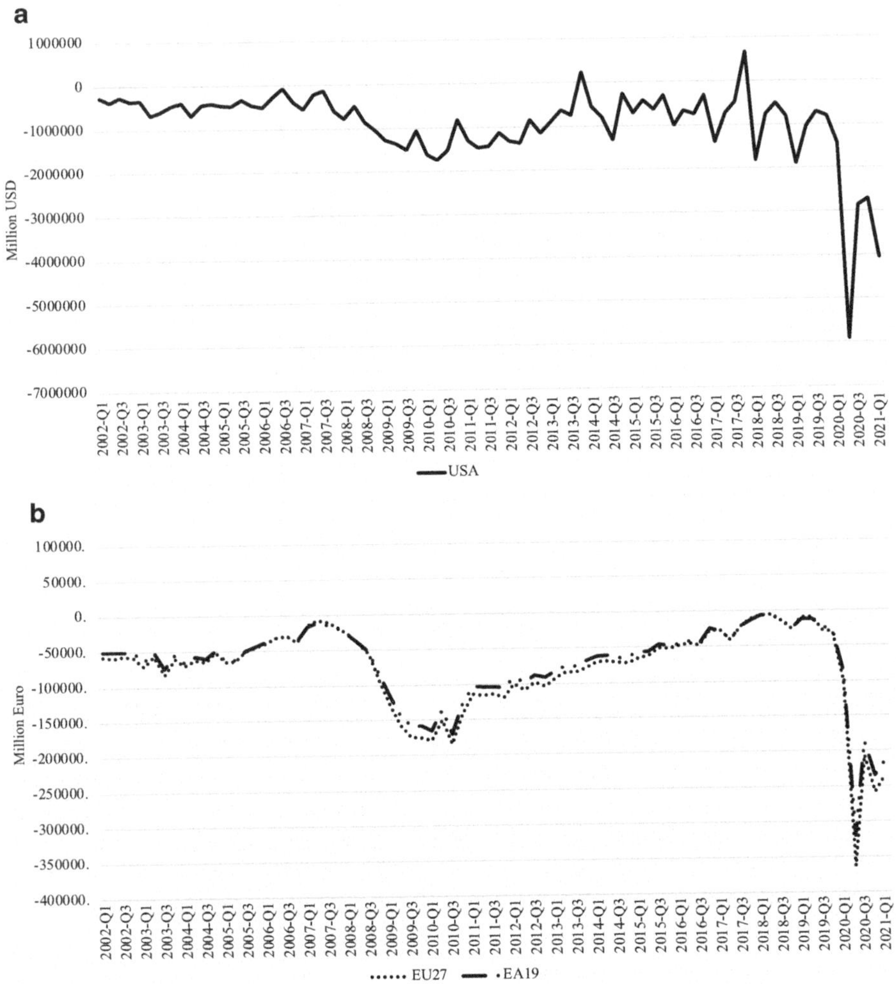


**Graph 5** (**a**) Net lending—US. (**b**) Net Lending—Europe. Note: Graphs based on authors own computations. Data provided by Federal Reserve Bank of St. Louis and Eurostat

risen: among 22 EU and OECD member countries, it climbed from about 97% of GDP in 2019 to 115% in 2020, a sizable increase. Yet, this does not necessarily mean that we will see a gradual return to previous (lower) levels. If you are a proponent of the modern monetary theory, there is no problem with funding deficits by printing money.

In the EU, sizable slippages in the fiscal disciplines have taken place since long, primarily in high-debt countries and mainly associated with current expenditure increases while a very tiny share was due to government investment. According to the Maastricht conditions, or more specifically the Stability and Growth Pact (SGP), countries are required to restrict their budget deficit to 3% of GDP and debt level to 60% of GDP. The number of countries significantly deviating from the rules in 2019 were the highest since the legislative reforms of 2011–2013.[7] Similarly, the size of the deviations was the largest since 2014. In addition, many governments failed to take advantage of good economic conditions that prevailed up until 2019 to build buffers.

As the COVID-19 crisis accelerated, EU experienced its deepest economic recession since the 1930s. That prompted the general escape clause to be activated to temporarily abolish the Maastricht conditions. Massive fiscal expansionary measures were then undertaken in most EU countries, often exerted in a new and experimental way (Braunerhjelm, 2021). The grand finale of these interventions were the launching of the Rescue and Recovery Fund (RRF), or Next Generation EU (NGEU) initiative, unprecedented in scale and scope (approximately 800 billion euro).[8] The RRF can be described as the first common fiscal policy initiative in EU, i.e., the first attempt to enforce a fiscal capacity to cushion large exogenous shocks while at the same time promoting public investment in growth-enhancing areas (defined as environment, digitization, research, and health).

The COVID-19 crisis led to the SGP thresholds being surpassed by most EU countries. The EU Commission, together with the European Council, had initiated an overhaul of these conditions already before 2019. The discussion on how the future SGP, expected to come into force 2023, should be designed have recently been restarted. Evidently, as many member states will come out of this crisis with historically high-debt levels, it is urgent to conclude the SGP reforms process before the deactivation of the general escape clause.

### 3.1.1 A New Framework

The redesign of the future fiscal framework within the EU will impact the potential size of the market. During the present crisis, the market has been pushed back due to a general contraction of the economy, paralleled by a massive fiscal expansion. Hence, the level and type of future governmental expenditures that will be tolerated also influence the limits of the market.

The present situation for most EU countries, with substantially higher levels of debt, obviously increases vulnerability if interest rates start to rise. This may trigger

---

[7]The so-called six- and two-packs that were decided in the aftermath of the financial market crisis 2008/09 in order to improve economic and fiscal surveillance. The six-pack is composed by five regulations and one directive proposed to ensure fiscal discipline, targeting expenditure benchmarks, surveillance of policies, etc. The two-pack, decided in 2013, focused on budget reforms to increase transparency, enhance coordination in the euro area, and the recognition of the special needs of euro area Member States under severe financial pressure.

[8]The NGEU also includes means for cohesion, etc.

financial instability and generate shock waves across countries. Such risks are further accentuated by different institutional set-ups among EU countries regarding governments, central banks, and the financial systems. Moreover, there is a debate within as well as across EU countries of increasing governmental expenditure to expand welfare schemes and reduce inequality. Growing ideological divisions may in itself distort the possibilities for fiscal stability and generate expansions of the state.

The criticism toward the present SGP focuses on nontransparency, ambiguities, pro-cyclical fiscal effects, declining government investment, and difficulties to build fiscal buffers in good times. The call for reform of the current framework is shared by a broad range of academics and institutions, such as the European Commission (2017), the IMF (see Eyraud et al., 2017), the European Fiscal Board (2017, 2019, 2020), the French Council of Economic Analysis (Darvas et al., 2018), and the German Council of Economic Experts (GCEE, 2017, 2018). However, no consensus has emerged to date on how to redesign the European fiscal framework. According to the GCEE, the most recent reforms of the Stability and Growth Pact are steps in the right direction, such as the "six-pack" and "two-pack" regulations, and the Fiscal Compact (Feld et al., 2018). Yet, the regulations have become more complex while transparency has been reduced.

The European Fiscal Board (EFB) has in a couple of reports argued for a comprehensive redesign of the fiscal framework while maintaining certain elements such as the debt target even if it presently seems out of range for some countries. The argument is that interest rates on government debt will be more susceptible to increases in the absence of a debt target. Three pillars can be defined in EFB's proposals, allotting some responsibilities to the national governments and other to the EU level:

- EMU needs a permanent fiscal capacity that can be deployed in times of large, exogenous shock. This implies a larger EU budget financed by own tax resources, the capacity to borrow in the event of large shocks, and a focus on EU investment priorities.
- A simpler, more transparent and more effective EU fiscal framework is needed. In addition, country-specific adjustment paths should replace a strict enforcement of "one-size-fits-all" measures, such as the 3% budget deficit rule. A debt anchor should be combined with an expenditure rule designed to take into account country-specific factors to reach the debt anchor. Moreover, a general escape clause is advocated in case of severe crisis situations. To create incentives to adhere to the framework, the fiscal capacity will only be available for those that stick to the rules.
- Finally, growth-enhancing expenditure, i.e., investments, should be excluded from the expenditure rules.

The GCEE also proposes that the EU countries retain a long-term debt limit, such as the 60% threshold in the SGP, and that the government budget should be close to balance over the business cycle. They would however prefer less rigid rules and suggest that the structural deficit should not exceed 0.5% of GDP over the business cycle, or 1% of GDP if the debt ratio is significantly below 60%. To monitor and synchronize a long-term debt rule and medium-term structural balance, they propose that annual ceilings of governmental expenditures are introduced. In addition, GCEE recommends that certain government expenditures that counteract cyclical swings are exempted. Overall, the suggestions modify rather than replace the present structure of the SGP.

In yet another proposal formulated by seven French and seven German economist (Pisani-Ferry 2018), it is suggested that the present sanctions for countries not fulfilling the SGP criteria should be replaced by a debt-corrected expenditure rules, adapted to countries' specific circumstances. Moreover, countries' individual responsibility should increase and no bail-outs (lending to insolvent countries) should be allowed. Simultaneously, measures for risk-sharing (e.g., deposit insurance, "safe assets", and unemployment insurance fund, allowing for debt restructuring), are suggested. A separation between the role of watchdog/surveyor and the role of political judge is also recommended.[9]

Blanchard et al. (2020) claim that the present structure of SGP is insufficient to protect public investment simultaneously as it excessively constrains the use of fiscal policy for output stabilization. Based on that observation, they present a policy package relatively similar to EFB's:

- EU should shift from fiscal rules to enforceable fiscal standards. The low interest rate regime, the complexity arising from constraints on monetary policy, combined with higher Knightian uncertainty all indicate that quantitative measures should be substituted for more qualitative assessments combined with ex-post assessment mechanism.
- Governmental expenditure should distinguish between current expenditure and investment expenditures, i.e., introducing a capital expenditure budget. It requires a common definition of capital among EU countries and a monitor mechanism at the EU level.
- A fiscal mechanism should be implemented to counteract shortfalls of demand at the EU level. It should be able to borrow at the EU level and engage in expansionary fiscal policies.

Finally, there is also an ongoing discussion within the Commission. Paolo Gentiloni (European Commissioner for Economy) has recently aired the need for a far-reaching legislative overhaul to help drive stronger public investment and growth (Financial Times, 2021a). He argues for a structure that incentivizes public investment in the green and digital transitions, while fostering stability and durable economic growth. Furthermore, in concert with EFB, he stresses simpler and more flexible rules, including an "expenditure rule" that sets a ceiling on the growth rate of nominal public spending to avoid repeating the aftermath of the financial crisis, when net investment drifted rapidly lower, stymying growth. Some growth-

[9] De Grauwe and Ji (2018) argue that it is impossible to decide whether a government is actually insolvent and that the very existence of a sovereign restructuring procedure may trigger panic.

enhancing expenditure may also be excluded from the ceiling on spending growth. Gentiloni represents the fraction of EU countries that favor stronger political clout at the EU level while the northern countries within EU are more skeptical and considerably more frugal.[10]

## 3.2 COVID-19, State Aid, and Competition

As the width and effects of the COVID-19 crisis became apparent early 2020, the EU fiscal framework conditions referred to above were put on hold. Similarly, the regulatory framework on state aid was basically abandoned until 31 January 2021. That allowed interventions and subsidies targeting firms directly, normally only allowed for limited causes (e.g., R & D), to certain firms (SMEs) and within certain thresholds. Direct capital injections to companies (up to 800,000 euros per company) was allowed, as was the provision of government-guaranteed loans (90%) with subsidized interest rates (six years), deferral of taxes and pay-roll fees, and wage subsidies (redundancy/furlough wages).[11] These provisions were combined with setting up governmental funds earmarked for innovation, venture capital, etc.

Hence, the abolition of both the Maastricht condition and temporary dismissing state aid rules made massive interventions to individuals, firms, industries, and sectors possible. Such support emerged in a plethora of different forms (Braunerhjelm, 2021). At the time, most of these measures were probably motivated; the issue now is their long-term effect on competition and the functioning of markets.

Some countries are more comfortable with more generous state aid and also favor more interventionistic industrial policies, e.g., creating national or EU champions.[12] Others would strongly object. Hence, just as in the case of the Maastricht conditions, it is not given that future state aid rules will be identical to those put on hold in 2019. There are advocates of permanenting certain types of micro-level support, implying that a wave of new regulations and support structures may be imposed. This may incur negative effects on long-run competition, spilling over to innovation, growth, and prosperity.

In addition, the last few decades have witnessed the emergence of digitized production technologies and new business models, a trend that has been reinforced during the present crisis. A conspicuous phenomenon is the emergence of platform companies, often global, which have had considerable positive consumer effects in

[10] Also, Janet Yellen, US Treasury secretary, advocates a framework that enables more stimulus measures in case of crises.

[11] The conditions are that companies receiving support have had a financially sound position in 2019, that loans and guarantees do not exceed twice the wage cost or 25% of turnover and that liquidity strengthening measures apply for a maximum of 18 months for SMEs and 12 months for larger business.

[12] Some changes have already been decided, e.g., regarding regional support.

the short-run, while the long-run welfare effects have been increasingly questioned (Crémer et al., 2019).

### 3.2.1 How to Regulate Competition

The overarching conditions for fair and competitive markets are contingent upon an institutional framework based on the rule of law, a credible judicial system, impartial and unbiased regulations, and limited governmental interventions that do not distort markets. In addition to these overall conditions, there are regulations and legislation that directly target competition.

The United States was the first country to impose a competition law (Sherman Act, 1890) that made it possible to break up larger companies. It was followed a few years later by the Clayton Act (1914) which prevented anticompetitive company acquisitions. The reason for the Sherman Act was the extremely strong market position of Standard Oil, significantly more dominant than today's large platform companies (measured as profit shares). After the legislation, the company was broken up into 34 parts that continued to be very profitable. One of the concerns had to do with company's extensive power and political influence, which partly resembles today's situation (Braunerhjelm, 2020).

Views on how competition should be regulated have varied over the decades. Pigous' (1938) work on public interest theory constitutes a starting point. The idea was that unregulated markets would lead to market failures which must be rectified through political intervention. This was questioned much later in the so-called public choice theory, which instead emphasized the negative effects of weak ownership and the risk that arises in organization where agency structures open up for opaque behavior drive by individuals' preferences. Similarly, different stakeholders may try to control or influence how regulations are formulated (Stigler, 1971).

Regarding competition, a group of academics at Harvard developed a theory in the 1950s about the design, functioning, and efficiency of markets that had a major impact. The analysis was based on firms producing a well-defined product that could be linked to a specific market where a number of firms compete. The focus of the analysis is the competitive relationship between the producers in this market, i.e., number of companies and market shares, so that no firm dominates the market.

Later, this view was challenged by the so-called Chicago school, which is based on assumptions about efficient and rational markets that also have a self-correcting function. In the short-term efficiency reasons and consumer benefit can justify a higher degree of market concentration (referred to as efficiency defense). A lower competitive pressure at times is argued to be compensated for by economies of scale, lower prices, and a better adaption of services and products to customers and producers. The conclusion was that regulations of competition should be limited, and dominant companies can be allowed, at least as long as there is a change of market leaders. The Chicago school thus advocated a more dynamic view of market competition where the number of companies was not decisive (static view).[13]

The current framework on competition draws on the Chicago school but has recently been increasingly questioned due to digitization and the emergence of platform firms. The cornerstones of current regulations of competition refer to the abuse of market power, mergers of firms (given certain turnover thresholds), and different types of collusions (prices in particular), and whether that generated harmful effects on consumers, primarily through price increases. However, in the platform economy, it may be considerably more intricate to verify that harm has been inflicted upon consumers, especially in the short-run, since services are often free. Instead, other potentially negative effects of platforms have increasingly been emphasized, such as deterring entry and innovation. This has sparked efforts to adjust institutions to incorporate the specific characteristics of platform firms and their potential future impact on industrial dynamics.

### 3.2.2 The Platform Economy and Competition

Digitization was initially expected to lead to stronger competition by, among other things, facilitating entry of a large number of companies. However, reality was shown to be more complicated, which is perhaps most clearly illustrated by the so-called platform companies. Given that a number of such companies have quickly established themselves as global market leaders in their respective industry, it has been increasingly questioned whether the current regulations are sufficient to ensure fair competition.

Moreover, platform companies have gradually expanded their domains to other markets by bundling products or making access to services conditioned on the usage of other services provided by the platform (e.g., travel and payment services), and by developing a significant number of ancillary services, i.e., an ecosystem of complementary services. In addition, the platform companies often have a "gatekeeper function" implying that they decide who can use the platform and on what conditions. Hence, doubts have been expressed whether competition between platforms, as well as on these platforms, actually works.

Obviously considerable positive values have been created by platform firms benefiting consumers, producers, and entrepreneurs. The issue is how to regulate competition in order to ensure a continuation of these beneficial effects. The combination of significant economies of scale, strong positive network effects, negligible marginal costs, and exclusive access to large amounts of data, can be expected to affect the competitive conditions over time. Such market characteristics imply that there is usually only room for one or a limited number of companies, i.e., a "winner-takes-most" economy. "Tipping points" might be reached where platform companies gain such a dominant position that entry of new firms is virtually

[13] See Piraino (2007) on the development of competition law.

impossible. The long-term negative welfare effects of these concentration forces risk exceeding the short-term efficiency gains, leading to more concentrated markets (Furman et al., 2019; Scott Morton et al., 2019).

Similarly, the advantage of data access implies that platform owners may influence users' behavior through various types of smart algorithms that "nudge" them in the desired direction. These forces accumulate as the platforms grow and may in the long-run stifle competition, innovation, and negatively affect consumer value. This suggest that policies should pre-empt potentially negative future effects on competition.

An increase in market concentration can also be observed since some time, being particularly accentuated in the U.S. and embracing most industries (Phillipon, 2019). In Europe, that pattern looks somewhat different. Likewise, a decline in new ventures has been observed in several countries, particularly in the U.S. (Decker et al., 2016; Naude, 2019), adding to the worries of languishing economic dynamism.[14] Hence, both the size of the market and its functioning may be threatened if the competitive forces are reduced (Acemoglu & Restrepo, 2018).

Not only a dominant position but also acquisitions may hamper competition and strengthen incumbents' market position. This can justify very high prices despite low sales in the acquired company. Such early "killer acquisition" was first observed in the pharmaceutical industry where the purpose was to kill an innovation (a new drug) in the acquired company or to integrate it into the acquirer's own product portfolio. Since then, the concept has been extended to especially digitized markets and partly recast into a "kill zone". If you get too close to the core business of an existing firm, you risk being liquidated through acquisitions. Of course, an acquisition does not need to be negative if, for example, there are clear synergies or if efficiency and user benefits increase in other ways.

According to present EU and US regulations, acquisitions and mergers must be prohibited if they lead to significant impediment to effective competition. However, many acquisitions go under the radar because they do not meet the turnover requirements for a review to begin, even though the company may have a large and growing group of users.

## 3.3 *COVID and Openness*

During the last decades, the world has become increasingly interconnected. The interlinked value-added production chains still account for approximately 70% of world trade. The interconnectedness comes in terms of mobility of information, labor, capital, and goods and services. In many areas in the past, countries have liberalized their trade policies and taken part of the world trade at an increasing rate.

[14] To what extent firms in the gig and sharing economy are included is unclear. These firms may be registered differently and therefore not show up in the statistics, at least in European countries.

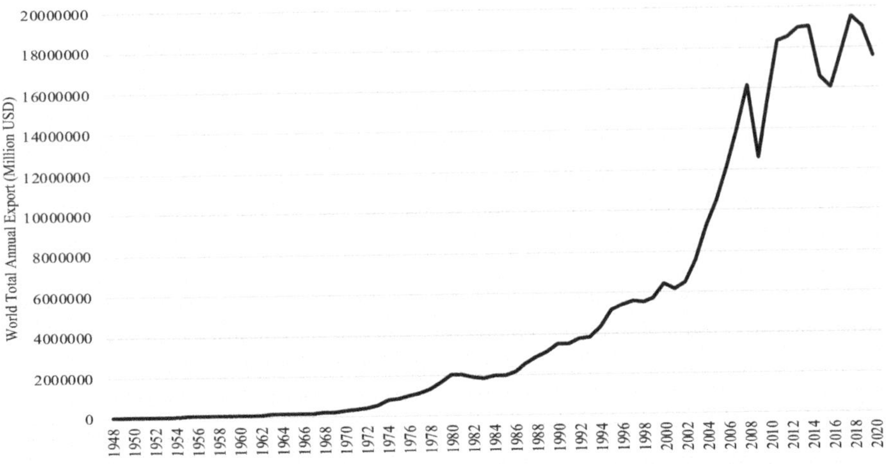


**Graph 6** World trade (in million USD). Note: Graph based on authors own computations. Data provided by the World Trade Organization (WTO)

However, in more recent years, some of the public and policy sentiments have been redirected to more protectionism which has led to increases in tariffs, Brexit, and other national protectionist measures being taken place. Graph 6 below shows the volume of world trade since 1948 obtained from WTO.

In the early 2000s, global trade increased substantially as countries became involved in the world economy and integrated in global production chains at a new pace. A setback occurred after the 2008–2009 crisis, but then it bounced back to an even higher level. Following the recovery, international trade stagnated and there was even a dip 2015 to 2016. In the early months of the COVID-19 crisis, total global trade volumes decreased by around 17% and the decline in 2020 averaged about 8%. Global trade, similar to GDP, has however recovered faster than initially expected. A conspicuous feature of previous crises has been an initial decrease in demand which then transcended into a decline in trade. In the present COVID-19 crisis, this was reversed; world trade was first impacted through disruptions on the supply side due to lockdowns and other regulatory restrictions which more generally hindered imports and exports.

Subsequently exports of specific items, such as vaccines, were prohibited by some countries. Such national measures to shield the own population may set a viscous cycle into motion, characterized by escalated protectionism, global inefficiencies in production. Rents would be created—due to the lack of global competition—and shifted to national players.

High levels of inequality have also been claimed to be a fundamental factor undermining global trade and igniting political conflicts. Inequality within countries is thus central to understand long-term trade relationships and the strain that trade is placing on domestic policies. Addressing inequality within and between countries implies that the corresponding savings gluts and international imbalances need to be attended. Hence, surplus countries have to consider measures to increased demand. "De-globalization" has become a buzzword, but that would imply creating rents and new types of inequalities where some national businesses would benefit at the expense of consumers.

A particular concern in international trade has to do with resilient supply chains where it has been argued that governments should subsidize or protect production of strategically important components (e.g., semiconductors). Others argue that we should separate between globalization leading to global public goods, such as handling climate change or pandemics, and "beggar-thy-neighbor" policies, such as currency depreciation and tax competition. Yet other studies confer a positive and strengthening effect of trade on the resilience of supply chains. Hence, it is an open question whether, and to which extent, globalization will recover after the COVID-19 crisis.

## 4 Discussion: What to Expect?

We have discussed three potential forces that have been accentuated during the COVID-19 crisis that may threaten the future size and functioning of the market. Besides of those there are of course a number of other potential factors that may circumcise the market. The combination of geopolitical tensions, climate-induced conflicts, and more generally tendencies toward protectionism, implies that the market-based economy cannot be taken for granted. In addition, there is a strong political movement in several countries for increased governmental expenditures to overcome inequalities and expand social services.

### *4.1 The Size of Governments Versus Markets*

Regarding the role of governments and the risk of continued and increased governmental interventions, we believe that the expansionary fiscal policies during the crisis, combined with low interest rates, constitute an irresistible temptation for a large group of politicians to continue on that path. That may however well be "a road to hell paved by good intentions". In the US, the discussion seems to primarily have centered around the effect of expansionary policies on future inflation, interest rates, and crowding-out effects. In the EU, the question concerns the reform of the entire fiscal framework as outlined in the Maastricht conditions.

As regards the latter, and based on the discussion referred to above on how to reform the SGP, we would emphasize the following aspects:

- Before any extension of governmental expenditures can be considered, make sure that the current levels of tax revenues are spent in an efficient and rational way. For instance, a large chunk of the EU budget is still allocated to the agricultural sector, often without taking for instance growth or climate effects into account.

- Make sure that fraud and corruption in using present EU-level resources are, if not extinguished, at least minimized. This has to do with credibility and legitimacy.
- We would recommend abstaining from a fiscal mechanism based on a new level of taxes collected at the EU level. Once taxes have been delegated to the EU level, they are likely to increase and expand to new areas that may hamper confidence in the EU project and generate an excessive regulatory burden.
- We are skeptical to abolish debt anchors or budget rules but agree with the need to adjust the compliance rules such that country-specific circumstances are taken into account. Transparency and simplicity should be prioritized.
- Similarly, we believe that separating the budget between current expenditure and investments is a good idea. However, it would require a stringent framework and distinct assessment so that expenditures are not redefined as investments (e.g., with regard to human capital).
- It seems difficult to accomplish independent and credible assessment of nations' compliance with fiscal regulations, moral hazard risks will be present. Previous attempts to stricter rules and enforcement have come at the expense of increased complexity and practical implementation problems.
- Some of the recommendations launched by different organizations or scholars may be hard to reconcile with the principle of subsidiarity. There is already a discussion of the EU meddling into policy areas that best can be handled at the national level.

Hence, we advocate caution in imposing new and detailed regulations regarding EU's fiscal framework. The only proposal that seems likely to strengthen the market and contribute to its expansion is the investment proposal. Partly because it would engage private actors, partly because if correctly designed it would strengthen the growth prerequisites. Installing a so-called fiscal mechanism, combined with taxes at the EU level, is motivated by the inability of national governments to build up buffers in good times. Institutionalizing a responsibility for fiscal policies, besides of what is already possible, may however further reduce the incentives at the national level to safeguard public finances and can open up for moral hazard behavior. This is likely to have a detrimental effect on the functioning and size of markets.

## 4.2 COVID-19, State Aid, and Competition

Turning to state aid the temporary moratorium, or redefinition, of the present rules is supposed to end 31 December 2021. There are however suggestions from different stakeholders and policy sectors that the rules should be reformed to allow a more active industrial policy. To the best of our knowledge, this has not yet resulted in any concrete measures to change the current system, besides of some relatively minor changes related to regional policies. Since countries within EU have different traditions and tolerance when it comes governmental interactions with the business sector, a softening of state aid rules is likely to distort market competition, diminishing the room for market expansion and market dynamism.

That brings us to the important issue of the functioning of the market as such, i.e., competition rules, which recently has become a highly topical issue. Pivotal in that discussion is digitization and the emergence of big tech platform firms. The question is what the future implications are of their dominant position, network externalities, and access to data. Our conclusion is that digital markets will only work well if they are supported with strong pro-competition policies that open up opportunities for innovation and counter the forces that over time can reinforce higher concentration where industries are dominated by one or few firms. The challenge is therefore to reach a balance between (1) companies that build platforms and invest in data collection, (2) their market position and effects on competition, and (3) the interest of users of platforms (switching platforms, transfer data, integrity, etc.).

These potential problems for well-functioning and expanding markets in the longer run have recently received considerably more attention in both the EU and the US. In the US, the House of Representatives presented a report on the effects of Facebook, Apple, Amazon, and Google on competition in October 2020. According to the report, all these companies have abused their dominant position in terms of fees and prices, contractual relationships, and competition on the platforms. In addition, the companies have made more than 500 acquisitions since 1998, none of which have been stopped by antitrust legislation.[15] Moreover, there are presently two legal actions going on in the US, involving Facebook (the Federal Trade Commission) and Google (Department of Justice), whereas Apple just lost a case regarding their right to preclude information where app contents can be downloaded free or at lower costs.

The European Commission has been involved in a number of noticed legal cases on competition with the big platform firms, with varying success. The Commission has also proclaimed the 2020s as the "digital decade" with a focus on an independent digital agenda where data, technology, and digital infrastructure are at the forefront. The work is built around four pillars: technology that serves the EU population, a fair and competitive digitization, an open, democratic, and sustainable digitization, and that the EU takes the lead globally. The two main policy documents proposals are the Digital Service Act (cyber security, integrity, responsibilities, etc.) and the Digital Market Act (platforms, competition, entrepreneurship, etc.)

We sympathize with views forwarded by Furman (2019), Aghion et al. (2021), Phillipon (2019), and Cremer et al. (2019), too mention a few. Hence, market abuse cannot solely be determined by looking at prices. Data portability, interoperability, and sharing are critically important for users and new platforms. The gatekeeper position has in several cases rendered anticompetitive practices. Short-run consideration (prices) should be replaced by assessments of the long-run effects on competition, prices, and innovation. Moreover, the entire ecosystem and their

[15] In 2020, the big platform firms' acquisitions reached an all-time high (data from Refinitiv, see Financial Times, 2021b).

vertical structures should be included in the analysis of potential impediments to competition.

Similarly, the effect on competition of mergers cannot be based on turnover thresholds, since that does not take into pre-emptive mergers or acquisitions done to disarm potential future competitors (e.g., Facebook acquiring Instagram and WhatsApp). Antitrust regulations should be considered to diminish market power of few firms.

Pro-competitive tools, i.e., ex-ante measures, should to a larger extent complement ex-post actions to facilitate for new businesses to enter digital markets and increase predictability to all companies about the rules and standards that apply. This is likely to spur innovation and provide consumers with higher quality and greater choice (Furman et al., 2019). In addition, it could replace large fines and drawn-out procedures and enable faster action that more directly targets and remedies the problematic behavior.

There is nothing inherently wrong about being a large company, in fact is necessary in order to reap the advantages of economies of scale, which may increase efficiencies and benefits for consumers or businesses. But regulations have to be designed such that long-term user welfare, entry, and innovation are preserved in order for markets to function and grow.

## 4.3 *COVID-19 and Openness*

An arms race-type of behavior where different countries engage in protectionist measures to secure national interest against foreign will be a costly strategy, not only in the short-run but also in the medium- and long-run. If these sentiments persist, it may even lead nations to exit institutions such as European Union or trade agreements. In the case of Brexit, at least the short-run costs seem to have been quite extensive measured as a decline in investments more generally, relocation of firms and disruption in supply chains.

If protectionist measures accelerate and become permanent, the absence of foreign competition can be expect to lead to increased sizes of domestic firms, combined with less productive firms surviving for longer and an overall more inefficient production structure. Similarly, a continued decrease in foreign direct investment would also hamper competition and productivity.[16] This means that the closing down of borders and trade can have fundamental effects on the structure of the firms in a market.

Also restrictions on the mobility of individuals will have negative effects over time. Besides of certain industries being particularly hurt, hindering mobility of individuals implies that embodied knowledge will not be diffused to the same extent.

---

[16]Foreign direct investments fell by a third during 2020.

Hence, mobility of individuals would be beneficial not only to certain industries but also the exchange of idea and thus innovation.

## 5 Concluding Remarks

COVID may expand or decrease the potential size and functioning of the market. This entirely depends on the policies taken and for how long they persist, and the political reactions to the crisis. If market imperfections or market failures prevail, policy interventions are justified to correct such deficiencies. In the case of COVID-19, the logic was almost reversed, i.e., policy measures implied that markets ceased to function, which is obvious when a lockdown is imposed. Then the state can be argued to have a responsibility to cushion and bridge such situations until markets can open up again, which prompted a number of government interventions during the COVID-19 crisis. As the recovery of the economy has gained speed, the stimulus packages and crisis-induced regulations should be withdrawn, since they may otherwise have unintended, long-term impacts on markets and how they function.

From a Schumpeterian perspective, the question is whether and to which extent dynamics and creative destruction forces have been affected by COVID or if there are risks for more persistent post-COVID malaises? We have tried to assess that by taking a selective look at actual and potential interventions at the macro-, meso-, and micro-levels, being relevant for our purposes. The macro-level refers to the size of public expenditure which basically determines the overall room for market-based activities and shapes the role of the public sector in an economy. Presently the situation is characterized by considerable uncertainty about the future role of governments and the instruments available, particularly in the EU. Proponents of the modern monetary theory, as well as those stressing more interventions to reduce inequalities, claim that fiscal expansions can be financed through printing new money without no or negligible negative effects. Hence, pursuing that view means that there is basically no financial constraints on the public sector, except political.

We have illustrated the interventions at the meso-level with the direction international trade and openness have taken. It could however also have been policies targeting the industrial level, which have been frequent but less transparent. We concluded that after an initial surge in protectionist measures, there seems to be a return to business as usual. Yet, it depends on the design of future state aid policies as well as possible erection of nontariff barriers and tariffs, the extent to which resilience in supply chains and mitigation in carbon dioxide emissions are used as general reason to shield domestic markets from foreign competition. An excessive use of such instruments risk to stifle economic dynamism and the functioning of markets.

Finally, at the micro-level we were concerned about the long-term effect of massive state aid and faltering competition regulations. We would claim that continuation of those risk infecting Schumpeter I with serious post-COVID symptoms, irrespective of data showing higher entry and fewer bankruptcies in 2020. The reason is that different kinds of support to firms are likely to have kept zombie-firms with no or small long-term for survival on the market. Schumpeter II seems less affected, rather the dominance of large platform firms has thrived during the pandemic. This is however not a desirable outcome and may have severe long-term implications for entry and innovations. In addition, if government intervention continues it might push back the private sector even further, giving large firm an advantage handling and interacting with governments. Hence, the "wrong" Schumpeter seems to have benefited from the COVID crisis so far.

Still, governments and policymakers are usually laggards when markets change. It is primarily private firms and individuals that exploit new technology and contribute with innovations that reshape the frontiers of the prerequisites for markets. Hence, the outcome is far from given even if we presently see growing public sectors and an increased rate of interventions.

## References


Acemoglu, D., & Restrepo, P. (2018). *Artificial intelligence, automation and work*, NBER WP, 24196, NBER.

Aghion, P., Antonin, C., & Bunel, S. (2021). *The power of creative destruction*. Harvard University Press.

Beckmann, M. (2017). The size of the market. *Asia-Pacific Journal of Accounting & Economics, 18*, 1–9.

Blanchard, O., Leandro, A., & Zettelmeyer, J. (2020). *Revisiting the EU fiscal framework in an era of low interest rates*. https://ec.europa.eu/info/sites/default/files/s3-p_blanchard_et_al_0.pdf.

Braunerhjelm, P. (2020). Plattformsföretag: Välsignelse eller förbannelse? Konkurrens, innovation och användarnytta (Plattform companies: Blessing or curse?). In J. Eklund & P. Thulin (Eds.), *Svensk konkurrenskraft. Hur kan Sverige säkerställa ett långsiktigt välstånd? Swedish Economic Forum Report 2020*. Entreprenökapsforum.

Braunerhjelm, P. (2021). *Rethinking stabilization policies; including supply-side measures and entrepreneurial processes, small business economics, online version*.

Buchanan, J. (1967). *Public finance in democratic process: Fiscal institutions and individual choice*. UNC Press.

Crémer, J., de Montjoye, Y.-A., & Schweitzer, H. (2019). *Competition for the digital era, report to the commission*. Directorate-General for Competition, Bryssel.

Darvas, Z., Martin, P., & Ragot, X. (2018). *European fiscal rules require a major overhaul, policy Contribution18*, Brueghel, Brussels.

De Grauwe, P., & Ji, Y. (2018, April 19). *Financial engineering will not stabilise an unstable euro area*, VoxEU.org.

Decker, R., Haltiwanger, J., Jarmin, R., & Miranda, J. (2016). Declining business dynamism: What we know and the way forward. *American Economic Review Papers and Proceedings, 106*, 203–207.

European Commission. (2017). *Reflection paper on the deepening of the economic and monetary union*. https://ec.europa.eu/info/publications/reflection-paper-deepening-economic-and-monetary-union_en

European Fiscal Board. (2017). *Annual report*. European Commission.

European Fiscal Board. (2019). *Annual report*. European Commission.

European Fiscal Board. (2020). *Annual report*. European Commission.

Eyraud, L., Gaspar, V., & Poghosyan, T. (2017). *Fiscal policies in the euro area*. IMF eLibrary, https://www.elibrary.imf.org/view/journals/001/2017/018/article-A001-en.xml.

Feld, L., Schmidt, C., Schnabel, I., & Wieland, V. (2018). *Refocusing the European fiscal framework*. https://voxeu.org/article/refocusing-european-fiscal-framework.
Financial Times. (2021a, July 28). *EU economy chief urges end to 'muddling through' with budget rules*.
Financial Times. (2021b, September 19). *Big tech companies snap up smaller rivals at record pace*.
Fornaro, L., & Wolf, M. (2020). *COVID-19 coronavirus and macroeconomic policy*. CEPR Discussion Paper No. DP14529. Available at SSRN: https://ssrn.com/abstract=3560337
Furman, J., Coyle, D., Fletcher, A., Marsden, P., Och McAuley, D. (2019). *Unlocking digital competition, report of the digital competition expert panel*. www.gov.uk/government/publications.
German Council of Economic Experts. (2017). *Towards a forward-looking economic policy, annual report 2017/2018*.
German Council of Economic Experts. (2018). *Setting the right course for economic policy, annual report 2018/19*.
Guerrieri, V., Lorenzoni, G., Straub, L., & Werning, I., (2020). *Macroeconomic implications of COVID-19: Can negative supply shocks cause demand shortages?* NBER WP 6918, NBER.
Naude, W. (2019). *The extinction of entrepreneurs*. Maastricht University and RWTH Aachen University.
OECD. (2020). *Tackling coronavirus (COVID-19): Contributing to a global effort. SME policy responses*. OECD.
OECD. (2021). *Government at a glance*. OECD.
Phillipon, T. (2019). *The great reversal: How America gave up on free markets*. Harvard University Press.
Pigou, A. C. (1938). *The economics of welfare*. Macmillan.
Piraino, T. A., Jr. (2007). Reconciling the Harvard and Chicago schools: A new antitrust approach for the 21st century. *Indiana Law Journal, 82*, 345–409.
Pisani-Ferry, J. (2018). *Euro area reform: An anatomy of the debate*. CEPR.
Reinhart, C. M., & Rogoff, K. S. (2009). *This time is different: Eight centuries of financial folly*. Princeton University Press.
Scott Morton, F., Nierenberg, T. Y., Bouvier, P., Ezrachi, A., Jullien, B., Katz, R., Kimmelman, G., & Och Morgenstern, J. (2019). *Market structure and antitrust subcommittee, Committee for the Study of digital platforms, George J. Stigler Center for the Study of the Economy and the State*. University of Chicago Booth.
Stigler, G. (1971). The theory of economic regulation. *Bell Journal of Economics and Management Science, 2*, 3–21.
World Bank. (2020). https://dataviz.worldbank.org/views/SME-COVID19/Overview?%3Aembed=y&%3AisGuestRedirectFromVizportal=y&%3Adisplay_count=n&%3AshowAppBanner=false&%3Aorigin=viz_share_link&%3AshowVizHome=n&fbclid=IwAR0vfwIVUpPgT9qn7w9473B7hyi8mVlB4PZVkosOLRJCQR6NgS1ZJPeR5qM.

**Pontus Braunerhjelm** is Professor at KTH Royal Institute of Technology, Blekinge Institute of Technology, and Swedish Entrepreneurship Forum. Pontus earned his Ph.D. at the Graduate Institute of International Studies, Geneva, Switzerland, in 1994. His research focusses on innovation, entrepreneurship, industrial dynamics, and growth. He has been involved in several policy projects, e.g., the Swedish Globalization Council (2007–2009), the Committee on Entrepreneurship Policies (2014–2016), and the Swedish Restart Commission (2020).

**Emma Lappi** holds a Ph.D. in Economics from Jönköping International Business School. Her research interests include the impact of entrepreneurship, regulations, and micro-level outcomes such as health and productivity. Her research is published in journals such as Empirica, Journal of Industrial Economics, Journal of Regulatory Economics, and Small Business Economics.

# COVID-19 Crisis: Modernization Push at the Macroeconomic and Firm Level, Providing for Not So Disparate Opportunities and Challenges for Majors and Start-Ups

**Gunter Deuber**

**Abstract** The existential COVID-19 crisis, which was unpredictable for entrepreneurs and companies in this form, has triggered unprecedented modernization dynamics in society at large and in the economic sphere. Companies that were already geared toward resilience and agility precrisis—regardless of their size—should emerge strengthened from the crisis. Since such traits also characterize newly founded companies and start-ups, this existential crisis—thanks to a more solid and faster-than-expected economic recovery—has also favored such companies or at least did not put them into substantive disadvantage compared to large and/or well-established companies. In a way, the COVID-19 crisis was also an "equalizer" between established (large) firms and small-scale start-ups. In this respect, there is a chance that there will be more fruitful interactions between start-ups and well-established companies in the years to come, a development that can lead to the formation of more productive enterprise ecosystems. The latter may induce positive macroeconomic growth effects as well. In the context of post-COVID-19 economic cycle, which is particularly geared toward strong nominal growth of GDP globally and in Europe, companies and enterprises that have (hyper) scalable business models in addition to the success factors outlined above should perform particularly well. Moreover, the war in Ukraine has once again demonstrated the need for resilient for resilience and agility in the private sector.

**Keywords** Firm size · Resilience · Scalable business model · Ecosystems · Digital economy

---

G. Deuber (✉)
Raiffeisen Bank International AG, Vienna, Austria
e-mail: gunter.deuber@rbinternational.com



D. B. Audretsch, I. A. M. Kunadt (eds.), *The COVID-19 Crisis and Entrepreneurship*, International Studies in Entrepreneurship 54,
https://doi.org/10.1007/978-3-031-04655-1_6

## 1 Introduction

The global COVID-19 crisis was an existential economic and social crisis, a "crisis of the century" or a "black swan" event. Particularly devastating were the short-term economic and social costs felt by many (small) firms and entrepreneurs as an "exogenous shock", as initially in many parts of the global economy and especially in Europe almost all nonessential parts of the economy (and society) were shut down in 2020. At the same time, the COVID-19 crisis—despite all short-term hardship—as a phase of "creative destruction" challenged the resilience of companies and their organizational structures and in some cases also raised it to a new level. Whether small- and medium-sized companies or entrepreneur-led start-ups were particularly affected in the context of the COVID-19 crisis in direct comparison to large major companies must be assessed in a differentiated manner, as will be shown in this article. However, the COVID-19 crisis will in all likelihood have initiated permanent changes and distinct modernization dynamics for society at large in combination with distinct innovative corporate and entrepreneurial dynamics, all of which in combination can induce positive growth and well-being enhancing macroeconomic effects in the long term. The basic idea behind this train of thought is that existential or exogeneous (economic) shocks can bring about (economic) transformation (Winston, 2020).

In this paper, the economic impact of the COVID-19 crisis will be explored on three levels. First, the author brings in his real-life experience within the context of the COVID-19 crisis working in a major international corporation and in an industry that is at the forefront of digital transformation, more specifically the financial sector, where many start-ups have also established themselves. Secondly, the author brings in his macroeconomic view of the COVID-19-related calamity, outlines its economic particulars, and shares his view of the specific features of the most likely imminent extended postcrisis economic recovery and investment cycle ahead. Here the focus is also on Europe in particular. In the author's view, the postcrisis recovery cycle should particularly benefit innovative, agile, and growth/scalability-driven firms and start-ups. Thirdly, the author brings in his experience from numerous discussions at top management and company executive level, which he was able to gather—in addition to actively observing media and the business environment—in the context of the COVID-19 crisis. Moreover, as (chief) economist of a major international or pan-European bank, the author had to analytically penetrate relevant short- to medium-term trends in a timely manner—together with his analysis teams—and give predictions to the extent possible. In this paper, the objective is now to deduct and present longer-term consequences and trend developments, based on the experiences outlined. Moreover, the author would like to sketch some future research questions, which will certainly need the availability and processing of more valid data (macroeconomic data as well as data at the firm or founder level) and experience from the longer post-COVID-19 recovery cycle that probably lies ahead.

## 2 COVID-19 Crisis: Unprecedented Constraints on Economic and Social Life in Peacetime—Creative Solutions Called for and Delivered by Companies and Entrepreneurs

At the onset of the COVID-19 crisis, policymakers and other decision-makers were confronted with unprecedented (exponential) global or transboundary risks and risk dynamics. In this respect, extremely radical policy measures in terms of severe restrictions—unseen in peacetimes—on social and economic life at the beginning of 2020 were rationally explainable and without any choice. Less radical actions would not have been politically justifiable. At the beginning of the COVID-19 crisis, sharp lockdowns were therefore evident globally, imposing immense restrictions on social and economic life. This was particularly true in (Western) Europe. The primacy of politics was to maintain confidence in the systemic steering capacity—without explicitly considering short-term economic costs and needed adjustments for economic actors, be it large enterprises, small firms or start-ups. Many economic actors and entrepreneurs were thus deprived of their planning and business basis within a short period of time due to drastic supply restrictions. In view of the severity of the restrictions at the beginning of the pandemic in developed economies and especially in Europe, generous bridging and financing options were provided for many companies and types of companies. In addition to supporting individuals and companies, the aim here was also to lay the groundwork for a sustainable upswing.

Given the severity of the restrictions and the explicit prevention of entrepreneurial activity, especially in Q1 2020, it is not at all surprising that the resulting short-term economic slump was dramatic. On a quarterly basis, GDP losses in Q1 2020 and early Q2 2020 were dramatic and much more severe than in any other economic crisis in modern history (e.g., compared to the Global Financial Crisis). Relatively modest GDP drops on an annual level in 2020 were supported by a high degree of adaptability plus the economic recovery dynamics kicking in the second half of 2020. In the phases of subsequent relaxation and partial tightening of the COVID-19-related restrictions in the further course of 2020, there was much more differentiation, which facilitated a lot of ongoing adjustment among economic actors and entrepreneurs. Overall, there had been a surprisingly high degree of adaptation on the part of the economic actors in the sense of innovative distribution channels, innovative methods of acquiring customers, etc. already visible in the course of 2020. In part, already progressive and agile actors (e.g., in terms of their digital presence) and smaller companies were able to benefit particularly, but large companies have also demonstrated a high degree of adaptation. This is the only explanation, apart from supportive global economic developments, for the significantly lower economic setbacks in the further course of 2020 and 2021—despite some COVID-19-related restrictions on social and economic life picking up again.

It is not entirely clear here whether small firms and start-ups or large companies were more drastically affected by the COVID-19-related restrictions in the short term at the beginning of the pandemic. There are indications that COVID-19 restrictions affected small firms and start-ups more negatively, at least in the short term. Such types of firms usually have more limited financial cushions in the event of (unexpected) revenue shortfalls and/or, in the absence of classic loan collateral, cannot easily establish bridge financing via classic bank funding. In addition, small businesses, and start-ups, compared to large enterprises, were not necessarily in the political focus of drafting financial support measures by the public sector at first, while such firms are more often dependent on private-sector financing. On the other hand, many small businesses and start-ups today have very flexible cost structures or, above all, low fixed cost blocks in scalable business models, which have increased their agility (Doern, 2021). From a macroeconomic point of view, it would be problematic if the "mortality" or insolvency rate of small businesses and start-ups was too high within the context of the COVID-19 crisis. Such processes would then impair the long-term growth potential in a given economy. To date, however, there are no indications that such processes have occurred. This has to do with the rapid onset of macroeconomic recovery dynamics in H2 2020, as well as the nature of small businesses and start-ups. Such forms of enterprise are characterized by resilience, based on an innovation focus and entrepreneurial spirit. The latter makes it possible to act quickly; innovative firms regularly and quickly adapt to external challenges. The latter is part of their self-image or their business model. In this respect, such firms have also succeeded in offering alternative products or services rather quickly during the crisis, partially also via changed distribution channels. In this respect, the inherent characteristics of small enterprises and start-ups may even have partially compensated and/or overcompensated for other disadvantages compared to large firms (Kramer, 2021).

In addition, the special nature of the crisis in the sense that many or all actors were affected and this through no fault of their own has led to a collaborative and partially altruistic so-called "supporter mentality" and this on many levels. In part, larger companies supported their (smaller) suppliers and partners on various levels (e.g., in terms of crisis management experiences or financing). Even more important for small businesses and start-ups were such activities of support in their own network or the corresponding communities (Giones et al., 2020). In addition, small enterprises and start-ups (or their staff), especially in Europe, have also benefited directly or indirectly from the comprehensive support packages for society at large and compensations for loss of income (compared to the US) (Kuckertz et al., 2020). However, in case of Europe start-up, dynamics cannot match with the US and/or other jurisdictions and this did not change within the context of the COVID-19 crisis (Baroudy et al., 2020).

In a way, the immediate crisis challenges for large and microenterprises and start-ups were very similar, which could have interesting implications. All these players were equally confronted with the challenge of a rapid (complete) shift to digital ways of working, customer interactions, and/or digital distribution and sales channels as well as the adaptation of the product and service offering or the so-called "digital imperative". The challenges here were much greater than classical concepts of business continuity usually cover. In principle, this process was quickly mastered above all by economic actors who had already committed themselves as fully as possible to digital and agile ways of working and the digital transformation across the board before the crisis. This is especially true for companies that had not only digitized their customer and external image (front-end), but also their entire internal processes and systems (technology stack, back-end) as well as (internal and external) forms of communication as far as possible in the sense of the digital imperative. In addition to digital or technical preparation, the combination with agile working methods counts here, which aim precisely to generate a high degree of resilience by proactively dealing with uncertainty and disruption. In addition to preparation (in the technical sense and in the sense of working methods), purpose-driven or value-based management styles have also proven to be a stability element in the crisis. In this respect, companies and entrepreneurs—regardless of the size of the company—should emerge stronger from the crisis if they were already leaders in their sectors in the three areas outlined above (digitization, agile working methods, and purpose-driven management) in the precrisis period and were thus able to make quick decisions and communicate meaningfully under uncertainty. Thus, the COVID-19 crisis could also lead to an even greater dispersion between the leading companies and start-ups in a sector or area of activity, compared to their less advanced competitors. In some economic sectors, this could also trigger even more pronounced "the winner takes all" dynamics in the sense of "winner-takes-most" economics. Whether the growth and innovation impulses of such processes, in addition to possible short-term growth-increasing effects, will then also increase growth and prosperity in the long term, compared to a situation with a more atomistic competitive situation, cannot be answered conclusively at present (Doug & Makhija, 2021; Hegarty, 2021; Aggarwal et al., 2021).

Given the trends outlined above, it is not straightforward to deduce whether larger and already established companies or smaller companies and start-ups were more affected in the short term at the height of the COVID-19 crisis. More problematic, however, is certainly a decline in the start-up rate, especially in Europe (e.g., compared to the US) in the context of the COVID-19 crisis and especially at the early stages of the COVID-19 crisis. Even if there is no experience with a global crisis of this dimension and the subsequent and/or subsequent business start-ups, previous studies after local and regional crises show that so-called "crisis entrepreneurs" can be an important element of recovery. Moreover, such studies show that regions with high business density and start-up dynamics often recover faster than geographies with low business density and start-up dynamics. In principle, crises and the subsequent (first) recovery phases are certainly times for company start-ups, innovators, and disruptors. Interestingly, some of the companies and business models that are currently receiving a lot of international attention or are considered to be modern emerged in the aftermath of the global financial crisis of 2008/2009. In the USA, the following examples are worth mentioning Uber, Airbnb, Venmo (Djankov & Zhang, 2021).

Interestingly, especially in Europe in the context of the COVID-19 crisis, a trend toward the implementation of agile working methods and purpose-driven management or so-called "mission-oriented economic policy" is also discernible in the public sector and especially at the EU level (manifested, for example, in the Next

Generation EU Instrument or the Green Deal). Here, the crisis has obviously contributed to the implementation of such approaches. This could also generate sustainable innovation impulses, which should have a positive impact on the business environment. Especially since more productive interactions between the public and private sectors should be possible (for example, public tenders could be designed more flexibly in the future and not only appeal to established firms). Moreover, many current EU policy schemes are deliberately not aimed at "building back" to precrisis structures, but aimed at reorientation and upgrading (Mazzucato, 2018).

## 3 Recovery After the COVID-19 Crisis: Macroeconomic Trends, Modernization, Financing Trends, and Their Relation to Intra- and Entrepreneurship

On top of the macroeconomic stabilization and adaptation trends, interesting microeconomic trends have also manifested themselves in 2020 and 2021. The trend is for new business start-ups to increase after the first impact of the crisis. Here, the retail, transport and personalized services, and business services sectors stand out in particular. Even though valid insolvency statistics are still scarce, it can be assumed that the start-up momentum outweighs the insolvency figures. However, the job-creating effects of this "start-up dynamic" should not be overestimated (in the short term). It can be assumed that many start-ups are also due to the "emergency situation" on the official labor market. However, some of the start-ups could also develop long-term job and growth potential that cannot yet be seriously foreseen and estimated. Nevertheless, there are indications that the start-up dynamic was particularly strong in the USA compared to Europe. This can probably be attributed to less generous support measures in the USA, which also empirically leads to more start-ups out of necessity. In Europe, on the other hand, the crisis measures were primarily aimed at keeping firms alive; in the US, the policy focus was more on new firm formation and entrepreneurship. Moreover, in the context of the COVID-19 crisis, countries with lean company formation procedures in particular were logically able to record many start-ups.

Nevertheless, there is also a chance in Europe that the COVID-19 crisis could have laid the foundation for many successful companies in the future. Especially since the macroeconomic growth environment in the aftermath of this crisis—this time also in Europe—should be particularly conducive. The extremely accommodative global monetary and fiscal policy will in all likelihood create optimal conditions for growth and, above all, financing, not only in the short term but also in the medium term, with probably slight advantages for start-ups already established before the crisis. This is especially true this time around in Europe, where we have never seen such a coherent monetary and innovation-oriented fiscal policy in the last decade or decades. In contrast, in many parts of Europe—and partly also digitally well-positioned EU countries—the years after the global financial crisis were often years of stagnation or a "lost decade" characterized by austerity. Moreover, the COVID-19-related restrictions in the context of the lockdowns have acted as a catalyst for trends that also favor innovative, scalable, and above all hyperscalable business models. For example, the digital maturity of some established economies has changed within one year at a pace that can normally only be observed over a period of years (this applies, for example, to the acceptance of purely digital offerings, payment habits, etc.). In this sense, the COVID-19 crisis can be seen as a "trend amplifier crisis" that favors digital and scalability-oriented business models.

The line of thinking of a particular post-COVID recovery cycle advocated here is based on the following considerations. First, monetary and fiscal stimuli in the established economies created a highly dynamic global economic and growth environment. The highest real GDP growth rates in the last decade(s) are expected from 2021 to at least 2023. In addition, inflation rates should trend higher in the coming years than in recent years. This means that the nominal growth dynamics are once again much more considerable. For example, high double-digit turnover growth rates are rather easy to achieve in such an economic environment of high nominal growth in economic output. This macroeconomic environment will favor high-turnover entrepreneurs and companies that have intact and rapidly scalable or so-called hyperscalable business models and can thus grow quickly organically (without too high additional costs) and/or take over competitors and complementary providers. Company takeovers (M & A) driven by modernization impulses or the "digital imperative" should thus shape the coming years and partly also benefit small companies and start-ups. Established companies in particular will often want to strengthen the necessary meta-skill set for agile working methods and resilience through such M & A activities.

Moreover, the global interest rate environment (in addition to M & A activity) continues to structurally favor equity financing and equity markets as well as venture capital financing, venture capital valuations, and corporate acquisition dynamics. This is vividly illustrated by the sharp rise in the number of "unicorns" in the context and aftermath of the COVID-19 crisis (The Economist, 2021). Entrepreneurs and companies that were able to demonstrate a basically intact business model geared toward growth even before the COVID-19 crisis and can now credibly present high sales growth to investors—as outlined above—should benefit most from this financing and risk-taking environment. The availability of good financing conditions with so-called private financing forms is of particular importance for start-ups. It should not be neglected here that Europe still lags far behind internationally in terms of these important forms of financing for the digital, platform, and innovation economy.

Through the challenges of the COVID-19 crisis, well-prepared large companies that had already oriented themselves toward agility and resilience before the crisis have learned that they can operate with similar agility as supposedly more nimble small-scale start-ups. In this respect, a certain level playing field has emerged with regard to forms of work. After all, even before the crisis, many large companies relied on small, autonomous units that set completely new approaches in terms of products and market penetration within a large company. In addition, even before the crisis, large companies were increasingly relying internally on a culture of experimentation (and failure) or intrapreneurship and bottom-up approaches. Such developments in large companies are supported by increasingly agile working methods and the widespread establishment of cross-functional teams in order to implement customer-centered innovations more quickly. The COVID-19 crisis has once again strengthened such trends and favored leading (large) companies in these areas. Thus, in the coming years, the often-sought cooperation and interaction between established (large) companies and start-ups should also be able to become more fruitful. This could prospectively have a positive effect on the economy as a whole; special ecosystems with symbiotic interactions could be established as a result. By establishing such new ecosystems with special innovation capacities, it would be possible for innovation capacity to increase more than through large-scale funding programs. Thus, on the one hand, the resilience of regions or national economies could also increase at the macro level and, on the other hand, more growth effects could arise in the long term than through large-scale, top-down government transformation programs. Nevertheless, it should be pointed out that innovative ecosystems with productive interaction between the public and private sectors can also be created on the basis of certain interventionist principles and strategies, as the prominent example of Estonia in the European context shows (Numa & Muzikarova, 2021). The war in Ukraine (and the associated sanctions against Russia) have once again shown how important resilient corporate and modern digital infrastructures are. Moreover, the swift adaptation of many Western companies (including the rapid market exit from Russia) can also be explained by the growing importance of agile management techniques at firms of all scale (incl. a termination and failure culture).

## 4 Summary: COVID-19 Crisis as Catalyst, "Leveler" and Potential Growth Driver—In "Ordinary" Risks of the Digital Economy

The COVID-19 crisis has favored companies that, even before this unforeseeable exogenous shock, had already comprehensively oriented themselves toward agility and resilience in the sense of capabilities, infrastructure and culture in a long term, increasingly dynamic and uncertain economic environment. Thus, the foundation for a high degree of resilience in an exogenous shock (COVID-19 crisis) was de facto laid at the company level even before the crisis. On the one hand, such a company orientation based on a certain meta-skillset—independent of the company size—favored the rather short term and partly reactive crisis management (business continuity as far as possible), but at the same time also favored a necessary medium- and longer-term adaptability in the context of the COVID-19 crisis (proactive adaptation of the business model, distribution channels, etc.). This is because the COVID-19 crisis has massively accelerated trends in working and economic life that were designed as catalysts, such as the digital transformation and changing customer and employee preferences. It is not clear—especially in Europe—whether the COVID-19 crisis hits large companies or smaller firms and start-ups harder. Longer-term studies can provide more evidence here in the coming years. For here it is not "only" about survival in the crisis, but above all about the recovery patterns—possibly differentiated by firm type—after the crisis. In principle, however, there is no evidence to date that the sharp economic slump induced by the first COVID-19-related restrictions, followed by a very dynamic recovery, puts start-ups at a particular disadvantage. Disadvantages in state subsidies were (at least) compensated by networks and above all the agility and resilience inherent in this type of company.

In the coming years, entrepreneurs and firms—regardless of firm size—with innovative and scalable or, above all, hyperscalable business models that have operated successfully in the context of the COVID-19 crisis should continue to be favored. This is especially true against the backdrop of the macroeconomic, growth and investment environment outlined in this paper. In the coming years, Europe in particular can expect one of the highest investment dynamics in years. At the same time, the financing environment in Europe should remain favorable for almost all types of companies for years to come, i.e., for bank financing, capital market financing, and venture capital financing.

However, it is important to note that the COVID-19 crisis also acted as a "leveler" to some extent between small-scale and innovative firms and large firms. In a sense, both groups of firms faced the same challenges and will have to deal with the same changing customer needs and preferences in the future. By converging the working practices of successful large firms and smaller firms plus start-ups in the context of the COVID-19 crisis, collaborations often sought between the two types of firms should be more successful. This could lead to positive macroeconomic effects or a macroeconomic increase in productivity. However, the latter can only be shown by empirical studies conducted several years from today. At the same time, it is important to consider whether the special economic and digitalization environment—in addition to positive short-term impulses—does not bring long-term growth and welfare losses due to the "winner-takes-most" economic dynamics in the general context of the digital and platform economics.

## References

Aggarwal, N., et al. (2021). *Perspectives on resilient leadership from asia-pacific board chairs*. Boston Consulting Group. https://www.bcg.com/publications/2021/perspectives-on-resilient-leadership-from-asia-pacific-board-chairs?linkId=131148281. Accessed Sep 14, 2021.

Baroudy, K. et al. (2020). *Europe's start-up ecosystem: Heating up, but still facing challenges*. McKinsey Insights. Oct 11, 2020. https://www.mckinsey.com/industries/technology-media-and-telecommunications/our-insights/europes-start-up-ecosystem-heating-up-but-still-facing-challenges. Accessed Mar 31, 2021.

Djankov, S., & Zhang, E. (2021). *Startups boom in the United States during COVID-19*. Realtime Economic Issues Watch, Peterson Institute of Economics. https://www.piie.com/blogs/realtime-economic-issues-watch/startups-boom-united-states-during-covid-19. Accessed 30 Jun 2021.

Doern, R. (2021). Knocked down but not out and fighting to go the distance: Small business responses to an unfolding crisis in the initial impact period. *Journal of Business Venturing Insights, 15*, e00221. https://doi.org/10.1016/j.jbvi.2020.e00221. Accessed Sep 15, 2021.

Doug, F., & Makhija, A. K. (2021). *The 5 fronts of digital transformation in the middle market*. Harvard Business Review. October 19, 2021. https://hbr.org/2021/10/the-5-fronts-of-digital-transformation-in-the-middle-market. Accessed Oct 28, 2021.

Giones, F., et al. (2020). Revising entrepreneurial action in response to exogenous shocks: Considering the COVID-19 pandemic. *Journal of Business Venturing Insights, 14*, e00186. https://doi.org/10.1016/j.jbvi.2020.e00186

Hegarty, A. (2021). *How digital transformation can build more resilient businesses*. World Economic Forum. https://www.weforum.org/agenda/2021/10/digital-transformation-business-resilience-cyber/. Accessed October 20, 2021.

Kramer, S. (2021). *Navigating the new normal: Which firms have adapted better to the covid-19 disruption?* MPRA Paper 109,485, https://doi.org/10.1016/j.technovation.2021.102368. Accessed Oct 31, 2021.

Kuckertz, A., et al. (2020). Startups in times of crisis–A rapid response to the COVID-19 pandemic. *Journal of Business Venturing Insights, 13*, e00169. https://doi.org/10.1016/j.jbvi.2020.e00169

Mazzucato, M. (2018). *Mission-oriented research & innovation in the european union, a problem-solving approach to fuel innovation-led growth*. European Commission. mazzucato_report_2018.pdf (europa.eu). Accessed 15 Aug 2020.

Numa, A., & Muzikarova, S. (2021). *Spotlight: Lessons from Estonia's digital miracle*. GLOBSEC Tatra Summit Insight Report 2021, pp. 26–27. https://www.globsec.org/wp-content/uploads/2021/10/GLOBSEC-Tatra-Summit-Insight-Report-2021.pdf

The Economist. (2021, July 24). *Unicornucopia, technology unicorns are growing at a record clip*.

Winston, A. (2020). *Is the COVID-19 outbreak a black swan or the new normal?* MIT Sloan Management Review. https://sloanreview.mit.edu/article/is-the-covid-19-outbreak-a-black-swan-or-the-new-normal/. Accessed Mar 20, 2020.

**Gunter Deuber** serves as Chief Economist of Raiffeisen Bank International (RBI), which operates in Austria and large scale in Central and Eastern Europe. He analyses short- and medium-term economic tides and advises executives on strategical matters such as long-term economic/political tendencies, disruptive trends in the banking/financial industry, and country (risk) and business strategies. He has published several edited volumes on the EU economy.

# Entrepreneurship and Economic Resilience in Times of Crisis: Insights from the COVID-19 Pandemic

**Matthias Menter**

**Abstract** Exogenous shocks such as the COVID-19 pandemic pose major challenges to firms and even entire economies, moving the concept of economic resilience to the foreground. Market actors need to adequately respond to prevalent crises to secure their market position and long-term survival. Entrepreneurship has thereby been identified as a critical lever in creating resilient economies. Based on their innovative capacities, entrepreneurs are able to dynamically adapt to new market conditions and offer (new) solutions to recent problems. Focusing on Germany, this chapter investigates how entrepreneurship was affected by the COVID-19 pandemic and how entrepreneurs responded to the dramatically changing business environment. It further evaluates current policy approaches meant to support entrepreneurs and strengthen economic resilience. The chapter concludes with a discussion on effective policy instruments aimed at promoting economic recovery and derives policy recommendations.

**Keywords** Entrepreneurship · Entrepreneurship policy · Economic recovery · Economic resilience · COVID-19

## 1 Introduction

The COVID-19 pandemic has hit the entire world without warning and has induced severe economic impacts, plunging economies worldwide into a deep recession. In 2020, after ten years of steady growth, the German price-adjusted gross domestic product (GDP) declined by 4.9% compared to 2019. The Coronavirus crisis further led to a state financing deficit of approx. 139.6 billion Euros in Germany in 2020 (Destatis, 2021). These macroeconomic effects of the COVID-19 pandemic were driven by several industry sectors that suffered the most from the multiple

M. Menter (✉)
Friedrich Schiller University Jena, Faculty of Economics and Business Administration, Jena, Germany
e-mail: matthias.menter@uni-jena.de



D. B. Audretsch, I. A. M. Kunadt (eds.), *The COVID-19 Crisis and Entrepreneurship*, International Studies in Entrepreneurship 54,
https://doi.org/10.1007/978-3-031-04655-1_7

lockdowns, e.g., the hospitality sector, arts and entertainment, retail, and personal services (Bartik et al., 2020), along with a general decrease in consumption. By contrast, the German online retailing sector recorded a real increase in sales of almost 30% compared with the same period of the previous year (Destatis, 2021). Hence, the COVID-19 pandemic has produced both winners and losers: Whereas some firms were able to respond adequately to the changing business environment and benefit from resulting market disequilibria, other firms were unable to react.

This attracts special attention to the concept of "resilience". Williams et al. (2017) describe resilience as the ability to maintain "reliable" functioning in times of crisis and disruption. Resilience thereby relates to the utilization of resources before, during, and after an exogeneous shock, thus responding adequately and recovering quickly from prevalent crises. Bergami et al. (2021) highlight the importance of dynamic capabilities that enable entrepreneurs to not only survive but effectively address and adapt to changing business environments. According to Teece et al. (2016: 18), dynamic capabilities describe a firm's ability to "integrate, build, and reconfigure internal and external capabilities to address changing business environments." Helfat et al. (2007) thus state that dynamic capabilities enable firms to translate firms' (newly created) resource base into innovation. Especially, the adoption of digital technologies and the transformation of business models has thereby served as a means to cope with the environmental changes caused by the COVID-19 pandemic (Priyono et al., 2020).

In order to support market actors during the COVID-19 pandemic, governments worldwide tried to support existing firms and initiated immediate measures. The US government provided funds to small businesses via the Paycheck Protection Program, the UK government implemented the Coronavirus Job Retention Scheme, and the German government provided lump sum payments, loans from the state-owned investment and development bank KfW, taxation support as well as short-time work compensation schemes among others. Common to all these policy initiatives was the effort to mitigate the negative consequences of the COVID-19 pandemic, aimed at protecting employment, enabling the continuation of economic activities across industries. Whereas most of these measures focused on incumbent firms, (innovative) start-ups, i.e., productive entrepreneurship, have received less attention (Kuckertz et al., 2020).

Focusing on Germany, the purpose of this chapter is to investigate how entrepreneurship was affected by the COVID-19 pandemic and how entrepreneurs responded to the dramatically changing business environment. Entrepreneurship serves as a critical lever in creating resilient economies and shapes future economic activities. Based on their innovative capacities, entrepreneurs are able to dynamically adapt to new market conditions and offer (new) solutions to recent problems. Hence, a clearer understanding of the short- and long-term impacts of the COVID-19 pandemic on (innovative) entrepreneurship is needed. This chapter evaluates current policy approaches meant to support entrepreneurs and strengthen economic resilience, concludes with a discussion on effective policy instruments aimed at promoting economic recovery, and derives policy recommendations.

## 2 The COVID-19 Pandemic, Economic Resilience, and Entrepreneurship

Although firms tend to decrease investments in innovation during economic crises (Archibugi et al., 2013), entrepreneurial innovations are crucial in times of crisis to address existing (economic or societal) challenges. Kuckertz et al. (2020: 3) state that "being innovative is a precondition of being resilient, as innovative businesses tend to constantly and continuously anticipate and adjust to a broad range of crises." The COVID-19 pandemic with its multiple lockdowns and social distancing restrictions has thereby changed the way innovation is pursued. According to a recent online survey of almost 2000 firms in Germany, the Coronavirus crisis has placed additional burdens on economic agents and simultaneously changed innovation patterns (BMWi, 2021): Especially, the utilization of platforms and the digitization of innovation processes have been intensified. This is in line with Acs et al. (2021) who note that platform-based ecosystems serve as a force of "creative destruction." Kuckertz and Brändle (2021: 20) add to this line of argument and state that entrepreneurship becomes "creative reconstruction," enabling firms to move beyond pre-crisis levels: "When entrepreneurial activity comes under pressure from a major exogenous shock, entrepreneurship in itself is an integral and essential part of the solution."

Studies focusing on economic resilience show that regions with high levels of entrepreneurship are better able to cope with exogeneous shocks (Bishop, 2019; Williams & Vorley, 2014). These findings are also confirmed in the context of the COVID-19 pandemic. The analysis of Ebersberger and Kuckertz (2021) suggests that innovative start-ups were able to respond much faster to changing business environments in comparison with incumbent firms and research institutions. Especially opportunities for digital entrepreneurship arose during the COVID-19 pandemic, highlighting the importance of the digital transformation across industries (Modgil et al., 2021). Kuckertz et al. (2020: 5) consequently note that "an entrepreneurial region is characterized by the resilience of its enterprises and entrepreneurial activity can contribute to restructuring and adaptation in the aftermath of the crisis." Hence, resilient entrepreneurial ecosystems are able to make economic, technological, and societal impacts (Audretsch et al., 2019).

However, entrepreneurial patterns across gender, race, and immigrant status vary significantly and have been affected differently by the COVID-19 pandemic. Focusing on the United States, Fairlie's (2020) study reveals that African American as well as Latinx business owners experienced major losses, eliminating 41% and 32% of active business owners, respectively. In addition, immigrant business owners as well as female business owners suffered disproportionately. Graeber et al. (2021) confirm the existence of this gender gap also for Germany, which has its origin in the self-selection of female entrepreneurs in industries that were more severely affected by the COVID-19 pandemic. Thus, the Coronavirus crisis has exacerbated inequality and has placed additional burdens on marginalized entrepreneurs.

Overall, the fluctuation in the commercial economy in Germany has decreased significantly in 2020, as both the number of start-ups and the number of firm liquidations have declined (Kay & Kranzusch, 2020). Contrary to the trend in start-ups, the number of part-time business start-ups increased in 2020. As expected, the pandemic led to a particularly sharp decline in the hospitality, arts and entertainment, and other personal services sectors. The share of foreigners among entrepreneurs fell slightly in 2020, which may be explained by the entry restrictions in the course of the COVID-19 pandemic. Interestingly, the Coronavirus crisis has delayed the implementation of plans to start a business, but rarely prevented it completely (Metzger, 2021). Experts thus expect that an end of the pandemic-related restrictions will be accompanied by an increase in start-up activities, especially in the sectors heavily affected by the restrictions.

## 3 Entrepreneurship Policy in Times of Crisis

In the course of the COVID-19 pandemic, governments worldwide were forced to take immediate action to avoid employment losses as well as severe negative economic and social consequences. Hence, a core focus was put on the enhancement of incumbent firms' financial capital, almost neglecting necessary support for start-ups. Belitski et al. (2021: 1) yet emphasize that policy initiatives as a response to the COVID-19 pandemic should not only shield employment and economic activities of incumbent firms, but also create "productive entrepreneurship and resilient location-specific entrepreneurial ecosystems." Conflating the uncertainty perspective, the resilience perspective, and the opportunity perspective of existing research on the COVID-19 pandemic, Kuckertz and Brändle (2021) present a comprehensive overview of various political fields of action related to effective entrepreneurship policy: (1) To address the uncertainty-resilience link, policymakers should offer support beyond financial capital and especially assist marginalized entrepreneurs, (2) to address the uncertainty-opportunity link, policymakers should try to reduce uncertainty wherever possible and increase the incentives for post-crises growth, and (3) to address the resilience-opportunity link, policymakers should reflect on entrepreneurial responses during the COVID-19 pandemic, enable creative reconstruction, and prepare for future crises.

In the course of avoiding business failures, many governments offered rather indiscriminate financial support to firms. Focusing on Germany, Dörr et al. (2021) identify resulting adverse effects of these "whatever-it-takes" aid measures, potentially undermining market dynamics and associated cleansing mechanism of economic crises. Based on the Mannheim Enterprise Panel, the authors find a backlog of insolvencies, affecting in particular small firms. Hence, policy trade-offs exist in times of crisis (Zoller-Rydzek & Keller, 2020): On the one hand, policymakers need to avoid high unemployment rates—in the case of the COVID-19 pandemic induced by a drop in demand along with a shortage of capital; on the other hand, policymakers need to avoid the creation of zombie firms by providing too high levels of loans (firms that would fail if they would not be kept artificially alive by the provision of additional financial capital by the government) that imply higher public spending in the long run. Ragnitz (2020) thus highlights that policymakers need to separate corona-related structural adjustments from market- or policy-driven transformations.

Ratten (2020) further argues that successful policy measures need to consider the wider attributes of an entrepreneurial ecosystem as well as the various entities engaged. Audretsch et al. (2022) follow this line of argument emphasizing the importance of the institutional, cognitive, technological, and social context. Kuckertz et al. (2020) synthesize four major challenges arising from the COVID-19 pandemic, conceptualizing associated policy options: (1) avoidance of immediate start-up failure due to a lack of liquidity by offering wage subsidies and direct payments, (2) adaption to changing business environments by facilitating digital transformation, (3) continuation of start-up growth by boosting an innovative business climate and nurturing knowledge diversity, and (4) responsiveness to potential mismatches by continuously evaluating demands of start-ups and considering future growth trajectories. Thus, a multitude of policy measures seems to be necessary to address current and future challenges for entrepreneurship in the course of the COVID-19 pandemic. Wölfl (2021) consequently suggests that policymakers should address well-known barriers to entrepreneurship (e.g., financing gap, bureaucratic burdens, fear of failure) and additionally develop policy instruments that particularly focus on innovative start-ups that are better able to flexibly adapt to changing business environments instead of prolonging the survival of nearly insolvent firms (Dörr et al., 2021).

## 4 Conclusion

The present COVID-19 pandemic has shown the vulnerability of economies and their economic actors, yet has also highlighted the importance of economic resilience. Following the definitions of Williams et al. (2017), the allocation and utilization of resources before, during, and after crises determine the responsiveness of economic actors. Consequently, the ability to innovate, adapt to changing business environments, break with business routines, create novel business models, hence exploit new opportunities, and act entrepreneurially constitutes a crucial factor in how economies cope with the COVID-19 pandemic. It is thereby not the single economic actor, but the ecosystem as a whole that decisively affects the responsiveness of economies. Taking a system perspective has thus proven to be beneficial (Acs et al., 2014).

Policymakers need to build resilient entrepreneurial ecosystems that are able to continuously recover from and adapt to exogenous shocks (Roundy et al., 2017), considering the underlying dynamics of entrepreneurial ecosystems (Cantner et al., 2021). Kuckertz and Brändle (2021: 23) follow this line of argument and state that "policy support should not only aim to tackle funding gaps for new ventures [...] but additionally strengthen entrepreneurs' broader support systems such as the entrepreneurial ecosystem before and during a crisis." It is about balancing governmental support to on the one hand build resilience (preparedness before crises, responsiveness during crises, and recovery after crises) and on the other hand promote entrepreneurial action, as entrepreneurship and economic resilience are interrelated concepts that are likely to reinforce each other.

Future research should broaden our understanding of the interconnectedness of entrepreneurship and economic resilience and particularly focus on the role and impact of (regional) resource allocation and deployment. Scholars should further investigate different types of resources that are necessary for building and maintaining economic resilience. Interestingly, scientists seem to be hardly affected by the COVID-19 pandemic, as the Coronavirus crisis appears to be rather a driver than a barrier to scientific entrepreneurship (Bijedić, 2020). Future studies should investigate the underlying mechanisms of these differences. Moreover, more research is needed that focuses on the short-term but especially also long-term consequences of policy interventions on entrepreneurial activities and resulting economic resilience, as economies with the most effective policy instruments will be best able to withstand future crises.

## References


Acs, Z. J., Autio, E., & Szerb, L. (2014). National systems of entrepreneurship: Measurement issues and policy implications. *Research Policy, 43*(3), 476–494.

Acs, Z. J., Song, A., Szerb, L., Audretsch, D. B., & Komlosi, E. (2021). *The evolution of the global digital platform economy: 1971–2021*. Available at SSRN: https://ssrn.com/abstract=3785411.

Archibugi, D., Filippetti, A., & Frenz, M. (2013). The impact of the economic crisis on innovation: Evidence from Europe. *Technological Forecasting and Social Change, 80*(7), 1247–1260.

Audretsch, D. B., Belitski, M., Caiazza, R., Günther, C., & Menter, M. (2022). From latent to emergent entrepreneurship: The importance of context. *Technological Forecasting and Social Change, 175*, 121356. https://doi.org/10.1016/j.techfore.2021.121356

Audretsch, D. B., Cunningham, J. A., Kuratko, D. F., Lehmann, E. E., & Menter, M. (2019). Entrepreneurial ecosystems: Economic, technological, and societal impacts. *The Journal of Technology Transfer, 44*(2), 313–325.

Bartik, A. W., Bertrand, M., Cullen, Z. B., Glaeser, E. L., Luca, M., & Stanton, C. T. (2020). How are small businesses adjusting to COVID-19? Early evidence from a survey. *National Bureau of Economic Research* (No. w26989).

Belitski, M., Guenther, C., Kritikos, A. S., & Thurik, R. (2021). Economic effects of the COVID-19 pandemic on entrepreneurship and small businesses. *Small Business Economics, 58*, 593–609. https://doi.org/10.1007/s11187-021-00544-y

Bergami, M., Corsino, M., Daood, A., & Giuri, P. (2021). Being resilient for society: Evidence from companies that leveraged their resources and capabilities to fight the COVID-19 crisis. *R & D Management, 52*(2), 235–254. https://doi.org/10.1111/radm.12480

Bijedić, T. (2020). *Gründungserfolg von Wissenschaftlerinnen und Wissenschaftlern in der Corona-Pandemie*. IfM Bonn.

Bishop, P. (2019). Knowledge diversity and entrepreneurship following an economic crisis: An empirical study of regional resilience in Great Britain. *Entrepreneurship & Regional Development, 31*(5–6), 496–515.

BMWi. (2021). *Transferinitiative – Ergebnisse der Online-Befragung zum Wissens- und Technologietransfer in Deutschland*. Federal Ministry for Economic Affairs and Climate Action.

Cantner, U., Cunningham, J. A., Lehmann, E. E., & Menter, M. (2021). Entrepreneurial ecosystems: A dynamic lifecycle model. *Small Business Economics, 57*(1), 407–423.

Destatis. (2021). 10 figures on the consequences of the corona pandemic. *Press release #N 023* as of March 31, 2021.

Dörr, J. O., Licht, G., & Murmann, S. (2021). Small firms and the COVID-19 insolvency gap. *Small Business Economics, 58*, 887–917. https://doi.org/10.1007/s11187-021-00514-4

Ebersberger, B., & Kuckertz, A. (2021). Hop to it! The impact of organization type on innovation response time to the COVID-19 crisis. *Journal of Business Research, 124*, 126–135.

Fairlie, R. (2020). The impact of COVID-19 on small business owners: Evidence from the first three months after widespread social-distancing restrictions. *Journal of Economics & Management Strategy, 29*(4), 727–740.

Graeber, D., Kritikos, A. S., & Seebauer, J. (2021). COVID-19: A crisis of the female self-employed. *Journal of Population Economics, 34*, 1141–1187.

Helfat, C. E., Finkelstein, S., Mitchell, W., Peteraf, M., Singh, H., Teece, D., & Winter, S. G. (2007). *Dynamic capabilities: Understanding strategic change in organizations*. Blackwell.

Kay, R., & Kranzusch, P. (2020). Gewerbliche Existenzgründungen und Unternehmensaufgaben im 1. Halbjahr 2020 – Auswirkungen der Coronavirus-Pandemie. *IfM-Hintergrundpapier*.

Kuckertz, A., & Brändle, L. (2021). Creative reconstruction: A structured literature review of the early empirical research on the COVID-19 crisis and entrepreneurship. *Management Review Quarterly*, 1–27. https://doi.org/10.1007/s11301-021-00221-0

Kuckertz, A., Brändle, L., Gaudig, A., Hinderer, S., Reyes, C. A. M., Prochotta, A., Steinbrink, K. M., & Berger, E. S. (2020). Startups in times of crisis – A rapid response to the COVID-19 pandemic. *Journal of Business Venturing Insights, 1–13*, e00169. https://doi.org/10.1016/j.jbvi.2020.e00169

Metzger, G. (2021). *„Junge" Selbstständige: branchenbedingt trifft Corona-Krise Frauen härter als Männer*. KfW Research: Fokus Volkswirtschaft, 324.

Modgil, S., Dwivedi, Y. K., Rana, N. P., Gupta, S., & Kamble, S. (2021). Has Covid-19 accelerated opportunities for digital entrepreneurship? An Indian perspective. *Technological Forecasting and Social Change, 175*, 121415. https://doi.org/10.1016/j.techfore.2021.121415

Priyono, A., Moin, A., & Putri, V. N. A. O. (2020). Identifying digital transformation paths in the business model of SMEs during the COVID-19 pandemic. *Journal of Open Innovation: Technology, Market, and Complexity, 6*(4), 104.

Ragnitz, J. (2020). Langfristige wirtschaftliche Auswirkungen der Corona-Pandemie. *ifo Schnelldienst, 73*(11), 25–30.

Ratten, V. (2020). Coronavirus and international business: An entrepreneurial ecosystem perspective. *Thunderbird International Business Review, 62*(5), 629–634.

Roundy, P. T., Brockman, B. K., & Bradshaw, M. (2017). The resilience of entrepreneurial ecosystems. *Journal of Business Venturing Insights, 8*, 99–104.

Teece, D. J., Peteraf, M., & Leih, S. (2016). Dynamic capabilities and organizational agility: Risk, uncertainty, and strategy in the innovation economy. *California Management Review, 58*(4), 13–35.

Williams, T. A., Gruber, D. A., Sutcliffe, K. M., Shepherd, D. A., & Zhao, E. Y. (2017). Organizational response to adversity: Fusing crisis management and resilience research streams. *Academy of Management Annals, 11*(2), 733–769.

Williams, N., & Vorley, T. (2014). Economic resilience and entrepreneurship: Lessons from the Sheffield City region. *Entrepreneurship & Regional Development, 26*(3–4), 257–281.

Wölfl, A. (2021). Corona – Krise oder chance für start-ups? *ifo Schnelldienst, 74*(1), 62–65.

Zoller-Rydzek, B., & Keller, F. (2020). COVID-19: Guaranteed loans and zombie firms. *CESifo Economic Studies, 66*(4), 322–364.

**Matthias Menter** is Assistant Professor for Business Dynamics, Innovation, and Economic Change at the Friedrich Schiller University Jena. His research focuses on entrepreneurial and innovative ecosystems, academic entrepreneurship, technology transfer, and science and innovation policy. He is also a senior research fellow at the Institute for Development Strategies at Indiana University.

# Business Angel Investing During the COVID-19 Pandemic

**Colin Mason**

**Abstract** The onset of the coronavirus pandemic quickly raised concerns that the associated economic disruption would result in a collapse in angel investing which—given their critical role in the entrepreneurial ecosystem—would have an adverse impact on entrepreneurial activity. Given the discretionary nature of investing in new and early-stage entrepreneurial businesses, the uncertainty about the impact of COVID-19 on their financial assets (e.g. shares, property) was expected to prompt angels to pause their investment activity. Meanwhile, those angels who continued to invest were expected to focus on their existing portfolios rather than making new investments. A further source of disruption was the shift in the investment process from face-to-face to online meetings. The evidence that emerged in the early months of the pandemic indicated that there had been a significant decline in angel investing. But by the autumn of 2020, there were clear signs of a recovery in angel investing. Moreover, contrary to expectations there has not been a sustained shift by angels to making follow-on investments in their portfolio companies and away from new investments. The resilience of angel investing reflects several factors. The confidence of angels increased as the COVID vaccine roll-out programme started, driving economic recovery and as they became more familiar with the new business environment. Moreover, entrepreneurs who had deferred seeking funding in the early months of the pandemic had return to the market. Angels also had the opportunity to see more deals as investment pitching moved online. Both angels and angel groups had also become more accustomed to the digital environment for connecting with people and more comfortable in investing in people that they had never met. And attractive investment opportunities had emerged as entrepreneurs developed creative and innovate solutions to the problems arising from the disruptions created by COVID.

**Keywords** Business angels · Entrepreneurial ecosystem · Venture capital · COVID-19 · Resilience · Regional investment

---

C. Mason (✉)
Adam Smith Business School, University of Glasgow, Glasgow, Scotland, UK
e-mail: colin.mason@glasgow.ac.uk



D. B. Audretsch, I. A. M. Kunadt (eds.), *The COVID-19 Crisis and Entrepreneurship*, International Studies in Entrepreneurship 54,
https://doi.org/10.1007/978-3-031-04655-1_8

# 1 Introduction

A fundamental characteristic of an ecosystem—whether a biotic or an economic community—is that a creature in a biotic ecosystem or agent in an economic ecosystem cannot survive without others. The suppression of one creature/agent has a negative impact on other creatures/agents in the ecosystem, potentially destroying the entire ecosystem. It is the interrelation of creatures/agents within their environment that enables other creatures/agents to reproduce themselves and thereby enhance the entire ecosystem (Cantner et al., 2021). Bees play a critical role in the natural ecosystem by transferring pollen between flowering plants, enabling them to grow, breed and provide food. Their pollination is critical to agriculture, food and biodiversity. One-third of the food we eat depends on bees for pollination. Some plants grown to feed to livestock for meat production, such as clover and alfalfa, also depend at least partly on bee pollination. The plants that rely on bees for pollination also provide food and habitat for a range of other creatures. Maintaining our native flora also depends on healthy pollinator populations. The health of our natural ecosystems is therefore fundamentally linked to the health of our bees. But bees are in decline across the world. This decline is caused by a combination of stresses—from loss of habitat and food sources to exposure to pesticides and the effects of climate breakdown. The loss of bees could therefore lead to lower availability of crops and wild plants that provide essential micro-nutrients for human diets, impacting health and nutritional security (Friends of the Earth, 2017).

Following the common practice of using biological metaphors in entrepreneurship (e.g. Clarke et al., 2014; Isenberg, 2016), we can describe business angels as *the bees of the entrepreneurial ecosystem* on account of their role in funding the start of the entrepreneurial pipeline. They are high net worth individuals acting alone or as part of a formal or informal syndicate who invest their own money, along with their time and expertise, directly in unquoted companies in which they have no family connection, in the hope of financial gain through a future exit. After making the investment, they generally take an active involvement in the business, for example, as an advisor or member of the board of directors. (Mason, 2011).[1] Angel investors are typically the first external investors in new and emerging businesses, providing them with funding to make the transition from the concept stage to revenue generation and so play a critical role at the start of the entrepreneurial pipeline. Many angel-backed start-ups go on to raise further rounds of finance from venture capital (VC) funds to scale up. Some will achieve "unicorn" status, becoming anchor

[1]The term angel was coined by Broadway insiders in the early 1900s to describe wealthy theatregoers who made high-risk investments in theatrical productions. Angels invested in these shows primarily for the privilege of rubbing shoulders with the theatre personalities that they admired. The term business angel was given to those individuals who perform essentially the same function in a business context (Benjamin & Margulis, 2000). They are not a new phenomenon: Sohl (1999) notes that Alexander Graham Bell, Henry Ford, Anita Roddick and Jeff Bezos all raised their initial funding from private investors.

companies in their ecosystems.[2] Other angel-backed companies do not offer or achieve the rapid growth required to attract VC investment. However, some of these businesses will be attractive strategic acquisitions for other companies (Mason et al., 2015). Moreover, the importance of angels goes beyond their money. Angel investors are founders and top management team members of successful entrepreneurial businesses, corporate leaders and business professionals (e.g. accountants, lawyers) who draw on their experience, expertise and networks to provide the entrepreneurs that they invest in with business, psychological and emotional support. This non-financial support is at least as significant as the money that they invest.

With angels increasingly organizing themselves into organized groups with anywhere from 10 to upwards of 100 members rather than investing informally on their own (Mason et al., 2016), they have the financial resources not only to make larger initial investments but also to participate in follow-on rounds to finance the early scale-up of their investee businesses (British Business Bank, 2020). Angel groups also have the credibility and professionalism to co-invest with both institutional and government seed and venture funds in larger syndicated deals (Mason et al., 2013; Mason, 2018). The widening post-seed financing gap resulting from the shift of venture capital to larger, later stage deals makes the role of business angels even more critical.

It is estimated that business angels account for 60% of European early-stage investment activity in terms of amount invested, with venture capital accounting for 34% and equity crowdfunding 6% (EBAN, 2019). In the USA, angels make up to 20 times more investments than venture capital at the early stage.[3] The importance of business angels in the entrepreneurial ecosystem is further underlined by the UK's ScaleUp Institute (2020) which reported that 63% of scale-ups received investment from business angels to fund their early growth.

Just as the decline in the bee population has had detrimental consequences for the natural ecosystem, the onset of the coronavirus pandemic quickly raised concerns that the associated economic disruption would result in a collapse in angel investing which—given their critical role in the entrepreneurial ecosystem—would have an adverse impact on entrepreneurial activity. In May 2020, Canada's National Angel Capital Organisation (NACO) suggested that angel investment activity would decline over the next 12–24 months while demand from founders was likely to increase (NACO, 2020). This would undermine Canada's entrepreneurial base: "COVID-19 is a momentum and capacity building killer. . . . As it stands, in a few short months we are at risk of losing an entire generation of early-stage companies who are too small to attract institutional venture capital and whose survival cannot

[2]Canadian examples of successful companies that were initially funded by business angels include Shopify in Ottawa, Solium in Calgary, Skip The Dishes in Saskatoon, Blackberry in Kitchener-Waterloo, Verafin in St John's, and Enthusiast Gaming in Toronto.

[3]This comment was made by a speaker that the Angel Capital Association 'Angel Investing Post-COVID webinar, 9 June 2021.

depend on the pocketbooks of friends [and] families ..." (NACO, 2020). These concerns were shared across Canada's entrepreneurial ecosystem. For example, Senator Colin Deacon, a member of Canada's upper house, and a former entrepreneur, commented in May 2020 that "angel communities are at the base of the pyramid. Without them, we will not have the same opportunities created" (Croteau et al., 2021). A similar concern was expressed by Luigi Amati, president of Business Angels Europe, who remarked that COVID-19 "would have a massive impact on the start-up economy in Europe. Indeed, if angel investing breaks down, you break down the whole pipeline of development" (Sifted, 2020a). And Jenny Tooth, chief executive of the UK Business Angels Association (UKBAA), commented that "angels are where VCs find deals so a contraction in angel investing will create a massive hole in the ecosystem going forward" (Sifted, 2020a). The consequence would be "a lost generation" of entrepreneurs (City AM, 2020). Professor Jeffrey Sohl from the Centre for Venture Research at the University of New Hampshire, who monitors angel investing in the USA, observed that "angels are the predominant source of seed and start-up capital for our nation's entrepreneurs. [So] any .... decline of the foundational, and critical, seed and start-up financing provided by angel investors could lead to significant, and lasting, repercussions throughout the risk capital ecosystem." (Sohl, 2020).

The evidence that is presented in this chapter indicates that these fears did not materialize. Although there was a significant fall in angel investing during the early months of the pandemic, business angels have proved to be remarkably resilient, with investment activity rebounding by the end of 2020 and into 2021, exceeding pre-COVID levels.

## 2 The Impact of COVID-19 on Angel Investing: Early Fears

The onset of the coronavirus pandemic in early 2020 and the resulting economic restrictions, along with the uncertainty about how long it would last and its economic impact, led to widespread fears of a drastic decline in the availability of angel capital. Given the discretionary nature of investing in new and early-stage entrepreneurial businesses (with business angels investing between 5 and 15% of their financial assets to this asset class), the fall in share prices triggered by the outbreak of the COVID-19 pandemic, along with the uncertainty about its impact on their other financial assets (e.g. property), was expected to prompt angels to pause their investment activity.

Meanwhile, those angels who continued to invest were expected to focus on their existing portfolios rather than making new investments (Mason, 2021; Mason & Botelho, 2021; Sohl, 2020). A European angel group commented that they expected "many investors' focus will change from seeking out new investments to supporting their existing investments that appear to be most successful. Follow-on rounds in those companies will take precedence over new startups" (Go Beyond, 2020). This reflected several considerations. First, the coronavirus crisis created a liquidity crisis for many of the companies in the portfolios of angels as a result of the deterioration in their revenue prospects, with the immediate risk that they would run out of cash and therefore be unable to fund their ongoing operations. Early-stage pre-revenue companies were particularly vulnerable because of the need to delay plans to launch their products and begin to generate revenue. Second, was the risk for those business angels who had businesses in their portfolio that were planning in the near future to raise a funding round from a venture capital fund to scale-up would not be able to do so. With a funding round typically providing businesses with finance for 18 to 24 months, this was a particular consideration for those investee businesses whose previous funding round was more than a year earlier and were therefore reaching the end of their financial runway. So here again business angels would wish to conserve their available capital for this scenario rather than making new investments. Third, a related concern was the potential downward pressure on valuations at later rounds, creating the risk of down-rounds, which would reduce the value of their shareholding. Fourth, reinforcing these concerns was the associated fear amongst business angels that there would be fewer opportunities to exit in the immediate future and that companies may need to have hit more milestones than in the past in order to become an attractive acquisition target for a large corporate. Seeking an exit from a position of relative weakness would generate sub-optimal returns. This was a further factor that would require angels to continue to support their investee companies for longer. The cumulative effect of these sources of risk was that business angels would seek to preserve their capital so as to be in a position to support those companies in their portfolio that appeared to have the best prospects for success rather than making new investments. This focus on supporting their portfolio companies was reinforced by the difficulties in making new investments. Lockdowns disrupted the interpersonal relationships between investors, intermediaries and entrepreneurs that are crucial to the investment decision-making process (Brown et al., 2020). It also significantly extended the length of time to undertake due diligence. And because angels were spending more time supporting the companies in their portfolios to navigate the crisis, they had less bandwidth to consider new investments.

A further disruptive effect of the COVID pandemic on making new investments has been the shift in the investment process from face-to-face to online meetings (Mason, 2021; Mason & Botelho, 2021). On the one hand, the shift by angel groups and other intermediaries from in-person to online pitching events has ensured that businesses angels have continued to have access to deal flow. However, it has also had potentially adverse consequences. First, various studies have identified the role of impression management techniques in successfully raising finance (Mason & Harrison, 2003; Parhankangas & Ehrlich, 2014), with potential investors influenced both by the language used by entrepreneurs in their pitch and non-verbal expressions, notably the use of gestures and facial expressions of emotion. Indeed, gestures have been shown to have a more important impact than language on the funding decision of investors (Clarke et al., 2019; Warnick et al., 2021). However, it is much harder for investors to read these visual cues in online pitches because the pitch deck fills most of the screen with the consequence that the presenter is much less visible and is generally looking at their computer screen rather than at the audience. As one angel group manager commented: "we invest in the entrepreneur presenters so reading their body language and how they respond to questions is critical" (Dorset Business Angels, 2021). And as most investments are relationship driven, it is also a barrier to the development of trust between investors and entrepreneurs. A prominent Canadian investor expressed this concern as follows: "taking pitches over a zoom call doesn't really replace that face-to-face contact. As good as the technology is, I don't believe that it replaces face-to-face contact particularly when you're meeting someone and building a relationship" (Techregister, 2021). A leading UK angel commented that "angels invest in people. We have got to get to know the people . . . to build trust and relationship. It is a two-way relationship. It is difficult to see how this can be overcome [in the current circumstances]" (Cowley, 2020). Another angel observed that ". . .when you're building a relationship—being able to read the body language, go have a meal together, do a facilities tour, if that's appropriate—you learn a lot from these real-world interactions." Angels can mitigate these risks by concentrating their investments in situations where there is an existing personal relationship, first, in their existing investee businesses, second, alongside other investors investing in businesses where these investors have relationship with the entrepreneur, third, investing in businesses where a trusted intermediary is involved (e.g. advisor) and fourth to invest in companies that have previously raised finance from other investors.

These concerns were confirmed by anecdotal and survey evidence from the spring and summer of 2020. For example, one NACO angel group manager commented in April 2020 that:

> COVID concerns, with a serious drop in the market, many angels have lost liquidity. Many startups themselves are also at risk of running out of cash given their clientele. There are many more ripple effects that are yet to have been felt.

Another group manager commented:

> COVID-19 is impacting investors' interest in investing in new companies, unless they can clearly address specific concerns. Most investors seem to be focused on supporting their current portfolio companies. However, on a positive note, the general reduction in available capital will cause a reduce in valuation and offer investment opportunities at more appealing valuations.

And a major Canadian angel investor commented that his fund *"went into cash conservation mode—it made sure the existing portfolio were looked after . . ."* (Techregister, 2021).

The survey data that emerged in the early months of the pandemic confirmed the anecdotal evidence that the COVID pandemic had precipitated a significant decline in angel investing. In the UK, a survey by Activate our Angels (2020), undertaken in the first half of May 2020 that attracted responses from over 250 angels, reported that one-third of UK angels were not investing during the lockdown period: 71% of these angels were continuing to review deals but adopting a "wait and see" stance and only 29% of were not planning to invest at all, with almost half (48%) of this group indicating that they were only going to invest again when they felt confident that the COVID-19 crisis was over. Those angels who were continuing to invest were making fewer investments, completing an average of just 1.81 deals during the early lockdown period compared with 3.24 deals in 2019. Moreover, just over half (51%) expected to invest less in 2020 than in 2019; only 19% anticipated investing more. A survey of members of the Henley Business Angels Group, associated with Henley Business School (University of Reading) in the UK, undertaken from 15 June 2020 to 20 July 2020 reported that 62% of respondents were not investing, with 25% investing in their existing portfolio and only 13% still investing in new deals. Additionally, half of those that had completed the survey stated that COVID-19 had negatively impacted on the volume of investment opportunities that they were receiving. More positively, although more than half (56%) of respondents stated they were investing less than before the pandemic first hit, the overall consensus amongst respondents was that COVID-19's impact was low or short term. Most investors were continuing to actively look for companies that have an experienced management team, a realistic business model and offer a sustainable and differentiated solution to a problem.

Evidence from a British Business Bank (BBB) online survey of the UK business angel market undertaken in July 2020—just prior to the second wave of COVID infections—also found that angels had continued to invest but that the value of both their initial and follow-on investments was lower than in the previous year. Looking forward, most respondents planned to continue to invest but anticipated that the proportion of their investable assets that they would allocate to angel investing in the remainder of the 2020/21 tax year (to 5 April) would be slightly lower than their allocation in 2019/20. Nevertheless, most of the angels surveyed were generally confident about the future growth in value of their portfolio over the next 12 months and close to half were open to building their portfolio in the remainder of the 2020/21 fiscal year, while only 12% said they intended to make no further investments (BBB, 2020).

This is consistent with evidence from the USA. The Angel Capital Association (2020) reported an initial strong retrenchment in late Q1 and Q2, 2020, but detected the beginnings of a rebound later in the year. Nevertheless, although the early-stage capital market remained down compared to 2019, with two-thirds of angel groups expecting to invest less in 2020, the willingness to invest was higher in September 2020 compared with April 2020 (ACA, 2020). However, the ACA inserted the caveat that it was unclear what would be the impact, if any, if there was to be a second wave of the pandemic in the final quarter of the year.

## 3 The Resilience of Angel Investing

By the autumn of 2020, it was becoming clear that there had not been a collapse in angel investing. Angel groups that had operated prior to the onset of COVID-19 on the basis of inviting entrepreneurs to make pitches to a live audience of investors

Fig. 1 Canadian Angel investments in 2020 by quarter. Key: Blue—number of investments; Red—amount invested (Color figure Online). Source: NACO (2021)

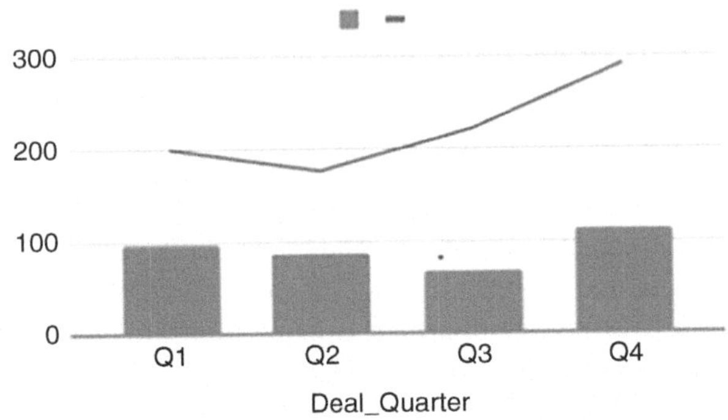


moved these meetings online (NACO, 2021). This shift to online pitching events enabled more angels to attend. In the USA, 43% of groups that had moved to virtual meetings reported increased attendances compared with their pre-COVID in-person events (ACA, 2020). Some groups shifted their activities to online platforms. Various groups also introduced new online meetings and events to compensate for the loss of in-person events, to develop investor relations, maintain and build their investor community by creating networking events (e.g. before and after pitching events), and to facilitate the mentorship of investors and entrepreneurs (NACO, 2021). However, while some angels made this transition with little or no difficulty, others reported that being unable to meet with entrepreneurs in-person created difficulties in relationship building and engagement and stopped investing. Other angels responded to these challenges by undertaking due diligence on a collaborative basis and investing in syndicates with other investors.

Investment statistics provide evidence of the resilience of angel investing during the pandemic. NACO publishes an annual report on angel investment activity in Canada based on information provided by its member organizations. Its report on investment activity in 2020 is based on responses from 29 active angel groups of which 24 had made investments during the year (NACO, 2021). Investment activity fell slightly from Q1 to Q2 of 2020 (−10% in deals and −12% in the amount invested) but dropped sharply in Q3 (20% fewer deals than in Q2, although the amount invested actually increased by 26%). Investment activity bounced back in Q4 as the economy partially recovered and angels began to adjust to online investing, with the number of deals 67% higher than in Q3 and higher than in Q1, with the amount invested up 32% on Q3, and also higher than in Q1 (Fig. 1). Taking the year as a whole, Angel groups made 416 investments in 2020 compared with 299 in 2019, a 39% increase. Nevertheless, this was a lower figure than in 2018. The average (mean) and median number of investments made by groups in 2020 was also higher than in 2019. On the other hand, the total amount invested by responding groups in 2020 ($102.9 m) was lower than in both 2019 and 2018 ($163.9 m and $142.8 m, respectively). There was also a decline in the size of investment, with both the mean and median amounts invested per company lower than in 2019. One interpretation of these trends—more but smaller investments and less invested—is that it reflects the drip-feeding of investments in their portfolio businesses in the early stage of the pandemic to keep them afloat until there was greater clarity concerning which ones to support.

These conclusions are confirmed when we focus on the investment activity of the 17 groups that provided information in both 2019 and 2020. These groups made more than twice as many investments in 2020 than in 2019 (+112%); there was an increase in the average number of investments, a decline in the total amount investment (−8%) and a decrease in the mean size of investment.

Angels and angel groups in Canada therefore ended 2020 in a strong place as the various actors in the ecosystem adjusted to the changes in the investment environment and angels were becoming more accustomed to the online environment for connecting with entrepreneurs.[4] This momentum has been maintained in 2021 despite a further wave of COVID infections and more lockdowns as the economy has stabilized and angels have become more comfortable with meeting entrepreneurs online and virtual meetings have given them access to national deal flow (Galea, 2021).

However, it is important to insert two important caveats. First, demand for angel funding increased in 2020, with groups reporting a rise in the number of companies approaching them for finance (higher than in five of the previous six years), and the funding success rate was lower (NACO, 2021). Second, angel groups report that lockdown and the associated restrictions have created a disconnect between investors and the start-up community which has reduced the opportunities for investors to engage directly with entrepreneurs which has not been entirely overcome the shift to online meetings and pitches. Some members had disengaged because they were not interested in investing if they could not meet the entrepreneurs in person. This has negatively impacted on the number of active investors, investment activity, round size and syndication and the pool of money available to invest. And some respondents suggested that the initial enthusiasm of angels to shift to online investing waned over the course of the year as zoom-fatigue set in (NACO, 2021). With the relaxation of COVID restrictions on meetings, some angel groups have now reverted to in-person pitching events.

In the USA, the amount invested by ACA members in 2020 was the highest ever recorded; as was the case in Canada, the amount invested per company fell, hence angels were spreading their investments amongst more deals. Meanwhile, venture capitalists decreased their role in early-stage funding in 2020, emphasizing the key role that angels have played in supporting entrepreneurial activity during the pandemic (ACA, 2021).[5]

Angel investment in Scotland exhibits similar trends (Mason and Botelho, 2021). Here, again the evidence is limited to angel groups, in this case members of LINC Scotland, the national association for business angels in Scotland, (Fig. 2).

---

[4] Some Canadian angel groups have always operated online, using Zoom Facetime and Skype, because of the large geographical territories over which they operate.

[5] Tech Coast Angels, one of the largest and longest established US angel groups reported that 2020 was a record year for funding and member growth (Tech Coast Angels, 2021).

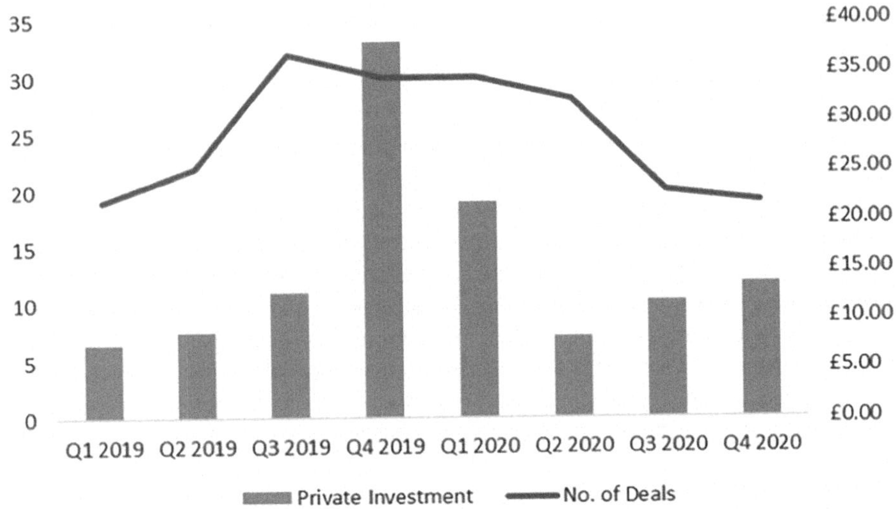


**Fig. 2** Investment activity by LINC members: 2019 compared with 2020. Source: Mason and Botelho (2021), based on LINC data

Investment activity by LINC members in Q1 2020 was relatively buoyant and similar to activity in the second half of 2019. Investment activity in Q2 2020 remained at a high level, with more deals than in the equivalent period in 2019 and just two fewer investments than in Q1 2020. The due diligence for these deals is likely to have started in 2019, well before the onset of COVID, reflecting the fact that the investment process generally takes several months to progress from the decision in principle to invest and negotiating the terms and conditions of the investment, to writing the cheque (Mason & Harrison, 1996). There would also be pressure to complete investments that qualify for SEIS and EIS tax relief before the end of the tax year (April 5). The full impact of COVID only became apparent in Q3 2020, with a sharp decline in the number of investments (−29%) between Q2 and Q3. Investment activity stabilized in Q4 with just one fewer investment than in Q3. Nevertheless, although angel activity increased in Q4 of 2020, the level of investment activity was lower than in the equivalent period in 2019. In contrast to the number of deals, the amount invested declined sharply between Q1 and Q2 2020 (although the amount invested in Q1 2020 was unusually high and the amount invested in Q2 2020 was only slightly less than in Q2, 2019), but increased in Q3 2020 and again in Q4 (Fig. 2). Overall, the number of deals was only 6% lower 2020 than in 2019 while the amount invested by angels was down 3%. The recovery of angel investing has continued into 2021 despite a further lockdown at the start of the year in response to a further rise of COVID infections from December 2020. Angels invested £54.2 m in the first half of 2021, marginally less than the amount invested in the whole of 2020 and almost the same as in 2019. However, this is distorted by a large outlier which accounted for more than half of the total. The number of investments made is therefore a better guide: the number of investments made in the first half of 2021 was 59% of total investment activity in 2020.[6]

HBAN—the organization responsible for the promotion of business angel investment on the island of Ireland—provides further evidence of the resurgence of angel investing. Investment activity in 2020 (a year in which it attracted over 100 new angels and the formation of a new group) was only marginally lower than in 2019, with angels investing €14 m in 59 deals compared with €16.8 m invested in 66 deals in 2019. Investment activity in the first half of 2021 was higher than the pre-pandemic level: the number of investments in H1 2021 was up 28% compared with H1 2019, the amount that angels invested was up 13% and the average investment was 29% higher (Irish Tech News, 2021).

It was anticipated that angels would increase the proportion of follow-on investments to prevent their investee businesses from running out of cash in the initial stages of the pandemic and extend the financial runway of their promising investee businesses to enable them to take advantage of new opportunities. But contrary to expectations, there has not been a sustained shift by angels to making follow-on investments in their portfolio companies and away from new investments. In Canada, follow-on investments accounted for 34% of angel investments in 2020, similar to previous years (NACO, 2021) The Scottish context is rather different. Reflecting both the maturity of angel investing in Scotland (Mason et al., 2016) and the lower level of later stage VC investment that is available, follow-on investments dominate, accounting for three-quarters of the investments made by angel groups in 2019, increasing slightly to 79% in 2020, peaking at 85% in Q3. New investments bounced back strongly in Q4 2020, with follow-on investments dropping to 58% of all investments. Follow-on investments as a proportion of the total amount invested increased in Q2 and Q3 of 2020 compared with 2019, with a particularly large increase in Q3 from 79% to 99%. Follow-on investments dropped to just 54% of the amount invested in Q4 2020 reflecting the rebound in new investments (Mason & Botelho, 2021). However, this shift was not maintained in 2021, with follow-on investments accounting for 83% of all investments in the first half of 2021 and 89% of the amount invested. In the USA, the amount invested in follow-on deals rose 26% while the amount invested in new investments fell by 12% (ACA, 2021). But in the much less mature Irish market, new investments dominated in the first half of 2021, accounting for 65% of total investments made.

The recovery in angel investing in Q4 2020 and into 2021 reflects several factors. First was the increased confidence of angels as the COVID vaccine roll-out programme started, driving economic recovery and they became more familiar with the new business environment. And businesses which between March and June 2020 were unsure what would be the impact of COVID on their business and so could not tell a 12- to 18 -month funding story had by the autumn a clearer line of

[6]Data supplied by LINC Scotland.

sight of the direction in which they could go.[7] Second, is the return to the market of entrepreneurs who had deferred seeking funding in the early months of the pandemic. Third, angels have had the opportunity to see more deals as investment pitching moved online and had more time on their hands on account of restrictions on travel and social activity which created more time to invest. Both angels and angel groups had also learned how to do pitching and due diligence online had become more accustomed to the digital environment for connecting with people and more comfortable in investing in people that they had never met. One respondent to the NACO annual activity report observed that "with the virtual shift, the possibility for collaboration has skyrocketed," an observation reflected in angel investor organizations reporting "that collaborative due diligence resulted in more syndication at the local and national level." And by removing many of the geographical barriers to investment, online pitching has enabled angels to expand their investment radius. The ACA (2021) reported that almost half of all deals in 2020 were done outside of the groups' local region, with the out-of-region investment dollars increasing by more than 30%. In the case of Tech Coast Angels, over half of their investments were, for the first time, in companies located outside their home base of Southern California (Tech Coast Angels, 2021). Fourth, angels have been ready to invest in the attractive investment opportunities have emerged as entrepreneurs have developed creative and innovate solutions to the problems created by the disruption, notably in digital health/healthcare, biotech/life science, software as service, fintech, fulfilment providers, education tech, AI and digital assets (crypto). One Canadian investor noted that "we've seen new business models we've never seen before."[8] And there has also been a growth in interest amongst in "green" investment opportunities as climate change has become central in the media, politics, economy and society.

The NACO report on angel investing in 2020 in Canada reported that the vast majority of angel groups expected to continue with pitching and other events online (investor networking, training, social activities) during 2021 and beyond because of the recognition that there have been benefits. Some groups indicated that they would continue to operate entirely virtually but most anticipated that they would move to a hybrid format with both in-person and virtual events. A few groups were concerned that many of their members were suffering from zoom fatigue and did not want to continue with virtual investment meetings and so were likely to hold back from investing again until in-person events resumed. Some UK groups have also returned to in-person events. This strong desire amongst many business angels to return to in-person events may be driven as much by the desire to interact in-person with other group members as the attraction of live pitching. However, there are some groups that have indicated they have no intention of moving back to physical pitching events.

[7] These comments were made at a Technopia Live webinar on Angel Investment Outlook in Ottawa, 26 January 2021. https://www.youtube.com/watch?v=JnqpTRXCJQw

[8] NACO (Virtual) Roundtable on Angel Investing in Canada. 12 August 2021.

## 4 Conclusion

Analogous to the role of bees in the natural ecosystem, business angels "pollinate" the entrepreneurial ecosystem, providing "smart capital" (money, plus know-how) to start-up businesses. Of course, many of the businesses that they back subsequently fail (Mason & Harrison, 2002) (although the entrepreneurs may go on to start other businesses) but some will be successful, often having raised further rounds of finance from VCs, and become strategic or financial acquisitions by larger businesses. Meanwhile, those successful entrepreneurial teams, along with their angel investors, will recycle some of their financial gains in new ventures in a virtuous process that drives entrepreneurial ecosystem growth (Mason & Brown, 2014). The onset of the COVID-19 pandemic in early 2020 immediately raised fears that it would have an adverse effect on both the ability and willingness of business angels to invest which, in turn, would damage the start-up ecosystem. These fears proved unfounded. Angel investment proved to be resilient; investments did fall in Q2 and Q3 of 2020 but quickly recovered, matching or exceeding pre-COVID levels in 2021 as investment activity moved online. Many angel groups reported that—somewhat to their surprise—angels did not drop away but actually invested more and their membership increased. Meanwhile, although VC funds have invested record amounts of money in 2020 and 2021, an increasing proportion has been invested in mega deals, so they have actually made fewer seed and early-stage investments, further increasing the importance of business angels in the entrepreneurial ecosystem. Moreover, this resilience has occurred largely in the absence of government support. For example, in both the UK and Canada, government support for investors was largely oriented to VCs, while new and pre-revenue companies—which dominate the portfolios of business angels—were excluded from many of the business support programmes (City AM, 2020; Sifted, 2020b; NACO, 2021; Mason, 2021).

The COVID pandemic has resulted in changes in angel investing as the investment process has gone online. Pitching events take place on zoom and many angels now invest in entrepreneurs that they have never met in person. A number of consequences are already apparent. The proportion of long-distance investments has increased, weakening the local focus of angel investing. This raises the possibility that angel investment will increasingly flow from smaller and less economically developed regions to large city regions. There has been an increase in syndicated investments in response to the challenge of investing in entrepreneurs that they have never met, with angels co-investing in deals with other investors who have such relationships. The likely outcome is larger deal sizes and investments in businesses that have already raised a round of finance. This has negative implications for the ability of entrepreneurs seeking a small initial funding round and those who are not well connected to raise funding. There is also anecdotal evidence that the investment preferences of angels (e.g. sectors, business models, criteria) have changed. But it remains unclear whether angels evaluate online and in-person pitches differently. How many angels will wish to return to in-person pitches and face-to-face meetings? And will angel investing practices revert to pre-COVID times with the return of in-person pitching and meetings? These questions form the basis of a research agenda on angel investing in a post-COVID world.

## References


ACA. (2020). *Pandemic investor impact report.* Angel Capital association https://www.angelcapitalassociation.org/pandemic-investor-impact-report/

ACA. (2021). *ACA angel funding report 2021.* Angel Capital Association. https://www.paperturn-view.com/angel-capital-association/angel-funders-report-2021?pid=MTk193714&v=2.1

Activate our Angels. (2020). *Angels are investing during Lockdown, but it's not all good news.* https://www.activateourangels.com/results

Benjamin, G. A., & Margulis, J. B. (2000). *Angel financing: How to find and invest in private equity.* Wiley.

British Business Bank. (2020). *The UK business angel market 2020.* British Business Bank in Association with UK Business Angel Network. https://ukbaa.org.uk/wp-content/uploads/2020/10/20201008-BBB-Business-Angels-Report-Final.pdf

Brown, R., Rocha, A., & Cowling, M. (2020). Financing entrepreneurship in times of crisis: Exploring the impact of COVID-19 on the market for entrepreneurial finance in the United Kingdom. *International Small Business Journal, 38*(5), 380–390.

Cantner, U., Cunningham, J., Lehmann, E. E., & Menter, M. (2021). Entrepreneurial ecosystems: a dynamic lifecycle model. *Small Business Economics, 57*, 407–423.

City, A. M. (2020, October 15) *A lost generation of startups: Are early-stage companies being left behind?* https://www.cityam.com/a-lost-generation-of-startups-are-early-stage-companies-being-left-behind/?utm_source=newsletter&utm_medium=email&utm_campaign=2020+Five+at+5

City, A.M. (2020, May 20). *£500m Future Fund launch mired by fears startups will miss out.* https://www.cityam.com/500m-future-fund-launch-mired-by-fears-startups-will-miss-out/

Clarke, J. S., Cornelissen, J. P., & Healey, M. P. (2019). Actions speak louder than words: How figurative language and gesturing in entrepreneurial pitches influences investment judgments. *Academy of Management Journal, 62*(2), 335–360.

Clarke, J., Holt, R., & Blundel, R. (2014). Re-imagining the growth process: (co)-evolving metaphorical representations of entrepreneurial growth. *Entrepreneurship & Regional Development, 26*(3–4), 234–256.

Cowley, P. (2020, June 25). *Panelist at a Barclays eagle lab webinar on raising Angel Investment in the current landscape.* https://labs.uk.barclays/support/continuity/understanding-the-angel-investment-landscape.

Croteau, M., Grant, K. A., Rojas, C., & Abdelhamid, H. (2021). The lost generation of entrepreneurs? The impact of COVID-19 on the availability of risk capital in Canada. *Journal of Entrepreneurship in Emerging Economies, 13*(4), 606–627.

Dorset Business Angels. (2021, September 17). *The importance of face-to-face events.* https://dorsetbusinessangels.co.uk/news/the-importance-of-face-to-face-pitch-events

EBAN. (2019). *European early stage market statistics 2018.* European Business Angel Network. https://www.eban.org/wp-content/uploads/2020/06/Statistics-Compendium-2018-FINAL-NEW.pdf

Friends of the Earth. (2017). *Why do we need bees?* https://friendsoftheearth.uk/nature/why-do-we-need-bees.

Galea, I. (2021, August 11). Angel investing deterred by risk in 2020, now taking flight amid economic recovery. *Globe and Mail.*

Go Beyond. (2020, April 29). *COVID-19's impact on the angel ecosystem.* https://www.gobeyondinvesting.com/2020/04/29/covid-19s-impact-on-the-angel-eco-system/

Henley Business School. (2020) *Professor Yipeng Liu shares findings of research into angel investment during and post COVID-19 to Henley Business Angels members*. https://www.henley.ac.uk/news/2020/professor-yipeng-liu-shares-findings-of-research-into-angel-investment-during-and-post-covid-19-to-henley-business-angels-members

Irish Tech News. (2021, October 29). *HBAN angel investments exceed pre-pandemic levels*. https://irishtechnews.ie/hban-angel-investments-exceed-pre-pandemic-levels/

Isenberg, D. J. (2016). Applying the ecosystem metaphor to entrepreneurship: Uses and abuses. *The Antitrust Bulletin, 61*(4), 564–573.

Mason, C. M. (2011). Business angels. In L. Dana (Ed.), *World Encyclopaedia of entrepreneurship* (pp. 1–16). Edward Elgar.

Mason, C. (2018). Financing entrepreneurial ventures. In R. Blackburn, D. de Clercq, & J. Heinonen (Eds.), *The sage handbook of small business and entrepreneurship* (pp. 321–349). Sage.

Mason, C. (2021). Financing an entrepreneur-led economic recovery: The impact of the coronavirus on business angel investing. In P. McCann & T. Vorley (Eds.), *Productivity and the pandemic* (pp. 73–87). Edward Elgar.

Mason, C., & Botelho, T. (2021). Business angel investing during the COVID-19 economic crisis: Evidence from Scotland, PIN – Productivity Insights Network Working Paper (May) https://productivityinsightsnetwork.co.uk/app/uploads/2021/08/PIN-WP-version-v2.pdf

Mason, C. M., Botelho, T., & Harrison, R. (2013). *The transformation of the business angel market: Evidence from Scotland.* SSRN 2306653.

Mason, C., Botelho, T., & Harrison, R. (2016). The transformation of the business angel market: Evidence and research implications. *Venture Capital: An International Journal of Entrepreneurial Finance, 18*(4), 321–344.

Mason, C. M., & Harrison, R. T. (1996). Informal venture capital: A study of the investment process and post-investment experience. *Entrepreneurship and Regional Development, 9*, 105–126.

Mason, C. M., & Harrison, R. T. (2002). Is it worth it? The rates of return from informal venture capital investments. *Journal of Business Venturing, 17*, 211–236.

Mason, C. M., & Harrison, R. T. (2003). Auditioning for money': What do technology investors look for at the initial screening stage? *Journal of Private Equity, 6*(2), 29–42.

Mason, C., & Brown, R. (2014). *Entrepreneurial ecosystems and growth-oriented enterprises*. OECD LEED programme. http://www.oecd.org/cfe/leed/entrepreneurial-ecosystems.pdf

Mason, C., Harrison, R., & Botelho, T. (2015). Business angel exits: Strategies and processes. In J. G. Hussain & J. M. Scott (Eds.), *Research handbook on entrepreneurial finance* (pp. 102–124). Edward Elgar.

NACO. (2020). *Entrepreneurship capital action plan: National Policy Consultation on sustaining Canada's innovation economy*. National Angel Capital Association.

NACO. (2021). *The changing landscape: 2021 annual report on Angel Investment in Canada*. National Angel Capital Organisation. https://digital.builtbyangels.com/link/228783/

Parhankangas, A., & Ehrlich, M. (2014). How entrepreneurs seduce business angels: An impression management approach. *Journal of Business Venturing, 29*(4), 543–564.

ScaleUp Institute. (2020). *ScaleUp annual review 2020*. https://www.scaleupinstitute.org.uk/scaleup-review-2020/introduction/

Sifted. (2020a, May 21). *What's happened to the angels?* https://sifted.eu/articles/angel-investing-startups-europe-covid/

Sifted. (2020b, May 7). *The debate still raging around the UK's future fund*. https://sifted.eu/articles/future-fund-criticism/

Sohl, J. E. (1999). The early stage equity market in the United States. *Venture Capital: An International Journal of Entrepreneurial Finance, 1*, 101–120.

Sohl, J. (2020). *UNH finds impact of COVID-19 was swift in the angel investing market*. University of New Hampshire Media Relations.

Tech Coast Angels. (2021). *Annual report 2020*. https://www.techcoastangels.com/wp-content/uploads/2021/06/TCA-Annual-Report-2020-final.pdf

Techregister. (2021, February 26). *East Coast angel investors building relationships via virtual pitches*. https://www.techregister.co.uk/east-coast-angel-investors-building-relationships-via-virtual-pitches-regional-business-business/

Warnick, B. J., Davis, B. C., Allison, T. H., & Anglin, A. H. (2021). Express yourself: Facial expression of happiness, anger, fear, and sadness in funding pitches. *Journal of Business Venturing, 36*(4), 106109.

**Colin Mason** is Professor of Entrepreneurship in the Adam Smith Business School, University of Glasgow. His research is on entrepreneurship and regional development with specific research focus on entrepreneurial finance, in particular business angel investing, and entrepreneurial ecosystems. He was co-founder of the journal *Venture Capital: An International Journal of Entrepreneurial Finance*.

# Part III
# Reflecting on the Future of Entrepreneurship Research: Diversity and Impact After the COVID-19 Crisis

# Dreaming of a Different Future

**Friederike Welter**

**Abstract** Drawing on personal observations and experiences during 2020, the author reflects on the challenges the COVID-19 pandemic poses for academic and researcher diversity as well as for which entrepreneurship research matters and how best to disseminate research results beyond academia. She discusses the multiple effects of the pandemic on the nature of entrepreneurship scholarship in general. The pandemic has a major impact on the career of women academics and early-career scholars, potentially threatening academic diversity if those effects are not just temporary but long-lasting. The pandemic also laid open again the differences between policymakers and academics in terms of what is considered interesting research. Entrepreneurship scholars were pushed towards more relevant research topics. At the same time, the rapid digitization of teaching, meetings and conferences offers opportunities for global and multidisciplinary collaborations that foster new insights into the challenges entrepreneurs and small business face, both for academia and for policymakers.

**Keywords** Academic diversity · Public policy · Multidisciplinary collaborations · Entrepreneurs · Small businesses

## 1 Looking Back and Thinking Forward

When Iris and David invited me to contribute to this book, my initial response was a cautious yes, because I could not anticipate my workload in the coming months. The pandemic turned work and life upside down. With an increasing share of the population being vaccinated, prospects for summer 2021 suddenly look much more relaxed. Thus, this chapter is a great opportunity to sit down and reflect

F. Welter (✉)
Institut für Mittelstandsforschung (IfM) Bonn, Bonn, Germany

University of Siegen, Siegen, Germany
e-mail: welter@uni-siegen.de



D. B. Audretsch, I. A. M. Kunadt (eds.), *The COVID-19 Crisis and Entrepreneurship*, International Studies in Entrepreneurship 54,
https://doi.org/10.1007/978-3-031-04655-1_9

whether and how we can build back better, regarding research structures, scholarship and the relevance of our research for entrepreneurs, small firms and policymakers. Looking back, I notice instances in which the pandemic has challenged diversity in the research landscape, which is a call for action. Also, it has stirred up academia, pushing many of us to question what we had taken for granted and at the same time opening opportunities to rethink research structures and research agendas to make them more relevant to practice. Looking forward this could be the starting point towards a different (research) future as I suggest in my chapter outlook. The chapter starts with a short snapshot of my personal observations and experiences during 2020, before discussing a few issues in more detail. Those include the effects of the COVID-19 pandemic on women academics and (women) early-career researchers and the challenges in making entrepreneurship research more relevant for those outside the academic ivory tower, together with potential changes in the nature of scholarship as such.

## 2 Notes from a Pandemic Year

**February 2020:** I have been invited to a workshop on entrepreneurship policy at Kingston University in England. Encouraging to see so many junior researchers interested in policy topics, and even someone from the OECD attending. Insightful discussions on critical perspectives and new avenues for entrepreneurship policy. The weekend I spend with friends in St Albans, discussing research ideas and, also, the threat of this unknown virus. One of my last work travels for a long while.

A colleague comes to my office, worried about his next business trip to Belgium. I try to calm him down—the organizers will cancel the event two days later.

**March:** Early March, together with friends, I visit the Hopper exhibition in Switzerland. The last time for several months in a museum (or theatre, cinema, concert hall). Only in July 2021 will I meet my friends in person again.

Things are speeding up. Worrying reports and pictures from Northern Italy. More and more virus infections also in Germany. As of 16 March, we allow everybody in our research institute to work from home. A few days later the government implements its first anti-pandemic measures—and we restrict entry to the institute. We start our digital work-life which will dominate 2020 and beyond. Much to organize, from cameras, soft- and hardware to thinking through workflows, digital leadership, and team building. How to substitute for all the small talk happening during a workday? How to make sure we take everybody along? How to best accommodate the needs of researchers with small kids? How to prevent information and work overload? I start writing weekend emails, chatting about the institute workweek.

My father calls. The special-care home where my mother lives forbids any visits for the time being. Only in May can I visit her again—outside, a table between us, skyping in the family. A few months later, I can sit next to her and hug—concealed behind a mask and in a sterile gown. Hybrid family meetings and birthday parties will become our pattern until spring 2021.

The SME department in the Federal Ministry of Economics and Energy wants to know more about the effects of the COVID-19 pandemic on small firms and entrepreneurship. As soon as possible. They have been tasked with designing support programmes, and now want to know from us which immediate support measures SMEs require and how a medium- to long-term support policy could look like, also in terms of which laws and other framework conditions would need to be adapted. Moreover, they need information on how anti-pandemic measures impact on entrepreneurs and SMEs in different sectors and across different business sizes. We start our series of background papers—no data are available yet, so we compile evidence wherever we find studies and deduct possible lessons for Germany. We also add COVID-19-relevant questions and aspects to some of our ongoing research projects to ensure up-to-date evidence. In-depth discussions with our research advisory board, in particular its business representatives, and our international research fellow network which we just set up a few months ago, help us to sharpen and fine-tune our conclusions and implications.

At the University of Siegen, I move the final sessions of my doctoral workshop online. Except for one onsite meeting in early December 2020, I have been teaching online since. At least, we can meet online! The first digital course session, we talk about how the pandemic affects the doctoral students and how they cope with it. It's a close-knit community that emerges from this course—and many are staying on for the next courses.

**April**: Most days I now start early in the morning with a long walk, taking my camera along. Getting to know the area where I live quite well—many hidden nature treasures around here. My quiet times of otherwise long days.

My pile of COVID-19 papers from (economic) experts is growing, as are the debates on which policy strategy to (not) follow. A challenge to keep up to date with what happens to small firms, despite first empirical studies. What helps are virtual meetings such as those of the Federal Ministry's SME Advisory Board together with the Minister of Economics. I am also regularly listening to various podcasts by virologists and epidemiologists on the virus. Watching science in the making: heated debates emerge around which results are correct and who is the best expert. It must be difficult for the public to understand how quickly scientific results can be proven wrong as, for example, we learn more about how the virus spreads.

So much to do! Finding it more and more difficult to concentrate; regularly falling asleep in front of the TV evening news. I realize that I lack the stamina and creativity to work on anything else beyond our background papers, institute management, teaching and preparing for the evaluation of our big collaborative research proposal at the university. Turning down several writing commitments, I had very much looked forward to. Little worries compared to what's happening in the world and elsewhere.

**May**: I had booked tickets for the "Passion Play" in Oberammergau. In 1633, in the middle of the plague, the villagers promised passion plays every tenth year, and have kept their promise ever since. In 2020, for the first time ever, they had to postpone their play to 2022 because of the COVID-19 pandemic. . .

We are allowing work at the institute, again—although still restricting the number of people onsite. We implement COVID-19 safety concepts, learning to work onsite, but socially distanced. Keeping track of COVID-19 regulations issued by the federal and our state governments proves to be very time-consuming—oftentimes, we are surprised by regulations issued a day before they become effective. A real-life example of how bureaucracy impacts on small businesses!

**Summer**: Conference season. My favourite research week moved online, also. This is a writing retreat for mid- and late-career entrepreneurship scholars: a full week to focus on one's own and collaborative writings, to meet with co-authors, and get to know a few new doctoral or postdoctoral students in attendance. This did not really work well online: I appreciated the food for thought from the short daily seminars, but definitely missed the timeout at a different place—work interfered too much this time. Also, I miss the chit-chat in between sessions, running into friends, the surprise talks and idea sessions. Too much of my work-life is happening in front of a screen.

Heated debates with a friend who emails fake videos dismissing the existence of the virus and the global pandemic. We stop talking, and sadly, never manage to revive that friendship.

Infections are slowing down. I am longing for some normality. A few days off, at the sea. Museums have opened again. However, looking back from summer 2021, with decreasing infection rates and a rapidly increasing share of virus variants of concern: What is considered normal, now? When does a pandemic end and normality sets in again?

**Autumn**: Our first international roundtable on SMEs and entrepreneurship takes place, followed a few weeks later by an international discussion round organized during Germany's presidentship of the EU council. Everything online, of course. These workshops illustrate, once more, how important international research networks are at these times—we learn from each other which entrepreneurship policies work, and about the manifold pandemic challenges for small firms.

**December 2020**: Back home. The university closes once more. At the institute, we send everybody back to working from home, again. Only in July 2021 will we begin bringing back more of the team onsite. I am one of the few regularly working in the institute—sometimes feeling lonely with no one else around.

The rapid development of vaccines is very encouraging. As entrepreneurship scholar, I am interested in the story behind the vaccine: a start-up from Germany is at the forefront of these developments, owned by a second-generation migrant scientist couple. Funny, though: While in Germany we talk about the BioNTech vaccine (the company), colleagues elsewhere talk about the Pfizer vaccine (the well-known big collaboration partner).

Our Xmas gift: My mother is among the first in Bonn to be vaccinated in late December!

## 3 Missing Voices? Towards Maintaining Research Diversity

How does the pandemic affect our research landscape? The diversity of researchers is key to research that matters and offers novel insights, but this may be threatened because of the pandemic. In spring 2020, I noticed a rather worrisome debate on twitter: Journal editors from different academic disciplines pointed out that women researchers were submitting fewer articles since the pandemic had started. School closures and home-schooling, together with remote work had put competing demands on all working parents. Would this indeed contribute to widening the gender divide in academia, once more? Did we simply observe a temporary backlash? A quick search when writing this chapter surfaced several papers published since spring 2020 that investigate women's potential underrepresentation in the academic debate during the pandemic—the topic is of interest for many disciplines. Initial results are rather bleak, regardless of discipline: women have published considerably less since the pandemic started. This became already visible a few months into the pandemic (e.g. Carpenter et al., 2021; Feng & Savani, 2020; King & Frederickson, 2021; Krukowski et al., 2021); and recovery towards pre-pandemic publication patterns is slow (Lerchenmüller et al., 2021).

Gender inequalities in academia have been exacerbated during the pandemic not least because the move to working from home appears to have reinforced traditional gender roles. Globally, women researchers reported greater declines than men in the amount of time they could set aside for their own research; and those with dependent children reported the highest declines in available research time (Deryugina et al., 2021; Myers et al., 2020). Women primarily take over childcare when both parents are forced to work from home. Additionally, during the pandemic, women researchers frequently have been tasked with caring for students and colleagues (Boncori, 2020; Pereira, 2021).[1] All this affects their research outcomes as reflected in publication activities or research applications. For example, for the USA, the total research output in social sciences increased by 35% in spring 2020, but women academics' output dropped by 13.2% compared to men's (Cui et al., 2021). Even worse, women were less involved in taking up new COVID-19-related research, for example in medical and health studies (Muric et al., 2020; Pinho-Gomes et al., 2020; Squazzoni et al., 2020) or economics (Amano-Patiño et al., 2020), where women make up only 12% of the authorship of new COVID-19-related studies. Women's voices are lost amid the pandemic—apart from the long-term effects on individual research careers, and gender equality in academia.

What about early-career researchers? Does the pandemic contribute to a "lost generation" (Harrop et al., 2021)—a generation that loses out on research opportunities, on getting to know the community and on making their first steps towards

[1] It is only when writing this chapter that I come across Boncori's (2020) article, published in April 2020 during the first pandemic months. From a feminist perspective, she reflects on living and organizing academic lives during the coronavirus pandemic. Definitely recommended reading!

their future academic careers? Gender disparities also are visible in this regard: During the first wave of the pandemic, the drop in research productivity was especially pronounced for younger cohorts of women academics, both regarding journal submissions (Squazzoni et al., 2020) and submissions to preprint archives across different disciplines (Vincent-Lamarre et al., 2020). Also, fewer early- to mid-career women researchers worked on COVID-19-related topics (Amano-Patiño et al., 2020; Vincent-Lamarre et al., 2020). Governments quickly introduced measures during the pandemic to cushion some of the negative institutional impact on early and mid-career researchers, such as contract expansions, postponement of academic evaluations and similar, although some of that, at least in Germany, depends on the good will of department heads at universities. Again, those measures may discriminate against women and dual-career couples with children who need more individualized support to be able to remain in academia and research (Myers et al., 2020).

When I talk to doctoral students and to postdoctoral researchers, we frequently touch upon the challenges the pandemic poses for them. For example, journal reviewers ask for more fieldwork—but international travel is not possible in the foreseeable future, and digital workaround solutions impossible to implement in some contexts. International research stays have been cancelled; conferences moved to the virtual. This may particularly impact newcomers in building up their own research networks—and it is the responsibility of us senior researchers to make an extra effort in introducing new researchers into our networks. Still, a few early-career researchers have been quite entrepreneurial in identifying opportunities for COVID-19-related research, pivoting (some of) their research themes, although that raises the question of how much and how far to pivot (Denfeld et al., 2020). Data have been collected and papers have already been submitted to entrepreneurship journals several of which have open calls for crisis- and COVID-19-related special issues.[2] Not the quickest way to get hold of these results and probably not the best one yet to be heard outside academia, but at least one way of making sure that novel voices are getting out in the public. Once these issues have been published, it would be interesting to assess the share of early-career authors (and, of course, the share of women among authorship) to see whether it is the established or new voices dominating.

It is still too early to know whether the disparities in academia that have been exacerbated by the pandemic are a momentary drawback. However, this needs to be monitored closely, and we need to make sure that this debate is not lost as soon as the pandemic has passed. Missing the voices of women researchers, early-career researchers and other (minority) groups I have not touched upon has far-reaching consequences for our research. Each research generation comes with their own perspective on which questions to ask and prioritize, and how to conduct research. If early-career (female) researchers drop out of academia because of the pandemic,

---

[2]Entrepreneurship Theory & Practice, International Journal of Entrepreneurial Behaviour and Research, International Small Business Journal, Small Business Economics Journal.

we will miss out on the novel ideas they bring along to address other grand challenges besides the health issue. Diversity gives us access to much more perspectives and knowledge, thus adding to the relevance of the research we conduct.

Also, the debate on who is disadvantaged in the publication race because of the pandemic points to a fundamental and, in my view, increasingly problematic notion, namely the current career advancement standards of our profession. Publications (and, to some extent, research funding applications) have become our currency—they are a universal measure of our research productivity. Given that the pandemic—once more—highlighted the inequalities and challenges of this model, wouldn't it be timely to revisit our standards and our focus on peer-reviewed publications as one of the *central* indicators for academic excellence and impact? Many more aspects of research and academic work are worth valuing beyond publications. Why not use the pandemic as a wake-up call to reimagine academic work and career paths, aiming to sustain research diversity and making our research more relevant to practice instead of narrowly evaluating (and valuing) scholarly impact?

## 4 Walking the Talk! Pushing Relevant Entrepreneurship Research

When in spring 2020, I declined the invitation to develop a paper for a special issue at a highly ranked entrepreneurship journal, pointing to the background policy papers we were prioritizing, the reaction was one of envy: How come our research was valued by policymakers and theirs not? Suddenly, measures of impact such as publishing in peer-reviewed journals appeared to have lost some of their value. Academics, practitioners, and policymakers differ with respect to which research is considered relevant. For academics, as a rule, the scholarly impact counts; in the real world it is the value of research for solving problems of small firms and entrepreneurs. Over the past decades, academics have again and again lamented the gap between papers that were academically rigorous and successfully cited but failed to have a real-world impact (e.g. McGahan, 2007). Much has been written on how to make our research not only scholarly impactful but also relevant to practice and practitioners (e.g. Baker & Welter, 2020; George et al., 2016), but not that much has changed.

Come the pandemic, and suddenly, we can walk the talk, having been forced to reconsider our stance on which kind of research to conduct and where to publish. As governments were searching for immediate knowledge on the challenges that entrepreneurs and small firms are facing and how best to support them, this pushed many entrepreneurship and small business researchers towards COVID-19 research topics, and towards searching for and implementing real-time publication routes. Entrepreneurship journals pulled together crisis-related online repositories (e.g. Entrepreneurship Theory & Practice[3]), offered rapid publication routes for new research (e.g. Journal of Business Venturing Insights through its "Entrepreneurship Rapid Response Initiative"[4]) or published COVID-19-related commentary series (e.g. International Small Business Journal,[5] Journal of Management Studies[6]). Several academic publishers made new COVID-19 publications of any discipline open access (at least for the time being). Think-nets and policy-related entrepreneurship research institutes like ours both benefited from the growing body of empirical evidence and added to it. Our institute launched its series of background policy papers,[7] both in German and in English, in which we assessed and commented on economic COVID-19 policies regarding their relevance for entrepreneurship and small enterprises—similarly the Enterprise Research Centre (ERC)[8] for the UK. Empirical evidence mounted up quickly: For example, five out of seven presentations at our April 2020 RoundTable Mittelstand (a regular meeting of policymakers, business associations, entrepreneurship, and SME research institutions) already drew on initial empirical evidence regarding the effects of the pandemic on SMEs.[9] These dialogues between entrepreneurship scholars, businesses and policymakers are important, not just in pandemic times: I see them as excellent means to get a feeling for what is required from research from a non-academic perspective.

Although the pandemic accelerated the much-needed move towards relevant research that serves audiences beyond academia, at the same time, it also highlighted the challenges in advising policymakers as described in Welter et al. (2020):

> Advising policymakers can be compared to a tightrope walk: it is a delicate balance between keeping a researcher's integrity and using one's in-depth knowledge of what has worked beforehand to present—potential—solutions to new problems and circumstances. Finally, one of the biggest challenge is the communication with, in this case, policymakers: Trained as researchers, we have entirely different ways of communicating and writing, we talk differently, we use jargon (not that policymakers don't use their own)—and it takes quite a while to bridge this communication gap, for example, to make sure that we find our own, authentic way, of talking to policy-makers, also knowing how far we can take our empirical evidence and not adhering to the demands of policymakers in making our evidence fit their expectations.

When during the early months of the pandemic, more and more academics from different disciplines came to public attention, this was not without drawbacks. The

[3]https://journals.sagepub.com/page/etp/covid-19-and-entrepreneurship

[4]https://www.sciencedirect.com/journal/journal-of-business-venturing-insights/special-issue/101KTJ1F47F. However, not all articles in this online collection are open access, i.e. accessible without payment.

[5]https://journals.sagepub.com/page/isb/covid-19-and-entrepreneurship

[6]https://onlinelibrary.wiley.com/page/journal/14676486/homepage/covid19-commentaries

[7]https://www.ifm-bonn.org/en/dossiers/coronavirus-pandemic

[8]https://www.enterpriseresearch.ac.uk/covid-19-resource-directory/

[9]https://www.ifm-bonn.org/fileadmin/data/redaktion/ueber_uns/pressemitteilungen/PM-22-04-2020_Mittelstand_in_der_Coronakrise.pdf

oftentimes very heated public discourse in German media, especially social media that allows every user to participate, is a telling example of the pitfalls in speaking to the public. As researchers we are used to mutually discuss and question our findings and, where necessary, revise our conclusions. However, these discussions normally take place within our close-knit academic communities, and, ideally, results only are disseminated publicly once vetted through peers. The pandemic forced much of that debate, especially that of virologists and epidemiologists who made it their task to educate us about the virus, to take place in public, because we all urgently needed to acquire knowledge on how the virus would affect our economy and society. Not surprisingly, this led to misinterpretations along the lines of "he (usually this was a man) has published wrong results" when new insights superseded initial conclusions. Knowledge accumulation and dissemination happened very rapidly during the pandemic, probably too quick for our minds that tried to make sense out of so many unknowns, uncertainties and frights coming along with the health threat. As important as it is that researchers disseminate and transfer their findings, the pandemic also highlights the responsibility we have when advising policymakers: We need to be aware when to stop talking or not to talk in public.

Policymakers rely on experts for ideas, and such expert knowledge influences the outcomes of policymaking. In my view, the pandemic also questioned the function and roles of such experts, and rightly so: Who is (seen as) an expert? Who is asked to advise and talk? How to make sure that we not only consider the economic impact on small firms and entrepreneurs, but also include social aspects? Groups that are silenced or not listened to because they are perceived as not having the required expertise may have come up with different ideas for policy solutions. Diversity is, again, key here, to ensure inclusive policymaking and to prevent "expert silos" (Murphy et al., 2021).

Some global evidence points to gender gaps in COVID-19-related decision-making (van Daalen et al., 2020): 85% of 115 task forces launched in 87 countries had mostly male members and a mere 11% mostly female members, while only 3.5% showed gender parity. I do not perceive a lack of gender diversity in advisory bodies that problematic in Germany, not least because official advisory groups must strive for gender parity. Expert groups such as the interdisciplinary "Expert Council Corona" of the North-Rhine Westphalian government (5 women, 7 men) or, at national level, the German Ethics Council (currently 23 members, 11 women) fared much better on gender equity and diversity. The latter, led by a woman, became an important and impartial voice in COVID-19-related public discussions. I valued their input for our own work on SMEs and entrepreneurship, because of the ethical and societal perspectives offered by a truly diverse group—including mid-career scholars, whose voices are still missing in too many official advisory groups.

Whenever single expert voices were heard in public, however, these frequently belonged to established male researchers. Over time, German media made extra efforts to turn to women researchers. It remains to be seen whether this will hold also after COVID-19, or whether we are stuck in the past—a past where expertise is a result of experience coming with age and male gender. Junior scholars have long attempted to break up these deeply ingrained structures of who is seen as expert by the public, policymakers, and media, but even they work and communicate within "expert silos." I had not been aware of initiatives like the globally oriented "Young Scholars Initiative"[10] of economists or that the multidisciplinary junior research group "KontiKat" at my own university published a position paper with new insights on, for example, information policies during a pandemic (Schorch et al., 2020). We need these initiatives in the entrepreneurship field, also. One entrepreneurship journal (International Journal of Entrepreneurship and Innovation) is planning to publish "Fresh Perspectives Research Notes" (Kevill et al., 2021) that will be exclusively written by early-career scholars—I am looking forward to their insights. However, we need to ensure that such voices become known beyond academia, thus supporting the next generation of entrepreneurship experts policymakers can turn to.

Relevant entrepreneurship research also needs global and multidisciplinary collaborations. The pandemic has pushed both, not least because workshops, conferences and meetings quickly moved online. As much as I am looking forward to also physically attending workshops and meeting colleagues and friends in person again, there are clear benefits of virtual collaborations. For example, I was invited to present our COVID-19 policy papers to the National Planning Commission of South Africa in a workshop on policy solutions for (informal) SMEs—something which would never have happened in "real" pre-COVID life due to time and cost constraints. Or the new doctoral course I designed in spring 2021, assembling entrepreneurship scholars and students from around the world, only made possible because of virtual teaching. A clear benefit! Digital technologies facilitate collaboration with scholars and policymakers from countries we usually do not meet at workshops or conferences, thus also allowing for much more diversity in research collaborations. Lower travel costs, less time spent on the road, the possibilities to go global, notwithstanding the smaller carbon footprint—virtual exchange formats definitely will stay with us. It is up to us to exploit the opportunities they offer to push multidisciplinary and global exchange and to build diverse entrepreneurship research communities (Gartner et al., 2006).

The economic policy discussions that happened in Germany are good examples for multidisciplinary collaborations. They rapidly evolved from mainly economists speaking up also on health-related issues to multidisciplinary policy proposals, for which economists teamed up with sociologists, ethicists, physicists, mathematicians, virologists and epidemiologists and many more disciplines (e.g. Abele-Brehm et al., 2020), also offering pan-European suggestions (e.g. Priesemann et al., 2021). What is expected from most official advisory councils, where members of different professions, businesses, disciplines work together, has—finally—gained importance in academia and beyond. To me, working across one's own discipline is not only required to make our research relevant, but also is a vital element of the future of

[10] https://ysi.ineteconomics.org/, an initiative supported by the Institute of New Economic Thinking (INET). Also see their COVID-19 webinar series: https://ysi.ineteconomics.org/project/5e947f40a6a5c2058bd14aea

academia and research institutions. Once more, we can learn much from early-career researchers and their perspectives on the research of the future and the future of academic work structures (see Chacón-Labella et al., 2021 for some inspiration).

Collaboration across fields does not stop at (entrepreneurship) research but is equally important for entrepreneurship and SME policy. SMEs fulfil functions for which policy areas beyond economic policy are responsible while framework conditions and legal regulations initiated in various ministries influence SME development. Therefore, SME policy necessitates a cross-sectional approach, that considers policy areas such as education, research, environment and energy, labour and social policies or transport/infrastructure (Welter et al., 2016), as difficult as this is to implement in practice. The pandemic clearly illustrates the need for joined-up SME and entrepreneurship policy approaches: Public health, economic and social policy requirements have continuously been weighed against each other (Welter & Levering, 2021; Welter et al., 2021). Take the example of healthcare policies, normally a policy field considered remote from the economy, which all of a sudden had a major impact on SMEs through hygiene requirements and compulsory closures of whole sectors. From an employment policy perspective, one of the most important tasks of SME policy during the pandemic is to stabilize the labour market and keep job losses at a minimum. Healthcare measures such as the wide-ranging hygiene regulations to be implemented in businesses assisted in this regard, preventing high sickness rates in many firms. But they also added to the ever-growing bureaucratic burden of small firms which could have been eased by a temporary moratorium on other regulations. Why not build on the lessons from the pandemic and implement cross-sectional SME policies also in the long run? In Germany, the key challenge for SME policy in the coming legislative period will be to ensure that SME interests and needs are considered in all ministries involved and are not relegated solely to the ministry of economics.

## 5 Here's to the Future of Entrepreneurship Research

There is something good to be found everywhere, even during turbulent times. Here's to a different future for entrepreneurship scholarship and policymaking, one which has started in many aspects already during the pandemic. This will be a future where we will make sure to support and sustain academic diversity and closely listening to those coming next; where we will collaborate much more beyond our own disciplines to craft a policy-relevant research agenda for entrepreneurship that can offer at least some solutions for the grand challenges of our times like climate change but that also strives to remedy the social injustices and inequalities created and exacerbated through the pandemic. The pandemic has shaken up our lives, still, I also see some value in that it has pushed us to rethink the essence of our research, its relevance and finding ways to quickly disseminate research findings and start building more global collaborations. Entrepreneurship research is well suited to contribute policy-relevant answers—the field traditionally has attracted researchers from different disciplines like sociology, history, management, economics, and psychology. There is richness in such diversity for generating scholarly interesting and, at the same time, policy-relevant research—research that understands the challenges small businesses and entrepreneurs face in a turbulent world and offers new solutions.

## References

Abele-Brehm, A., Dreier, H., Fuest, C., Grimm, V., Kräusslich, H.-G., & Krause, G., et al. (2020). *Die Bekämpfung der Coronavirus-Pandemie tragfähig gestalten. Empfehlungen für eine flexible, risikoadaptierte Strategie*. (Koordination: Clemens Fuest und Martin Lohse). München.

Amano-Patiño, N., Faraglia, E., Giannitsarou, C., & Hasna, Z. (2020). *The unequal effects of Covid-19 on economists' research productivity*. Cambridge-INET Working Paper WP2022, https://doi.org/10.17863/CAM.57979.

Baker, T., & Welter, F. (2020). *Contextualizing entrepreneurship theory (Routledge studies in entrepreneurship)*. Routledge.

Boncori, I. (2020). The never-ending shift: A feminist reflection on living and organizing academic lives during the coronavirus pandemic. *Gender, Work and Organization, 27*(5), 677–682. https://doi.org/10.1111/gwao.12451

Carpenter, M. A., Cotter, D. A., & Berheide, C. (2021). "I have no time for anything:" differences in faculty research productivity during the COVID-19 pandemic. *ADVANCE Journal, 2*(3), 24815.

Chacón-Labella, J., Boakye, M., Enquist, B. J., Farfan-Rios, W., Gya, R., Halbritter, A. H., et al. (2021). From a crisis to an opportunity: Eight insights for doing science in the COVID-19 era and beyond. *Ecology and Evolution, 11*(8), 3588–3596. https://doi.org/10.1002/ece3.7026

Cui, R., Ding, H., & Zhu, F. (2021). Gender inequality in research productivity during the COVID-19 pandemic. *arXiv preprint,* arXiv:2006.10194v10195.

Denfeld, Q., Erickson, E., Valent, A., Villasana, L., Zhang, Z., Myatt, L., et al. (2020). COVID-19: Challenges and lessons learned from early career investigators. *Journal of Women's Health, 29*(6), 752–754.

Deryugina, T., Shurchkov, O., & Stearns, J. (2021). Covid-19 disruptions disproportionately affect female academics. *AEA Papers and Proceedings, 111*, 164–168.

Feng, Z., & Savani, K. (2020). Covid-19 created a gender gap in perceived work productivity and job satisfaction: Implications for dual-career parents working from home. *Gender in Management: An International Journal, 35*(7–8), 719–736.

Gartner, W. B., Davidsson, P., & Zahra, S. A. (2006). Are you talking to me? The nature of community in entrepreneurship scholarship. *Entrepreneurship Theory and Practice, 30*(3), 321–331.

George, G., Howard-Grenville, J., Joshi, A., & Tihanyi, L. (2016). Understanding and tackling societal grand challenges through management research. *Academy of Management Journal, 59*(6), 1880–1895. https://doi.org/10.5465/amj.2016.4007

Harrop, C., Bal, V., Carpenter, K., & Halladay, A. (2021). A lost generation? The impact of the COVID-19 pandemic on early career ASD researchers. *Autism Research, 14*(6), 1078–1087.

Kevill, A., Refai, D., Galloway, L., Pattison, S., & Kromidha, E. (2021). Introducing fresh perspectives research notes for the international journal of entrepreneurship and innovation. *The International Journal of Entrepreneurship and Innovation, Online Early*. https://doi.org/10.1177/14657503211034033

King, M. M., & Frederickson, M. E. (2021). The pandemic penalty: The gendered effects of COVID-19 on scientific productivity. *Socius, 7*(1), 24.

Krukowski, R. A., Jagsi, R., & Cardel, M. I. (2021). Academic productivity differences by gender and child age in science, technology, engineering, mathematics, and medicine faculty during the COVID-19 pandemic. *Journal of Women's Health, 30*(3), 341–347.

Lerchenmüller, C., Schmallenbach, L., Jena, A. B., & Lerchenmueller, M. J. (2021). Longitudinal analyses of gender differences in first authorship publications related to COVID-19. *BMJ Open, 11*(4), e045176.

McGahan, A. M. (2007). Academic research that matters to managers: On zebras, dogs, lemmings, hammers, and turnips. *Academy of Management Journal, 50*(4), 748–753.

Muric, G., Lerman, K., & Ferrara, E. (2020). COVID-19 amplifies gender disparities in research. *arXiv preprint* arXiv:2006.06142.

Murphy, J., Devereaux, A., Goodman, N., & Koppl, R. (2021). Expert failure and pandemics: On adapting to life with pandemics. *Cosmos + Taxis, 9*(5–6), 7–17.

Myers, K., Tham, W. Y., Yin, Y., Cohodes, N., Thursby, J. G., Thursby, M., et al. (2020). Unequal effects of the COVID-19 pandemic on scientists. *Nature Human Behavior, 4*, 880–883.

Pereira, M. d. M. (2021). Researching gender inequalities in academic labor during the COVID-19 pandemic: Avoiding common problems and asking different questions. *Gender, Work and Organization, 28*(S2), 498–509.

Pinho-Gomes, A.-C., Peters, S., Thompson, K., Hockham, C., Ripullone, K., Woodward, M., et al. (2020). Where are the women? Gender inequalities in COVID-19 research authorship. *BMJ Global Health, 5*(7), e002922. https://doi.org/10.1136/bmjgh-2020-002922

Priesemann, V., Balling, R., Brinkmann, M. M., Ciesek, S., Hel, Z., Hotulainen, P., & et al. (2021). *Aktionsplan für einen europaweit koordinierten Schutz vor neuen SARS-CoV-2-Varianten.*

Schorch, M., Langer, A., Riebe, T., Syed, H. A., Seifert, F., Grinko, M., & et al. (2020). *Corona pandemic.* Position paper KontiKat.

Squazzoni, F., Bravo, G., Grimaldo, F., Garcıa-Costa, D., Farjam, M., & Mehmani, B. (2020). Only second-class tickets for women in the COVID-19 race. A study on manuscript submissions and reviews in 2329 Elsevier journals. *SSRN Electronic Journal, 16*(10), e0257919. https://doi.org/10.2139/ssrn.3712813

van Daalen, K. R., Bajnoczki, C., Chowdhury, M., Dada, S., Khorsand, P., Socha, A., et al. (2020). Symptoms of a broken system: The gender gaps in COVID-19 decision-making. *BMJ Global Health, 5*(10), e003549. https://doi.org/10.1136/bmjgh-2020-003549

Vincent-Lamarre, P., Sugimoto, C. R., & Larivière, V. (2020). The decline of Women's research production during the coronavirus pandemic. *Nature Index.*

Welter, F., & Levering, B. (2021). Die Mittelstandspolitik nach Corona – für eine nachhaltige Zukunft. *Perspektiven der Wirtschaftspolitik, Online Early.* https://doi.org/10.1515/pwp-2021-0035

Welter, F., Levering, B., & May-Strobl, E. (2016). Mittelstandspolitik im Wandel. In *IfM-Materialien* (Vol. 247). Institut für Mittelstandsforschung Bonn.

Welter, F., Urbano, D., Alfahaid, T., Aljarodi, A., Breit, E., Buhrandt, A., et al. (2020). Introducing the book: The what, why and how of relevance and impact. In F. Welter & D. Urbano (Eds.), *How to make your doctoral research relevant* (pp. 2–9). Edward Elgar Publishing.

Welter, F., Wolter, H.-J., & Holz, M. (2021). Mittelstand policy during and after the Covid-19 pandemic. In *IfM background papers.* Institut für Mittelstandsforschung.

## Websites

https://journals.sagepub.com/page/etp/covid-19-and-entrepreneurship
https://journals.sagepub.com/page/isb/covid-19-and-entrepreneurship.
https://onlinelibrary.wiley.com/page/journal/14676486/homepage/covid19-commentaries.
https://www.enterpriseresearch.ac.uk/covid-19-resource-directory/

https://www.ifm-bonn.org/en/dossiers/coronavirus-pandemic.
https://www.ifm-bonn.org/fileadmin/data/redaktion/ueber_uns/pressemitteilungen/PM-22-04-2020_Mittelstand_in_der_Coronakrise.pdf
https://www.sciencedirect.com/journal/journal-of-business-venturing-insights/special-issue/101KTJ1F47F.
https://ysi.ineteconomics.org/

**Friederike Welter** is President of the IfM Bonn and Professor of Entrepreneurship and SME Management at the University of Siegen, Germany. She has broad experiences in applied and policy-related research on entrepreneurship and small business. She has published widely and is on the review board of several leading entrepreneurship journals.

# Editorial Quandaries During the COVID-19 Pandemic: A Personal Exposé

**Albert N. Link**

**Abstract** This chapter summarizes my editorial experiences as Editor-in-Chief of the *Journal of Technology Transfer*. I discuss two of the many dimensions associated with scholarly respect through the actions of an editor. These dimensions are an *initial timely review* of a submitted manuscript and, if warranted, a review by *appropriate reviewers* of the manuscript. I have noticed during COVID-19 that the pandemic has affected my ability to act in a timely manner on a submitted manuscript as well as on my ability to solicit publication advice from appropriate reviewers. Identifying appropriate reviewers after I had reached a decision that a submitted manuscript warranted peer review was not an issue during the intense COVID-19 time period, but identifying appropriate reviewers who were in fact willing to accept my invitation to review a manuscript was indeed a major issue. And in fact, the difficulty I faced intensified as the pandemic raged on. And, finding appropriate reviewers who are willing to accept a reviewing assignment remains problematic.

**Keywords** Scientific journals · Academic review process · Knowledge transfer · Manufacturing firms

I appreciate the opportunity to share with others, especially younger faculty, in this chapter my experiences as Editor-in-Chief of the *Journal of Technology Transfer*. My tenure as Editor-in-Chief began in 1996, so I do experience to which I can compare my editorial experience in a non-COVID-19 environment to a COVID-19 environment. I urge a reader not to generalize from my experiences as editor to the experiences of other journal editors who have shepherded their journal through the pandemic. Experiences are, in all likelihood, unique to the individuals involved. I hope that a reader will view my experiences as only a point estimate of the situations that other journal editors might have experienced.

---

A. N. Link (✉)
Department of Economics, University of North Carolina at Greensboro, Greensboro, NC, USA
e-mail: anlink@uncg.edu



D. B. Audretsch, I. A. M. Kunadt (eds.), *The COVID-19 Crisis and Entrepreneurship*, International Studies in Entrepreneurship 54,
https://doi.org/10.1007/978-3-031-04655-1_10

Journal editors have many responsibilities including, but not limited to, ensuring that those who submit a manuscript for review are treated with scholarly respect. From an editorial perspective, the pursuit of scholarly respect covers a wide spectrum ranging from my own ethical behavior as editor to an awareness of the professional intent of authors.

Herein, I wish to share two aspects of scholarly respect that are not only meaningful to me, but also that I believe are meaningful in an informational sense to those who have or will have submitted a manuscript to the *Journal of Technology Transfer*, or perhaps to any other journal.

I will discuss below two of the many dimensions associated with scholarly respect through the actions of an editor. These dimensions are an *initial timely review* of a submitted manuscript and, if warranted, a review by *appropriate reviewers* of the manuscript. Please do not infer that I view these as the most important dimensions of scholarly respect, or that I think other journal editors should or do view these as being most important; these are only two of many dimensions of editorial actions that I think have been, based on my experiences, affected during COVID-19.

The phrase *initial timely review* likely means different things to different editors. To me, the phrase refers to a prompt (within several days if possible) reading of a submitted manuscript and a prompt decision on whether or not a manuscript merits external peer review. If a manuscript does not warrant moving from submission to the peer review stage, based on the publication aims and goals of the journal, I believe that the author should be notified as soon as possible. As we all know, academics at all ranks face publication expectations, and younger faculty have a clock running on those expectations, and an awareness of that clock is to me an editor's responsibility.

Also, the phrase *appropriate reviewers* likely means different things to different editors. Here is where my experiences with the process of identifying appropriate and willing reviewers became complex as COVID-19 intensified. To me, appropriate reviewers refer to those individuals from whom an editor solicits advice on the publication merits of a submitted manuscript. I think appropriate reviewers include academic and/or professional individuals who are not only familiar with the topic of the submitted manuscript and its related literature but who are also familiar with the analytical tools (ranging from data collection methods to statistical methodology) used within the manuscript.

I have noticed that the pandemic has affected my ability to act in a timely manner on a submitted manuscript as well as on my ability to solicit publication advice from appropriate reviewers. Online submissions to the *Journal of Technology Transfer* go through an editorial manager portal. To the best of my knowledge, software issues associated with our editorial manager portal have not been an issue during COVID-19. Once a paper has been submitted, an individual in the Journal Editorial Office—who is a Springer Publisher employee and not a *Journal of Technology Transfer* employee and who has I perceive responsibilities for a number of journals—is in charge of getting the submitted manuscript to my screen as a new email with the subject line Submission to the Journal of Technology Transfer.

I did notice an increase in delays in my receiving such emails as the pandemic intensified compared to what I experienced in pre-pandemic time periods and what I am experiencing now. While I, as editor, am not privy to all of the electronic details of the submission process, I did perceive that individuals in the Journal Editorial Office were overwhelmed during the COVID-19 pandemic, and that those individuals who were not incapacitated because of the pandemic competently and professionally took on the responsibilities of others. During the upswing in COVID-19 infections, I experienced periods of a week or more during which I did not receive any newly submitted manuscripts, and then I received as many as a dozen on a single day.

The prevalence of vaccines has greatly alleviated this issue, if not completely returned the electronic submission process to what existed in the pre-pandemic period. However, the editorial consequence of these COVID-19 delays meant that the meaning of an initial timely review had changed, and I was not able as I am today, to read a newly submitted manuscript within several days of its initial submission and make a decision on the next editorial step that would follow.

Identifying appropriate reviewers after I had reached a decision that a submitted manuscript warranted peer review was not an issue during the intense COVID-19 time period, but identifying appropriate reviewers who were in fact willing to accept my invitation to review a manuscript was indeed a major issue. And in fact, the difficulty I faced intensified as the pandemic raged on. And, finding appropriate reviewers who are willing to accept a reviewing assignment remains problematic.

In this regard, I think that the difficulty I faced was due, in large part, to an increase in the university-related responsibilities of an identified reviewer. Those added responsibilities likely included learning how to teach online learning as well as how to work efficiently and effectively outside of a university office. When an automated electric reminder was sent to an individual to whom an invitation to review was sent, all too often I would receive a personal email from that individual saying that the initial email invitation went into his or her SPAM. Hmmm. While I am certainly not a medical expert, I did not know that COVID-19 infected the email delivery system!

In addition to excuses by invited reviewers (most of which were not as clever as "my dog ate the email"), I also experienced the following. When an identified reviewer agreed to review a manuscript, more often than not he or she would take longer to complete the review than he or she typically took either in a pre-pandemic time period or even now. In pre-COVID-19 times, I would normally request that reviews be completed within 45 to 60 days depending on the complexity of the submitted manuscript, but the time period for me to receive a review often approached 100 days or more during the pandemic. In fact, in more times than I like to remember, a reviewer would send me an apologetic email that read that unexpected events now prohibited him or her from completing the review at all. Such a response meant that I had to start the peer review process all over again.

As more and more journal editors faced the problem in identifying appropriate reviewers who were also willing to accept a reviewing assignment, the pool of such reviewers became overburdened with editors' requests. It was not uncommon for me to receive, justifiably I might add, an email from an identified and previously willing reviewer that read that he or she simply did not have time to accept yet another reviewing assignment.

The bottom line of my personal exposé is that manuscripts were being accepted at a slower rate than before COVID-19, and they are coming into print at a slower rate because production workers are unable to work, often at home or in a remote location, as efficiently as they previously had prior to the pandemic. Not only is this reality frustrating from my perception as an editor, but also this reality has or will have social consequences. In other words: What are the social consequences of an increased lag between scholarly research and the research reaching the public domain?

I address this question from an empirical point of view. From a social perspective, it is well known that across countries a major predictor of economic growth is investments in research and development (R&D) activity. As such, consider an aggregate production function of the form (Terleckyj, 1974):

$$Q_i = A_i\, F\, (K_i, L_i, T_i) \tag{1}$$

where $Q$ represents aggregate output, $A$ is a neutral disembodied shift factor, $K$ represents the stock of physical capital, $L$ represents the stock of labor, $T$ represents the stock of technical capital built over time from investments in R&D, and the subscript $i$ refers to the unit of observation.

If this production function framework takes on the form of a Cobb-Douglas production function, and dropping the observational subscripts, then it takes the form:

$$Q = \mathrm{A}_0 \mathrm{e}^{\lambda t}\, K^{\alpha}\, L^{\beta}\, T^{\gamma} \tag{2}$$

where α, β, and γ are output elasticities. Following the related literature, a reduced-form equation can be estimated of the form:

$$\mathrm{TFPG} = \lambda + \rho\,(\mathrm{RD}/Q) \tag{3}$$

where TFPG represents total factor productivity growth, RD represents investments in R&D, and ρ is the marginal rate of return to R&D.

The related empirical literature has provided evidence that ρ is positive, and thus at the aggregated levels, countries with greater R&D to measures of aggregate output (e.g., gross domestic product, GDP) enjoy greater total factor productivity growth.

The related empirical literature has also assumed that the output elasticity of technical capital is a constant ($0 < \gamma < 1$). However, if one assumes that γ is a variable that is positively related to the use of alternative sources of knowledge, then in a period of decrease in the use of alternative sources of knowledge to leverage the productivity of R&D, total factor productivity growth will slow.

**Table 1** Sources of information used by innovative-active manufacturing firms

| |
|---|
| Internal sources |
| Within your enterprise or enterprise group |
| Market sources |
| Suppliers of equipment, material, components, or software |
| Clients or customers |
| Competitors of other enterprises in your sector |
| Consultants, commercial labs, or private R&D institutes |
| Institutional sources |
| Universities or other higher education institutions |
| Government or private research institutes |
| Other sources |
| Conferences, trade fairs, exhibitions |
| *Scientific journal and trade/technical publications* |
| Professional and industry associations |

Source: United Nations Educational, Scientific and Cultural Organization (UNESCO, 2015), http://uis.unesco.org/sites/default/files/documents/unesco-science-report-towards-2030-part1.pdf

The United Nations Educational, Scientific and Cultural Organization has identified categories for access to the use of innovation-related sources of knowledge (UNESCO, 2015). Table 1 summarizes UNESCO's taxonomy of information sources relied on by manufacturing firms. The category of "Scientific journal and trade/technical publications" is, based on my personal experiences, a category of information sources that has been affected by COVID-19.

And, Table 2 shows the percentage of manufacturing firms for which scientific journals and trade/technical publications were a highly important source of information.

While the percentages in the table are modest in size, and only greater than 20 percent in two instances—Columbia and Romania— they are nevertheless positive in value for all of the reporting countries.

Knowledge reported in scientific journal and trade/technical publications has public goods characteristics, and thus the knowledge is non-rivalrous (i.e., when knowledge consumed by one individual does not deplete its usefulness for consumption by another individual). Thus, to the extent that COVID-19 has slowed down the availably of new knowledge in journals per se, there is every reason to believe that there will be social consequences in terms of a slowdown in productivity growth in varying degrees across countries.

**Table 2** Percentage of manufacturing firms for which scientific journals and trade/technical publications were a highly important source of information, 2012–2014

| Country | 2012 | 2013 | 2014 |
|---|---|---|---|
| Argentina | – | – | – |
| Australia | – | – | – |
| Austria | 13.46555 | – | – |
| Azerbaijan | – | – | 11.11111 |
| Belarus | – | – | – |
| Belgium | 7.53968 | – | – |
| Brazil | – | – | – |
| Bulgaria | 9.65131 | – | – |
| Canada | – | – | – |
| Chile | 7.47801 | – | – |
| China | – | – | 3.94561 |
| China, Hong Kong Special Administrative Region | – | – | – |
| Colombia | 54.30346 | – | – |
| Costa Rica | – | – | – |
| Croatia | 7.39130 | – | – |
| Cuba | – | – | – |
| Cyprus | 33.49057 | – | – |
| Czech Republic | – | – | – |
| Denmark | – | – | – |
| Ecuador | – | – | – |
| Egypt | – | – | 9.43972 |
| El Salvador | 10.27732 | – | – |
| Estonia | 2.74170 | – | – |
| Ethiopia | – | – | 6.58017 |
| Finland | 4.41658 | – | – |
| France | – | – | – |
| Germany | 7.35115 | – | – |
| Ghana | – | – | – |
| Greece | 7.81910 | – | – |
| Hungary | 12.8858 | – | – |
| Iceland | – | – | – |
| India | – | – | – |
| Indonesia | – | – | – |
| Ireland | – | – | – |
| Israel | 6.78377 | – | – |
| Italy | 2.81660 | – | – |
| Japan | – | – | – |
| Kazakhstan | – | – | 8.95141 |
| Kenya | – | – | 16.42857 |
| Latvia | – | – | – |
| Lithuania | 8.67347 | – | – |
| Luxembourg | 8.00000 | – | – |

(continued)

**Table 2** (continued)

| Country | 2012 | 2013 | 2014 |
|---|---|---|---|
| Malaysia | – | – | 12.57996 |
| Malta | 9.61538 | – | – |
| Mexico | – | – | – |
| Morocco | – | – | – |
| Netherlands | 4.00000 | – | – |
| New Zealand | – | 48.31358 | – |
| Nigeria | – | – | – |
| Norway | 11.25581 | – | – |
| Panama | – | 2.17391 | – |
| Philippines | – | – | – |
| Poland | 8.95342 | – | – |
| Portugal | 7.31523 | – | – |
| Republic of Korea | – | 3.24764 | – |
| Romania | 23.14991 | – | – |
| Russian Federation | – | 14.58647 | – |
| Serbia | 7.58405 | – | – |
| Slovakia | 9.10426 | – | – |
| Slovenia | – | – | – |
| South Africa | – | – | – |
| Spain | 4.66288 | – | – |
| Sweden | – | – | – |
| The former Yugoslav Republic of Macedonia | 15.51313 | – | – |
| Turkey | 7.63389 | – | – |
| Uganda | – | – | – |
| Ukraine | 9.06555 | – | – |
| United Kingdom of Great Britain and Northern Ireland | – | – | – |
| United Republic of Tanzania | – | – | – |
| United States of America | – | – | – |
| Uruguay | 17.58794 | – | – |

Source: United Nations Educational, Scientific and Cultural Organization (UNESCO, 2015), http://uis.unesco.org/sites/default/files/documents/unesco-science-report-towards-2030-part1.pdf

## References

Terleckyj, N. E. (1974). *Effects of R&D on the productivity growth of industries: An exploratory study*. National Planning Association.

United Nations Educational, Scientific and Cultural Organization (UNESCO). (2015). *UNESCO Science Report: Towards 2030*. United Nations Educational, Scientific and Cultural Organization.

**Albert N. Link** is the Virginia Batte Phillips Distinguished Professor at the University of North Carolina at Greensboro. His research focuses on entrepreneurship, technology transfer, program evaluation, and technology and innovation policy. He is also the Editor-in-Chief of the *Journal of Technology Transfer*, co-Editor of *Foundations and Trends in Entrepreneurship*, and Editor of *Annals of Science and Technology Policy*.

# Part IV
# Acting Under Uncertainty: Personal Perspectives from Sweden, Egypt and Germany

# My Experiences of the COVID-19 Pandemic So Far

**Charlie Karlsson**

**Abstract** In this essay, I share my personal and my family's experiences of living in the middle of a pandemic in Sweden. Interestingly, due to severe health problems in the family, the pandemic for half a year was a non-issue. As a background for my essay, I present information about the diffusion of the coronavirus in Sweden during the three first waves and about the special Swedish strategy to combat the virus. The Swedish strategy was criticized heavily abroad by politicians and media despite that there before the large outbreak of the pandemic in Europe had been a widespread agreement among the state epidemiologists in the EU to follow a strategy to combat the pandemic of the kind Sweden adopted. I also highlight how public policy authority is divided between the government, the central governmental agencies, the regions and the municipalities, which all according to the Swedish constitution have an independent standing and each have their own areas of responsibility. This explains why the governmental agency the Public Health Agency took the lead in the anti-COVID measures in Sweden and not the Swedish government. At the end, I also present my own preliminary personal evaluation of the way the Swedish authorities dealt with the pandemic.

**Keywords** COVID-19 · Pandemic · Sweden · Public policy · Government · Central governmental agencies · Regions · Municipalities · Strategy · Evaluation

**JEL Codes** HI 1 · H12 · 118

When information about the diffusion of a new virus was spread, the experts at the Swedish Public Health Agency, responsible for communicable disease prevention and control in Sweden, declared that it was unlikely that the virus would diffuse outside China. They believed that the Chinese authorities would succeed in containing the virus within China. So, there was no major corona hype early on in

C. Karlsson (✉)
Jönköping International Business School, Jönköping, Sweden
e-mail: Charlie.Karlsson@ju.se



D. B. Audretsch, I. A. M. Kunadt (eds.), *The COVID-19 Crisis and Entrepreneurship*, International Studies in Entrepreneurship 54,
https://doi.org/10.1007/978-3-031-04655-1_11

Sweden. The first case of COVID-19 in Sweden was detected on January 31, 2020. It was a young woman, who had visited Wuhan in China, but on return had self-isolated and managed to avoid spreading the virus to any other person in Sweden. The next day, the Swedish Public Health Agency declared the coronavirus to be a dangerous disease constituting a public danger, but they considered the risk of a general diffusion of the coronavirus, i.e. the virus SARS-CoV-2, in Sweden to be low and did not take any further measures. Actually, most countries postponed taking any measures. Both COBRA, which is the British Governments' Civil Contingencies Committee, and the German Robert Koch Institute made the judgement that the danger of a diffusion was low.

In a radio programme in the summer 2020, Anders Tegnell, the state epidemiologist of Sweden, claimed that, before the large outbreak of the pandemic in Europe, there had been widespread agreement among the state epidemiologists in the EU countries to follow a strategy to combat the pandemic of the kind that Sweden later adopted, but when the crisis developed, the agreement was abandoned, mainly due to forceful interventions by politicians. It is worth stressing that the general opinion among state epidemiologists in the EU was that a strategy similar to the Swedish model should be used to deal with the pandemic.

The aim of this essay is to share my experiences of living in the middle of a pandemic in Sweden against the background of the diffusion of the coronavirus and the measures taken by the Swedish authorities to combat the pandemic. At the end, I also present my personal evaluation of the way the Swedish authorities dealt with the pandemic.

## 1 From Business as Usual to a Family Crisis

In February, life in Sweden continued very much as before. The second case of COVID-19 was confirmed on February 26. Like so many other Swedes in the winter time, my wife and I travelled to Tenerife on February 9 for a 2-week holiday. Corona was not a major issue on Tenerife, since no cases had been detected there. The most dramatic thing that happened on Tenerife was that my wife became very tired after 10 days. We returned to Sweden on February 23. The next day, I flew to Paris for a meeting. During the meeting, our hosts told us about the first cases of COVID-19 in Paris. I returned to Sweden on February 26. My wife was still very tired and later that week I took her to our health centre to meet a general practitioner who referred her to the medical lab for test taking.

We now started to adapt to the general recommendations from the Public Health Agency advising people to keep physical distance to people outside their own household, to wash their hands carefully and to stay at home if they had the slightest symptoms. Interestingly, no recommendations to wear masks in public spaces were issued. The Public Health Agency was firm in its standpoint that no scientific evidence existed that the use of masks among the general public would have any effect on the spread of the virus. Later some health experts in Sweden questioned this position, but the Public Health Agency was persistent in its view. No special recommendations for our age group 70+ had been issued yet.

And now the proverbial bomb exploded putting corona in the background for my family. When my wife met her regular general practitioner, she was told that her test values were very, very bad. She had to go through several examinations but without results. She was told that the test results could indicate cancer in the kidneys or in the skeleton. Great shock, of course, but in August her test values were again normal. The doctors guessed that she had had some virus although not COVID-19. Certainly, this was a very special period. The pandemic and the risks of infection were totally in the background of our minds. Exclusively and excessively, our focus was on my wife's health, and at the same time, we also got more and more isolated from our friends. Fortunately, we had our four children and their families who gave a fantastic support during the crisis months.

## 2 The Diffusion of the Coronavirus in Sweden Takes Off and the Authorities React

Meanwhile the corona situation in Sweden had changed. The second known COVID-19 case in Sweden was confirmed on February 26. The same day, the National Board for Health and Welfare, which is the national agency overseeing the fields of social services, health and medical services, patient safety and epidemiology for which the regions and the municipalities have the operational responsibility, went into a state of alert. It was assessed that Sweden was not at all prepared for a larger pandemic, since the country had a very severe lack of protective equipment in both health care and elderly care. As a result, the agency was instructed by the government to procure and distribute such equipment.

On March 2, the Public Health Agency changed its view on the risk of a community transmission of the coronavirus in Sweden from low to medium even while judging the risk of importing infected cases to be high. Four days later, it was reported that the number of COVID-19 cases in Sweden was increasing rapidly. Initially (March 6), the focus was on people coming back infected with COVID-19 from a winter holiday in the Alps as they were seen as the drivers of COVID-19 spread. Interestingly, many of these winter holiday resorts were located in the regions with the first large outbreaks of COVID-19 in Europe. However, later it was also found out that people infected with COVID-19 had come back from many other countries including the USA, the UK, France, the Netherlands, Iran and China, after the winter holiday period from mid-February to mid-March during which schools in Sweden close for 1 week, varyingly depending upon region. More than one million Swedes, i.e. 10% of the total population, were abroad during these 4 weeks. In total, this implies that Sweden got a very substantial inflow of infected people, and this contributed to increasing the diffusion of the coronavirus in Sweden.

Thus, the winter holidays functioned as an amplifying event, i.e. an occurrence that brought the transmission of the infection to a higher level.

During the first half of March, there was a substantial increase in the level of activity in Sweden for the purpose of reducing the speed of transmission, defining risk groups and reorganizing the health-care system to secure capacity to take care of and treat patients with COVID-19. New decisions and recommendations guided by the Public Health Agency's pandemic plan from 2019 came in quick succession and were updated more or less daily. Pandemics are a rare phenomenon and COVID-19 was a new little-known virus, which implies that the authorities worked under a state of uncertainty and lack of information due to limited knowledge about how the COVID-19 virus spread and how it should be controlled.

On March 10, the Swedish foreign ministry recommended people to avoid all unnecessary trips to Italy. The same day, the Public Health Agency increased the risk level for transmission of the coronavirus in Sweden to very high and limited the maximum attendance of gatherings to 500 people. The next day, the World Health Organization (WHO) presented its assessment that COVID-19 could be characterized as a pandemic, and the same day, the first death in Sweden of a person infected with COVID-19 was reported. The number of infected had now increased substantially, but the exact number is unknown, since the severe lack of test equipment did not allow for a broad testing. A few weeks later, the number of COVID-19 patients in intensive care and the number of diseased people with COVID-19 showed a similar increase.

On March 11, the Swedish government decided that sick people would get sickness benefit from the first day of illness so that no one should go to work if they had the slightest infection symptoms. Employers were recommended not only to let but also to recommend employees to work from home when possible. On March 12, the Swedish stock market dropped by 11.1%. The same day, the Public Health Agency announced a new strategy to hinder the spread of the virus from becoming too intense. The diffusion curve should be "flattened out" in order to avoid a collapse of the health-care sector. Two days later, the foreign ministry recommended people not to travel abroad unless it was a necessary trip. The main argument was not the risk that travellers might be infected but that travellers risked getting stuck abroad when other countries closed down. Sweden kept its borders open unlike countries like Denmark, Norway and Finland, which closed their borders for people travelling from Sweden. Travel within Sweden was free but in the spring people were recommended to avoid unnecessary trips longer than 2 hours. In the middle of March, based upon advice from the Public Health Agency, the regional bodies responsible for health care in Sweden changed their strategy and stopped general testing and tracking of people that had been in contact with infected people, since the capacity ceiling had been reached.

On March 16, the Public Health Agency recommended people over 70 to stay at home and not even to go out to buy food. The next day, universities and upper secondary schools were recommended to switch to online teaching. The same day, the Swedish government issued an ordinance banning people from outside the EES area and Switzerland to enter Sweden except under certain circumstances. On March

19, the government decided that elementary schools (years 1–9) and nursery schools may close if hit by a virus outbreak, but should under normal circumstances stay open. Five days later, the national government decided that all guests in restaurants, bars and cafés must be served sitting at the table. From March 27, all gatherings of more than 50 people were forbidden. The same day, the Public Health Agency announced that people 70+ could have social activities and contacts outdoors, keeping physical distance. On March 31, the government prohibited all visits to care homes for elderly people starting April 1.[1] In a Swedish context, this is a very harsh intervention, since people living in care homes have every right to receive visitors. Then, on April 4, the government presented a temporary law making it possible for the government to take more rapid decisions to combat the diffusion of the virus during a 3-month period. The parliament later adopted the law, but it was never used.

On April 6, the government, consisting of social democrats and the green party, presented its strategy in response to the COVID-19 pandemic. Interestingly, the government did not formally take a decision on the strategy. The government stated that its efforts and decisions should aim to (i) limit the spread of infection in the country, (ii) ensure that health and medical care resources are available, (iii) limit the impact on critical services, (iv) alleviate the impact on people and businesses,[2] (v) ease concern and (vi) implement the right measures at the right time. This strategy is, in essence, a copy of the strategy of the Public Health Agency, and it is important to observe that, in principle, it says that Sweden should keep key parts of its society open and the economy up-and-running in the face of the COVID-19 pandemic. Indirectly, the strategy recognizes that lockdowns can pose broader threats to the individual and civil liberties, and it was developed in light of the basic fact that lockdowns are difficult, if not impossible, to sustain in democracies. The basic idea is to put trust in the general public or at least a substantial majority of the people to do the right thing and to avoid rules that are all too onerous for people.

It is important to stress that this strategy was implemented and operative also during the second and third wave. For example, restaurants, shops and shopping malls stayed open, subject to recommendations about social and physical distancing. Also, nursery schools and elementary schools remained open in order to provide children with a modicum of normalcy and enable parents and in particular staff in health care and long-term care and other frontline occupations to go to work.

Interestingly, all parliamentary parties stood united behind the government's strategy and very little critique was voiced. It was not until later in the year that some criticism was launched which however did not concern the strategy as such but rather focused on specific aspects of the strategy. Opposition parties started to raise

[1] It is questionable whether this restriction is in line with the Swedish constitution, which guarantees people in Sweden a number of rights (see next section). It is highly doubtful that the government had the legal right to stop people from receiving visitors in their own home.

[2] From March 16 onwards, the government took many measures to support companies hit by the coronavirus and their employees.

demands that the testing capacity and the ability to track potentially infected people should increase, but testing and tracking was not part of the Swedish strategy.

What is important to note here is that the Public Health Agency has full autonomy when deciding on measures to reduce the spread of the virus. This contrasts with other countries, where governments have taken such decisions based upon advice from their own expert authorities on contagious diseases or in some cases against their advice. This special Swedish approach to public policy is the subject of the next section.

## 3 The Special Swedish Approach to Combat Virus Diffusion

The Swedish approach to deal with the pandemic has received a great deal of attention abroad. Many people have got the impression that Sweden in principle has done very little or even nothing to reduce the spread of infection in the absence of formal lockdowns. A strategy based on advice and recommendations may sound vague, but in practice, many different measures were applied by the Public Health Agency and several regulatory decisions were taken by the Swedish government, and these interventions have had very substantial effects on people's life and habits even if there were no formal sanctions for those who failed to follow the recommendations. However, to understand how public policy is decided, executed and limited in Sweden, one must understand how responsibility for public policy is divided in Sweden as well as understand the basic principles of the Swedish constitution and the Swedish Communicable Diseases Act. Central governmental agencies, such as the Public Health Agency, have an independent standing in Swedish public policy and have full decision power on individual issues within their respective areas of responsibility and the limits of applicable laws, as well as their yearly budget and yearly instruction from the government.

At the same time, the regional authorities, which among other things are responsible for health care, and the municipalities, which among other things are responsible for long-term care, have directly elected council, which implies that they also are independent in their decisions in relation to the government. The national government and its individual ministers are not allowed to interfere in the daily business and decisions of central agencies, regions and municipalities. This organization of public governance is assumed to be able to handle every policy problem in peacetime in Sweden, even if there is a crisis such as a pandemic. Thus, every public agency keeps its responsibilities in all situations according to the so-called responsibility principle. This principle is associated with the so-called proximity principle that states that crises should be handled at the lowest possible level.

Quite naturally, it has been a matter of debate if a public governance organization like this really is suitable to deal with a crisis, like a pandemic. Each of the 21 regions is, for example, responsible for procuring their own equipment for personal protection, but due to their small size, they have very little bargaining power in the international market for protection equipment. It has also been discussed if all the 290 municipalities, where the median municipality has around 15,000 inhabitants, have the necessary competence to plan for and to act under a pandemic. Thus, this is not a command system but a very intricate negotiation system, in which public policy is made through agreements between the national government and the national association of regional authorities and municipalities. During the pandemic, these negotiations often took place under substantial time pressure, and several times there were disagreements afterwards about what actually had been agreed. Interestingly, these agreements are not legally binding.

The Public Health Agency is the expert public authority for protection against infectious diseases in Sweden. The Agency is responsible for the coordination of the protection against infectious diseases at the national level and shall on its own initiative take measures necessary to uphold effective protection against infectious diseases. The Public Health Agency shall, according to its instruction from the government, also survey the diffusion of contagious diseases in Sweden and develop plans and take initiative to control measures. However, this authority is restricted to the areas that concern the diffusion of a contagious disease, while the central government is responsible for other considerations, including, for example, economic measures. Thus, the Swedish public policy system differs substantially from that in other countries including our Nordic neighbours.

The applicable protection measures are limited by the statues in the Swedish constitution. The Instrument of Government, which is one part of the Swedish constitution, guarantees people in Sweden in peacetime, among other things, freedom (i) to organize and participate in all kinds of meetings, (ii) to organize and participate in demonstrations and (iii) to travel around in the country. However, the Public Order Act gives the authorities the right, under certain restricted circumstances, to regulate how people can exercise these liberties, but rules in the constitution preclude, among other things, formal lockdowns, the compulsory isolation of people and curfews. Within the limits of the Public Order Act, the Instrument of Government gives the government the right to limit the freedom to meet and to demonstrate to counteract an epidemic. Still, the Swedish public policy system does not give the Swedish government the right to apply many of the harsh policy measures to combat the corona pandemic enforced in many other countries including the other Nordic countries.

Instead of compulsory measures that would curtail constitutional rights, the Swedish Communicable Diseases Act, which is applicable also in the case of a pandemic, rests in principle on the idea of trust in the population's willingness to assume individual responsibility and heed advice and recommendations concerning behaviour and the gradual introduction of recommendations and restrictions. This trust-based approach relies on people listening to the public health experts and voluntarily complying with the recommendations, since the recommendations are just that and there is no legal sanctions for people who fail to follow them. It can be described as a nudging approach, where the authorities remind people of the recommendations and where recommendations are adjusted when the authorities consider it motivated.

An important component of this trust-based strategy was the daily press conferences broadcasted on weekdays (and later 2 days a week) in one public and one private TV channel, where the Public Health Agency, the National Board for Health and Welfare and the Swedish Civil Contingencies Agency presented the latest development of the pandemic in terms of the number infected, the number infected in hospital care and intensive care, the number of diseased infected with COVID-19, new recommendations and so on. After the presentations, journalists from both Swedish and foreign media were invited to ask questions to the presenters. The information from the press conferences was then presented in both printed and digital media, which means that the general public was continuously informed about both the development of the pandemic and changes in the recommendations. The government also held many press conferences broadcast in the media not least to present and justify new restrictions to combat the transmission of the virus.

The effect of this institutional and legal background is that the Public Health Agency and the government introduced recommendations and restrictions to reduce the diffusion of the coronavirus gradually instead of everything at one point in time. Rather, the authorities changed the recommendations and restrictions when the diffusion situation changed.[3] The use of recommendations is possible in Sweden, since the Swedish population has a very high trust in the government and its agencies. To preserve the high trust among the Swedish population in Sweden's corona strategy, very substantial efforts were made to inform the population and to explain the authorities' measures and recommendations. The experiences during the pandemic show that a majority of the Swedes did follow the recommendations from the Public Health Agency. Analyses of the position of mobile phones showed a very substantial drop in the spatial mobility of people in Sweden after the recommendations to refrain from travelling had been issued, but other time there were signs that some people had become tired of following the recommendations and the restrictions.

One reason for this policy approach or strategy was the belief that this was the only policy approach that would be sustainable over time, since it was very uncertain for how long the pandemic would last. A second rationale was that the strategy would influence not only the number of COVID-19 cases and deaths but also the country's general health situation and the economy including the public health effects of a declining economy. This broad view behind the strategy was probably a result of instruction from the national government that the Public Health Agency should focus not only on communicable diseases (as similar agencies in many other countries do) but also on the population's general health. Furthermore, it was feared

[3] Critics have argued that the authorities in Sweden were at bit slow in introducing recommendations and restrictions compared to other countries, where the politicians took the lead and that speed is more important in dealing with contagion rather than taking exactly the right measures. Others have argued that rapidly changing and regionally different recommendations are difficult to communicate and to understand.

that the negative effects of other policy approaches might surpass the positive effects in the long run if the authorities acted too quickly and that the motivation among the population to follow the recommendations might decrease over time and during later waves of virus diffusion.

Interestingly, this Swedish strategy was misunderstood abroad and among some critics in Sweden. The strategy was interpreted as having herd immunity as its goal, but there was never any decision taken that heard immunity should be the goal of the strategy. What was discussed and communicated among experts was that, in the absence of a vaccine, herd immunity would be the result when enough people had been infected. Extremely few experts believed in February and March 2020 that a vaccine would become available in time to have any effect on the pandemic. Quite a few experts on virology, immunology and epidemiology in Sweden criticized the Swedish strategy on other grounds and argued that Sweden should practice a type of lockdown that included closing schools. Despite their scientific background, they had very little influence on the Swedish strategy.

What should be noted here is that the Public Health Agency, given its responsibility for the health of the population, assumed that a closure of nursery and junior schools would lead to a substantial loss of health and wellbeing and a loss of learning among children and not least among children in exposed and vulnerable areas and families. The agency was also afraid that a closure of nursery and junior schools could lead to problems with the supply of personnel in the health-care sector and in elderly care. These sectors are highly dependent on women working full-time, while their children are in junior and/or nursery schools. And due to the much higher risks of severe illness and death among older people, it was considered impossible to rely on grandparents to take over the care of children of women working in the care sectors. Furthermore, in reality, many families live far away from grandparents.

Naturally, the open Swedish model to combat the pandemic has been questioned by politicians and researchers both inside and outside Sweden, while others have seen it as a model for other countries.

## 4 A Radical Change in Our Way of Life

The increase in the spread of the virus and thus in the risk of becoming infected radically changed our way of life, since we both belong to the risk group 70+. No more meetings with children, grandchildren and friends in-house. No more eating out, no more shopping and no more visits to the opera, the concert hall and the theatres (subscription tickets and prepaid tickets were repaid). Rather, we substantially had to increase home cooking. To get a variation in our home menu and avoid getting stuck with the dishes we normally cook, we searched for inspiration for new dishes in the morning TV cooking programmes, in TV cooking competitions, on the Internet and in our cook books.

All at once, it was no longer a major advantage to live in the central parts of the city of Gothenburg with an 8-minute walk to the concert hall, the arts museum and the city theatre, a 20-minute walk to the city centre, a 25-minute walk to the opera house and plenty of good restaurants within walking distance. And no advantage at all to have the stop for two tram lines and two major bus lines within 70 metres, since the age group was recommended not to use public transport because of the infection risk.

We had to learn new behaviours on our city strolls. Abruptly, it was now very important not to come too close to other people including family and friends. We changed the way we walked. If we met people on the pavement, we automatically started to walk in a curve so that we would not come too close to the people we met. During the rare visits in shops, we started to ask people to move if they came too close. Some people apologized, but some people became angry and said that the distance was sufficient, or they were just angry because we asked them to move. The Public Health Agency's recommended distance to keep outdoors as well as indoors was 2 metres.

We tried to order food for home delivery but the increased demand for home delivery went far beyond the capacity of the food stores. As a result, many of the ordered products were not delivered at all or replaced. Instead, we asked our three children living in the Gothenburg region to do the food shopping for us and that worked very well. Later, we started to pre-order food to be picked up outside the store, which worked fairly well.

We now started to meet our children and grandchildren as well as friends outdoors. Fortunately in this situation, most of our children and grandchildren live in the Gothenburg region, and meeting them became one of the few highlights in our social isolation. To keep ourselves active and busy, we started to explore the geography in the Gothenburg region including islands in the Gothenburg archipelago which we could visit by car. We went hiking in many places, most of which we had never visited before. At lunchtime, we had coffee and sandwiches which we had brought with us in a rucksack. On our hikes, we met many senior people doing the same as us. Some places became favourite places to which we returned several times. However, we had problems during weekends, since some places became overcrowded and it was difficult to keep physical distance, since many more Swedes turned to outdoor activities. Thus, we had to travel further and further away from the city centre to find places that were not crowded.

During this period, it became a ritual of our daily life to follow the press conferences weekdays at 2 pm, when representatives of the Public Health Agency, the National Board for Health and Welfare and the Swedish Civil Contingencies Agency reported on (i) the spread of the coronavirus globally and in Europe, Sweden, Swedish regions and Swedish institutions for care of elderly, (ii) the number of people in Sweden with COVID-19 in hospital care and in intensive care, (iii) the number of diseased people with a documented COVID-19 infection, (iv) the total number of fully equipped beds for intensive care, (v) the situation concerning protection equipment (that often was critical due to failing deliveries from abroad and (vi) the situation within critical areas (i.e. areas affected when personnel became infected with COVID-19), such as food and water, ambulance transports, police, fire protection and so on. The press conferences were broadcast on

TV and radio. Mostly, we followed them on TV, sometimes using a mobile phone sitting on the rocks on an island in the archipelago of Gothenburg.

On July 4, I had planned to celebrate my 75th birthday with our four children and their spouses and our 11 grandchildren. Already, in July 2019, I had booked a hotel in Timmendorfer Strand in Northern Germany just outside Lübeck and a birthday dinner at 1-star Michelin restaurant for us all, but this was given the corona situation impossible to carry through. All reservations were cancelled. Instead, on my birthday, my wife and I checked in at a hotel on the coast 1-hour drive south of Gothenburg. It was a rainy day, and when we entered the reception area of the hotel, we were shocked to see it was so crowded. The reception area also functioned as a bar. We expected to be infected but luckily, we escaped this fate. Since it rained, we stayed mostly in our room, but in the evening, we had an excellent birthday dinner in the restaurant, where there was plenty of space for keeping physical distance to the other guests.

A few days later, I celebrated my birthday with my wife and our four children sitting outdoors at separate tables in the backyard of our cooperative apartment building in Gothenburg. Even if our grandchildren and our children's partners were missing, this became a fantastic birthday celebration, not least since we seldom have the opportunity to spend quality time with our four grown-up children, one of whom lives in Germany. They brought two presents: a DNA test kit to help me in my genealogical research and a framed, newly taken photo of them together under a tree, which I now enjoy looking at on the kitchen wall every day.

All summer, we continued going on hikes. We spent some time in our summer house but as soon as some of our grandchildren came to stay there, we went back to Gothenburg, since we could not live indoors in the summer house together with them because of the infection risk. Even if we had to give up many of our normal activities, the pandemic induced us to adopt a much more active lifestyle spending much more time outdoors. We substantially improved our physical fitness and learned a lot about the geography of the Gothenburg region which would not have happened without the pandemic. It became a sport to find new nice and beautiful places where we could walk.

Originally, I was scheduled for a hip replacement late in April, but due to the high infection level in the spring, I contacted the hospital in question and asked them to postpone it until June due to the high spread of the coronavirus. Later, I postponed it till late August. During the summer, the diffusion speed of the coronavirus in Sweden slowed down very substantially, and I decided that the risk level was now so low that a stay in a hospital was acceptable. Then, in late August, I had my right hip replaced at the privately owned Carlanderska hospital in Gothenburg. The surgery went well and then followed 2 months of rehabilitation with physiotherapy and finally we could take up hiking again even if the days now in the autumn were becoming shorter and darker.

## 5 The Second Wave in the Autumn

After the summer, the speed of the coronavirus diffusion started to increase but only slightly. The Swedish government now started a process to mitigate the recommendations and restrictions, but it rapidly came to a stop when the diffusion speed of the coronavirus increased considerably. For a long time, representatives of the cultural sector and the sports sector had been lobbying intensively for mitigating the restrictions which limited the number of people allowed to follow culture and sports events live to 50. From November 1, the government made gatherings of up to 300 people possible, if they were seated with a certain minimum distance. At the same time, the number of people in public dances was limited to 50. However, the attempts to mitigate the recommendations and restrictions abruptly came to an end when Sweden got a second infection wave with a rapid increase in the number of infected.[4] Already on November 24, participation in gatherings was limited to eight people. The serving of alcohol at restaurants and bars after 10 pm was forbidden by the government on November 20, and from December 24, alcohol was not allowed to be served after 8 pm. It is noteworthy that care homes for the elderly were now opened for visits, since the cost of forbidding visits was considered higher for the elderly and their relatives than the risk that visits would lead to elderly people being infected.

From December 14, the Public Health Agency introduced more stringent national regulations and general guidelines regarding everybody's responsibility in preventing the spread of COVID-19. Senior high schools now had to switch to distance education. At first it was said that distance education should stop at the end of January, but later distance education was prolonged until the end of April. Among other things, a recommendation was now issued to wear a face mask when travelling with public transport in rush hours, where a seat reservation is not offered.[5] In December, the national government started to go against the recommendations of the Public Health Agency to demonstrate "the ability to act" that many Swedes had started demand, despite the objections from the Public Health Agency.

A temporary pandemic law was introduced on January 10, 2021. It was at least partly a result of the demands from the political opposition for an increased use of close downs to reduce the spread of COVID-19. The law applies the provisions of the Instrument of Government giving the national government and the authorities options to introduce legally binding restrictions for both activities and places to reduce the diffusion of the coronavirus. For instance, the law makes it possible to limit the number of people gathering outdoors in parks and beaches, and to close

---

[4]The decision by the national government to lessen the restrictions was in hindsight a very unwise decision and might have contributed to a more severe second wave than necessary.

[5]The value of using face mask has been hotly debated in Sweden. Critics have claimed that the ad hoc and "sometimes" advice for face mask usage meant that Sweden did not establish "peer norms" for usage, implying weak adherence. Their argument that the use of face masks helps others more than yourself and that a more strict usage of a non-obtrusive, non-costly intervention like face masks would have been wise.

shopping centres, gyms, restaurants, bars and cafés. The law is valid until September 30, 2021. Interestingly, the background material to the pandemic law does not present any evidence that the measures made legal are effective or any analysis of their health, social, economic and democratic costs.

## 6 COVID-19 in the Family and Christmas Celebrations Outdoors

A week before Christmas, our elder daughter phoned us to say that she, her husband, son and younger daughter had got COVID-19. They tried to get tested but it was impossible, since so many people tried to get a test in the Gothenburg region. Fortunately, none of them were severely affected and they quickly recovered. Later, they tested for antibodies and the tests confirmed that they had had COVID-19.

That our elder daughter and her family were infected with COVID-19 partly changed our Christmas plans. Instead of the planned forest meeting with the three of our children and their families who live in the Gothenburg region to grill sausages and hand out Christmas presents, we met with two of them and their families in our younger daughter's garden just outside Gothenburg and grilled sausages on her terrace. Then my wife and I left that day, but instead of driving home, we drove away to a parking lot and redressed as Santa Claus and his wife. Soon, we walked along a path towards our daughter's house in our costumes and with the Christmas presents in sacks. When the children saw us, they became wild and wanted us to come directly to the terrace, where the sacks were distributed—one for each family. This was really a fundamentally different Christmas experience that neither we nor our children and grandchildren will ever forget.

That day, we could see many open fires and lit grilles at houses in the garden suburb. After Christmas, we learnt that other relatives and friends had celebrated Christmas in a similar manner. During the winter, it more or less became a habit to meet our children and grandchildren outdoors and grill sausages over open fire often in some recreation area around Gothenburg.

## 7 More Changes in Our Behaviour

The Christmas presents bring us to our shopping behaviour. Since long, we have booked trips, hotels, restaurants and tickets for cultural events on the Internet, but we have mainly shopped in local stores. Ever since the early 2020, very little shopping has been done at all, but in the autumn, my wife started to shop food once a week early in the morning when there were few customers in the food store. However, for the purchase of Christmas presents, we used the Internet, and since then we have bought a few pieces of clothes and a few other things on the Internet. The prices were very competitive, and the deliveries were just-in-time.

Looking back to the end of February 2020, it is interesting to note that we did not once used public transport in Gothenburg even though we were allowed free travel on weekdays except in rush hours and all weekends, since we were over 65 years old. On the other hand, we used our car to an extent we never anticipated, when moving to Gothenburg in May 2011.

A new experience for us during the corona times was that all meetings took place via Zoom or Google Teams as well as our communication with children and grandchildren. Generally speaking, platforms work but digital board meetings and brainstorming sessions are clearly inferior to face-to-face meetings and make discussions less lively and spontaneous and the level of creativity is clearly lower.

In March 2021, I was hit by periostitis, probably the result of a too long and too ambitious walk. This put a hold on our corona walks, so my wife had to go alone for some time, while I rested my left leg. COVID-19 was detected at the nursery school of one of my grandchildren, and when he became sick and later more people in his family, it was feared that they also were infected but fortunately the tests were negative.

## 8 A Third Wave

Early in 2021, the rate of virus spread in Sweden started to decline but not at all to the levels experienced in the summer 2020. After mid-February, the diffusion rate increased again, and Sweden experienced a third wave. Already late in January, the Swedish government decided that citizens in Norway, Denmark and the UK were not allowed to enter Sweden. Due to the harsh restrictions in Denmark and Norway, it was feared that Danes and Norwegians would travel to Sweden to shop and eat in restaurants, which was a very common weekend activity for them before the pandemic. This was an attempt to make it more difficult for the so-called British mutation of the coronavirus to spread in Sweden. From February 6, citizens in other countries were only allowed to enter Sweden if they had a negative corona test not older than 48 hours. On March 2, the Public Health Agency issued a warning for a third wave if people in Sweden failed to follow the recommendations. On March 31, extended restrictions for foreign citizens aged 18 and above who wanted to enter Sweden were announced, requiring everyone to present a negative COVID-19 test that could at most be 48 hours old. Foreign citizens from a non-EEA country, including the UK, were only allowed to enter on certain exemptions. New rules were introduced for all people entering Sweden (including Swedish citizens) born 2013 and earlier. They were required to get tested on day 5 following the arrival, and they should self-quarantine and avoid close contact with other people for 7 days.

Meanwhile, vaccinations against COVID-19 had started but not at the expected speed, since Sweden, as all the member states in the EU, only got one third of the expected number of doses for the first quarter of 2021. Priority was given to people in elderly care homes and with home care services and personnel caring for them and health-care personnel dealing with COVID-19 patients. My mother who is 97 years old had her vaccination completed in February. There seemed to be a very rapid effect since there was a clear reduction in the number of diseased people infected with COVID-19 in elderly care homes very soon and also, but to a lower extent, among people with home care services for whom vaccination lagged compared to vaccinations in the care homes. However, it took a longer time before the number of people treated for COVID-19 in hospitals including intensive care started to fall.

For people in vaccination priority group 2, i.e. people 65+, the wait was long. This delay was extended several times as the vaccine producers failed to deliver as promised because of production problems. The real blow came when AstraZeneca announced that it would reduce its deliveries to the EU, and thus Sweden, to two thirds due the vaccine export bans in the US, the UK and India. When the use of the AstraZeneca vaccine was stopped in Sweden (like in many other countries) in mid-March on the grounds of a very small number of suspected serious secondary effects of the vaccine, many people 65+ became worried, including my wife and me, that they would have to wait even longer to be vaccinated, while others were relieved since they would prefer a different vaccine. Soon the Swedish Public Health Agency decided that the AstraZeneca vaccine could be used only for people 65+.

The restrictions from January 20 were prolonged several times during the spring 2021. It was not until May 11 that the national government took a decision that some of these restrictions should be lifted from June 1. At the same time, the Public Health Agency presented a plan with three steps for how restrictions and recommendations should be lifted and how everyday life for Swedes could return to normal from the summer 2021. On May 27, after the COVID-19 incidence had fallen for many weeks, the national government presented a five-step plan for abandoning the COVID-19 restrictions starting with the first step on June 1.

## 9 Life During the Third Wave

On March 26, I had an appointment with my general practitioner for my yearly check-up. I asked him how the vaccinations were going, and he told me that they were currently vaccinating people born in 1939. On April 6, when we were staying in our summer house in the province of Småland in Southern Sweden, I called the local health centre and asked if we could get our vaccination there and we directly got an appointment there on April 9. On April 7, my wife had an appointment at our local health-care centre in Gothenburg and when she asked, they were still vaccinating people born in 1939. On April 9, we both got our first AstraZeneca shots at the local health centre in Småland, and none of us experienced any side effects. In the afternoon of April 10, we both got text messages from our local health centre in Gothenburg that we were welcome on April 13 to get our first AstraZeneca shots! We still fail to understand how the vaccine logistics work in Gothenburg. The distribution of vaccines was very uneven between the different local health centres and not related to the number of people 65+ listed at each centre. It should be added that according to the Swedish health-care act, people are free to use health care wherever they want in Sweden. It needs to be said that in some regions the vaccination process was much smoother and faster.

However, the need to comply with the recommendations and restrictions was repeatedly stressed. Planning for the future was difficult not knowing when vaccination would be offered or what recommendations and restrictions would prevail for the rest of the year and the coming year, not least regarding travel. A since long planned and booked golden wedding celebration in April at a SPA hotel in Southern Sweden with our children, their partners and our grandchildren had to be cancelled because of all uncertainty about vaccinations and the level of virus spread. In February, our older son and his family moved from Germany to live in Gothenburg for half a year, which gave us further opportunities for social contacts with them outdoors. It was a new experience to celebrate the birthdays of grandchildren outdoors when it had snowed.

For our golden wedding, we instead rented five cottages at a resort on the coast north of Gothenburg. We celebrated our golden wedding anniversary late in April with cake and champagne outdoors in the wind at a temperature of 9 degrees Celsius and then later in the afternoon with sausage barbeques outdoors close to the sea to reduce the infection risk if someone was infected with COVID-19. So, the golden wedding dinner was replaced by grilled sausages! Altogether, this became a very memorable event for my wife and me and certainly much more memorable than a formal dinner at a SPA hotel. The day after, we visited the rock carvings in Tanum World Heritage site (https://www.vitlyckemuseum.se/en/).

On May 9, we had Sunday dinner at a restaurant with some of our friends in the Värmland Guild. It was the first meeting with them in 16 months and it was now possible to meet since all participants were 65+ and all had got at least one vaccine shot. In the week that followed, we learnt that our younger son's wife and older son had tested positive for COVID-19 but none of them became severely ill. A few days later, our younger son also tested positive for COVID-19.

Late in May, we made our first holiday trip since the start of the pandemic. We travelled by car to the province of Värmland and stayed at hotels for 5 nights. We enjoyed beautiful nature, good food and wine and meeting some old friends. We also saw the house in Karlstad that was built for us in 1973–1974 in which we lived between 1974 and 1990. We felt a fantastic freedom when we drove around in Värmland and did not think much about the pandemic. Actually, Värmland had the lowest level of infection of any region in Sweden and was number one in terms of the share of the population that had got one vaccine shot. After returning from Värmland, we spent several hours the following very rainy day in the botanic garden in Gothenburg together with friends from the Värmland Guild.

Early in June, we returned to our summer house in Småland and on June 11, we got our second vaccine at the local health centre. Two weeks later, when the vaccine was supposed to give full protection, we more of less returned to live as before the pandemic. We went to the food store together, we had dinners with friends and we spent time in our summer house together with our children and all our eight smaller grandchildren. So, the summer in 2021 was very normal and very different from the summer in 2020.

In August 2021, we made our first trip abroad since February 2020. We took the ferry from Gothenburg to Kiel and then went by car to be present when one of our two grandchildren in Germany started school. The situation in Germany really contrasted with the situation in Sweden. Indoors all people from the age of 6 had to wear a mask. It was mandatory. The effect was obvious. Very few people cared to keep physical distance anywhere. We had our COVID-19 vaccination passes with us but only once at a hotel in Lübeck were we asked to show them.

## 10 A Fourth Wave?

During the summer 2021, the rate of infection was very low in Sweden. Compared to earlier, few of the infected needed general hospital or intensive care. The number of COVID-19-related deaths was also very low. During the summer, the Swedish government and the Public Health Agency in several steps alleviated and partly abandoned some of the restrictions and recommendations. However, some were kept, and as the infection rate slowly increased in August, some restrictions and recommendations that should have been abandoned early in the autumn were extended. Interestingly, the number of infected per 100,000 people was now among the lowest in Europe.

Since most older and middle-aged people were fully vaccinated at this time, the infection mainly spread among people younger than 30. During the summer, younger people had started to live as before the pandemic entertaining themselves in bars, in restaurants and on beaches. Some people came back infected after having been on holiday in southern Europe.

Another group that got infected were immigrants of all ages who often lived in extended families in segregated areas. Actually, a high share of those needing intensive care due to COVID-19 in August 2021 were older and middle-aged immigrants who had not been vaccinated. The substantially lower vaccination rate among immigrants was probably partly due to difficulties for the responsible regions to reach out with vaccination information, since many immigrants do not as a rule follow Swedish media and a substantial share of them have problems understanding Swedish. Certainly, information material in many different languages was produced and distributed, not least through special vaccination guides with immigration background. Another problem was that there existed a rather widespread scepticism to vaccination against COVID-19 among many immigrant groups.

## 11 How Has Sweden Managed to Handle the Pandemic So Far?

Sweden is one of very few developed countries that did not have formal lockdowns, so it is certainly warranted to evaluate the Swedish policies to combat the pandemic and to treat those infected, but of course a bit premature. A proper evaluation cannot be made until after one or a few years, when it is possible also to take into account the more long-term effects of the pandemic and of the various policy measures, including the substantial share of infected people with long-term COVID-19. So, the text below is my highly personal evaluation to date. My principal starting point is my conviction that an evaluation of a policy to combat a pandemic must focus on how effective it has been in balancing the benefits of reduced deaths, long-term illness and human suffering against the effects of policy in terms of limited democratic rights (e.g. limited mobility and freedom to assemble), economic costs (e.g. unemployment, bankruptcies, deteriorated school results) and deteriorated public health (e.g. physical ill health, addictions, isolation and physical inactivity).

Starting with the spread of COVID-19 across Sweden, studies indicate that this had more to do with the timing of the first infection than the socio-economic characteristics of places. Rather, the spread was more closely linked to the early onset of infections during the initial face of the pandemic. The factor that seemed most closely associated with the geographic variation of COVID-19 incidence was the proximity to other locations with higher levels of infections. Thus, there appears to have been a high degree of randomness and bad luck in terms of places most affected and bad luck in terms of which places were first hit by the infection and those adjacent to such places.

In 2020, a fierce debate started in newspapers and electronic media about the Swedish corona policy because of the daily reports on the number of people diseased with a COVID-19 infection. Not least were comparisons made with our neighbouring Nordic countries where the death numbers were substantially lower. It was claimed that their corona policies, which were similar to the corona policies implemented all around Europe, were much more effective than the Swedish policy response. What was often forgotten in the debate was that Sweden because of the extensive travelling abroad in February and March got a much greater inflow of infected people than the other Nordic countries. According to official Swedish statistics, 9309 individuals infected with COVID-19 according to tests passed away during 2020. Of these individuals, 90% were 70 years or older and 70% were 80 years or older. Roughly, 50% of them were living in elderly care homes and 25% lived at home receiving home care services. Of the deaths with COVID-19 in elderly care homes, 70% were concentrated to 40 out of 290 municipalities in Sweden. Studies indicate that half of the variation in COVID-19-related deaths per capita between municipalities could be explained by the 40 municipalities with care home problems and the overall infection rates in each municipality. It must also be observed that individuals with immigration background were more severely hit than ethnic Swedes because many of them were in service occupations and the fact that different generations in immigrant families often lived close together.

In February 2021, it was possible to compare the mortality figures for the member states in the EU. According to official statistics, Sweden had an excess mortality in 2020 of 7250 individuals or 7.9%. This figure indicates that some of the infected individuals who passed away died of other causes than COVID-19. It is interesting to note that 22 of the member states in the EU had a higher excess mortality in 2020 than Sweden. A study by the Office for National Statistics in Britain standardized the populations with regard to age and sex in 25 countries and found that Sweden was in place 18 with an excess mortality in 2020 of 1.7%. Poland topped the list with an excess mortality of 11.6%, followed by Spain with an excess mortality of 10.6% and Belgium with an excess mortality of 9.7%. So perhaps Sweden did not fail to deal with the pandemic as badly as some people claimed. Still, the other Nordic states did substantially better, and Norway did not have an excess mortality at all possibly because Norwegians do not as a rule travel abroad in wintertime to the same extent as Swedes do. Furthermore, the immigrant population in Norway is smaller, and, unlike Sweden, Norway has a system of more medically staffed nursing homes.

The 21 Swedish regions, which are responsible for health care in Sweden, were not prepared for a pandemic even if it is obligatory for each region to have a pandemic plan and to store, for example, equipment for personal protection. Many regions had given up storing such equipment for cost reasons but luckily, they never really ran out of equipment for staff protection, but this was thanks to the National Board of Health and Welfare organizing purchases of protection equipment from abroad that was distributed to those regions most in need. The regions did a heroic job to restructure the hospitals to admit and treat thousands of patients with COVID-19. Compared with other countries in the EU, Sweden has few beds and ICU units per 100,000 inhabitants. In a very short time, the number of beds was increased substantially, and the number of manned ICU units was doubled. To staff the new COVID-19 nursing wards and the ICU units, doctors, nurses and other staff had to be moved from wards and units, which implies that much elective care, such as orthopaedic surgery, had to be postponed. However, critical treatments, such as cancer surgery and treatments of sick children, could still be performed, and, as is illustrated by my wife's and my experience during 2020, many health-care activities were performed as in normal times. Still, around 100,000 Swedes had their planned treatment postponed. Also, quite a few did not contact the health-care system, and the number of cases for many diseases was lower in 2020 than in earlier years, which indicates that there is a substantial backlog of cases that will need treatment in the near future. Such a "treatment debt" of a partly unknown size is impossible to deal with under a pandemic and will take substantial time to deal with after the pandemic, since staff in the health-care sector urgently need holidays and recovery.

Even if the Swedish regions were unprepared for a pandemic, the situation was substantially worse in the 290 municipalities, which have the main responsibility for care homes and home care services for older people. These services are partly run by the municipalities themselves and partly out-sourced to private firms even if the costs are covered by the municipalities. To make the situation more complicated, the regions are responsible for the health care of people in care homes and with home care services. It has been known for years that many elderly facilities and services in Sweden have quality problems, among other things due to insufficiently trained staff, many employees without permanent contracts, high labour turnover, problems with basic hygiene routines, etc. When the pandemic started to hit the old age care sector, there was furthermore in many municipalities a severe lack of protective equipment for personnel as well as liquid soap and hand sanitizers for many months. During the first wave of the pandemic, it turned out that the communication between the care homes and the health-care sector did not work in many cases. The result was that many infected with COVID-19 in the care homes were ordered palliative care instead of oxygen and infusion of liquids. It is impossible to know how many died as a result of such prescribed treatment, but certainly some could have been saved with the right treatment. The Health and Social Care Inspectorate carried out a substantial evaluation of a large number of care homes and the critique was very severe.

It is also important to reflect on what happened to the economy during the pandemic. Actually, the Swedish economy did not develop too badly during 2020. Among the EU member states, only one—Lithuania— had a lower drop in GDP than Sweden despite all the regulations and restrictions. For the EU as a whole, GDP dropped by 7%, while in Sweden the drop was only 3%. Even if the hospitality industry was severely hit in Sweden not least due to a severe shortage of foreign guests, it was to a considerable degree business as usual for many industries. The food stores did extremely well now when people largely stopped eating out and instead started cooking at home. Also D.I.Y. markets did very well, since people who could not travel abroad during their holidays or were temporarily laid off used the extra free time to renovate their houses and flats. From spring to early autumn 2020, manufacturing was severely affected particularly by shortages of inputs when many countries closed their borders, but for the rest of the year, operations more or less went back to normal levels. Still many companies in different industries needed some temporary public support during 2020.

Not unexpectedly, unemployment and particularly long-term unemployment increased during 2020. Specifically, young people and immigrants were hit by increasing unemployment because the hospitality sector was the sector most severely hit by the pandemic. But even if the national government pumped in substantial amounts to support industries, regions, municipalities and affected individuals, the increase in public debt in percentage was lower in Sweden than in most of the EU member states.

More importantly, Sweden succeeded in protecting the freedom of its citizens. People could move around and travel freely. The mountain region in Northern Sweden was a very popular holiday target in the summer 2020— much more popular than in the summer 2019— and already in March 2021 it was almost fully booked for the summer 2021. Shops, restaurants and cafés were kept open but had to follow certain recommendations and restrictions, which over time became stricter. In contrast to many other countries, nursery schools and the 9-year compulsory schools were in principle kept open to protect the health, wellbeing and learning of all children and not least of the children in exposed and vulnerable areas and families.

The Public Health Agency was anxious that all children should get their school lunches. An indirect effect of this policy was that it secured labour in not least the health-care sector, the care of elderly and vital societal functions, such as the police, medical and rescue services, water and food supply, etc.

Although nursery schools and elementary schools were kept open, the situation for children in Sweden became worse during the pandemic. For example, recreational activities for children were cancelled. There was reported an increase among children in anxiety, depression, physical and psychic violence and family conflicts. The switch to distance learning in senior high schools and partly in junior high schools led to an increase of study stress, feelings of loss of control, mental problems as well as reduced physical social relations and also decreased physical health due to restrictions in sports activities for older young people. Still, it is important to note that Sweden did not at all sacrifice the childhood, education and career of young people to the same extent as so many other countries did by imposing severe lockdowns and the closure of schools for a long time including repeated lockdowns. The long-term benefits for children in Sweden of open nursery and compulsory schools cannot be overestimated.

The bottom line in my personal evaluation of the way Sweden managed the pandemic is that the public policy approach chosen to deal with the pandemic limited its economic, social and democratic costs compared with many other countries that applied severe lockdowns but still got a high rate of COVID-19 infection and related deaths. Sweden did choose its own route to deal with the pandemic, and in earlier sections, I have explained how this came about. What is more difficult to understand is why Sweden's approach to the pandemic became an exceptional and unique case in the world.

It would seem like a paradox that Sweden, so far, has been spared the worst scientifically unjustified restrictions just because politicians in Sweden way back in history delegated the responsibility to deal also with pandemics to the experts in the Public Health Agency and that the Public Health Agency according to its instruction in its decisions had to consider the health effects for the whole nation. Of course, the decisions taken by the Public Health Agency had to be within the limitations of the law on infectious diseases but might also have been influenced by the beliefs among the central experts in the Public Health Agency concerning the most effective means to combat a pandemic.

Possibly, these experts also were influenced by their experiences of the swine flu, where Sweden applied maximum carefulness and among other things vaccinated a very large share of the population with the serious side effect that several hundred children got narcolepsy from the vaccine. When evaluated it turned out that the swine flu was not at all as serious as expected beforehand. Given this final result of the swine flu and the criticism against the Swedish approach, it is understandable if the responsible experts now chose a more cautious way to deal with the pandemic.

In contrast to many other countries, the Swedish experts did not act immediately on the reports by Neil Ferguson and Tomas Pueyo, indicating an enormous demand for hospital beds and ICU units and high mortality due to the spread of the COVID-19 infection. Instead, experts affiliated to the Public Health Agency started to check the assumptions used in these reports and quite soon came to the conclusion that many of the assumptions were unrealistic and that the effects of the spread of the infection were severely overestimated.

One could also imagine that since Sweden for the last hundred years had not experienced any war or other serious catastrophe, Swedish society was not prepared mentally nor practically to deal with a pandemic, which limited the options to deal with the pandemic. In contrast to Finland, Sweden had in the last 20 years, liquidated the enormous preparedness stockpile built up under the cold war. The choice of strategy might also have to do with the fact that according to the World Values Survey, the Swedes' values are extreme in an international comparison, giving strong priority to individual self-fulfilment over survival.

Whatever the real reasons behind the Swedish strategy, we may see the chosen strategy as a fortunate coincidence, since politicians in other countries in the world, given the chance, were so much more inclined to show potent ability to act by limiting the democratic freedom and rights of the people than to take reasonable and scientifically justified measures to deal with the pandemic.

## 12 My Experiences of Living in a Pandemic: Summing-Up

Now in late September 2021, it is possible to look back on 20 months of my life that have been extremely special. During this time, my life was quite different compared to my life before February 2020. Since my wife and I belonged to the risk group 70+, we had to take extra precautions. We can look back on a period where we had to give up or severely reduce many of our usual activities. We reduced our physical social contacts and in particular social contacts indoors. We continued to meet our children and grandchildren but always outdoors. We met our friends more seldom or not at all. There were no more visits to the concert hall, the opera and theatres since they were closed. Very seldom did we eat at restaurants and before the pandemic we had been regular visitors to restaurants for both lunch and dinners. Before the pandemic, we took several trips abroad each year and this halted abruptly with the pandemic. For me personally, the new way of life, oddly enough, led to doing much less research and writing than before the pandemic.

The explanation is that I spent much more time and shared activities with my wife than before the pandemic. In addition to the activities described above, we certainly watched more TV programmes than before and started to use HBO and Netflix and also to follow most of the press conferences that the Public Health Agency organized at first on every weekday and later Tuesday and Thursday. To keep ourselves updated, we watched German TV channels and in particular the news programme *Heute* sent on the German channel ZDF. My wife kept busy by knitting, while I sometimes lost myself in Facebook. After we had got our first vaccination shot, we gradually started to take up some of the activities that we had given up earlier during the pandemic.

Apart from the critical health issues we had during the pandemic, in evaluative terms, we can say that our life was not too bad. We succeeded in avoiding the infection. Our elder daughter and her family were infected with COVID-19 just before Christmas 2020 but only mildly. Also, our younger son and his family caught COVID-19 but they were not severely ill and were all recovered within a few weeks. Certainly, our lives became limited to a substantial degree, but we managed to substitute with other activities and then specifically spending much more time outdoors. Without doubt, we succeeded in improving our physical fitness. And even if it was boring now and then not to be able to do what we wanted to do, the pandemic did not affect our mental health. One very important reason for this was that we did not become totally socially isolated since we could meet with our children and grandchildren fairly frequently outdoors.

If we compare with how young people who were affected by the pandemic in terms of limited physical social contacts, increased unemployment, distance learning, etc., we did not fare too badly. If we compare with other countries where people were locked-in for longer periods and got their democratic freedoms and rights severely curtailed, we did fare quite well.

Many older people complained about the recommendation that they should not hug their grandchildren and keep them at a distance of 2 metres. We never saw this as a problem. It was quite OK to see the grandchildren at a distance of 2 metres and see that they were healthy and growing, which is what really matters. What we did miss from the beginning of the pandemic until we were fully vaccinated in June 2021 was sitting with the grandchildren reading a book, playing a game, watching TV and not least eating lunch or dinner or having a Swedish "fika", i.e. activities in which we really could interact with the grandchildren. We also missed no longer being able to pick up the grandchildren at the nursery school and the school or take them to an activity like gymnastics or football, thereby also giving our children a helping hand. We could neither care for the grandchildren when our children and spouses were occupied or travelling, nor have any grandchildren staying overnight in our apartment. This was very sad but fortunately it was temporary. After getting our vaccinations, it was and is business as usual.

**Charlie Karlsson** is Emeritus Professor in Economics at Jönköping International Business School and in Industrial Economics at Blekinge Institute of Technology, Karlskrona. In 2009–2013, he was President of the European Regional Science Association (ERSA).

# “Hibernating” in Cairo: COVID-19, as seen from Egypt

Christian Schubert

**Abstract** Spending most of the COVID-19 pandemic in Cairo (Egypt) has been an amazing and eye-opening experience, and probably a less stressful one than one might have expected before. Compared to, say, Germany, Egypt has by and large managed this crisis rather well, despite its relatively poor health infrastructure. I can only speculate as to why that’s the case, but a median age of 24, spending lots of time outside, and swiftly enforcing vaccination mandates have likely contributed.

**Keywords** COVID-19 · Cairo · Egypt · Crisis management

To be sure, “hibernating” is an extremely ill-chosen metaphor here, but I’m not aware of a synonymous expression that would replace winter with (hot!) summer. Anyway, let’s move back in time a bit...

It’s Thursday, the 19th of March 2020. In Germany, the last few days have seen a very rapid turn into crisis mode: Suddenly, the whole world worries about the “novel coronavirus” and a mysterious disease referred to as “COVID-19.” Our chancellor Angela Merkel has gone on national TV, something she does very rarely. She urged Germans to take this crisis seriously. Will there be a lockdown?

I’m in my hometown Münster, a beautiful city of 310,000 in North-West Germany, supposedly enjoying a weeklong break from my second home, Egypt. Since early 2018, I live in Cairo, working as professor of economics at the German University in Cairo (GUC). In mid-March, I had traveled to Münster, on an Egyptair flight via Amsterdam (Netherlands), as I very much prefer that well-designed and relaxed airport to stressful Frankfurt. Upon landing, I noticed that Dutch police only superficially checked incoming passengers for the known cold-like symptoms indicating COVID-19. No one wore a mask. In those early days and weeks of this pandemic, masks seemed to be hard to come by anyway.

A few days later, everything comes thick and fast: Will our government impose a hard lockdown? All around, countries start to close their borders. Egyptair cancels

---

C. Schubert (✉)
Economics, German University in Cairo (GUC), Cairo, Egypt

 
D. B. Audretsch, I. A. M. Kunadt (eds.), *The COVID-19 Crisis and Entrepreneurship*, International Studies in Entrepreneurship 54,
https://doi.org/10.1007/978-3-031-04655-1_12

my return flight! Then rumor has it that more and more countries plan to close their airports entirely. It's Wednesday, 18th of March, and I'm glued to my iPad, following the news. If Egypt follows suit, I will probably be stuck in Germany for months, which I would rather avoid. Then comes the news: Egypt does close all its airports, effective tomorrow (Thursday) evening. In the late hours of Wednesday, I manage to find a seat on the last flight to Cairo: Egyptair 786. But is it a good idea to leave Germany today of all days and to live through this incoming pandemic in a developing country like Egypt? What if Germans who are still in Cairo are being evacuated right now? Consider this, for instance: While according to the World Health Organization (WHO), Germany spends about 2400 USD per capita on public health, Egypt spends roughly 580 USD.[1]

No time to worry too much about this now, though. Thankfully, Thursday morning does not see any lockdown, so I can get on the train, now to Frankfurt rather than Amsterdam, and hop on this very last flight back to Egypt. Once on board, I realize that I'm the only "Western" person on this flight. People look at me in a funny way. The captain does a lengthy announcement, in Arabic—which I still don't speak—which has everyone laughing (Egyptians have a great sense of humor), while secretly glancing at me. Then just a few English words: "Welcome aboard, please fasten your seatbelts," and off we go. Upon arrival in Cairo, we are all led to a testing site deep within the airport, where tiny blood samples are taken. Being the only (potentially troublemaking?) foreigner, I'm among the first to be tested and then finally released, at around midnight, into the stifling 30 degree centigrade night in Cairo. The 18 months since then have been incredibly interesting and instructive.

While in the coming one and a half years or so, wave after wave hits Germany, and devastating news about overcrowded ICUs, tens of thousands of deaths, the depressing reality of "Long COVID" (and the disturbing radicalization of anti-vaxxers) reach me, the situation in Egypt remains mostly calm, maybe eerily so. At the outset of this pandemic, experts around the globe had of course predicted that African countries, with their horribly underfinanced public health sectors, would be hit particularly hard by the virus. Obviously, reliable numbers are still impossible to get, and most Egyptians rather piece together what they need to know about the COVID-19 situation from social media, friends, and extended family (families are *very* extended here).[2] But still, except some short months about a year ago, when hospitals almost reached their capacity limits, the situation remained much more comfortable compared to, for instance, Germany.

Now, why is that? It seems especially puzzling given the still very low vaccination rates: At the time of writing—December 2021—45.1% of the world population can be considered fully vaccinated. But that number is only 15.8% in Egypt—and

[1] See https://www.who.int/health_financing/documents/health-expenditure-report-2019.pdf?ua=1.

[2] The official number of COVID-19 cases in Egypt, as of November 2021, is allegedly around 351,000, in a country of about 105 million; see https://www.statista.com/statistics/1170463/coronavirus-cases-in-africa/.

68.6% in Germany.[3] Mask wearing has never been strictly enforced here, and "social distancing"—even if it were culturally accepted—never seemed realistic in a densely populated megalopolis such as Cairo. Around 21 million Cairenes live in an area the size of the city of Berlin—with its 3.7 million people.[4]

So why did Egypt fare so (relatively) well? To be honest, I have no idea. It's a puzzle. Maybe they already reached herd immunity months ago? The warm climate certainly helps, keeping most people outside for much longer periods of time than in the comparably cold countries of Europe. Also, the median age in Egypt is 24.6 years, a whopping 21 years—nearly a generation—below the median age of Germany, which means that there just aren't as many old and vulnerable people to suffer the horrible consequences of COVID-19 that we keep hearing out of Germany.[5] Egypt, while of course the oldest known civilization, is also an incredibly young country.

Another factor that may contribute to the generally relaxed view on the pandemic is that one much-feared consequence of all those lockdowns and social distancing measures implemented throughout (at least) most OECD countries—namely, social isolation, loneliness, and resulting depression—is hardly an issue in collectivist Egypt. As Max Rodenbeck, the author of what is still the best "Western" monograph on Cairo, observed back in 1998: "[F]ew cities are so relaxed, so accommodating, so disdainful of merely impersonal relations. Loneliness, that bane of city life in the West, is almost unknown."[6] As a rule, people here are deeply embedded in wide-ranging social networks, which obviously means that the level of social control can sometimes be perceived as quite stifling. At least it would be from an individualist viewpoint. For Egyptians, this embeddedness is a much-needed source of relief and support in socioeconomic circumstances that, already long before the pandemic, had been felt as being quite dire. To illustrate, 29.3% live in absolute poverty, i.e., on less than 857 Egyptian Pounds (that's the equivalent to 43 Euros or 46 USD) per month.[7] The minimum wage, recently increased to 2400 Egyptian Pounds, implies a salary of around 14 Pounds per hour, i.e., 0.71 Euros.[8] Still, Egyptians seem surprisingly resilient in the face of their daily calamities—possibly the traditionally deep religious commitments of both majority-Muslim (Sunni) and Christians here are a

[3] The numbers can be found in https://ourworldindata.org/covid-vaccinations.

[4] That number is for the *Greater Cairo Metropolitan Area*, including neighboring cities such as Gizeh, Shubra El Kheima, and Sheikh Zayed; see: https://worldpopulationreview.com/world-cities/cairo-population. The number grows quickly: Egypt's population has doubled between 1988 and 2021 (https://www.worldometers.info/world-population/egypt-population/).

[5] Sources for median ages can be found here: https://www.worldometers.info/world-population/.

[6] See Rodenbeck (1998).

[7] See, for instance, https://enterprise.press/stories/2020/12/06/egypts-poverty-rate-falls-for-the-first-time-in-two-decades-26212/, and: https://www.statista.com/statistics/1237041/poverty-headcount-ratio-in-egypt/.

[8] For a 40-hour workweek, which is an optimistic assumption. For Egypt's minimum wage, see https://egyptianstreets.com/2021/06/30/egypt-sets-private-sector-minimum-wage-at-egp-2400-per-month/.

contributing factor.[9] What the poor lack in material resources, they make up in terms of "morality."[10] While this often contributes to deep-seated attitudes (toward gays, Jews, etc.) that this Westerner can only perceive as backward, it may also be responsible for what Rodenbeck observed: "If a single trait can describe Cairo's people, it must be their enduring, life-giving nonchalance" (Ibid.: 71). Does "Oriental fatalism" play a role? Talking with locals can be a truly charming experience, but then you may find yourself struck by your interlocutor's smiling endorsement of homophobia or antisemitism—a reminder that the cultural distance between our two societies, the German and the Egyptian one, is really quite large.[11]

So, my hunch would be that this social connectedness, combined with the fact that Egypt has always been a country of faith, is responsible for the evidence that notorious movements such as the anti-vaxxers—so annoyingly present in contemporary Germany, but also in the USA—are largely unknown here. Egyptians simply don't lack spirituality, so the demand for "substitute religions," such as Germany's anthroposophy movement (one cultural driver of anti-vaxxers) with its anti-rational and anti-science implications, is near zero. In fact, the only source of related fake news, including all kinds of weird conspiracy theories, I come across here is a WhatsApp group of German and Swiss retirees who live in the Cairo area for decades. Most Egyptians seem to be happy to trust scientific authorities and take the vaccine, if and when (God-willing, as they say here) it becomes available in their vicinity. The public support by star footballer Mo Salah, in favor of getting vaccinated, was not even needed.[12]

To conclude my short report, these past 2 years "hibernating" in Cairo—with the occasional trip back to Germany, to see family and friends—have, unexpectedly, only increased my admiration for this country, despite the occasional reminder that there really is a large cultural distance. Maybe Egyptians are simply more skilled at coping with all kinds of disasters—such as this global pandemic—than my comparatively super-rich compatriots?

[9]It's estimated that 10% of Egyptians are Christians, most of them belonging to the Coptic Orthodox Church, with its pope in Alexandria. It's by far the largest Christian community in the Middle East.

[10]See Rodenbeck (Ibid.: 201).

[11]Recently, Harvard anthropologist Joseph P. Henrich and his team have tried to quantify it: see www.culturaldistance.com. To illustrate, using their scale, Germany's cultural distance to China is 0.126, while its distance to Egypt is 0.243. (The largest distance is to Pakistan, 0.286, and the lowest to the Netherlands, 0.026). For theoretical background and methodology, see https://journals.sagepub.com/doi/full/10.1177/0956797620916782. See also: https://nautil.us/issue/81/maps/the-cultural-distances-between-us. See of course also Henrich (2020).

[12]See, for instance, https://twitter.com/FootballJOE/status/1468606504836153356.

## References

Henrich, J. (2020). *The WEIRDest people in the world: How the West became psychologically peculiar and particularly prosperous*. Farrar, Straus & Giroux.
Rodenbeck, M. (1998). *Cairo: The city victorious*. Vintage.

**Christian Schubert** is Full Professor of Economics at the German University in Cairo/Egypt. He studied economics and philosophy in Osnabrück/Germany and Lausanne/Switzerland. He worked at Max Planck Institute of Economics in Jena/Germany till 2012 and as Lecturer at the Universities of Freiburg, Cottbus, Kassel, Düsseldorf, and Münster.

# COVID-19 Pandemic Lockdown: The Era of Connection and Creation

**Maha Aly**

**Abstract** This chapter reflects on how I harnessed the opportunities afforded from the pandemic to advance on my own journey, rather than succumb as a victim. A key to transforming the crisis into opportunity for personal and professional growth was recognizing the gift of a Mentor-Mentee relationship and prioritizing the development through nurturing of this connection. Looking back, the pandemic paused a paralyzing challenge in a country like Germany, but also the unexpected opportunity to develop a special relationship with my Mentor, complete my PhD, develop our own inner selves, and start our new business together to serve and promote entrepreneurship.

**Keywords** Emotional connection · Creation vs. creativity · Seizing opportunities · Making best use of time · Divine gift

## 1 The Pandemic

In February 2020, while the world started to hear the words "coronavirus in China," I was packing to travel from Germany to Australia to participate in the Australian Centre for Entrepreneurship Research Exchange Conference (ACERE) and present my second PhD research paper in front of the top scholars in the field of "Entrepreneurship." At that time, Europe was clean and there were zero corona cases. My brother, who is a dentist in Belgium, warned and urged me to cancel the trip as the pandemic started to spread in Australia. I was sure that this trip is very important for my soul, my career, and my PhD research. I insisted on going, and I decided to prepare myself to take the maximum protection procedures. I was the only person who bought masks from different pharmacies in the city I used to live in, alcohol to keep my hands disinfected, and moisturizing nasal spray to keep my airway moist during the long flight. The pharmacists looked at me strangely enough and asked me

M. Aly (✉)
The Institute of Development Strategies, Bloomington, IN, USA



D. B. Audretsch, I. A. M. Kunadt (eds.), *The COVID-19 Crisis and Entrepreneurship*, International Studies in Entrepreneurship 54,
https://doi.org/10.1007/978-3-031-04655-1_13

why do you need such stuff? I think they all knew the answer 1 month later (March 2020), when the first corona lockdown hit, and the whole world was temporarily closed.

I started my journey with so much trust in my heart that this trip would be exceptional. I then took my utmost precautions. I sprayed alcohol on my hands every time I touched anything, and applied moist to my nose every hour during the long flight. I was the only crazy woman wearing a mask during the 24-hour flight, in the airports, and when I arrived at the hotel in Adelaide (South Australia). I was such an anomaly that in the main shopping streets of Adelaide, a hairdresser wondered if I had cancer and was forced to wear a mask because of my ill immunity! In the hotel, the receptionist told me that there is no need for masks and that Adelaide is safe. I decided then to take off the mask and show up on the first day of the conference with my face. Funny how the whole world has been wearing masks since then!

It was at that conference where I first met Prof. David Audretsch, one of the super top scholars in the research field of "Entrepreneurship," that I knew from reading his rich renowned research articles and books. I was very lucky to have my first roundtable on the first day of the conference with him. Each roundtable was dedicated to discuss one research paper. I have always known the big top name "David Audretsch," but I did not know how he looked like. When the roundtable discussion started, I found a very grounded centered confident calm man sitting beside me. I looked in the conference agenda to find out that this table's moderator and discussant is Prof. David Audretsch. I remember I said to myself "WOW! This is the great Prof. Audretsch that I have been reading his name on the important entrepreneurship books and papers!". I then waited until he spoke. I was charmed by his superb humbleness and the very careful and considerate feedback he gave to the authors of the discussed paper. I was the last to leave the table before him. We had a short talk together that encouraged me to talk to him again during the evening event, and I did. I seized the opportunity at the end of the event and approached him. We talked about the PhD papers and supervisors, but most importantly, we exchanged emails. On the next day, at the Gala Dinner, we met again and talked about personal emotional challenges in life. We immersed and mingled in a marvelous talk for around 15 minutes, and suddenly the conference host took Prof. Audretsch away to start the event ceremony. Nevertheless, we kept in touch exchanging emails about my PhD research. I went back to Germany and we started to have Zoom meetings to discuss different topics. By the end of March, I was super lucky and blessed to have Prof. Audretsch as my Mentor and my second PhD advisor. This occurred concurrently with the COVID-19 lockdown.

For a person who is addicted to traveling and vivid nightlife, is always excited to meet new people, and enjoys many outdoor activities like myself, the first pandemic lockdown in 2020 seemed to be confining like a prison. However, I altered my thoughts after the first 5 days of staying at home—which were very intense, draining, and difficult for my mental health—and decided to make the lockdown period as highly productive as possible. I started to run every day in the heart of nature, focused on refining and finishing my PhD research, wrote better papers, and learned a lot from my new Mentor.

## 2 The Connection

The more I learned from my Mentor, the higher levels of harmony and resonance fueled this very special Mentor-Mentee relationship. Prof. Audretsch and I started to develop an authentic mental and spiritual connection. We have been enjoying working, creating, and producing together. The flow of thoughts, talks, and subjects we have been sharing is incredibly inspiring and changing each one of us to become a better version of ourselves. We share a conviction that when positive exchange of energy flows between two souls, it enables them to create something valuable and unique. Hence, we decided to create a professional dream together to help young people and give more to the world through a very dynamic collaboration that falls between research and translation (application) into reality.

When we first met in Mainz (Germany), after the pandemic, we so much enjoyed working together on our dream. Our Mentor-Mentee relationship has developed and grown to become a father-daughter relationship, something I very much cherish, and I am super proud of.

Prof. Audretsch has a very humble, loving, kind, sensitive, and helpful attitude. He shines out through serving people and giving his best to the world. He always keeps his promises! Always!

I have to say I am super lucky to have a business partner and a Mentor like him.

## 3 The Creation

While the PhD research was progressing, a new deep feeling started to blossom in my heart, "the fear of endings." I observed my emotions swinging between the extreme willingness to finish my degree and the fear of finishing it. The PhD was the last biggest dream to chase at that time and I had no idea what exciting thrilling bigger dream I would be living to achieve next.

Keeping highly motivated, self-driven, and ambitious requires determining new goals and envisioning scary big dreams to follow. I asked myself, what could this dream be? What and how could the product of my accumulated knowledge, experience, study, and passion look like? I found different answers and decided to keep calm and let them simmer at the back of my head. In June 2020, the answers started to crystalize into two main business ideas.

Despite my concerns regarding sharing business ideas with professors in academia, I felt that discussing with Prof. Audretsch would definitely be fruitful. I shared the two business ideas with him, one was about fashion events and the other about helping entrepreneurs overcome their emotional challenges. He was very open, listened carefully, and gave important feedback on both ideas.

After a few days, I decided to go for the second idea. I asked Prof. Audretsch if he would be interested to co-found and co-create this business together and introduce new value to serve entrepreneurs worldwide, not just on the research level but also on the applied, practical, and clinical level. He welcomed the idea and connected me immediately with his great network of entrepreneurs, professors, professionals, coaches, and guides. We started discussing with them the potential of the idea, market need, applicability, direction, service type, revenue model, markets, and customers, and that was just the beginning. We kept working on the idea, developing, and reshaping it for about a year, until we reached a compelling name for the business, *The Institute of Entrepreneurial Emotional Education and Research*, bold mission, clear vision, novel set of greatly needed services, and a flexible scope.

We had noticed that while the private sector, through entrepreneurship training programs; educational sector, through entrepreneurship education; and public sector, through a myriad of policies to spur entrepreneurship, offered a broad spectrum of services and programs to enhance entrepreneurial capabilities, the skills and competencies to navigate through an emotionally fraught entrepreneurial journey have been sorely neglected. The absence of educational and training programs dedicated to equip entrepreneurs with the requisite emotional skills and tools along with public policies to create local, regional, and national institutions and cultures supporting entrepreneurship has left entrepreneurs in the lurch with few options. This void reflects an academic literature in entrepreneurship that has systematically fleshed out a number of the emotional challenges confronting entrepreneurs, such as the fear of failure, the stigma of failure, stress of uncertainty, and alienation following entrepreneurial achievement, but has yet to even begin to identify clinical approaches, programs, and policies to enhance the emotional resilience of entrepreneurs.

The value proposition of our new business is to address this dearth of entrepreneurial support by offering the key requisite skills and competencies needed by entrepreneurs to thrive as they traverse their entrepreneurial journeys rather than succumbing as victims, defeated by the inevitable emotional landmines. *The Institute of Entrepreneurial Emotional Education and Research* intends to offer services to a broad spectrum of customers and clients, ranging from therapeutic sessions, seminars, and training programs for entrepreneurs to nonprofit institutions, foundations, and government agencies at all levels on practical and pragmatic policies that will enhance the resilience of entrepreneurs to navigate entrepreneurial challenges.

Professor Audretsch—through his connections and relationships—has crowned our efforts in many different ways. He suggested a series of awareness sessions and introductory activities to spread the word and get a sense of how this service should be provided in the market. The activities are ordered chronologically as follows:

1. May 18, 2021: Presenting the idea for the first time in the Middle East in the Holy Spirit University of Kaslik in Beirut[1], which resulted in an overwhelming confirmation of the validity of the core business idea and booking the last 10 days of July 2021 to provide coaching and therapy sessions for entrepreneurial emotional fitness with the Asher Center for Innovation and Entrepreneurship (ACIE) in Beirut.

[1] https://www.usek.edu.lb/news/virtual-awareness-session-emotional-skills-for-entrepreneurial-success

2. May 27, 2021: Presenting the idea in Central America (including Spanish translation) via the EmpreSomos: The Center for Advancing the Development of the Entrepreneurial Ecosystem in the Central American Region.
3. June 24, 2021: Panel discussion in a recorded episode in BEE Vision TV of the USASBE: United State Association for Small Business and Entrepreneurship, which resulted in inviting us as speakers in the upcoming 2022 conference on the same topic.
4. July 13, 2021: Publication of our paper introducing the idea, "Emotional Skills for Entrepreneurial Success: The Promise of Entrepreneurship Education and Policy" (Aly et al., 2021), in the globally renown *Journal of Technology Transfer*.
5. July 20–30, 2021: Applying results and giving free emotional education and therapy sessions to Lebanese entrepreneurs under the umbrella of the Asher Center for Innovation and Entrepreneurship (ACIE) and the Holy Spirit University of Kaslik in Beirut.
6. September 16, 2021: Panel Discussion, *European Encounters: Policy & Education for Emotional Skills for Entrepreneurial Success Discussion*—Online event sponsored by the Indiana University Global Gateway in Berlin, Germany.
7. January 5–9, 2022: Participating in the USASBE Conference Pioneer and Persevere, USA, as speakers to discuss how we can serve entrepreneurs in the context of managing their emotional fitness and how vital and essential this topic.

Currently, we are working on our next paper that should reflect the impact of emotional fitness sessions on the entrepreneurs in Beirut, and trying to expand our customer reach to enrich our track record for our start-up, *The Institute of Entrepreneurial Emotional Education and Research (IEEER).*

The activity assessment by the entrepreneurs who received the service in Beirut indicates promising success for the Institute. Responses of the assessment survey show that 80% of the entrepreneurs were better able to identify the emotional challenges after the session, 90% could better identify their limiting beliefs compared to before, 50% felt that their emotional blockage was resolved in one session, and 90% felt that their need to be equipped with emotional skills for entrepreneurs had increased. The verbal feedback on how the participating entrepreneurs felt after the session reflects the upside potential impact of the IEEER B2C service, which is one-to-one transformational coaching sessions. The following is a list of the verbal feedback provided by the ten entrepreneurs who had received the transformational coaching sessions by the IEEER first run in Beirut:

> Curious to know more (entrepreneur 1).
>
> I feel that I am much stronger and more emotionally stable (entrepreneur 2).
>
> I am questioning a lot of things and keep on wondering (entrepreneur 3).
>
> Relaxed, focused, and positive (entrepreneur 4).
>
> The session helped me be more productive and motivated moreover to be filled with positive energy; I become more interacting in the workshops and helped me discuss my ideas and thoughts more freely and openly. The session was a turning point as when I get accepted to the accelerator, I was thinking to quit due to fears and worries of not getting an investor and be wasting my time specially the workshops I have previously attended in different

accelerator program and lead me to nothing; the turning point was that the session motivated me and cleared my mind and helped me succeed in setting my first meeting with group of investors and get me more attached to the accelerator program and keen to develop myself. After the session, I'm more positive and extra motivated (entrepreneur 5).

A lesson to be learned that makes no difference how much our business ideas are great and our management skills are perfect if our emotions are not stable and we are not aware to manager our emotions intelligently, it will be so difficult for us as entrepreneurs to make the right decisions in our journey to succeed (entrepreneur 6).

Satisfied (entrepreneur 7).

I see the importance of considering emotions in entrepreneurship which is uncommon in our society (entrepreneur 8).

I felt the need of going outside the box of being underpressurized, and start taking care of the work-life balance (entrepreneur 9).

Refreshed and motivated to start practicing the exercises recommended by Dr. Maha (entrepreneur 10).

Such positive feedback gave us the feeling that we can help the next generations of entrepreneurs realize their own entrepreneurial dreams by enhancing their productivity as they embark upon their entrepreneurship journey with higher mental awareness and well-being.

# 4 The Gift

Like for everyone, the COVID-19 pandemic came as a shock. It has inflicted days of fatigue, anxiety, boredom, fear, frustration, and bewilderment. However, I learned something important. There is no choosing about external challenges, such as the COVID-19 pandemic, which are imposed on me. I can, however, choose my response to those external challenges. That response can be either negative, and succumbing as victim, or positive, by harnessing the opportunities afforded by the challenge. I did not always choose the latter and am no stranger to the dejection, despair, and detachment of the former.

Still, what I learned from the COVID-19 pandemic is to choose hope and purpose over cynicism, connection over isolation, and creating value for others over self-serving. These lessons have been a gift, which has blossomed in seven important ways. The first was completion of my PhD thesis, "Exploring the Entrepreneurial Mindset in the Context of Managing Adversities within the German Ecosystem: The Impact of Cultural Values on Entrepreneurial Behavior" (Aly, 2021). The second was my first academic publications (Aly (2020), Aly and Galal-Edeen (2020), and Aly et al. (2021)). The third was founding my second start-up business. The fourth was the blessing of discovering my Mentor, Professor Audretsch, and building an amazing fulfilling connection with him.

The fifth new dimension was taking a new challenge to join a start-up as a Product Owner of UX Operations, and then leaving it after 6 months (in the middle of the COVID-19 lockdown) due to feeling boxed and limited. Then I started the very challenging but courageous journey of job search, trying to find a better fitting job for my skills, ambitions, and expansion potentials, until I successfully joined a UK global bank as a Manager of Digital Capabilities in the second half of 2021. I wanted a job that helps me expand and polish my skills, teaches me new ones that help me run our new start-up, and positions me well in a corporate with a big name. And guess what! I got what I wanted. The sixth was building stronger and deeper bond with my Mentor and business partner by involving each other in our daily life challenges and victories; sharing our thoughts, emotions, and learned lessons together; and focusing on creating value in every conversation we had. The seventh was about wisdom and self-reflection. I took the time to develop the way I know myself and leverage my self-worth and self-value by improving my inner voice, re-positioning myself in the job market to get the job that I deserve through enhancing my social media visibility, and being coached to improve my emotional flow quality. Perhaps the greatest value was a consequence of prioritizing the time to befriend my emotional challenges in different contexts, reflect, meditate, slow down, and taste life, which was a great development in my self-actualization.

Each has their own life journey to travel. However, thanks to my beloved Mentor, I learned during the COVID-19 pandemic that this journey is more rewarding and joyful traveling it together. That is the gift.

## References

Aly, M. (2020). Towards more qualitative research paradigms in nascent entrepreneurship research. *International Journal of Entrepreneurship and Small Business, 1*(1), 1. https://doi.org/10.1504/IJESB.2020.10038749

Aly, M., (2021). *Exploring the entrepreneurial mindset in the context of managing adversities within the German ecosystem: The impact of cultural values on entrepreneurial behavior*. Ph.D. Thesis, University of Erfurt.

Aly, M., Audretsch, D. B., & Grimm, H. (2021). Emotional skills for entrepreneurial success: The promise of entrepreneurship education and policy. *Journal of Technology Transfer, 46*(5), 1611–1629. https://doi.org/10.1007/s10961-021-09866-1

Aly, M., & Galal-Edeen, G. (2020). Why is Germany less entrepreneurial? A behavioral reasoning perspective. *Journal of Technology Transfer, 46*(5), 1376–1416. https://doi.org/10.1007/s10961-020-09823-4

**Maha Aly** is a Change Catalyst. She co-founded the "Institute of Entrepreneurial Emotional Education and Research" after her first successful startup, which enables her training and consulting nascent entrepreneurs since 2015. Her Ph.D. focuses on entrepreneurial psychology. She also brings diversified corporate experience in customer centricity and digital emotional connection in various industries (e.g., e-banking and telecom).

# Part V
# The Educational Ecosystem for Entrepreneurship: Moving the Digital Way Forward After the COVID-19 Crisis

# Entrepreneurial Intention of Dutch Students During the COVID-19 Pandemic: Are Today's Students Still Tomorrow's Entrepreneurs?

**Annelot Wismans, Milco Lodder, and Roy Thurik**

**Abstract** In early 2020, it became clear that policy and public health responses to the pandemic would generate an unprecedented economic crisis. Entrepreneurship is documented as helping economies recover from economic slowdowns (Koellinger & Thurik, Review of Economics and Statistics 94, 1143–1156, 2012). Hence, the immediate reaction of our Rotterdam and Montpellier entrepreneurship research groups was to start looking for ways to assess the development of entrepreneurial intention (EI). In particular, we focus on students, since they may be the ones to create a novel wave of firms to fill in the gaps caused by the crisis or to replace firms weakened by the crisis. The present analysis is the first to investigate whether and in which direction EI has changed in the beginning of the COVID-19 pandemic using a survey of approximately 1000 students from Erasmus University Rotterdam. Moreover, we study how a set of COVID-19-related, context-related, and demographic variables is connected to changes in EI. While most students report their EI to be unaffected by the pandemic, 16% report a decrease in EI, and 19% report an increase in EI. These changes appear to be most strongly associated with pandemic-induced changes in mental health and with gender. We find that students who report a negative change in their mental health are more likely to indicate lower EI rather

A. Wismans (✉)
Erasmus School of Economics, Erasmus University Rotterdam, Rotterdam, The Netherlands

The Erasmus University Rotterdam Institute for Behavior and Biology (EURIBEB), Rotterdam, The Netherlands
e-mail: wismans@ese.eur.nl

M. Lodder
Erasmus School of Economics, Erasmus University Rotterdam, Rotterdam, The Netherlands

R. Thurik
Erasmus School of Economics, Erasmus University Rotterdam, Rotterdam, The Netherlands

The Erasmus University Rotterdam Institute for Behavior and Biology (EURIBEB), Rotterdam, The Netherlands

Montpellier Business School, Montpellier, France
e-mail: thurik@ese.eur.nl



D. B. Audretsch, I. A. M. Kunadt (eds.), *The COVID-19 Crisis and Entrepreneurship*, International Studies in Entrepreneurship 54,
https://doi.org/10.1007/978-3-031-04655-1_14

than higher EI. Moreover, females are more likely to indicate decreased EI due to the pandemic, while males are more likely to report increased EI, indicating a potential increase in the gender gap in entrepreneurship. Additionally, students with higher trust in the government are less likely to report lower EI relative to similar EI. Finally, we also find associations between change in EI and expected income in 10 years, compliance with COVID-19 regulations, age, and international student status.

**Keywords** COVID-19 · Entrepreneurial intention · Students

# 1 Introduction

The COVID-19 pandemic has considerably affected the global economy, specifically hurting businesses and consequently business owners (Belitski et al., 2021). Nationwide lockdowns forced businesses to remain closed for many consecutive months, resulting in a substantial increase in economic uncertainty (Altig et al., 2020). While bankruptcies decreased by 17% in 2020 in the Netherlands—mainly due to fiscal measures taken by the government to counteract the effects of the pandemic—they are expected to increase when fiscal support phases out (Smid & Ciobica, 2021). According to Statistics Netherlands, in the fourth quarter of 2020, the pandemic resulted in the highest economic downturn in the Netherlands (−3.8%) since World War II. Moreover, the unemployment rate in the Netherlands rose from 2.9% to 4.6% between March and August 2020 (Statistics Netherlands, 2021). While multiple governmental support measures have limited negative consequences to a large extent, the COVID-19 pandemic revealed the risks associated with being a business owner, showing how external factors outside entrepreneurs' control can impact their businesses. In a survey among small- and medium-sized enterprise (SME) owners in 23 countries conducted during the pandemic in 2020, 61% of business owners indicated that the existence of their business was under threat due to the pandemic (Stephan et al., 2021). Moreover, Kuckertz et al. (2020) reported that the growth and innovation potential of start-ups are at risk due to the pandemic and the measures taken by governments. Finally, it was shown that self-employed workers were affected more strongly than wage workers by the financial insecurities caused by the pandemic in terms of psychological distress (Patel & Rietveld, 2020), that their perceived level of burnout increased (Torrès et al., 2021a, 2021b), and that health perception was affected (Torrès et al., 2021c).

While most focus has been on the consequences of the pandemic for current and nascent entrepreneurs, the consequences of the COVID-19 pandemic may also shape the future of entrepreneurship by altering entrepreneurial intentions (EI) and the profile of the future entrepreneur (Liñán & Jaén, 2020). Potential future entrepreneurs have witnessed sizeable negative outcomes and economic uncertainty related to business ownership, which may negatively affect the EI of today's students. Therefore, the pandemic may not only have affected the current business landscape but could also lead to a future (temporary) decline in the number of start-ups. In line with this possibility, studies have shown that macroeconomic conditions when young shape job preferences for the rest of one's live, with those entering the job market during a recession giving higher priority to income for the rest of their lives (Cotofan et al., 2020). As Cotofan et al. (2020) also argued, the so-called impressionable years (between ages 18 and 25) are crucial for shaping future preferences. The literature has shown that the historical environment in which a young person becomes active in the adult world shapes the formation of lasting values, attitudes, and preferences. During the impressionable years, people are highly susceptible to attitude change, although afterward this susceptibility drops drastically and remains low for the rest of one's life (Krosnick & Alwin, 1989). Taking this fact into account, students who form their future job preferences—and thus entrepreneurial aspirations—during the COVID-19 pandemic may have different attitudes and preferences for the rest of their lives.

On the other hand, the COVID-19 pandemic may have also increased the EI of students. As the current job market has become increasingly challenging, the expected difficulties associated with a job search could lead to higher EI due to more necessity-based entrepreneurship. Aucejo et al. (2020), for example, showed that in a US sample, 40% of students lost a job, internship, or job offer and that perceived probability of finding a job before graduation decreased by 20%. Moreover, studies have shown that graduates who enter the job market during a recession suffer from the consequences for up to 10 years due to lower job opportunities and lower wages (Brunner & Kuhn, 2014; Kahn, 2010; Schwandt & von Wachter, 2019). The expected difficulties of finding employment may shift some students in the direction of self-employment, also known as necessity entrepreneurship[1] (Bosma & Harding, 2007; van der Zwan et al., 2016). At the same time, the pandemic has changed consumption patterns, and stimulated growth in certain sectors, such as online retail, digital transformation, and healthcare (Donthu & Gustafsson, 2020; Sheth, 2020). These changes may create gaps in the market and hence opportunities for new businesses. Students may perceive these new business opportunities, which could translate into reporting increases in EI, also known as opportunity entrepreneurship[1] (Bosma & Harding, 2007; van der Zwan et al., 2016). EI could therefore have increased both due to necessity and to opportunity. Taken together, EI may thus have shifted in two directions.

In addition to the potentially bidirectional changes in EI due to the pandemic, it is likely that perceptions of entrepreneurship are affected differently among various groups of students, influencing the profile of the next generation of entrepreneurs. In other words, some individual characteristics may affect whether EI stays the same, increases, or decreases during the pandemic. With respect to the profile of current entrepreneurs, Grashuis (2021) showed that the effects of the pandemic varied across

[1] The entrepreneurship literature often distinguishes between necessity-driven and opportunity-driven entrepreneurship. While the first group is pushed into entrepreneurship because of the lack of other options in the labor market, the latter group is pulled into entrepreneurship because they see a business possibility (Bosma & Harding, 2007; Fairlie & Fossen, 2020; van der Zwan et al., 2016).

groups, with unemployment being more likely for younger, female, and nonwhite individuals. Moreover, Kuckertz (2021) showed that start-ups founded during the pandemic are characterized less by entrepreneurial teams and more by habitual entrepreneurs, indicating that the profile of the current entrepreneur may already have changed. With respect to future entrepreneurs, certain groups of students may be more discouraged by the pandemic from starting a business than others. For instance, due to their more risk-averse nature (Borghans et al., 2009; Verheul et al., 2012), women may be more discouraged by the perceived increase in uncertainty associated with starting a business, consequently increasing the already existing gender gap in entrepreneurship in the future.

With the considerable negative economic impact of the COVID-19 pandemic, entrepreneurship will be a key component in economic recovery. It is well documented that entrepreneurial activity affects economic growth, competitiveness, employment creation, and high-quality innovation (Thurik & Wennekers, 2004; van Praag & Versloot, 2007; van Stel et al., 2005). The disruption of the pandemic may even call for more innovative start-ups, since the pandemic forced businesses and education to go online overnight, creating space for newcomers to enter these markets (Liñán & Jaén, 2020). If young adults are discouraged from starting a business, this situation may result in a decline in the factors that are influenced by entrepreneurship, such as innovation and job creation, leading to even longer-lasting consequences of the pandemic.

While there is a large body of literature on the drivers of EI, little is known about the effects due to (health) crises on changes in EI. Brück et al. (2010) studied the effect of extreme events on individual perceptions and expectations of entrepreneurship and showed that natural disasters and terrorist attacks increase fear of failure, while violent conflict decreases it. Moreover, they showed that natural disasters mostly discourage females and older and low-income individuals from starting a business. Brück et al. (2010) showed that terrorist attacks positively affected the entrepreneurial activity of all population groups. In contrast, studying a sample of Afghans living in conditions of war and terror, Bullough et al. (2014) found that perceptions of danger from the environment lowered EI, while this effect was diminished for those with high resilience and entrepreneurial self-efficacy. Moreover, the perception of economic crisis as an obstacle negatively affects the likelihood of starting a business (Arrighetti et al., 2016). Related to the COVID-19 pandemic, Ruiz-Rosa et al. (2020) showed that the EI of students decreased during the pandemic compared to before the pandemic.

## 1.1 Current Study

As stressed by Liñán and Jaén (2020), it is important that the effects of the COVID-19 pandemic on EI be investigated, specifically focusing on the determinants that encourage and discourage changes in these intentions. While EI has been criticized as a measure of entrepreneurship,[2] we believe that as the focus of this research lies on tomorrow's start-ups rather than today's start-ups, it is crucial to use EI as an outcome. Moreover, according to Ajzen's Theory of Planned Behavior, intention is a significant predictor of eventual behavior. This link has been widely validated in the psychology literature for various behaviors (Kim & Hunter, 1993) and for entrepreneurial behavior in particular (Kautonen et al., 2013, 2015).

In the current paper, we study the drivers of self-reported change in EI of a sample of 1090 university students from the Netherlands. First, we investigate whether students self-report that their intentions have changed and, if so, in which direction. As stated above, the pandemic could have a two-sided effect on EI. On the one hand, it may lower EI due to the unprecedented high levels of economic uncertainty and exposure to the adverse consequences of the pandemic on businesses. On the other hand, it may strengthen EI through increases in necessity entrepreneurship—due to unpredictability of the job market—and opportunity entrepreneurship, due to changed consumption patterns and the growth of certain sectors. Second, we study how a set of COVID-19-related, context-related, and demographic variables relates to changes in EI. Specifically, we study four COVID-19-related variables: the self-reported effect of the pandemic on students' mental health, the self-reported effect of the pandemic on students' financial security, perceived risk of COVID-19 (infection and hospitalization), and compliance with COVID-19 measures. Additionally, we study how expectations of future income are connected to EI change. This variable can be interpreted as a measure of ambition. As discussed, governmental measures have considerably reduced the negative impact of the pandemic on businesses. Therefore, we also study the relationship between government trust and change in EI due to the pandemic. Moreover, we investigate how the COVID-19 pandemic may change or add to existing gender differences in entrepreneurship given that, despite initiatives to decrease the gender gap, women are already underrepresented in entrepreneurship (Elam et al., 2019) and have lower levels of intention to start a business after graduation (Dabic et al., 2012; Elam et al., 2019; Wilson et al., 2007a, 2007b) Finally, we control for age, whether students are involved in a business- or economics-related study and whether students are domestic or international. We conduct a multinomial logistic regression analysis to investigate which variables relate to an increase or decrease in EI compared to no change in intentions.

As there is hardly any literature available on the drivers of change in entrepreneurial aspirations during pandemics, we do not formulate explicit hypotheses but will take an inductive approach and interpret and reflect on the outcomes in the discussion.

[2]Top entrepreneurship journals tend not to allow studies that use EI as an outcome measure.

# 2 Data and Measures

## 2.1 Dataset

We make use of data that were collected as part of the Erasmus University Rotterdam International COVID-19 Student Survey (Wismans et al., 2020a, 2021b, 2021c). The first survey of this initiative took place during the early phase of the COVID-19 pandemic (April/May 2020, weeks 17–19). University students from ten countries worldwide participated. For this study, we make use of data collected from Dutch university students who took part in this first survey. The sample consists of students from multiple faculties of the Erasmus University Rotterdam and was distributed using university platforms and university e-mail addresses. The survey could be completed in Dutch or in English. The total sample consisted of 1090 students. All students signed an informed consent form before beginning the survey, and the study was approved by the Internal Review Board of the Erasmus University Rotterdam.

## 2.2 Measures

*Change in entrepreneurial intention:* Change in EI was measured by asking the following question: "During the past two months, did your intention of starting your own firm change in a positive or negative way?". Participants answered on a 5-point Likert scale, ranging from 1 (It is much lower) to 5 (It is much higher). For statistical analyses, we created three groups: lower intentions (original values: "1," "2"), similar intentions (original value: "3") and higher intentions (original values: "4," "5").

*Effect of COVID-19 on mental health:* To assess how the pandemic affected students' mental health at the time of our survey, we asked the following question: "How did/does the current corona crisis affect your general mental health?". Answers were given on a 5-point Likert scale, including "Strongly negatively affected" (1), "Slightly negatively affected" (2), "Did not affect in any way" (3), "Slightly positively affected" (4), and "Strongly positively affected" (5).

*Effect of COVID-19 on financial security:* Similarly, to assess how the pandemic affected students' financial security at the time of our survey, we asked the following question: "How did/does the current corona crisis affect your financial security/ situation?". Answers were given on a 5-point Likert scale, including "Strongly negatively affected" (1), "Slightly negatively affected" (2), "Did not affect in any way" (3), "Slightly positively affected" (4), and "Strongly positively affected" (5).

*Perceived personal risk of COVID-19:* We asked two questions concerning the perceived personal risk of COVID-19. We asked about perceived likelihood that the following events would occur in the next 2 months: "You get infected with the coronavirus?" and "You must be hospitalized, if you are infected with the coronavirus?". Answers were given on a 7-point Likert scale, ranging from "No chance at all" (1) to "Absolutely certain" (7). For the current study, we took the average of these two items to capture the perceived personal risk of COVID-19 (Pearson's $r$: 0.22, $p < 0.001$).

*Compliance with COVID-19 measures:* We measured compliance with COVID-19 measures on a 7-point Likert scale by asking the following question: "To what extent have you followed the measures advised by the government to prevent the spread of the coronavirus?". Answers ranged from "I have not taken any measures" (1) to "I have done everything that was possible" (7).

*Expected income in 10 years:* To assess expected yearly income, we asked the following question: "What do you think your yearly income will be in 10 years in euros (i.e., do not adjust for your expectation of inflation over this period)?". Answers were given on a 7-point Likert scale, including €0–€10.000 (1), €10.000–€30.000 (2), €30.000–€50.000 (3), €50.000–70.000 (4), €70.000–90.000 (5), €90.000–€110.000 (6), and more than €110.000. We will treat this measurement as a continuous variable.

*Government trust:* We asked students the following question: "In general, how much trust do you personally have in the Dutch Government on a scale from 1 (no trust at all) to 10 (full trust)?"

*Gender:* A binary variable, with 0 reflecting male and 1 reflecting female.

*Control variables*: We controlled for age, study direction, and international student status. Most students in our sample studied a subject related to business or economics (78%). As EI is expected to be higher for these students, we control for this factor using a dummy variable (1, economics/business related subject; 0, other). Finally, our sample included international students (30.5%). As these students may have different levels of EI in general and may have a different frame of reference (e.g., different impacts of COVID-19 in their home country), we controlled for this aspect.

## 3 Results

### *3.1 Entrepreneurial Intention and Change in Entrepreneurial Intention*

In Fig. 1, we present students' self-reported change in EI as percentages. Most of the students (66%) indicated that their EI had not changed in a positive or negative way during the past 2 months. Nevertheless, the EI of one-third of students changed in a positive or negative direction during the beginning phase of the COVID-19 pandemic. As may be expected, the change occurred in both directions: in total, 15.76% of students indicated that their EI had become (much) lower, while 19.17% of students indicated that their EI had become (much) higher. For the rest of this paper, we use a categorization into three groups (lower, similar, higher).

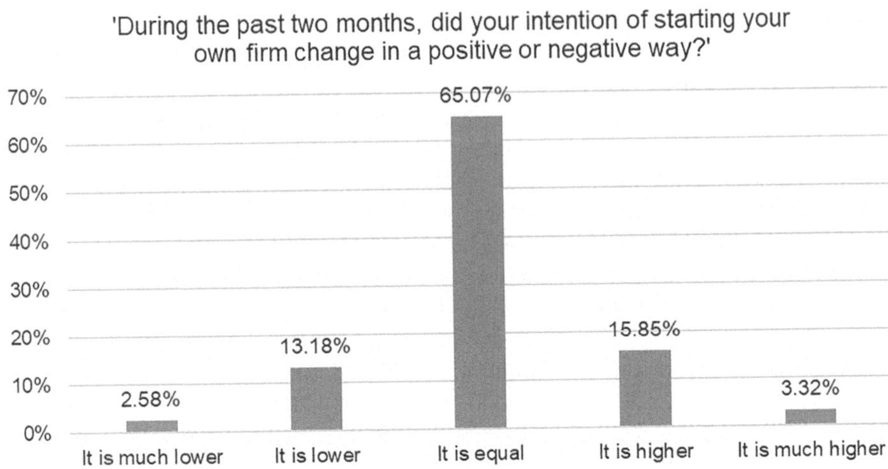


**Fig. 1** Frequencies (in %) of change in entrepreneurial intention (N = 1085)

**Table 1** Means (M), standard deviations (SD), and frequencies (in %) of all variables

| | M | SD | % |
|---|---|---|---|
| Change EI | | | |
| *Lower* | | | 15.76% |
| *Same* | | | 65.97% |
| *Higher* | | | 19.17% |
| Effect C-19: mental health | 2.39 | 0.89 | |
| Effect C-19: financial security | 2.78 | 1.04 | |
| Perceived risk C-19 | 3.23 | 0.89 | |
| Compliance C-19 measures | 5.86 | 0.99 | |
| Government trust | 7.28 | 1.64 | |
| Expected income 10 years | 4.49 | 1.41 | |
| Gender | | | |
| *Male* | | | 42.45% |
| *Female* | | | 57.54% |
| Age | 20.76 | 2.81 | |
| Economics/business student | | | |
| *Economics/business student* | | | 77.53% |
| *Other* | | | 22.47% |
| International student | | | |
| *Domestic student* | | | 69.52% |
| *International student* | | | 30.48% |

Note: C-19 = COVID-19

## 3.2 Correlations, Means, and Standard Deviations

To assess which factors contributed to increases and decreases in EI in the context of a pandemic, we investigated a set of COVID-19-related, context-related, and demographic variables. In Table 1, we present means and standard deviations (SD) for variables treated as continuous and percentages for categorical variables. Our sample consisted of slightly more females (57.5%) than males, which is representative for the gender distribution in higher education (World Economic Forum, 2020). Moreover, the majority of the sample studied a subject related to economics or business (77.5%), and most students were noninternational (69.5%). Government trust was relatively high ($M = 7.28$), which is in line with previous research showing increased political trust during the acute phase of the pandemic (Oude Groeniger et al., 2021). In Table 2, correlations between all variables are presented. The strongest correlations were present between EI change and the effect of COVID-19 on mental health ($r = 0.13$, $p < 0.001$), gender ($r = -0.18$, $p < 0.001$), and expected income in 10 years ($r = 0.19$, $p < 0.001$). However, these correlations only present linear relationships, while a multinomial logistic regression analysis - presented in the next part - will help us investigate whether there were nonlinear relationships among the variables studied and increasing versus decreasing EI.

## 3.3 Multinomial Logistic Regression Explaining Change in EI

To assess which of the variables were associated with a reported increase or decrease relative to unaffected EI during the COVID-19 pandemic, we conducted a multinomial logistic regression using 1071 observations in total. The results of this analysis are presented in Table 3. Column 1 presents the betas (B), standard errors (SE), odds ratios (OR), accompanying 95% confidence intervals (95% CIs), and p values for lower EI compared to similar EI, while Column 2 does so for higher EI compared to similar EI and Column 3 does so for higher EI compared to lower EI. The full model is significantly better at explaining changes in EI than the model including only the intercept ($X^2(20) = 113.61$, $p < 0.001$).

With respect to the COVID-19-related variables, a change in one's mental health due to the COVID-19 pandemic was significantly associated with changes in EI. Specifically, those who reported worsened mental health due to the pandemic were also more likely to report lower EI compared to similar EI (B = -0.24, OR = 0.78, $p = 0.02$), while those who reported improved mental health during the pandemic were more likely to report higher EI compared to similar EI (B = 0.24, OR = 1.27, $p < 0.01$).[3] In line with this result, those reporting higher EI compared to

[3]This result was further shown in additional analyses not presented here, in which we included a categorical version of the mental health variable (lower, similar, higher), using similar as reference group.

**Table 2** Correlations of all variables included in analysis

| | 1 | 2 | 3 | 4 | 5 | 6 | 7 | 8 | 9 | 10 | 11 |
|---|---|---|---|---|---|---|---|---|---|---|---|
| 1. Change EI | – | | | | | | | | | | |
| 2. Effect C-19: mental health | 0.13*** | – | | | | | | | | | |
| 3. Effect C-19: financial security | 0.07** | 0.20*** | – | | | | | | | | |
| 4. Perceived risk C-19 | −0.02 | −0.06* | −0.06* | – | | | | | | | |
| 5. Compliance C-19 measures | −0.03 | −0.03 | 0.03 | 0.06** | – | | | | | | |
| 6. Government trust | 0.04 | 0.05* | 0.12*** | −0.09*** | 0.05* | – | | | | | |
| 7. Expected income 10 years | 0.19*** | 0.04 | 0.02 | −0.06* | −0.005 | 0.0002 | – | | | | |
| 8. Gender (female = 1) | −0.18*** | −0.06* | −0.07** | 0.14*** | 0.17*** | −0.07** | −0.37*** | – | | | |
| 9. Age | −0.03 | −0.02 | −0.09*** | −0.01 | 0.02 | 0.004 | 0.08*** | −0.10*** | – | | |
| 10. Econ/business student | 0.07** | 0.04 | 0.10*** | −0.06** | 0.04 | 0.08** | 0.24*** | −0.12*** | −0.10*** | | |
| 11. International student | 0.08*** | −0.08*** | −0.10*** | 0.19*** | 0.11*** | −0.24*** | 0.09*** | 0.09*** | −0.05 | 0.02 | – |

Note: C-19 = COVID-19, *: $p < 0.10$, **: $p < 0.05$, ***: $p < 0.01$

**Table 3** Results of multinomial logistic regression with change in EI as the dependent variable

| | Lower EI vs. similar EI | | | | Higher EI vs. similar EI | | | | Higher EI vs. lower EI | | | |
|---|---|---|---|---|---|---|---|---|---|---|---|---|
| | B (SE) | OR | 95% CI | *p* | B (SE) | OR | 95% CI | *p* | B (SE) | OR | 95% CI | *p* |
| Effect C-19: mental health | **−0.24 (0.11)** | **0.78** | **0.64; 0.97** | **0.02** | **0.24 (0.09)** | **1.27** | **1.06; 1.51** | **0.01** | **0.48 (0.13)** | **1.61** | **1.26; 2.07** | **<0.001** |
| Effect: C-19: financial security | −0.12 (0.09) | 0.89 | 0.75; 1.05 | 0.18 | −0.01 (0.08) | 0.99 | 0.85; 1.16 | 0.94 | 0.11 (0.11) | 1.12 | 0.91; 1.38 | 0.29 |
| Perceived risk C-19 | −0.03 (0.10) | 0.97 | 0.80; 1.18 | 0.77 | −0.05 (0.09) | 0.95 | 0.79; 1.14 | 0.56 | −0.03 (0.12) | 0.98 | 0.76; 1.24 | 0.84 |
| Compliance C-19 measures | **−0.18 (0.09)** | **0.83** | **0.70; 0.99** | **0.04** | **−0.21 (0.08)** | **0.81** | **0.69; 0.95** | **0.01** | −0.03 (0.11) | 0.98 | 0.79; 1.2 | 0.81 |
| Government trust | **−0.11 (0.05)** | **0.90** | **0.81; 1.00** | **0.04** | 0.02 (0.05) | 1.02 | 0.92; 1.12 | 0.76 | 0.13 (0.07) | 1.14 | 1.00; 1.29 | 0.06 |
| Expected income 10 years | −0.09 (0.07) | 0.92 | 0.80; 1.05 | 0.22 | **0.24 (0.06)** | **1.27** | **1.12; 1.44** | **<0.001** | **0.33 (0.09)** | **1.39** | **1.17; 1.64** | **<0.001** |
| Female | **0.42 (0.20)** | **1.52** | **1.02; 2.26** | **0.04** | **−0.57 (0.18)** | **0.57** | **0.40; 0.81** | **0.002** | **−0.99 (0.25)** | **0.37** | **0.23; 0.61** | **<0.001** |
| Age | 0.04 (0.03) | 1.04 | 0.98; 1.10 | 0.21 | **−0.09 (0.05)** | **0.91** | **0.83; 1.00** | **0.04** | **−0.13 (0.05)** | **0.88** | **0.79; 0.97** | **0.01** |
| Economics/business student | 0.20 (0.21) | 1.23 | 0.81; 1.86 | 0.34 | 0.16 (0.23) | 1.18 | 0.76; 1.84 | 0.47 | −0.04 (0.28) | 0.96 | 0.55; 1.68 | 0.89 |
| International student | **−0.58 (0.22)** | **0.56** | **0.36; 0.86** | **0.01** | 0.31 (0.19) | 1.36 | 0.95; 1.96 | 0.09 | **0.89 (0.26)** | **2.43** | **1.45; 4.06** | **<0.001** |
| N | 1075 | | | | | | | | | | | |
| −2 Log likelihood (ic. only) | 1898.409 | | | | | | | | | | | |

(continued)

**Table 3** (continued)

| | Lower EI vs. similar EI | | | | Higher EI vs. similar EI | | | | Higher EI vs. lower EI | | | |
|---|---|---|---|---|---|---|---|---|---|---|---|---|
| | B (SE) | OR | 95% CI | *p* | B (SE) | OR | 95% CI | *p* | B (SE) | OR | 95% CI | *p* |
| −2 Log likelihood (full model) | 1784.801 | | | | | | | | | | | |
| $X^2$ (df = 20) | 113.609*** | | | | | | | | | | | |
| Nagelkerke $R^2$ | 0.12 | | | | | | | | | | | |

Note: C-19 = COVID-19, OR = odds ratio, 95% CI = 95% confidence interval, ic = intercept. Coefficients that are significant at 5% level are bold printed.
*: $p < 0.10$, **: $p < 0.05$, ***: $p < 0.01$

lower EI were more likely to report that the pandemic had a positive impact on their mental health (B = 0.48; OR = 1.61, $p < 0.001$). We did not find any relationship between the effect of the pandemic on students' financial security and changes in EI. Additionally, perceived personal risk of COVID-19 (in terms of getting infected with or hospitalized due to COVID-19) did not relate to changes in students' EI due to the pandemic. Interestingly, compliance with COVID-19 regulations in the Netherlands (i.e., regulations related to social distancing and improved hygiene) had a comparable relationship with reporting lower EI relative to similar EI (B = -0.18, OR = 0.83, $p = 0.04$) and with reporting higher EI relative to similar EI (B = -0.21, OR = 0.81, $p = 0.01$). This result indicates a U-shaped relationship between compliance and changes in EI, with students who were more compliant with COVID-19 regulations being more likely to report changes in EI in both directions, while those who reported lower compliance with COVID-19 regulations being more likely to report that the pandemic had not affected their EI.

Trust in government was negatively associated with reporting lower EI compared to similar EI: those with higher trust in government were less likely to report a decrease in EI compared to reporting similar EI (B = -0.11, OR = 0.90, $p < 0.04$). There was a trend toward significance ($p = 0.06$) for the odds of reporting higher EI relative to lower EI, such that those who reported higher trust in government were more likely to report increased EI relative to decreased EI (B = 0.13, OR = 1.14). However, this link was not significant at conventional significance levels.

Expected yearly income in 10 years was significantly positively related to reporting higher EI relative to similar EI due to the COVID-19 pandemic (B = 0.24, OR = 1.27, $p < 0.001$). This relationship was also present and positive for those reporting higher EI relative to lower EI (B = 0.33, OR = 1.39; $p < 0.001$). This result may indicate that those with higher ambitions or career expectations in terms of expected income were more likely to report that the pandemic led to increased levels of EI.

We found a strong relationship between gender and changes in EI. Females were more likely to report lower EI relative to similar EI (B = 0.42, OR = 1.52, $p = 0.04$) and less likely to report higher EI relative to similar EI (B = -0.57, OR = 0.57, $p = 0.002$). In line with this result, we found a strong negative link between being female and reporting higher EI relative to lower EI (B = -0.99, OR = 0.23, $p < 0.001$).

Finally, regarding the control variables, we found that age was negatively related to reporting higher EI compared to similar EI (B = -0.09, OR = 0.91, $p = 0.04$) and higher EI compared to lower EI (B = -0.13, OR = 0.88, $p = 0.01$). This result indicates that younger students were more likely to report increased EI relative to similar and lower EI. There was no association between being an economics or business student or studying in another area and changes in EI. We did find that international students, compared to domestic students, were less likely to report lower EI compared to similar EI (B = -0.58, OR = 0.56, $p = 0.01$) and thereby more likely to report higher EI compared to lower EI (B = 0.89, OR = 1.45, $p < 0.001$).

# 4 Discussion

The 2020 COVID-19 pandemic has had an unprecedented effect on businesses. As entrepreneurship is a vital component for economic recovery and growth (Koellinger & Thurik, 2012; Thurik & Wennekers, 2004), it is crucial to obtain an understanding of how the pandemic has affected the entrepreneurial aspirations of the future workforce. We studied the change in entrepreneurial intentions (EI) due to the pandemic in a large group of Dutch university students. We showed that while EI remained the same for two out of three students, one out of three students reported a change. Interestingly, students reported both decreases (16%) and increases in EI (19%) due to the pandemic. One could argue that, overall, EI has stayed the same on average or even increased slightly. Nonetheless, it is important to study whether the profile of future entrepreneurs may have changed due to the unparalleled impact of the COVID-19 pandemic. Therefore, we investigated how a set of COVID-19-related, context-related, and demographic variables relate to changes in EI in both directions. We will discuss and interpret our findings in sequence below.

We start by describing the variables that are most strongly associated with change in EI: gender and changes in mental health due to the pandemic. Despite initiatives to decrease the gender gap, women are still underrepresented in entrepreneurship (Elam et al., 2019). It is therefore important to assess whether the COVID-19 crisis will exacerbate this imbalance. In our sample, we find a very strong association between EI change and gender, showing that females are more likely than males to report decreased EI and less likely to report increased EI during the pandemic. This result indicates that given that EI is already higher for males in general (Dabic et al., 2012; Elam et al., 2019; Wilson et al., 2007a, 2007b), this difference may grow due to the pandemic. Previous research has shown that women perceive more (gender-specific) obstacles to entrepreneurship, such as (perceived) lack of support, less favorable perception of oneself and the entrepreneurial environment, household responsibilities, and lower chances of obtaining external capital from investors (Guzman & Kacperczyk, 2019; Langowitz & Minniti, 2007; Shinnar et al., 2012; Verheul et al., 2012). It is possible that the COVID-19 pandemic has further enhanced these barriers, especially those related to the perception of the entrepreneurial environment. Moreover, recent studies have shown that employment and income losses have been larger for women than men during the COVID-19 pandemic, explained by increased household responsibilities and concentration of employment in affected sectors (Alon et al., 2020a, 2020b, 2021; Graeber et al., 2021). While these changes most likely do not apply to our sample of students, it was also shown that the first lockdown has been associated with a shift toward more traditional beliefs in gender norms, which may also affect EI (Boring & Moroni, 2021). Finally, studies have shown that personality differences between men and women also underlie disparities in entrepreneurial aspirations. Women generally have lower levels of self-efficacy and are more risk averse than men (Borghans et al., 2009; Verheul et al., 2012). As the business environment is more uncertain than ever (Altig et al., 2020), a risk-averse personality and lower belief in one's capacity to overcome potential obstacles (i.e., self-efficacy) could deter women from pursuing a career in entrepreneurs in the current uncertain economy. In line with our findings, Giotopoulos et al. (2017) showed that during the 2008 economic crisis, gender was more strongly related to entrepreneurial high growth intentions, indicating that female entrepreneurship suffered more during the crisis.

Second, we found that pandemic-induced changes in mental health were strongly related to changes in EI. Specifically, students who indicated worse mental health due to the pandemic were more likely to report lower EI and less likely to report similar or higher EI. Only recently have scholars started to pay attention to the mental health of entrepreneurs (Wiklund et al., 2018, 2019; Wismans et al., 2020b, 2021a). It was shown that worse mental well-being is related to lower firm performance among entrepreneurs, which some have explained by conservation of resources theory (Gorgievski et al., 2010; Hobfoll, 2001; Stephan, 2018). Entrepreneurs with better mental health have more cognitive and affective resources, which enables them to be more persistent and creative, to identify opportunities, and to spend more effort on their work (Stephan, 2018). This same reasoning may explain why students who report a negative impact of the pandemic on their mental health have fewer resources available to identify opportunities and therefore a lower intention to start a business and vice versa. Overall, 65.3% of our sample indicates that their mental health has been (strongly) negatively affected by the COVID-19 pandemic, while only 12.1% indicates a (strong) positive effect. This result may indicate that the pandemic not only takes its toll on the mental health of the majority of students but also that it has further-reaching effects due to its indirect consequences on EI.

Moreover, we studied the relationship of three other COVID-19-related variables with changes in EI. First, students' perceived risk of COVID-19 (the perceived likelihoods of getting infected with and hospitalized due to COVID-19) is not related to changes in EI. Second, self-reported compliance with COVID-19 regulations in the Netherlands (such as social distancing and increasing hand hygiene) is related to changes in EI. We show that there is a U-shaped relationship between self-reported compliance and EI change. Students who report having followed COVID-19 regulations more closely are more likely to report higher and lower EI compared to similar EI. This result means that students with lower compliance are more likely to be unaffected in terms of their EI. Possibly, the lives of students who indicate lower compliance with COVID-19 regulations were thereby less heavily altered by the pandemic, which could explain why they are more likely to report unaffected EI. Third, while almost 40% of students in our sample indicate that the COVID-19 pandemic has negatively affected their financial situation, we do not find a relationship between changes in financial security and changes in EI. This result may come as a surprise, given that previous research has shown that preference for financial security, financial assets, and household capital affect EI and the transition to self-employment (Dunn & Holtz-Eakin, 2000; Millman et al., 2010; Raijman, 2001; van Gelderen et al., 2008).

Regarding general government trust, we show that those with higher trust in Dutch government are less likely to report lower EI compared to similar EI. As discussed in the introduction, governments imposed numerous measures to reduce the negative consequences of the pandemic on the economy. Students with lower trust in the government may be less confident in the capability of the government to limit adverse consequences for business owners, explaining the negative association between government trust and reporting decreased EI. Personal experiences with business failure or struggle (due to the pandemic) in one's environment may also underlie this relationship.

In our survey, we ask students about their expected yearly income in 10 years. We find that those with a higher expected income in 10 years are more likely to report increases in EI compared to similar EI and decreased EI. In other words, students with higher expectations of future income are more likely to report increased EI during the pandemic. The measure of expected income is less straightforward to interpret, as it could capture multiple beliefs and characteristics of the students, such as ambition, major, and overconfidence, which each may have their own effect. It is therefore not possible to completely disentangle the underlying processes of this relationship. For instance, one's level of general optimism could both underlie expectations about future income and increases in EI during the pandemic. At the same time, students that have recently come up with a business idea may indicate both enhanced EI during the pandemic and increased expectations of future income.

Finally, we controlled for several variables, among which age and international student status are found to be related to EI change. Specifically, older students are less likely to report increased EI compared to decreased and similar EI. Moreover, international students are more likely to report increased EI and less likely to report decreased EI, indicating that the EI of international students may be differently and more positively affected by the pandemic than that of domestic students. We do not find differences in changes in EI between students who pursue studies related to economics and business and students who pursue other studies.

There are several caveats to our study that should be borne in mind when interpreting the outcomes. First, we have assessed change in EI. While students may indicate that their EI has changed due to the pandemic, we do not know what this change means for their actual level of EI. For example, if decreases in EI are mainly present in students who were already unwilling to start a business before the pandemic (low levels of EI becoming even lower), this result has less severe consequences than if these decreases are mainly present in students with high levels of EI before the pandemic. Second, the change in EI is self-reported retrospectively. Students were forced to think about how the pandemic has affected their EI, which is arguably not something students have thought about before participating in the survey. For future research, it would be meaningful to compare postpandemic or midpandemic EI levels to prepandemic EI levels and use these comparisons to infer change. Third, our data were collected during the beginning phase of the pandemic (April/May 2020). At that time, nobody was completely aware of the long-lasting consequences of the pandemic. Thereafter, more (or less) severe changes in EI could have occurred. Importantly, changes in EI could be reversible, meaning that when the pandemic has ended, EI levels may return to their prepandemic states. While this possibility is not in line with previous research that shows that macroeconomic conditions during one's impressionable years (18–25) shape preferences for the rest of one's life (Cotofan et al., 2020; Krosnick & Alwin, 1989), future research using longitudinal data assessing EI before, during, and after the COVID-19 pandemic would be worthwhile. Finally, while studying EI is, in the context of our study, a useful outcome measure, for future research, it would be valuable to investigate whether the COVID-19 pandemic caused changes in or gave rise to factors that lower the transition from EI to actual entrepreneurial behavior.

Meanwhile, the 2020 COVID-19 pandemic has continued to impact the world for at least 2 years (at the time of writing the present article). While the economy is recovering more quickly than expected, with labor participation rates in the Netherlands even increasing beyond prepandemic levels, there are still concerns about the consequences of the pandemic on self-employment and specifically on EI. Therefore, this study aims to shed light on potential changes in the future of the entrepreneurial landscape caused by the COVID-19 pandemic. Fortunately, we find that in our sample, EI remains the same for most students, and both increases and decreases in EI are reported. Slightly more students report increased EI than decreased EI. However, disturbingly, we show that gender is strongly associated with reported changes in EI, with females being more likely to report decreases in EI, while males are more likely to report increases in EI. This result could have consequences for the gender gap in entrepreneurship. Furthermore, changes in mental health due to the pandemic have a strong effect on reported EI. As the pandemic has strongly affected the mental health of the majority of young adults, this situation could have indirect consequences for other aspects of life as well, such as career choice, and consequently for the economy. Finally, we find that reported changes in EI are associated with compliance with COVID-19 regulations, government trust, expected income in 10 years, age, and international student status. Initiatives focused on stimulating entrepreneurship among students should take our findings into account and try to avert negative consequences, for example, by giving more attention to mental health and gender-specific barriers caused by or perceived due the pandemic.

**Acknowledgements** The current study is part of the Erasmus University Rotterdam International COVID-19 Student Survey, a larger project in which data of students from ten countries was collected. RT is also member of *LabEx Entrepreneurship*, funded by the French government (LabEx Entreprendre, ANR-10-Labex-11-01).

## References

Alon, T., Doepke, M., Olmstead-Rumsey, J., & Tertilt, M. (2020a). *This time it's different: The role of women's employment in a pandemic recession*. National Bureau of Economic Research.

Alon, T., Doepke, M., Olmstead-Rumsey, J., & Tertilt, M. (2020b). The impact of COVID-19 on gender equality. National Bureau of economic research.

Alon, T., Coskun, S., Doepke, M., Koll, D., & Tertilt, M. (2021). *From Mancession to Shecession: Women's employment in regular and pandemic recessions*. National Bureau of Economic Research.

Altig, D., Baker, S., Barrero, J. M., Bloom, N., Bunn, P., Chen, S., et al. (2020). Economic uncertainty before and during the COVID-19 pandemic. *Journal of Public Economics, 191*, 104274.

Arrighetti, A., Caricati, L., Landini, F., & Monacelli, N. (2016). Entrepreneurial intention in the time of crisis: A field study. *International Journal of Entrepreneurial Behavior & Research, 22*(6), 835–859.

Aucejo, E. M., French, J., Araya, M. P. U., & Zafar, B. (2020). The impact of COVID-19 on student experiences and expectations: Evidence from a survey. *Journal of Public Economics, 191*, 104271.

Belitski, M., Guenther, C., Kritikos, A. S., & Thurik, R. (2021). Economic effects of the COVID-19 pandemic on entrepreneurship and small businesses. *Small Business Economics, 58*, 1–17. https://doi.org/10.1007/s11187-021-00544-y

Borghans, L., Heckman, J. J., Golsteyn, B. H. H., & Meijers, H. (2009). Gender differences in risk aversion and ambiguity aversion. *Journal of the European Economic Association, 7*(2–3), 649–658.

Boring, A., & Moroni, G. (2021). *Turning back the clock: Beliefs in gender norms during lockdown*. Unpublished manuscript.

Bosma, N., & Harding, R. (2007). *Global entrepreneurship monitor: GEM 2006 results*. Global Entrepreneurship Monitor (GEM).

Brück, T., Llussá, F., & Tavares, J. (2010). *Perceptions, expectations, and entrepreneurship: The role of extreme events* (IZA Discussion Papers, No. 5351).

Brunner, B., & Kuhn, A. (2014). The impact of labor market entry conditions on initial job assignment and wages. *Journal of Population Economics, 27*(3), 705–738.

Bullough, A., Renko, M., & Myatt, T. (2014). Danger zone entrepreneurs: The importance of resilience and self–efficacy for entrepreneurial intentions. *Entrepreneurship Theory and Practice, 38*(3), 473–499.

Cotofan, M., Cassar, L., Dur, R., & Meier, S. (2020). Macroeconomic conditions when young shape job preferences for life. *The Review of Economics and Statistics*, 1–20.

Dabic, M., Daim, T., Bayraktaroglu, E., Novak, I., & Basic, M. (2012). Exploring gender differences in attitudes of university students towards entrepreneurship: An international survey. *International Journal of Gender and Entrepreneurship, 4*(3), 316–336.

Donthu, N., & Gustafsson, A. (2020). Effects of COVID-19 on business and research. *Journal of Business Research, 117*, 284–289.

Dunn, T., & Holtz-Eakin, D. (2000). Financial capital, human capital, and the transition to self-employment: Evidence from intergenerational links. *Journal of Labor Economics, 18*(2), 282–305.

Elam, A. B., Brush, C. G., Greene, P. G., Baumer, B., Dean, M., & Heavlow, R. (2019). *Global entrepreneurship monitor 2018/2019 women's entrepreneurship report*. Babson College: Smith College and the Global Entrepreneurship Research Association.

Fairlie, R. W., & Fossen, F. M. (2020). Defining opportunity versus necessity entrepreneurship: Two components of business creation. In S. W. Polachek & K. Tatsiramos (Eds.), *Change at home, in the labor market, and on the job* (Vol. 48, pp. 253–289). Emerald Publishing Limited. https://doi.org/10.1108/S0147-912120200000048008

Giotopoulos, I., Kontolaimou, A., & Tsakanikas, A. (2017). Drivers of high-quality entrepreneurship: What changes did the crisis bring about? *Small Business Economics, 48*(4), 913–930.

Gorgievski, M. J., Bakker, A. B., Schaufeli, W. B., van der Veen, H. B., & Giesen, C. W. M. (2010). Financial problems and psychological distress: Investigating reciprocal effects among business owners. *Journal of Occupational and Organizational Psychology, 83*(2), 513–530.

Graeber, D., Kritikos, A. S., & Seebauer, J. (2021). COVID-19: A crisis of the female self-employed. *Journal of Population Economics, 34*, 1141–1187.

Grashuis, J. (2021). Self-employment duration during the COVID-19 pandemic: A competing risk analysis. *Journal of Business Venturing Insights, 15*, e00241.

Guzman, J., & Kacperczyk, A. O. (2019). Gender gap in entrepreneurship. *Research Policy, 48*(7), 1666–1680.

Hobfoll, S. E. (2001). The influence of culture, community, and the nested-self in the stress process: Advancing conservation of resources theory. *Applied Psychology, 50*(3), 337–421.

Kahn, L. B. (2010). The long-term labor market consequences of graduating from college in a bad economy. *Labour Economics, 17*(2), 303–316.

Kautonen, T., van Gelderen, M., & Tornikoski, E. T. (2013). Predicting entrepreneurial behaviour: A test of the theory of planned behaviour. *Applied Economics, 45*(6), 697–707.

Kautonen, T., van Gelderen, M., & Fink, M. (2015). Robustness of the theory of planned behavior in predicting entrepreneurial intentions and actions. *Entrepreneurship Theory and Practice, 39*(3), 655–674.

Kim, M.-S., & Hunter, J. E. (1993). Relationships among attitudes, behavioral intentions, and behavior: A meta-analysis of past research, part 2. *Communication Research, 20*(3), 331–364.

Koellinger, P. D., & Thurik, R. A. (2012). Entrepreneurship and the business cycle. *Review of Economics and Statistics, 94*(4), 1143–1156.

Krosnick, J. A., & Alwin, D. F. (1989). Aging and susceptibility to attitude change. *Journal of Personality and Social Psychology, 57*(3), 416.

Kuckertz, A. (2021). Standing up against crisis-induced entrepreneurial uncertainty: Fewer teams, more habitual entrepreneurs. *International Small Business Journal, 39*(3), 191–201.

Kuckertz, A., Brändle, L., Gaudig, A., Hinderer, S., Reyes, C. A. M., Prochotta, A., et al. (2020). Startups in times of crisis–a rapid response to the COVID-19 pandemic. *Journal of Business Venturing Insights, 13*, e00169.

Langowitz, N., & Minniti, M. (2007). The entrepreneurial propensity of women. *Entrepreneurship Theory and Practice, 31*(3), 341–364.

Liñán, F., & Jaén, I. (2020). The Covid-19 pandemic and entrepreneurship: Some reflections. *International Journal of Emerging Markets*. https://doi.org/10.1108/IJOEM-05-2020-0491

Millman, C., Li, Z., Matlay, H., & Wong, W. (2010). Entrepreneurship education and students' internet entrepreneurship intentions: Evidence from Chinese HEIs. *Journal of Small Business and Enterprise Development, 17*(4), 569–590.

Oude Groeniger, J., Noordzij, K., van der Waal, J., & de Koster, W. (2021). Dutch COVID-19 lockdown measures increased trust in government and trust in science: A difference-in-differences analysis. *Social Science & Medicine, 275*, 113819. https://doi.org/10.1016/j.socscimed.2021.113819

Patel, P. C., & Rietveld, C. A. (2020). The impact of financial insecurity on the self-employed's short-term psychological distress: Evidence from the COVID-19 pandemic. *Journal of Business Venturing Insights, 14*, e00206.

Raijman, R. (2001). Determinants of entrepreneurial intentions: Mexican immigrants in Chicago. *The Journal of Socio-Economics, 30*(5), 393–411.

Ruiz-Rosa, I., Gutiérrez-Taño, D., & García-Rodríguez, F. J. (2020). Social entrepreneurial intention and the impact of COVID-19 pandemic: A structural model. *Sustainability, 12*(17), 6970.

Schwandt, H., & von Wachter, T. (2019). Unlucky cohorts: Estimating the long-term effects of entering the labor market in a recession in large cross-sectional data sets. *Journal of Labor Economics, 37*(S1), S161–S198.

Sheth, J. (2020). Impact of Covid-19 on consumer behavior: Will the old habits return or die? *Journal of Business Research, 117*, 280–283.

Shinnar, R. S., Giacomin, O., & Janssen, F. (2012). Entrepreneurial perceptions and intentions: The role of gender and culture. *Entrepreneurship Theory and Practice, 36*(3), 465–493.

Smid, T., & Ciobica, I. (2021). *2021: A turn of the tide in insolvencies*. Accessed July 9, 2021, from https://group.atradius.com/publications/economic-research/2021-a-turn-of-the-tide-in-insolvencies.html

Statistics Netherlands. (2021). *Monthly labour participation and unemployment*. Accessed July 2, 2021, from https://www.cbs.nl/en-gb/figures/detail/80590eng

Stephan, U. (2018). Entrepreneurs' mental health and well-being: A review and research agenda. *Academy of Management Perspectives, 32*(3), 290–322.

Stephan, U., Zbierowski, P., Pérez-Luño, A., Klausen, A., Cabañas, M. A., Barki, E., et al. (2021). Entrepreneurship during the Covid-19 pandemic: A global study of entrepreneurs' challenges, resilience, and well-being. .

Thurik, R., & Wennekers, S. (2004). Entrepreneurship, small business and economic growth. *Journal of Small Business and Enterprise Development, 11*(1), 140–149.

Torrès, O., Benzari, A., Fisch, C., Mukerjee, J., Swalhi, A., & Thurik, R. (2021a). Risk of burnout in French entrepreneurs during the COVID-19 crisis. *Small Business Economics, 58*(2), 1–23.

Torrès, O., Benzari, A., Swalhi, A., & Thurik, R. (2021b). Confinement et risque de burnout des dirigeants propriétaires de PME: le syndrome d'épuisement d'empêchement. *Revue Internationale PME, 34*(2), 62–80.

Torrès, O., Fisch, C., Mukerjee, J., Lasch, F., & Thurik, R. (2021c). Health perception of French SME owners during the 2020 COVID-19 pandemic. *International Review of Entrepreneurship, 19*(2), 151–168.

van der Zwan, P., Thurik, R., Verheul, I., & Hessels, J. (2016). Factors influencing the entrepreneurial engagement of opportunity and necessity entrepreneurs. *Eurasian Business Review, 6*(3), 273–295.

van Gelderen, M., Brand, M., van Praag, M., Bodewes, W., Poutsma, E., & van Gils, A. (2008). Explaining entrepreneurial intentions by means of the theory of planned behaviour. *Career Development International, 13*(6), 538–559.

van Praag, C. M., & Versloot, P. H. (2007). What is the value of entrepreneurship? A review of recent research. *Small Business Economics, 29*(4), 351–382.

van Stel, A., Carree, M., & Thurik, R. (2005). The effect of entrepreneurial activity on national economic growth. *Small Business Economics, 24*(3), 311–321.

Verheul, I., Thurik, R., Grilo, I., & van der Zwan, P. (2012). Explaining preferences and actual involvement in self-employment: Gender and the entrepreneurial personality. *Journal of Economic Psychology, 33*(2), 325–341.

Wiklund, J., Hatak, I., Patzelt, H., & Shepherd, D. A. (2018). Mental disorders in the entrepreneurship context: When being different can be an advantage. *Academy of Management Perspectives, 32*(2), 182–206.

Wiklund, J., Nikolaev, B., Shir, N., Foo, M.-D., & Bradley, S. (2019). Entrepreneurship and well-being: Past, present, and future. *Journal of Business Venturing, 34*(4), 579–588.

Wilson, F., Kickul, J., & Marlino, D. (2007a). Gender, entrepreneurial self–efficacy, and entrepreneurial career intentions: Implications for entrepreneurship education. *Entrepreneurship Theory and Practice, 31*(3), 387–406.

Wilson, F., Kickul, J., & Marlino, D. (2007b). Gender, entrepreneurial self–efficacy, and entrepreneurial career intentions: Implications for entrepreneurship education. *Entrepreneurship Theory and Practice, 31*(3), 387–406.

Wismans, A., Letina, S., Thurik, R., Wennberg, K., Franken, I., Baptista, R., et al. (2020a). Hygiene and social distancing as distinct public health related behaviours among university students during the COVID-19 pandemic. *Social Psychological Bulletin, 15*(4), 1–26.

Wismans, A., Thurik, R., Verheul, I., Torrès, O., & Kamei, K. (2020b). Attention-deficit hyperactivity disorder symptoms and entrepreneurial orientation: A replication note. *Applied Psychology, 69*(3), 1093–1112.

Wismans, A., Kamei, K., Thurik, R., & Torrès, O. (2021a). The link between attention-deficit hyperactivity disorder symptoms and entrepreneurial orientation in Japanese business owners. *Management Review, 71*, 857–872.
Wismans, A., Letina, S., Wennberg, K., Thurik, R., Baptista, R., Burke, A., et al. (2021b). The role of impulsivity and delay discounting in student compliance with COVID-19 protective measures. *Personality and Individual Differences, 179*, 110925.
Wismans, A., Thurik, R., Baptista, R., Dejardin, M., Janssen, F., & Franken, I. (2021c). Psychological characteristics and the mediating role of the 5C model in explaining students' COVID-19 vaccination intention. *PLoS One, 16*(8), e0255382.
World Economic Forum. (2020). *The global gender gap report*. World Economic Forum.

**Annelot Wismans** is a Ph.D. candidate at the Erasmus School of Economics in Rotterdam. She works on interdisciplinary research combining psychology and economics. Her research can be broadly divided into two themes: (1) the psychology of entrepreneurship and (2) individual determinants of COVID-19-related behavior, such as compliance with regulations and vaccination attitudes.

**Milco Lodder** is an alumnus of Erasmus University Rotterdam in the field of strategy economics and entrepreneurship and currently employed as manager in the commercial sector.

**Roy Thurik** is Professor of Entrepreneurship and Economics at the Montpellier Business School in France. He is Emeritus Professor of Economics and Entrepreneurship at the Erasmus School of Economics in Rotterdam and the Free University in Amsterdam. He is Research Fellow at two renowned Dutch research schools: the Tinbergen Institute for Economic Sciences and the Erasmus Research Institute for Management. He is director of the Centre for Advanced Small Business Economics and the Erasmus University Rotterdam Institute for Biology and Behavior.

# COVID-19: Entrepreneurial Universities and Academic Entrepreneurship

James A. Cunningham

**Abstract** The purpose of this chapter is to reflect on how the pandemic has shaped entrepreneurial universities, academics and academic entrepreneurship. Against this background, some strategic dilemmas are considered for entrepreneurial universities, namely, first mission delivery and programme configurations, investment and funding, organisational configuration, institutional research priorities, third mission—technology and knowledge transfer—and university community and universities communities: resilience and progression. Considerations of how the pandemic has shaped academic and academic entrepreneurs are also discussed, concerning teaching, research priorities, research impact, technology and knowledge transfer and health and well-being.

**Keywords** Academic entrepreneurship · Entrepreneurial universities · COVID-19 · Pandemic · Universities · Technology transfer · Third mission

## 1 Introduction

COVID-19 has challenged many collective societal assumptions and has brought to fore many of the inequalities that exist in our society. It also has brought out many positive aspects of our society. For many people in our societies, this has been a horrendous time. Societies and individuals have gone through a range of emotions that will take time to fully process and understand. It also has raised many questions some very fundamental ones, such as what is the role of government? There are myriads of examples in neighbourhoods, communities and localities of individuals, charities, private sector organisations and public bodies going above and beyond demonstrating selflessness to support an individual through this challenging period.

J. A. Cunningham (✉)
Newcastle University Business School, Newcastle University, Newcastle Upon Tyne, UK

Centre for Innovation Research (CIRCLE), Lund University, Lund, Sweden
e-mail: james.cunningham@newcastle.ac.uk



D. B. Audretsch, I. A. M. Kunadt (eds.), *The COVID-19 Crisis and Entrepreneurship*, International Studies in Entrepreneurship 54,
https://doi.org/10.1007/978-3-031-04655-1_15

These acts of selflessness some visible and invisible to society have made small and significant differences to individuals and our societies. There are countless examples of voluntary efforts to support individuals in different ways. This may be a phone call, a grocery delivery, a card in the post and a socially distant conversation.

Globally, organisations faced unprecedented challenges due to COVID-19. Business models became redundant, sales stopped and operations became challenging for a variety of reasons. The focus was on survival. Some governments offered different types of temporary support to businesses and their employees to help them survive. For many, this was not sufficient or in place in time to save their businesses from failure. There were the entrepreneurs that had just launched a new venture based on normal environmental conditions, and all of their plans were negated in a short period due to COVID-19. Hard personal decisions were made by businesses as they tried and cope with the pandemic. The challenges being experienced by those who are self-employed working in different sectors become evident through the media. Charities and voluntary organisations were also impacted. Like businesses some had to change how they delivered their services and some did not survive.

The invisible workers and work that goes on to keep our societies running became visible during the pandemic. Societies began to realise the value of what is termed in the UK and other countries as key workers and the essential role that they play every day. This work became visible and important. It also highlighted their pay and conditions and the challenges that they face every day in fulfilling these roles to keep societies running. Within society, some experienced at first hand the real pain of COVID-19 and we all witnessed this through media reporting. The harrowing stories of individual citizens dying from COVID-19 alone in hospitals and medical centres without any loved ones providing the reassuring familial comfort. Our collective thoughts were with health professionals and the thousands of families who experienced the trauma of saying goodbye to loved ones virtually as well as not being able to attend funerals as part of our normal societal rituals. This would be unthinkable in normal circumstances. Countrywide lockdowns would be unthinkable in normal circumstances. Seeing medical and health professionals dressed in full PPE and having to make the most challenging medical decisions under the most unimaginable pressures for days and months on end would be unthinkable in normal circumstances. We have experienced as individuals a lot of unthinkable events. We have reacted, adapted, coped and not coped with these unthinkable changes. Seeing the vibrancy of society being shut down for the greater good of saving lives is something that would have been unthinkable in normal circumstances. It also brought into sharper focus the fragility and temporality of life. As the pandemic evolves with societies ebbing back to normal, the real question is will it change anything in our societies and our individual lives? Only time will tell if anything substantive will change in our societies due to the pandemic. Will we continue to value key workers who play an important and invisible role in our daily lives? To them and all the countless people who collectively made a significant difference to us during COVID-19, we should never forget their selflessness, courage and steadfastness.

Against this backdrop, my focus for this chapter is to reflect on how the pandemic has raised some strategic dilemmas for entrepreneurial universities, academics and academic entrepreneurship. These have been a research focus of mine over the last decade.

## 2 Entrepreneurial Universities

One of my research interests has been focused on entrepreneurial universities (see Forliano et al., 2021; Guerrero et al., 2015; Guerrero & Urbano, 2019; Urbano & Guerrero, 2013). This research has examined issues such as their mission focus, economic impact and organisational architecture to support entrepreneurial mission expansion (Cunningham et al., 2017, 2020a, 2020b; Miller et al., 2021). COVID-19 has highlighted once again the pivotal institutional role that universities play in society and in the communities and regions that they inhabit. Entrepreneurial universities' missions adapted to deal with the initial challenges posed by COVID-19 with modules and courses moving online and then to supporting regional and national efforts in dealing with the different dimensions of COVID-19 (see Choi et al., 2020; Liguori & Winkler, 2020; Secundo et al., 2021). Some used this time to innovate (see Bacq et al., 2020). Many universities made available their estates and facilities to support local communities such as supporting collective efforts in setting up COVID-19 testing centres. There are many examples of how students, faculty and professional support staff collaborated to support each other through this period and with their wider communities. Furthermore, many faculty members of entrepreneurial universities contributed their expertise directly to government efforts to deal with COVID-19. Some became household names due to their regular contributions to media and news programmes.

## 3 Some Strategic Dilemmas

From a strategic perspective for university leaders and academic communities, COVID-19 has raised some strategic dilemmas in how entrepreneurial universities pursue their missions and realise them for their stakeholders.

### *3.1 First Mission Delivery and Programme Configurations*

With many entrepreneurial universities moving quickly to online delivery of modules and programmes, this has challenged the norms concerning face-to-face delivery. Some entrepreneurial universities were better placed due to their investment in digital teaching infrastructures, while others were not. This placed added burdens to the wider university community in adapting and coping with this sudden change in delivery modes. The resultant strategic dilemma is how best to blend both online and traditional face-to-face delivery that supports the delivery of programmes that meet the needs of different learning groups. We have seen individual faculty members being bold, imaginative with innovative pedagogical approaches as they embraced and delivered online delivery. They have been creative in the manner they engaged to develop engaging content and to use technology effectively while also dealing with changing and evolving personal demands and circumstances. The pandemic has also illuminated what is possible to further enhance and reimagine the first mission degree programmes of entrepreneurial universities using technology.

One of the core tenants of an entrepreneurial university is having in place an entrepreneurial culture that supports individual autonomy. COVID-19 has highlighted once again how passionate faculty can respond, be original and creative given the organisational freedom, impetus and autonomy. The strategic dilemma of entrepreneurial universities is how to blend this individual-level creativity and passion of individual faculty members that have been very visible during the last academic year (2020/2021) and harness this with delivery modes that enhance the development of individual learners and their communities using a variety of delivery mechanisms. While there is an institutional comfort to return to previous delivery methods through face-to-face delivery, the strategic dilemma is how best to blend different delivery approaches and support individual faculty level autonomy to enhance learning and further diversify delivery mechanisms.

Without a doubt, first mission delivery blending also opens up first mission reconfiguration opportunities. It also places a renewed emphasis on entrepreneurial universities being bolder and more ambitious concerning interdisciplinary programmes at the undergraduate and postgraduate levels. Blending delivery also enhances the reach and scope of entrepreneurial universities. Will entrepreneurial universities be bold enough to grasp the opportunities that have emerged as a result of COVID-19 to fundamentally change their first mission delivery and programme suite configurations?

## 3.2 *Investment and Funding*

For entrepreneurial universities, much of their resource base has followed traditional norms of investing in what is termed as the student experience, ongoing consolidation or expansion of human capital (academic and professional services) and depending on the institutional research intensity an investment in the third mission (Dalmarco et al., 2018: Mok, 2015). Many universities have invested heavily and expanded their physical infrastructure to support their core teaching and research missions. Tangible results of such investments can be seen on campuses with new buildings and facilities such as laboratories, incubators, lecture halls, flexible teaching spaces, etc. (Abdelkafi et al., 2018; Bikse et al., 2016; Dolan et al., 2019; Kirby,

2006). For periods during the initial stages of COVID-19, much of these estates were mothballed and only coming back into use once local health restrictions permitted.

COVID-19 has presented entrepreneurial universities with a significant investment strategic dilemma. Do entrepreneurial universities continue their current mission investment plans such as estates investments, or do they divert such investment into activities that enhance digital agility and resilience across all missions? What overall strategic posture does an entrepreneurial university need to adopt given heightened uncertainties in the short and medium term? What missions does an entrepreneurial university prioritise? In considering such an important issue, do entrepreneurial universities have the internal institutional expertise and governance mechanisms to carefully consider this strategic dilemma and the associated questions? The investment decision influence what activities entrepreneurial universities invest in and prioritise. This the has a knock-on impact on institution itself and also outside the university (Guerrero et al., 2016; Cunningham & Menter, 2020).

COVID-19 also highlighted their funding dependency and challenges that entrepreneurial universities face. Many entrepreneurial universities have a predominant funding dependence on a mix of public funding and student fees. A significant portion of some of the student fee income can come from the international student market (see Blackmore, 2020). Within the internal funding allocation, there can be cross-subsidisation across missions and disciplines (Lewis & Pendlebury, 2002). Such funding dependency has shown the financial fragility of many entrepreneurial universities. This has been more widely acknowledged by Estermann et al. (2020) who suggest that funding sources for universities have been impacted by COVID-19 in the short and medium term. The strategic dilemma for entrepreneurial universities is how to build a more resilient funding model that can withstand unexpected shocks such as COVID-19 and allows them also to invest in all this mission, particularly the third mission entrepreneurial architecture.

### *3.3 Organisational Configuration*

Linked to the strategic dilemma of investment and funding is what is the appropriate organisational configuration that is necessary to ensure stability while also ensuring agility within organisational structures to respond effectively to external and internal changes. In essence, how do entrepreneurial universities build their entrepreneurialism and the associated culture? Entrepreneurial universities' core organisational units are grounded within academic disciplines through departmental structures. Complementary disciplines and departments are grouped in schools or faculties to fulfil the first mission (see Tajpour et al., 2020) While academic discipline contributes to the second mission, research, formal organisational units such as research institute and centres typically provide a focal point. Some of these organisational units are designed to nurture and support interdisciplinary research. A variety of organisational units are deployed by entrepreneurial universities to support their third mission (Cunningham et al., 2021a, 2021b). To support these missions, many universities have centralised their supporting organisational units and organisational decision-making (see Jarzabkowski, 2002).

Entrepreneurial universities before the pandemic have been involved in wider societal activities within and beyond their environs (see Ferreira et al., 2018: Ratten, 2017; Guerrero et al., 2016). During COVID-19, universities have responded and contributed to the wider community and societal efforts that have transcended normal internal organisational units and institutional boundaries. This has been empowering for individuals and necessary given the common purpose that bounded academic communities with wider societal and government COVID objectives. The strategic dilemma for entrepreneurial universities from an organisational design perspective is how best to create an appropriate organisational unit configuration that enhances and integrates further their core missions that meet ongoing and increasing stakeholder demands while also blending wider beneficial societal engagements. How do entrepreneurial universities formally embed their wider societal engagement into their core existing missions? Do they need to form another distinct mission or does it become integrated seamlessly into the existing missions? Should the traditional disciplinary organisational units remain the primary organising unit of entrepreneurial universities? Do entrepreneurial universities continue to invest and expand their mission activities across the stage of entrepreneurship? How can entrepreneurial universities imbue an entrepreneurial culture as part of their organisational-wide configuration?

## 3.4 Institutional Research Priorities

One of the strengths of entrepreneurial universities is their breadth of disciplinary expertise which can take decades to build and develop. Pre-pandemic such disciplinary breadth may have been considered by some as unnecessary. Some universities had started processes of closing academic departments. Typically, entrepreneurial universities have organised and supported their research through stated key institutional priorities. Such a prioritisation has been informed by a mix of established research strengths, funder and societal needs and priorities. Furthermore, entrepreneurial universities' research priorities have also been influenced by national funding research prioritisation (see Cunningham et al., 2020a, 2020b).

COVID-19 has highlighted very clearly the value and continual need for such disciplinary breadth and depth within entrepreneurial universities as well as across national university systems. As a result of COVID-19, there has been a significant disciplinary and interdisciplinary focus which has translated into a significant body of peer-reviewed scientific publications (see Älgå et al., 2020; Casado-Aranda et al., 2021; Sepúlveda-Vildósola et al., 2020) For example, in business and management, several journals have launched special issues related to COVID-19, while others have published peer-reviewed related papers on COVID-19 (see Amankwah-Amoah et al., 2021; Brammer & Clark, 2020; De Massis & Rondi, 2020; Lawton et al., 2020; Verbeke & Yuan, 2021; Verma & Gustafsson, 2020). Entrepreneurial universities have supported rapid and short-term COVID-19 publicly funded research calls and done in many cases in collaboration with universities nationally and internationally. The responses to these publicly funded research calls were institutionally supported and coordinated during periods when universities had closed their campuses during national and local COVID-19 restrictions.

The breadth of this disciplinary expertise was also evident in the public domain through media, and society was exposed to a variety of disciplinary expertise that addressed the health, social, economic and political aspects of COVID-19. Some of these scientists became household names and this also contributed to raising the visibility of their institutions. Governments, local authorities and other public bodies also sought such disciplinary expertise to support the shaping and implementation of responses to the evolving nature of COVID-19. Governments in communicating COVID-19 policies and regulations used this broad based disciplinary expertise to explain their underpinning rationale that guided their decision-making. 'Following the science' or 'following scientific advice' became part of the public discourse.

The strategic dilemma now for entrepreneurial universities is whether or should they adapt their stated research priorities as a result of COVID-19. While funders have devoted public and private funding to support initial efforts in understanding and responding to COVID-19, such funding may probably continue to grow to build the research capacity, resilience and response capability given the likelihood of further pandemic events. Do entrepreneurial universities build up dedicated pandemic research capacity? This in turn may divert or even diminish the institutional status of current research priorities and may have a knock-on impact on the level of institutional support that these areas currently receive.

A second strategic dilemma relates to how best to organise institutional research priorities given COVID-19 has highlighted the value of multidisciplinary research. The traditional model that entrepreneurial universities have adopted has in the main centred on developing disciplinary excellence. Some entrepreneurial universities have embraced multidisciplinary research that is evidenced through their centres and research institutes. The strategic dilemma that COVID-19 has highlighted for entrepreneurial universities is what is the appropriate research priorities institutional balance between disciplinary and interdisciplinary research and between basic and applied research. Based on current trends, the future research funding landscape would suggest a great emphasis and priority will be based on interdisciplinary research. The realities for entrepreneurial universities' multiple factors contribute to vibrant and thriving interdisciplinary research environments. Providing institutional support for basic and applied research requires sustained institutional support and investment. The cultural aspects of an entrepreneurial university may need further focus by institutional leaders to support researchers and research groups to cope with shifting institutional research priorities.

## 3.5 Third Mission: Technology and Knowledge Transfer

There has been a significant mission expansion of entrepreneurial universities' third mission centred on technology and knowledge transfer (Bengoa et al., 2020; Miller et al., 2021). This has resulted in the growth of technology transfer offices within entrepreneurial universities with the associated institutional investment in commercialisation specialists, etc. to protect and commercialise university intellectual property (Flanagan, 2017; Grimaldi et al., 2021; Hayter et al., 2020). Entrepreneurial universities have also created other institutional support to encourage and support academic entrepreneurship. This has led to the creation of technology transfer offices, incubators, accelerator programmes and hubs and wider involvement of universities in science and technology parks (see Albats et al., 2022; Cadorin et al., 2021; Hobbs et al., 2020; McAdam et al., 2006; Mian, 1994; Theodoraki et al., 2020). In essence, entrepreneurial universities have expanded their institutional entrepreneurial architecture supports across the stages of entrepreneurship (see Cunningham et al., 2021a, 2021b; Nelles & Vorley, 2011; Salomaa, 2019). Such an evolution of institutional support and entrepreneurial architecture has enabled entrepreneurial universities to become an actor of growing importance and significant for research commercialisation. This is evident and measurable in the hard metrics that are used to evaluate the performance of entrepreneurial university technology and knowledge transfer activities (Hsu et al., 2015; Kirby & El Hadidi, 2019; Mascarenhas et al., 2019; Siegel et al., 2008).

Many of the COVID-19 vaccinations have involved university-based researchers collaborating with private organisations and their R & D teams. Such collaborations within a short amount of time delivered vaccinations that are now part of national governments' COVID-19 public health strategies. These scientists have been lauded by society for their endeavours. Their achievements have made an immeasurable difference to individual lives. Moreover, it has shown the wider societal value of such collaborations between universities and industry in creating and commercialising knowledge. An interesting development that has emerged from these technology and knowledge transfer collaborations and subsequent collaborations is wider societal considerations and needs. This raises an interesting strategic dilemma for entrepreneurial universities concerning the commercialisation of intellectual property. Therefore, for technology and knowledge transfer, should entrepreneurial universities give greater consideration to wider societal needs rather than taking a purely economic focus in their commercialisation activities with industry partners? How should entrepreneurial universities place these interests through all of the technology and knowledge transfer mechanisms that they utilise? This is not alone a strategic dilemma for individual entrepreneurial university institutions but a key public policy issue for governments when considering their public R & D and science and technology strategies that are focused on societal grand challenges.

One of the many positives from such university and industry collaborations has been the number of successful vaccinations that have been made available in such a short time period. Also, that it is available to all members of society. Looking forward to the societal grand challenges society faces (Bina et al., 2017), there will be an ongoing need for the collaborative force of university-industry collaborations for knowledge creation and subsequent exploitation through various technology and knowledge transfer mechanisms. However, some of these commercial breakthroughs will need to be available and utilised by all members of society at no and minimal cost. The policy challenge is how to structure such collaborations upfront to ensure that the public good element is considered and realised for individual members of society. This has implications for what type of entrepreneurial architecture entrepreneurial universities should have in the future to support technology and knowledge transfer with industry and other stakeholders. It might even influence how they engage with industry and the criteria used to assess IP exploitation strategies as part of their research commercialisation.

### *3.6 University Communities: Resilience and Progression*

The greatest resource that entrepreneurial universities have is their university community—faculty, students and professional services. The collective endeavours of university communities make entrepreneurial universities dynamic and vibrant organisations that can survive, adapt and thrive. These university communities like other communities and organisations have been impacted directly and indirectly as a result of COVID-19. These university communities have shown great resilience and goodwill in how they managed the different institutional ramifications of COVID-19. Nevertheless, it has highlighted some of the challenges for different groups within the university communities. For example, for some students, COVID-19 had an impact on their health and well-being (Copeland et al., 2021; Essadek & Rabeyron, 2020; Grubic et al., 2020). There is a body of evidence that female faculty members have been more impacted by COVID-19 (see Deryugina et al., 2021; Fulweiler et al., 2021; Kamerlin & Wittung-Stafshede, 2020; Krukowski et al., 2021; Pololi et al., 2021; Sahu, 2020). It also impacted professional support staff in terms of the volume of work that has to contend with in supporting different groups within the university communities while also adjusting to working at home and different work patterns (see Cleland et al., 2020; Gottenborg et al., 2021; Johnson et al., 2020; Yoshinaga et al., 2021). Such issues will have a knock-on impact in terms of faculty career progression (see Oleschuk, 2020) and create new challenges for women in academia (see Hansen, 2020). These issues will also have a direct and indirect impact on university outcomes and performance as the pandemic evolves. The precarious nature of academic contracts has been highlighted in the media as some universities did not renew contracts during this period. It also has impacted tenure track academics (see Harrop et al., 2021). Issues of how entrepreneurial universities and funding agencies support doctoral students and tenure track academics, women and underrepresented minorities have come to the fore. More broadly while many universities did put in place supports during COVID-19 to support international and home students (Morris et al., 2020), this experience raises a strategic dilemma about what are the appropriate institutional supports that universities need to provide for their diverse student community.

So, what are the strategic dilemmas for entrepreneurial universities? For entrepreneurial universities, the most pressing strategic dilemma is how to appropriately and fairly recognise the impact of COVID-19 on faculty members and their career aspirations and progressions. This may in turn mean a mix of different disciplinary and university-wide initiatives that provide the necessary support and enablers for all faculty members. This also extends to professional support staff, some of whom were working at the frontline during the early stages of COVID-19. Furthermore, for professional service staff, many units and functions have adapted their work practices and processes to be able to function effectively virtually during the pandemic. The challenge going forward is how best to retain practices and processes that have been beneficial and effective. The strategic dilemma then is how best to maintain that intrapreneurial mindset and endeavour as part of continual organisational improvements. The pandemic impacted directly on all doctoral students and tenure track faculty. The strategic dilemma for entrepreneurial universities and the wider academic academy is how best to support them in terms of the research advancement and their careers in the short to medium term. For students, the strategic dilemma for entrepreneurial universities is how best to support the totality of their needs particularly concerning health and well-being. These issues need to be addressed along with the equality, diversity and inclusion issues that have been highlighted within academic communities.

## 4 Academics and Academic Entrepreneurs

Much has been written about the changing nature of the academic role and demands that individual academics now have to face (see Civera et al., 2020; Hayter et al., 2018; Miller et al., 2018; Siegel & Wright, 2015; Urban & Chantson, 2019). Depending on the national research system that individual academics operating in, there are expectations around research impact and quality that are driven by the national research evaluation systems such as the Research Excellence Framework (REF) in the UK (Hughes et al., 2019). The predominant focus of this body of research has been on the entrepreneurial university third mission and in particular how individual academics undertake technology and knowledge transfer (see Bojko et al., 2021; Obschonka et al., 2019; Wang et al., 2021). Over the last decade, I have focused my research efforts on this domain at the micro level. My particular research focus is on the scientists in the principal investigator role and how they experience academic entrepreneurship (see Cunningham, 2019; Cunningham et al., 2018, 2021a, 2021b; Mangematin et al., 2014). It is against this background that I offer the following considerations as to how the pandemic has shaped and the resultant strategic dilemmas that academics and academic entrepreneurs face.

## 5 Dilemmas and Considerations

### *5.1 Pedagogical and Delivery Modes*

Across the different national university systems across the globe, there is a continual focus on teaching quality, pedagogical approaches, the use of technology and employability. Traditional lecture formats continue to maintain their dominance as the primary delivery mechanism. In some disciplinary areas, there has been a significant advancement in new pedagogical formats and approaches being adopted by faculty to engage and enthuse students.

The use of technology as an integral part of module delivery became the norm during the pandemic when face-to-face lectures, seminars and tutorials were moved online to adhere to local health restrictions. Individual lectures had to reconfigure modules, content and assessment for virtual delivery. This was challenging and demanding for faculty, students and professional support staff supporting teaching. For some institutions, this change in delivery format ran a lot smoother given the pre-existing investment in a virtual infrastructure to support virtual delivery and the institutional support for specialised teaching and learning staff who can support and advise individual faculty concerning all aspects of curriculum design, virtual environment, assessment, etc.

As universities slowly and cautiously return to traditional face-to-face models of delivery, the strategic dilemma for individual academics is how best to truly blend traditional and virtual learning environments that meet teaching quality norms, are innovate from a pedagogical perspective and contain a further enhanced curriculum content that blends seminal and contemporary theoretical and practice perspectives. Against this is how to do faculty plan and bring their research into these blended environments. In addition, this will also require further faculty professional development to attain new skills and knowledge, and the challenge for universities is how will this be effectively supported and managed given the other demands that faculty have to face. It also opens up new opportunities to create and use more digital resources to support student learning. The opportunities to be innovative are significant. However, at the individual level, faculty considerations will turn pragmatically to how they will be supported and enabled to realise these opportunities. Also will pursuing such endeavours be fully recognised in terms of their career progression?

### *5.2 Research Priorities*

The pandemic as I highlighted earlier in the chapter has shown the value of multidisciplinary research and what can be accomplished by way of knowledge creation and commercialisation. Such multidisciplinary approaches will become the norm among funding agencies. Coupled with this trend will be further requirements to include industry, NGOs and public bodies as part of these large-scale publicly funded research programmes. In such a scenario where pandemics are predicted to become a more frequent society event, this will be reflected in national and international publicly funded research priorities. Depending on public finance constraints, this may displace existing prioritised funding programmes. In essence, more public investment is diverted to pandemic research priorities from existing research programmes.

The strategic dilemma for faculty who could be directly impacted by such a scenario is how they best position and to continue to realise their existing research priorities so they are not impacted by such changes in publicly funded research programme priorities. This may require faculty to expand their existing networks into new disciplinary areas and industrial sectors. Therefore, faculty boundary-spanning efforts may need to be broader and deeper in scope so that they are best positioned to be responsive to changing publicly funded research priorities. An ancillary dilemma for faculty is how to balance effectively their disciplinary and multidisciplinary research efforts and activities. How faculty members and universities collectively respond to these dilemmas will determine the configurations of national and international research communities, how they build their research teams, create and participate in research- and practice-based consortia.

### 5.3 Research Impact

The research that I have conducted concerning scientists in the principal investigator role has found that they are motivated by creating new knowledge (Cunningham et al., 2016) and want their research to have an impact on society (Cunningham et al., 2020a, 2020b). At the research funding proposal stage, it is becoming common practice for funders to require that applicants outline the impact of their proposed research programme. Depending on the nature of the research programme, describing and outlining research impact can be challenging for scientists to articulate credibly and realistically. Furthermore, within some national research systems, there is a systematic review of research quality and the impact such as the Research Excellence Framework (REF) in the UK.

Universities are becoming more attuned to marketing their impact to stakeholders as part of their branding and positioning strategies. COVID-19 has accentuated the relevance of research impact to our societies. It has become tangible at the micro level for individual members of society through public health vaccination programmes. As a consequence of COVID-19, the pressures will inevitably be on faculty members to collectively and individually demonstrate research impact to stakeholders. The pandemic will further strengthen individual academic resolve to plan for and realise research impact. To harness such a resolve, it required nurturing and supportive academic environments and cultures.

The strategic dilemma for individual faculty is how best to approach planning and realising research impact. In some disciplinary areas, this can be straightforward as it is very clear who are the end beneficiaries of faculty research impact. For other disciplines and based on the nature of the research process, it can be more challenging to determine or even envision realised impact. A further consideration in planning for impact is to ensure that it is credible and feasible while also meeting the ambitious expectations of stakeholders. As part of planning and realising research impact is an ongoing challenge concerning what are the appropriate measures of impact that faculty members need to use and how acceptable these are to internal and external stakeholders.

## 5.4 *Technology and Knowledge Transfer*

As discussed earlier, there has been a growing emphasis within entrepreneurial universities on the third mission expansion that has seen a resultant institutional focus and investment to support technology and knowledge transfer. For scientists in the principal investigator role, this continues to be challenging (Cunningham et al., 2020a, 2020b). Through the collaborative efforts of university-based scientists, the value of university-industry technology and knowledge transfer has been further affirmed.

The strategic dilemma for individual faculty members is whether to pursue technology and knowledge transfer as part of the expansion of the entrepreneurial university third mission. If they are going to engage in this activity, what individual agency and influence can they assert to ensure that public good and wider societal issues are considered in the technology transfer decision-making process? COVID-19 has highlighted the importance of considering wider societal and public good considerations when responding to a societal-wide issue.

Collectively, as we face societal grand challenges that are universal, the strategic challenge for individual scientists is that similar approaches to technology transfer that have been adopted during pandemic response become normal, thus ensuring that the resultant knowledge outcomes are available to all members of society without any constraints. Similarly with knowledge transfer that individual scientist have the agency and experience no barriers in pursuing this with external and internal stakeholders. In practical terms, it is ensuring that all their peer-reviewed research is open access and freely available.

## 5.5 *Health and Well-Being*

Similar to other professions, academics have been impacted directly and indirectly by the pandemic. The quick move to online teaching and conducting other academic activities virtually has been a significant change in work practices. This was done while also dealing with personal circumstances that meant that some of the normal activities of faculty such as conducting research had to be abandoned or curtailed. The priority focus was on ensuring that the degree programme kept going and that students were supported. Some faculty that could not travel back to their home countries to be with and to support their families during the pandemic also added to their pressures. Academics also took on further pastoral activities with students and supported them through this period. Faculty members lost family members and friends during which is difficult under normal circumstances.

The resilience of faculty members and the wider academic community over the pandemic period has been one of the positive aspects. However, there is a need to have a more open discussion about faculty health and well-being issues. The pressures on academics have been immense during the pandemic and continue as universities open up their campuses. These pressures need to be openly discussed in the context of individual and collective health and well-being. In doing so, it recognises the variety of personal circumstances of individual academics.

## 6 Concluding Thoughts

As we face the next stages of the pandemic, we need to acknowledge that this has changed our professional lives and the academic institutions that we work in. We may have a renewed appreciation of the normal rhythm and pace of academic life which provides contextual certainty in uncertain times. The danger is as we return to normal our appreciation of the normalisation of academic activities dissipates and is short-lived. While there may be many uncertainties ahead, it is also a period where changes can be made that supports the building of personal and institutional resilience. Our societies need resilient and diverse universities and their communities to address the challenges ahead. Universities need to continually and consistently communicate the tangible and intangible contributions that they make to our societies and individuals. The pandemic has clearly demonstrated the relevance, significance and importance of academics and universities to our societies. It has also shown just how important they are in supporting in all aspects of our society.

As we look forward to the biggest challenge that we collectively face which is ensuring the survival of our planet, the challenges that we have collectively experienced during the pandemic will fade in comparison. Universities and their academic communities have a central, relevant and significant role in tackling this common challenge. The lesson that the pandemic has taught us is that entrepreneurial universities and their communities have the selfless motivation, capability and capacity to deal with this future challenge and the resilience to cope with meeting it that benefits all members of society in an equitable and fair manner.

## References


Abdelkafi, N., Hilbig, R., & Laudien, S. M. (2018). Business models of entrepreneurial universities in the area of vocational education–an exploratory analysis. *International Journal of Technology Management, 77*(1–3), 86–108.

Albats, E., Alexander, A. T., & Cunningham, J. A. (2022). Traditional, virtual, and digital intermediaries in university-industry collaboration: Exploring institutional logics and bounded rationality. *Technological Forecasting and Social Change, 177*, 121470.

Älgå, A., Eriksson, O., & Nordberg, M. (2020). Analysis of scientific publications during the early phase of the COVID-19 pandemic: A topic modelling study. *Journal of Medical Internet Research, 22*(11), e21559.

Amankwah-Amoah, J., Khan, Z., & Wood, G. (2021). COVID-19 and business failures: The paradoxes of experience, scale, and scope for theory and practice. *European Management Journal, 39*(2), 179–184.

Bacq, S., Geoghegan, W., Josefy, M., Stevenson, R., & Williams, T. A. (2020). The COVID-19 virtual idea blitz: Marshaling social entrepreneurship to rapidly respond to urgent grand challenges. *Business Horizons, 63*(6), 705–723.

Bengoa, A., Maseda, A., Iturralde, T., & Aparicio, G. (2020). A bibliometric review of the technology transfer literature. *The Journal of Technology Transfer, 46*, 1–37.

Bikse, V., Lusena-Ezera, I., Rivza, B., & Volkova, T. (2016). The transformation of traditional universities into entrepreneurial universities to ensure sustainable higher education. *Journal of Teacher Education for Sustainability, 18*(2), 75–88.

Bina, O., Mateus, S., Pereira, L., & Caffa, A. (2017). The future imagined: Exploring fiction as a means of reflecting on today's grand societal challenges and tomorrow's options. *Futures, 86*, 166–184.

Blackmore, J. (2020). The carelessness of entrepreneurial universities in a world risk society: A feminist reflection on the impact of Covid-19 in Australia. *Higher Education Research & Development, 39*(7), 1332–1336.

Bojko, M. M., Knapińska, A., & Tomczyńska, A. (2021). Academic entrepreneurship and the research productivity in Poland. *Industry and Innovation, 28*(4), 486–506.

Brammer, S., & Clark, T. (2020). COVID-19 and management education: Reflections on challenges, opportunities, and potential futures. *British Journal of Management, 31*(3), 453.

Cadorin, E., Klofsten, M., & Löfsten, H. (2021). Science parks, talent attraction and stakeholder involvement: An international study. *The Journal of Technology Transfer, 46*(1), 1–28.

Casado-Aranda, L. A., Sánchez-Fernández, J., & Viedma-del-Jesús, M. I. (2021). Analysis of the scientific production of the effect of COVID-19 on the environment: A bibliometric study. *Environmental Research, 193*, 110416.

Choi, B., Jegatheeswaran, L., Minocha, A., Alhilani, M., Nakhoul, M., & Mutengesa, E. (2020). The impact of the COVID-19 pandemic on final year medical students in the United Kingdom: A national survey. *BMC Medical Education, 20*(1), 1–11.

Civera, A., Meoli, M., & Vismara, S. (2020). Engagement of academics in university technology transfer: Opportunity and necessity academic entrepreneurship. *European Economic Review, 123*, 103376.

Cleland, J., McKimm, J., Fuller, R., Taylor, D., Janczukowicz, J., & Gibbs, T. (2020). Adapting to the impact of COVID-19: Sharing stories, sharing practice. *Medical Teacher, 42*(7), 772–775.

Copeland, W. E., McGinnis, E., Bai, Y., Adams, Z., Nardone, H., Devadanam, V., . . . Hudziak, J. J. (2021). Impact of COVID-19 pandemic on college student mental health and wellness. *Journal of the American Academy of Child & Adolescent Psychiatry, 60*(1), 134–141.

Cunningham, J. A. (2019). Principal investigators and boundary spanning entrepreneurial opportunity recognition: A conceptual framework. In *A research agenda for entrepreneurship and innovation*. Edward Elgar Publishing.

Cunningham, J. A., & Menter, M. (2020). Micro-level academic entrepreneurship: A research agenda. *Journal of Management Development, 39*(5), 581–598.

Cunningham, J. A., Mangematin, V., O'Kane, C., & O'Reilly, P. (2016). At the frontiers of scientific advancement: The factors that influence scientists to become or choose to become publicly funded principal investigators. *The Journal of Technology Transfer, 41*(4), 778–797.

Cunningham, J. A., Guerrero, M., & Urbano, D. (2017). Entrepreneurial universities—Overview, reflections, and future research agendas. In *The world scientific reference on entrepreneurship. Volume 1: Entrepreneurial universities: Technology and knowledge transfer* (pp. 3–19).

Cunningham, J. A., Menter, M., & O'Kane, C. (2018). Value creation in the quadruple helix: A micro level conceptual model of principal investigators as value creators. *R&D Management, 48* (1), 136–147.

Cunningham, J. A., Collins, P., & Giblin, M. (2020a). Evolution of Ireland's industrial, science and technology policy. *Annals of Science and Technology Policy, 4*(2), 80–210.

Cunningham, J. A., O'Reilly, P., Hooper, D., Nepelski, D., & Van Roy, V. (2020b). *The Role of Project Coordinators in European Commission Framework Programme Projects. Results of the Innovation Radar PC Survey in FP R & I Projects* (No. JRC120015). Joint Research Centre (Seville site).

Cunningham, J. A., Escribá-Esteve, A., Foncubierta-Rodríguez, M. J., Martín-Alcázar, F., & Perea-Vicente, J. L. (2021a). A gender study of principal investigator lead public R & D centres and funding. *Economics of Innovation and New Technology, 31*, 1–16.

Cunningham, J. A., Lehmann, E. E., & Menter, M. (2021b). The organizational architecture of entrepreneurial universities across the stages of entrepreneurship: A conceptual framework. *Small Business Economics*, 1–17. https://doi.org/10.1007/s11187-021-00513-5

Dalmarco, G., Hulsink, W., & Blois, G. V. (2018). Creating entrepreneurial universities in an emerging economy: Evidence from Brazil. *Technological Forecasting and Social Change, 135*, 99–111.

De Massis, A., & Rondi, E. (2020). COVID-19 and the future of family business research. *Journal of Management Studies, 57*(8), 1727–1731.

Deryugina, T., Shurchkov, O., & Stearns, J. (2021, May). Covid-19 disruptions disproportionately affect female academics. *AEA Papers and Proceedings, 111*, 164–168.

Dolan, B., Cunningham, J. A., Menter, M., & McGregor, C. (2019). The role and function of cooperative research centers in entrepreneurial universities: A micro level perspective. *Management Decision, 57*(12), 3406–3425.

Essadek, A., & Rabeyron, T. (2020). Mental health of French students during the Covid-19 pandemic. *Journal of Affective Disorders, 277*, 392–393.

Estermann, T., Pruvot, E. B., Kupriyanova, V., & Stoyanova, H. (2020). *The impact of the Covid-19 crisis on university funding in Europe: Lessons learnt from the 2008 global financial crisis.* European University Association.

Ferreira, J. J., Fayolle, A., Ratten, V., & Raposo, M. (2018). Introduction: The role of entrepreneurial universities in society. In *Entrepreneurial Universities.*

Flanagan, T. P. (2017). The evolution of technology transfer in Ireland 2006–2016: A practitioner's perspective. *Small Enterprise Research, 24*(3), 316–325.

Forliano, C., De Bernardi, P., & Yahiaoui, D. (2021). Entrepreneurial universities: A bibliometric analysis within the business and management domains. *Technological Forecasting and Social Change, 165*, 120522.

Fulweiler, R. W., Davies, S. W., Biddle, J. F., Burgin, A. J., Cooperdock, E. H., Hanley, T. C., ... Ziegler, M. (2021). Rebuild the academy: Supporting academic mothers during COVID-19 and beyond. *PLoS Biology, 19*(3), e3001100.

Gottenborg, E., Yu, A., Naderi, R., Keniston, A., McBeth, L., Morrison, K., ... Burden, M. (2021). COVID-19's impact on faculty and staff at a School of Medicine in the US: What is the blueprint for the future? *BMC Health Services Research, 21*(1), 1–12.

Grimaldi, R., Kenney, M., & Piccaluga, A. (2021). University technology transfer, regional specialization and local dynamics: Lessons from Italy. *The Journal of Technology Transfer, 46*(4), 855–865.

Grubic, N., Badovinac, S., & Johri, A. M. (2020). Student mental health in the midst of the COVID-19 pandemic: A call for further research and immediate solutions. *International Journal of Social Psychiatry, 66*(5), 517–518.

Guerrero, M., & Urbano, D. (2019). A research agenda for entrepreneurship and innovation: The role of entrepreneurial universities. In *A research agenda for entrepreneurship and innovation*. Edward Elgar Publishing.

Guerrero, M., Cunningham, J. A., & Urbano, D. (2015). Economic impact of entrepreneurial universities' activities: An exploratory study of the United Kingdom. *Research Policy, 44*(3), 748–764.

Guerrero, M., Urbano, D., Fayolle, A., Klofsten, M., & Mian, S. (2016). Entrepreneurial universities: Emerging models in the new social and economic landscape. *Small Business Economics, 47*(3), 551–563.

Hansen, D. S. (2020). Identifying barriers to career progression for women in science: Is COVID-19 creating new challenges? *Trends in Parasitology, 36*(10), 799–802.

Harrop, C., Bal, V., Carpenter, K., & Halladay, A. (2021). A lost generation? The impact of the COVID-19 pandemic on early career ASD researchers. *Autism Research, 14*(6), 1078–1087.

Hayter, C. S., Nelson, A. J., Zayed, S., & O'Connor, A. C. (2018). Conceptualizing academic entrepreneurship ecosystems: A review, analysis and extension of the literature. *The Journal of Technology Transfer, 43*(4), 1039–1082.

Hayter, C. S., Rasmussen, E., & Rooksby, J. H. (2020). Beyond formal university technology transfer: Innovative pathways for knowledge exchange. *The Journal of Technology Transfer, 45*(1), 1–8.

Hobbs, K. G., Link, A. N., & Shelton, T. L. (2020). The regional economic impacts of university research and science parks. *Journal of the Knowledge Economy, 11*(1), 42–56.

Hsu, D. W., Shen, Y. C., Yuan, B. J., & Chou, C. J. (2015). Toward successful commercialization of university technology: Performance drivers of university technology transfer in Taiwan. *Technological Forecasting and Social Change, 92*, 25–39.

Hughes, T., Webber, D., & O'Regan, N. (2019). Achieving wider impact in business and management: Analysing the case studies from REF 2014. *Studies in Higher Education, 44*(4), 628–642.

Jarzabkowski, P. (2002). Centralised or decentralised? Strategic implications of resource allocation models. *Higher Education Quarterly, 56*(1), 5–32.

Johnson, N., Veletsianos, G., & Seaman, J. (2020). US Faculty and Administrators' experiences and approaches in the early weeks of the COVID-19 pandemic. *Online Learning, 24*(2), 6–21.

Kamerlin, S. C. L., & Wittung-Stafshede, P. (2020). Female faculty: Why so few and why care? *Chemistry-A European Journal, 26*(38), 8319–8323.

Kirby, D. A. (2006). Creating entrepreneurial universities in the UK: Applying entrepreneurship theory to practice. *The Journal of Technology Transfer, 31*(5), 599–603.

Kirby, D. A., & El Hadidi, H. H. (2019). University technology transfer efficiency in a factor driven economy: The need for a coherent policy in Egypt. *The Journal of Technology Transfer, 44*(5), 1367–1395.

Krukowski, R. A., Jagsi, R., & Cardel, M. I. (2021). Academic productivity differences by gender and child age in science, technology, engineering, mathematics, and medicine faculty during the COVID-19 pandemic. *Journal of Women's Health, 30*(3), 341–347.

Lawton, T. C., Dorobantu, S., Rajwani, T. S., & Sun, P. (2020). The implications of COVID-19 for nonmarket strategy research. *Journal of Management Studies, 57*(8), 1732–1736.

Lewis, B., & Pendlebury, M. (2002). Surplus or deficit–who cares? Cross-subsidy in colleges of higher education. *Financial Accountability & Management, 18*(1), 25–38.

Liguori, E., & Winkler, C. (2020). From offline to online: Challenges and opportunities for entrepreneurship education following the COVID-19 pandemic. *Entrepreneurship, Education and Pedagogy, 3*(4), 346–351.

Mangematin, V., O'Reilly, P., & Cunningham, J. (2014). PIs as boundary spanners, science and market shapers. *The Journal of Technology Transfer, 39*(1), 1–10.

Mascarenhas, C., Marques, C. S., Galvão, A. R., Carlucci, D., Falcão, P. F., & Ferreira, F. A. (2019). Analyzing technology transfer offices' influence for entrepreneurial universities in Portugal. *Management Decision, 57*(12), 3473–3491.

McAdam, M., Galbraith, B., McAdam, R., & Humphreys, P. (2006). Business processes and networks in university incubators: A review and research agendas. *Technology Analysis & Strategic Management, 18*(5), 451–472.

Mian, S. A. (1994). US university-sponsored technology incubators: An overview of management, policies and performance. *Technovation, 14*(8), 515–528.

Miller, K., Alexander, A., Cunningham, J. A., & Albats, E. (2018). Entrepreneurial academics and academic entrepreneurs: A systematic literature review. *International Journal of Technology Management, 77*(1–3), 9–37.

Miller, K., Cunningham, J., & Lehmann, E. (2021). Extending the university mission and business model: Influences and implications. *Studies in Higher Education, 46*(5), 915–925.

Mok, K. H. (2015). The quest for global competitiveness: Promotion of innovation and entrepreneurial universities in Singapore. *Higher Education Policy, 28*(1), 91–106.

Morris, A., Hastings, C., Wilson, S., Mitchell, E., & Ramia, G. (2020). *The experience of international students before and during COVID-19: Housing, work, study and wellbeing*. Accessed October 7, 2021, from https://opus.cloud.lib.uts.edu.au/bitstream/10453/142533/2/internationalstudentsandhousing%20report%20ss.com%3A2020%3A08%3Ainternational-students-and-housing-survey-report-final-no-logos-5-aug-2020.pdf

Nelles, J., & Vorley, T. (2011). Entrepreneurial architecture: A blueprint for entrepreneurial universities. *Canadian Journal of Administrative Sciences/Revue Canadienne des sciences de l'administration, 28*(3), 341–353.

Obschonka, M., Moeller, J., & Goethner, M. (2019). Entrepreneurial passion and personality: The case of academic entrepreneurship. *Frontiers in Psychology, 9*, 2697.

Oleschuk, M. (2020). Gender equity considerations for tenure and promotion during COVID-19. *Canadian Review of Sociology, 57*(3), 502–515.

Pololi, L. H., Vasiliou, V., & Bloom-Feshbach, K. (2021). Midcareer medical school research faculty perspectives on vitality and professionalism during the COVID-19 pandemic. *JAMA Network Open, 4*(8), e2120642.

Ratten, V. (2017). Entrepreneurial universities: The role of communities, people and places. *Journal of Enterprising Communities: People and Places in the Global Economy, 11*(3), 310–315.

Sahu, P. (2020). Closure of universities due to coronavirus disease 2019 (COVID-19): Impact on education and mental health of students and academic staff. *Cureus, 12*(4), e7541.

Salomaa, M. (2019). Third mission and regional context: Assessing universities' entrepreneurial architecture in rural regions. *Regional Studies, Regional Science, 6*(1), 233–249.

Secundo, G., Gioconda, M. E. L. E., Del Vecchio, P., Gianluca, E. L. I. A., Margherita, A., & Valentina, N. D. O. U. (2021). Threat or opportunity? A case study of digital-enabled redesign of entrepreneurship education in the COVID-19 emergency. *Technological Forecasting and Social Change, 166*, 120565.

Sepúlveda-Vildósola, A. C., MejÍa-Aranguré, J. M., Barrera-Cruz, C., Fuentes-Morales, N. A., & Rodriguez-Zeron, C. (2020). Scientific publications during the COVID-19 pandemic. *Archives of Medical Research, 51*(5), 349.

Siegel, D. S., & Wright, M. (2015). Academic entrepreneurship: Time for a rethink? *British Journal of Management, 26*(4), 582–595.

Siegel, D., Wright, M., Chapple, W., & Lockett, A. (2008). Assessing the relative performance of university technology transfer in the US and UK: A stochastic distance function approach. *Economics of Innovation and New Technology, 17*(7–8), 717–729.

Tajpour, M., Kawamorita, H., & Demiryurek, K. (2020). Towards the third generation of universities with an entrepreneurial approach. *International Journal of Technoentrepreneurship, 4*(2), 122–133.

Theodoraki, C., Messeghem, K., & Audretsch, D. B. (2020). The effectiveness of incubators' co-opetition strategy in the entrepreneurial ecosystem: Empirical evidence from France. *IEEE Transactions on Engineering Management, 2020*, 1–14.
Urban, B., & Chantson, J. (2019). Academic entrepreneurship in South Africa: Testing for entrepreneurial intentions. *The Journal of Technology Transfer, 44*(3), 948–980.
Urbano, D., & Guerrero, M. (2013). Entrepreneurial universities: Socioeconomic impacts of academic entrepreneurship in a European region. *Economic Development Quarterly, 27*(1), 40–55.
Verbeke, A., & Yuan, W. (2021). A few implications of the covid-19 pandemic for international business strategy research. *Journal of Management Studies, 58*(2), 597–601.
Verma, S., & Gustafsson, A. (2020). Investigating the emerging COVID-19 research trends in the field of business and management: A bibliometric analysis approach. *Journal of Business Research, 118*, 253–261.
Wang, M., Cai, J., Soetanto, D., & Guo, Y. (2021). Why do academic scientists participate in academic entrepreneurship? An empirical investigation of department context and the antecedents of entrepreneurial behavior. *Journal of Small Business Management, 26*, 1–32.
Yoshinaga, N., Nakagami, G., Fukahori, H., Shimpuku, Y., Sanada, H., & Sugama, J. (2021). Initial impact of the COVID-19 pandemic on time Japanese nursing faculty devote to research: Cross-sectional survey. *Japan Journal of Nursing Science, 19*, e12454.

**James A. Cunningham** is a Professor of Entrepreneurship and Innovation at Newcastle University Business School, Newcastle University, Newcastle Upon Tyne, United Kingdom and is an affiliated member of Centre for Innovation Research at Lund University, Sweden. He has held academic positions at University College Dublin, National University of Ireland Galway (NUI Galway) and Northumbria University. His research intersects the fields of entrepreneurship, innovation, and strategic management. His has papers published in leading international journals such as Research Policy, Small Business Economics, R&D Management, Long Range Planning, Journal of Small Business Management, Journal of Technology Transfer, Technological Forecasting and Social Change, International Marketing Management, Journal of Business Research and the Journal of Rural Studies among others. Awards for his research include seven best paper conference awards and two case study international competition awards. He has papers published in leading international journals such as *Research Policy, Small Business Economics, R&D Management, Long Range Planning, Journal of Small Business Management, Journal of Technology Transfer, Technological Forecasting and Social Change, International Marketing Management, Journal of Business Research and the Journal of Rural Studies* among others. Awards for his research include seven best paper conference awards and two case study international competition awards.

# Internationalization Meets Digitalization: Entrepreneurial Responses in Higher Education to the COVID-19 Pandemic

**Erik E. Lehmann, Jonah M. Otto, Laurenz Weiße, and Katharine Wirsching**

**Abstract** The COVID-19 pandemic disrupted and altered nearly every facet of higher education, with the programmatic aspects of international education being one of the components most adversely affected. With mobility being strictly limited due to health and safety concerns, academics and program administrators needed to think on their feet and act quickly in order to salvage international student programming and its benefits. This chapter presents a case study of an intricate, trilateral, short-term study abroad program where the academic leaders and program administration collectively adopted an entrepreneurial and innovative mindset in order to move the program into an online, digital environment as a response to the conditions of the pandemic. In doing so, the key actors in this case study provide a successful example of a collaborative online international learning (COIL) program to maximize student and other stakeholder outcomes in a turbulent situation. Further, this case study evidences the benefits of international higher education partnerships that are built on a foundation of trust and a commitment to innovation and resilience.

**Keywords** Internationalization · Higher education · COVID-19 · Digitalization · Online-learning · Innovation · Entrepreneurship

## 1 Introduction

With the discovery of the severe acute respiratory syndrome coronavirus 2, more commonly known as COVID-19, and with the subsequent and ongoing pandemic situation, society and economies worldwide have experienced, and are still experiencing, an unprecedented exogenous shock (McKibbin & Roshen, 2020). The infection control measures, such as social distancing, which are taken to slow the spread of

E. E. Lehmann · J. M. Otto (✉) · L. Weiße · K. Wirsching
Chair of Management and Organization, Faculty of Business and Economics, University of Augsburg, Augsburg, Germany
e-mail: erik.lehmann@wiwi.uni-augsburg.de; jonah.otto@wiwi.uni-augsburg.de; laurenz.weisse@wiwi.uni-augsburg.de; katharine.wirsching@wiwi.uni-augsburg.de



D. B. Audretsch, I. A. M. Kunadt (eds.), *The COVID-19 Crisis and Entrepreneurship*, International Studies in Entrepreneurship 54,
https://doi.org/10.1007/978-3-031-04655-1_16

COVID-19, exert tremendous pressure not only on large parts of a nation's economy but also on the world's education systems, which have historically relied on in-person classes, events, meetings and contacts (Marinoni et al., 2020). In particular, several aspects of higher education internationalization are severely affected by these pandemic control measures due to the closure of many university campuses and the implementation of international travel restrictions (Altbach & de Wit, 2020). Restricted student mobility has drastic consequences for international students who are then unable to begin or continue their degrees abroad, as well as for domestic students who face myriad challenges in implementing their exchange semesters or short-term study abroad programs; in particular, when such programs are mandatory graduation requirements (Kercher & Plasa, 2020). These impacts are being felt at the individual, institutional, network, national, and international levels of analysis. About 82% of respondents in a survey conducted in June 2020 indicated that their study plans are affected by COVID-19.[1] In Europe, the flagship program Erasmus+ might encounter serious cuts instead of an anticipated increase in funding, and in the United States, one of the larger providers of study abroad programs, the Council on International Educational Exchange, has also announced serious cuts (Altbach & de Wit, 2020).

Lockdown and social confinement measures have therefore had an enormous impact on higher education. Higher education has been disrupted as never before, but the fact that campuses are physically closed does not mean that higher education institutions have stopped functioning (Marinoni & van't Land, 2020). On the contrary, faced with multiple challenges, some universities have responded quickly and found new solutions to previously unknown problems and have discovered new ways in which to continue teaching and conducting research, even in an international and interdisciplinary context. Particularly, many universities have been able to shift international programming online, leveraging the strength of their institutional partnerships, international portfolios and technological capability/adaptability to implement collaborative online international learning (COIL) programs which are able to help provide some of the benefits of international education while mitigating the health risks introduced by the pandemic (de Wit & Altbach, 2021; Rubin & Guth, 2015).

Indiana University (USA), the University of Augsburg (Germany) and the University of Bergamo (Italy) provide an excellent case study of how to successfully cope with the pandemic in order to continue producing positive outcomes for students and stakeholders through COIL programs. Since 2013, these universities have annually offered a short-term summer study abroad program for groups of students comprised of all three institutions. The program, affectionately known as "the Summer School," normally takes place in Augsburg (first 1.5 weeks) and in Bergamo (second 1.5 weeks) every summer. Based on an intense international exchange between the students and the lecturers, and among the students themselves in order to organize their required team projects, in-person contact was assumed to

[1] https://www.fintiba.com/blog/corona-survey-results/

be a necessary condition and success factor of a program designed to enhance intercultural competence and international project management skills. Can such a program add some value to the students under the conditions of social distancing? How can such a program be organized just through online components?

By diving deeper into this specific case, this chapter exemplifies the ways in which universities have responded to the COVID-19 pandemic with innovative and entrepreneurial solutions, particularly in the area of internationalization. Given the importance of internationalization to the successful attainment of the traditional mission goals of the university (teaching, research and service to society) (Otto et al., 2021), the universities in this case study quickly answered the challenge of the pandemic in order to provide their students with opportunities for meaningful international experiences despite the inherent obstacles introduced by the pandemic. The rest of the chapter is organized as follows: Section 2 introduces the concept of the Summer School and how it normally functions (prior to the pandemic) and offers facts and statistics, Section 3 then describes how the Summer School was shifted in 2020 into a COIL format, and Section 4 concludes.

## 2 The Summer School[2]

The leadership of the program, three professors which have known each other personally and professionally for years, nurtured a formal partnership in 2013 between the University of Augsburg, the University of Bergamo and Indiana University that has resulted in an intensive, 3-week study abroad course that brings together graduate and undergraduate students from all three institutions to work on group projects that address regional economic development and public policy. This Summer School is co-hosted by the University of Bergamo and the University of Augsburg, splitting the program duration between the two locations. The program is designed so that the students not only benefit from hands-on academic training, but they also are able to build invaluable skills in international project management and cross-cultural competence by working in intercultural teams on rigorous research projects. This is ensured by requiring that every group has no more than 50% of its members from just one university.

As noted by Vismara et al. (2019), “the content of the seminar is comprised of lectures, guest speakers, site visits and cultural excursions so as to maximize the breadth and depth of experience for the students that attend. Through lectures and talks from various voices and areas of expertise, the students are exposed to the expansive and interdisciplinary nature of the academic discipline of the course and are provided with a theoretical foundation and examples of practical application. By making site visits to smaller, family-run firms as well as large, multinational corporations in the local community, the students learn about the important role of

[2] This section is largely adapted from the work of Vismara et al. (2019).

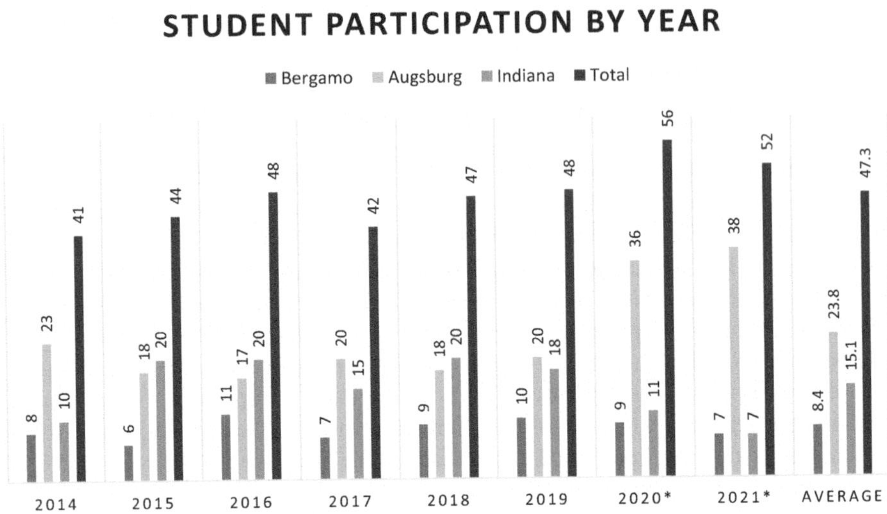


**Fig. 1** Student participation in the Summer School program by university and year. *Numbers include expansion to two Summer School programs per year. Source: Authors' own independent data collection

private enterprise in economic development, as well as the benefits of nurturing a diversified regional economy. The cultural excursions teach the valuable, yet often ignored, lesson of context; that the historical and cultural context of a place bears significant implications for regional economies and the public policies that are intended to shape them. At the conclusion of the program, the students formally present their findings to demonstrate what they have learned and show the progress that they have made towards their group papers. They then use the feedback from the presentations to finalize their work."

While the Summer School has been able to serve a large number of students in total (378), the program has also been popular from the beginning and has maintained a consistently high level of student interest each year, never having less than 41 students in a given year (see Fig. 1). These consistently strong numbers for a program of this scale and complexity are no small feat, particularly when accounting for the COVID-19 pandemic which has significantly impacted international programs since early 2020. This will be discussed in detail later in the chapter.

The number of students from each university is significant, but what is not shown is that there are far more nationalities and cultures represented in the data than just Italian, American and German. Owing to the internationalized student bodies at each of these universities, every iteration of the Summer School has had a very diverse population. Not only are the students culturally diverse, but they are academically diverse as well. The Indiana University students come from a public affairs background, the University of Bergamo students study management engineering, and the University of Augsburg students are trained in various disciplines within business and economics.

Vismara et al. (2019) describe the content of the program as such: "The student academic work of the Summer School revolves around group projects, which are consulting-style reports where the students outline an economic development problem within a place (municipality, city, region, etc.) and propose public policy recommendations within the context of strategic management. At the beginning of the course, students arrange themselves into groups of four or five, with the caveat that no more than two group members can come from the same university. This not only ensures that each group has multiple cultural perspectives, but that each group will also have different academic nuances. With the groups being comprised as such, they are instructed to take a multicultural and interdisciplinary approach to their work. Each group selects a place and an issue that is hindering economic development within that place, then they are tasked with combining their own independent research with the lessons learned from the readings, lectures, site visits and cultural excursions to formulate strategic recommendations that policy-makers from that place can use to appropriately manage and improve local economic development (Audretsch, 2015). In the first year of the Summer School, the resulting papers were published within a book edited by the leadership of the program: *Globalization and Public Policy: A European Perspective* (Audretsch et al., 2015)." See Fig. 2 for a selection of topics and places chosen over the years.

Vismara et al. (2019) go into further detail that, "while typical lectures and assigned readings are essential to providing the students with a theoretical foundation in economic development and the strategic management of places, these methods alone do not sufficiently equip the students to understand best practices, and worst mistakes, that policy makers and economic actors make in regional ecosystems. The best way to be exposed to this type of practical application, under normal circumstances, is to meet local decision makers and see the outcomes of their strategies and policies first-hand. Leveraging the geographic locations of the Summer School and the relationships that have been forged and nurtured by the co-directing professors, the students are not only given the opportunity to hear from economic development experts, government officials, corporate executives, socially-minded entrepreneurs and non-governmental organization leaders, but they are often able to visit their work places too. Throughout the years the Summer School has been fortunate to welcome high profile guest speakers (such as the U.S. Consul General of Munich and a former Senior Vice President of American Express Bank) and gain rare access to public sites and private firms (such as KUKA Robotics Corporation, MAN Group, the Bavarian Center for Transatlantic Relations, Roschmann IDL and Weisser Spulenkörper). This wide array of guest speakers and site visits has given the Summer School students an invaluable look at economic development and the strategic management of places in action; living case studies displaying how public-private partnerships and governmental policy and support can lead to economic prosperity (Audretsch & Lehmann, 2016). In this manner, the hands-on nature of the Summer School has been a crucial component of the student learning process and greatly informs the final products of the student groups."

Vismara et al. concluded by elaborating that, "The final, yet vitally important, components of the Summer School, under normal operation, are the cultural

| *Topic* | *Place(s)* |
|---|---|
| **Income Inequality** | United States, Germany, Norway |
| **Gender Pay Gap** | Iceland, Finland, Norway, Sweden, United States |
| **Recession and Unemployment** | Germany, United States |
| **Crime and Security** | Germany, Italy, United States |
| **Healthcare Systems and Policies** | Germany, Italy, United States |
| **CO2 Emissions and Regulations** | Germany, United States |
| **Aging Population** | Germany |
| **Education** | Munich |
| **Youth Unemployment** | Andalucia |
| **Tech Industry Regulation** | Ireland |
| **Discrimination** | Indiana |
| **Poverty** | East Germany |
| **Pollution** | India |
| **Minimum Wage** | California |
| **Water Resource Management** | Sicily |
| **Immigration** | United States |
| **Tea Industry Ethics** | Kenya |
| **Entrepreneurship** | Munich |
| **Water Resource Management** | Flint, Michigan |
| **Dependence on the Oil Industry** | Kuwait |
| **Unemployment** | Donegal County, Ireland |
| **Healthcare System** | United States |
| **Youth Unemployment** | Italy |
| **Natural Resource Management** | Namibia |
| **Hyperinflation** | Venezuela |
| **Poverty** | Mongolia |
| **Agriculture and Energy Dependence** | Moldova |
| **Water Resource Management** | Sub-Saharan Africa |
| **Poverty and Regional Inequality** | Brazil |
| **Gender Pay Gap** | Estonia |
| **Economic Decline** | Wieda, Germany |
| **Fashion Industry Ethics** | Bangladesh |
| **Chinese Investment** | East Africa |
| **Youth Unemployment and Brain Drain** | Southern Italy |
| **Dependence on the Tech Industry** | Silicon Valley |
| **Gender Pay Gap** | France |
| **Debt Crisis** | Greece |
| **Opioid Crisis** | West Virginia |
| **Corporate Taxation** | Ireland |
| **Public Transit** | Indiana |
| **Green Spaces** | Shanghai, China |
| **Start-up Culture** | Southern Italy |
| **Regional Inequality** | Germany |
| **Labor Regulations** | Bangladesh |
| | |

**Fig. 2** Student group research project topics and places. Source: Authors' own independent data collection

excursions. One of the key lessons to be learned in the strategic management of the economic performance of a place is that culture and context matter (Audretsch, 2015). It is often the case that a policy solution that works in one place cannot simply be implemented elsewhere without at least some modification, and this is owed to the unique cultural and historical considerations of each place (Audretsch & Lehmann, 2016). Cultural excursions are built into the program of the Summer School for this reason; so that students can understand the specific nuances of where they are studying and be able to compare and contrast with the context of their home cultures. This enables the students to dig into the background of a place, identifying root causes of economic and social issues so that they may tailor their policy recommendations in a way that addresses these causes, and doesn't merely put a bandage on the symptoms. The cultural excursions also provide an insight into the preservation, operation, marketing and management of historical and cultural sites, showing how these resources can be included in a local portfolio for economic development."

As one can see, the typical operation of the Summer School has traditionally relied upon educational components tied to the ability to travel and meet in-person. The pandemic, especially in its opening stages, completely upended this model. The following section details the extenuating circumstances of the partner universities and how they answered the challenge of the pandemic in order to continue providing the value of internationalization to their students.

## 3 The Pandemic and the Entrepreneurial Response

One by one, in early 2020, the realities of the COVID-19 pandemic began to sweep through the three countries of the Summer School partner institutions. Unfortunately, the University of Bergamo is very near to one of the early pandemic epicenters in the northern Italian province of Lombardy, with the local community severely impacted (Odone et al., 2020). The government and university system responded quickly by implementing strict measures to limit contacts and ensure social distancing to mitigate the rampant increase in positive cases. By mid-March, the federal states in Germany, in consultation with the national government and constituent universities, similarly imposed and recommended numerous requirements and regulations aimed at preventing the further spread of COVID-19, namely, a lockdown which restricted contact and movement.[3] The United States, whose response was largely fragmented along state lines, was not far behind Europe in instituting international travel restrictions as well as lockdown recommendations, which also implicated Indiana and its universities.[4]

[3] https://www.hrk.de/activities/the-covid-19-pandemic-and-the-german-universities/

[4] https://trumpwhitehouse.archives.gov/presidential-actions/proclamation-suspension-entry-immigrants-nonimmigrants-certain-additional-persons-pose-risk-transmitting-2019-novel-coronavirus/

The first reaction of the organizers of the Summer School was to express deep condolences and unwavering support for their colleagues and their families and friends in Bergamo, an area which was hard hit by the initial force of the pandemic during a time when little was known about the disease—including how it spread and how to treat it (Odone et al., 2020). After everyone was able to take initial stock of the situation and provide for the safety and stability of themselves and their loved ones, the focus quickly turned to how the best could be made of a difficult situation. The brutal nature of the pandemic was demoralizing in itself, and the leaders of the Summer School wanted to do their part to contribute to as much good as they could, for as many as they could. However, as co-organizer Silvio Vismara of Bergamo pointed out, "With the traditional start of the Summer School in May quickly approaching, we knew that we would need to be swift, innovative and flexible in order to deal with the chaotic environment that the pandemic had created."

In the face of the pandemic's disruptive force, the three institutions of the Summer School unilaterally agreed that the program would take place, but not in its traditional form. Questions about the educational consequences and possible ways to implement the program arose. The inability to attend the lectures, site visits, group work meetings and excursions in-person not only turned the regular Summer School routine on its head, but it also posed challenges to the program's educational, professional and cultural focuses. The organizers resolved to address these concerns with solutions that would (a) responsibly address the context of the pandemic and (b) not sacrifice the Summer School's distinctive ability to leverage internationalization for positive student outcomes.

In the ensuing planning discussions, it became clear that the Summer School could defy COVID-19's detrimental effects by playing to the program's true, underlying strengths. Year after year, the program had shown what can be achieved when universities commit to working together, being innovative and staying as flexible as possible, and the program leaders decided that 2020 would be no different. The consensus was that for the Summer School to take place during the pandemic, it must be delivered exclusively in a digital format so as to place public health as the top priority. However, in attempting to achieve the main goals of the program in a digital environment, the Summer School team encountered numerous obstacles. Available digital technologies have enormous potential in their applicability, as they offer direct, synchronous and asynchronous exchanges between supervisors and students; however, if not implemented correctly, these tools also risk forfeiting the core characteristics of the Summer School program, that is, the personal connections built between people when meeting in-person and the intercultural understanding that comes from conducting such programs abroad.

In facing these challenges head-on, the leadership team developed its own approach for the realization of the inaugural digital version of the Summer School. The first task relied upon the flexibility and adaptability of all partners in working with their respective central administrative units to handle the cancelation/rebooking/refunding process for all of the intertwined finances involved in setting up the traditional Summer School format, while also receiving necessary contracts for digital tools and checks for compliance with data privacy regulations. Given the shortened time frame and the complexities of three different university financial/regulatory systems in three different institutional and country contexts, this was no small task but it was necessary in order to clear the path for the digital version of the program.

With the administrative aspects sorted out, deciding upon the technical components of such an online program became the next item on the agenda. While basic videoconferencing software would be used for lectures and formal talks/presentations/interviews/etc., the students needed a place to work and collaborate—a digital version of the campus library. As there was no institutional student portal that students from all three universities had legal access to, it was imperative to obtain a license for software which would provide the students with online collaborative space for their group work. The organizers wanted a system that was already in use in one of the institutions in order to avoid any system-inherent problems and adaptation difficulties during installation, as that partner would then be able to assist with implementation questions and troubleshooting. Thus, the team decided to rely on a free version of the third-party communication and collaboration platform being utilized by the University of Bergamo which provided a hub for online meetings, chats, file sharing and real-time collaboration on documents for students. In addition, for supervisors the platform enabled sharing of classroom resources, curriculum management and increased student engagement by posting updates, tasks and discussion boards. This platform then satisfied all of the base technical needs of the Summer School which were required for the students to be able to complete the academic group work of the course, but as stated by the Summer School leader from Indiana University, David Audretsch, "Finding a technical solution to provide students with access to communal resources was one thing, but finding a way in an online format to recapture some of the interpersonal, cultural and experiential value created in a typical Summer School was something else entirely."

It has always been an essential component of the Summer School to promote intercultural exchange among all of the students and stakeholders involved in the program. For this reason, the internationally diverse and inclusive work groups with students from all involved universities were assigned again. Since in past Summer Schools the personal interaction in the student groups often took place outside the lectures, a private area for each group in the online platform was made available for the students to meet informally with their groups, enabling them to get to know each other, discuss aspects of the course or simply decompress with each other after the lectures. Small intercultural virtual workshops were another way to promote exchange. Whether it was cooking events in their own kitchens or game nights conducted by student teaching assistants, students had the opportunity to get to know their fellow students privately through functions and events designed by the Summer School organizers. In order not to neglect the cultural focus of the program, the digital Summer School placed additional emphasis on speakers in nonmanagement-related topics. Thus, online cultural lectures/events were offered by various partners of the three universities on the topics of "Brexit—Background, Current Situation, and Implications," "Comparing and Contrasting US and European Cultures," a virtual tour of the Documentation Centre for the History of National Socialism and a tour and introduction to the Bavarian American Academy, among others.

Despite the abrupt change to a digital format, the Summer School was a resounding success. Not only was the program very popular, seeing only a slight reduction in attendance when compared to a normal year, but it also received strong marks in the student evaluations which highlighted the academic value of the course and the efforts of the program organizers to actively foster connections within and across the student groups. Furthermore, the efforts in both the cultural and educational aspects also resulted in value for the students, or as program co-director Erik Lehmann recalled, "Our Summer Schools thrive on personal interaction and cultural experiences, but this year has truly proved how much interest students from different countries have in our Summer Schools. It was a unique highlight in what has been a difficult period for students, particularly given the large amount of extracurricular student activities that have been canceled. You could really tell that the students appreciated that we simply found a way to make it work."

Of particular interest is that the quality of the student projects did not suffer when compared to a typical year. As Vismara noted, "We initially expected that the distance education component of the program would result in papers and presentations of lower academic rigor, but rather, the groups thrived. We were thrilled with this outcome, as the academic merit of the program is of the utmost importance." These benefits became important pillars of success, as the pandemic continued throughout the summer and the next year, pushing new Summer School programs also into the online space, as well as the 2021 programs needing to be digital yet again. However, this time the Summer School partners were well equipped and prepared, resulting in another round of successful Summer School programming.

## 4 Conclusion

The COVID-19 pandemic has served as a singularly disruptive force in almost every aspect of modern life, and higher education is no exception. In order to provide for the safety and security of students and staff, universities largely shifted to the world of online or hybrid education, deviating from the traditional university model of in-person education and learning. As discussed in this chapter, international programs quickly came under intense focus as mobility was restricted and higher education institutions asked themselves, "How can we still reap the benefits of internationalization without physically sending students and faculty abroad?" One of the answers to this question is COIL programs, as evidenced in the case study focal point of this chapter, in addition to the expansive literature on this particular program architecture (de Wit & Altbach, 2021; Rubin & Guth, 2015).

By utilizing the mutual understanding and commitment within their trilateral partnership, in addition to their combined strengths in innovation and adaptability, the institutions of the Summer School were able to successfully create a COIL program capable of imparting invaluable international experiences for their students.

The intentional planning that went into adapting and caring for each individual component of the program made the difference. The leaders paused frequently in the planning process to evaluate and ensure that each decision made would result in outcomes which aligned with the mission and values of the program as it was originally constituted in its traditional, in-person form. Although the digital version of the Summer School was a spontaneous response to difficulties introduced by a once-in-a-century viral pandemic, the experiences gathered by the students and faculty involved will leave a lasting trace. While those involved with the program certainly still missed the full experience provided by the in-person format, it is comforting to know that, through a commitment to partnership and innovation, educators can find solutions to any ongoing difficulties related to the pandemic, as well as to future challenges that may arise.

## References

Altbach, P. G., & de Wit, H. (2020). Postpandemic outlook for higher education is bleakest for the poorest. *International Higher Education, 102*, 3–5.

Audretsch, D. B. (2015). *Everything in its place: Entrepreneurship and the strategic management of cities, regions, and states*. Oxford University Press.

Audretsch, D. B., & Lehmann, E. E. (2016). *The seven secrets of Germany: Economic resilience in an era of global turbulence*. Oxford University Press.

Audretsch, D. B., Lehmann, E. E., Vismara, S., & Richardson, A. (Eds.). (2015). *Globalization and public policy: A European perspective*. Springer.

de Wit, H., & Altbach, P. G. (2021). Internationalization in higher education: Global trends and recommendations for its future. In H. Eggins, A. Smolentseva, & H. de Wit (Eds.), *Higher education in the next decade: Global challenges, future prospects*. Brill/Sense Publishers.

Kercher, J., & Plasa, T. (2020). *COVID-19 and the impact on international student mobility in Germany*. Bonn.

Marinoni, G., & van't Land, H. (2020). The impact of COVID-19 on global higher education. *International Higher Education, 102*, 7–9.

Marinoni, G., van't Land, H., & Jensen, T. (2020). *The impact of COVID-19 on higher education around the world*. International Association of Universities.

McKibbin, W., & Roshen, F. (2020). *The global macroeconomic impacts of COVID-19* (pp. 1–43). Brookings Institute.

Odone, A., Delmonte, D., Scognamiglio, T., & Signorelli, C. (2020). COVID-19 deaths in Lombardy, Italy: Data in context. *The Lancet Public Health*. published online, April 24, 2020.

Otto, J. M., Zarrin, M., Wilhelm, D., & Brunner, J. O. (2021). Analyzing the relative efficiency of internationalization in the university business model: The case of Germany. *Studies in Higher Education, 46*(5), 938–950.

Rubin, J., & Guth, S. (2015). Collaborative online international learning: An emerging format for internationalizing curricula. In A. Schultheis Moore & S. Simon (Eds.), *Globally networked teaching in the humanities*. Routledge.

Vismara, S., Wirsching, K. & Otto, J. M. (2019). David B. Audretsch, A Gatekeeper and Globetrotter. In E. E. Lehmann & M. Keilbach (Eds), From industrial organization to entrepreneurship: A tribute to David B. Audretsch (479–488). Springer: .

**Erik E. Lehmann** is a professor at the University of Augsburg (Germany), leading the Chair of Management and Organization and directing the Global Business Management Program. He is also an adjunct professor at Indiana University (USA) and a research professor at the University of Bergamo (Italy). He is an associate editor of *Small Business Economics*. He researches linkages of entrepreneurship, higher education, and corporate governance in the global context.

**Jonah M. Otto** is a research and teaching fellow with the Chair of Management and Organization at the University of Augsburg (Germany), where he also manages international programs and partnerships. His research interests include the internationalization of higher education, international relations, public policy, and economic development.

**Laurenz Weiße** is a research and teaching fellow with the Chair of Management and Organization at the University of Augsburg (Germany) and Coordinator of the Master's Degree Program in Global Business Management. His research interests include entrepreneurship and organizational studies, particularly in the field of corporate governance in religious organizations.

**Katharine Wirsching** is an assistant professor at the Chair of Management and Organization at the University of Augsburg (Germany). She is also a senior research fellow at the Institute for Development Strategies (IDS) at Indiana University (USA). Her research focuses on entrepreneurial ecosystems, corporate governance and innovation in family firms, female and immigrant entrepreneurship, and public policy.

# The Silver Lining for Pandemic-Era International Education

**Andrea Adam Moore**

**Abstract** In this chapter, the first 18 months of the COVID-19 pandemic are revisited from the perspective of Indiana University's Europe Gateway Director in Berlin, Germany. She describes how, within a matter of days in March 2020, the global mobility on which the Gateway's programs depended came to a screeching halt and, in the bigger picture, the entire international education industry unraveled. Yet the author and her colleagues made their proverbial lemonade from the lemons they were given, developing innovative program ideas that addressed needs the pandemic brought upon international education only weeks into the initial shock and sudden new normal of remote work and virtual interaction. Online-only programming brought challenges, but great benefits as well. The crisis affected internal and external university partnerships in both nuanced and sea-change ways, and with potentially lasting impact. A glimpse at the post-pandemic horizon has come into view at the Indiana University Europe Gateway—and beyond.

**Keywords** International education system · Indiana University Global Gateway Network · Digitalization · Student exchange

## 1 Berlin, Bloomington, . . . and Beijing

In February 2020, I visited Indiana University (IU) to spend several days on the beautiful Bloomington campus as well as some time on the Indiana University-Purdue University Indianapolis campus. These trips to Indiana have been an important part of each of the until then 4.5 years I had been working for IU as the Director of the Indiana University Europe Gateway, a small satellite unit of the university with a mission to support international engagement of faculty and students. In my meetings with IU colleagues during the early 2020 visit, we planned for research workshops and study abroad activities for IU students in Europe as well as for the

A. Adam Moore (✉)
Indiana University Europe Gateway, Berlin, Germany
e-mail: andreaam@iu.edu



D. B. Audretsch, I. A. M. Kunadt (eds.), *The COVID-19 Crisis and Entrepreneurship*, International Studies in Entrepreneurship 54,
https://doi.org/10.1007/978-3-031-04655-1_17

upcoming festivities related to IU's Bicentennial. We also discussed the schedule for an upcoming meeting of all IU Gateway Directors—we have such Gateways in China, India, Europe, the ASEAN region, and Mexico—and other key representatives of our University's Office of the Vice President for International Affairs, planned for late March 2020 in Beijing. Everyone was looking forward to this very special professional development opportunity.

I also remember a very enjoyable and sizable after-work gathering at one of my Bloomington-based colleague's home. Among the many topics that evening was a growing concern about the outbreak of a novel coronavirus in China. We were trying to imagine what this would mean—for our students from and in China, our colleagues at the China Gateway, our planned trip to Beijing. None of us considered that this would affect each and every one of us in the most profound ways in a matter of weeks.

A few days later, while waiting to board my return flight to Berlin, where our Europe Gateway is located and I live with my husband and then 6-year-old son, I canceled my flight to Beijing. Another 4 weeks later, on March 11, we received an email from our son's school telling us that he would need to be quarantined for 7 days since one of his teachers had just tested positive for COVID-19. Our son would not go back to school until August 2020. And that would be just one of the several times he (and we as parents) had to cope with distance learning.

The week of March 8, 2020, brought many more disruptions. On March 12, U.S. President Trump suspended travel from Europe to the United States, causing many U.S. students all over the European continent to scramble and find what seemed like one of the last flights home. At the IU Europe Gateway, we were preparing to host an international workshop on entrepreneurship research on March 13 and 14. The workshop would be the last in-person event for many months to come. One of the organizers, who had traveled from Bloomington to Berlin specifically for this gathering, turned around after only a few hours on the ground in Berlin to make it back to the United States. He would attend the workshop via Zoom—the first such participation in what would become the new normal.

Fulfilling the IU Europe Gateway mission—to connect and engage the IU community with scholars, students, alumni, businesses, and other institutions in Europe—had many different pre-pandemic faces: most notably we hosted about 15 academic workshops and conferences in a given year, supported and hosted study abroad groups from IU, created a number of public events, and fostered the university's partnerships with higher education institutions (HEIs) in Europe. For our in-person workshops and conferences, we usually welcomed between 12 and 45 participants, with a small portion coming from the United States and most others from all over Europe. Once in a while we had an individual scholar joining us via Zoom or Skype. Most interactions with our European partner institutions were during in-person conferences or meetings and, of course, through email. Our students—which often meant those who could afford to do so—met and interacted with their European counterparts through short-term, faculty-led study abroad courses or within the framework of longer experiences through student exchange or other study opportunities. They also encountered a significant number of international students on their home campuses in Indiana. In mid-March 2020, we knew none of these personal encounters were going to happen anymore for an indefinite period of time.

During the early days of the first lockdown in Germany, I spent a lot of time trying to get my quarantined son (who had developed a cough) tested for the virus, gathering important documents and hardware from the Gateway (so that I could work from home), and (more or less) constantly checking the news. As for testing, there was no way to get that done: tests were very limited at that time and it was extremely difficult to reach the health authorities. The news looked more dire by the day, if not the hour. And my work time was largely spent on canceling all arrangements we had made for our spring and summer programming at the Gateway. It was truly depressing to watch our calendar emptying for what was supposed to be our busiest season ever at the Europe Gateway. I was also starting to worry and wonder what the Gateway(s) would do now that all our normal activities were suspended for at least a semester. "A semester" was indeed what we thought and hoped the halt to activity would be. From today's point of view, it seems extremely naïve, but at that time, the majority of people did not want to or could not imagine that we would continue to see case and death numbers climb and fall in cycles for well over a year, that whole countries would go in and out of different levels of national lockdowns for so long, and that life as we knew it would not return for such a long time. What we did then in the spring of 2020 was make tentative plans for academic gatherings in the last quarter of 2020, and consider how we could possibly support the IU community in such a difficult time. Our Berlin team of two was also getting used to remote work: how to organize our workdays and best communicate between our separate "home offices" rather than in a shared office. On a personal level, we were also figuring out how to homeschool and care for our son while maintaining work and other parts of life. My husband and I were fortunate that we could both work from home, which primarily meant that we enjoyed much more protection from the virus than many other people. It also meant that we could take turns with childcare. While both our employers have been relatively flexible about when we do our work, the result was seemingly endless days with no clear separation of work and (other) life—yet we were able to continue to work two full-time jobs and offer our child the support and company he needed. We continue to recognize that, even if it has been exhausting and difficult at many times—especially during longer periods of school closures—it has also been a very privileged situation.

## 2 Getting Creative

From my current perspective, the IU Global Gateway Network only became an actual *network* during the course of the COVID-19 pandemic. Until March 2020, our five Gateways operated very independently, with only occasional communication between the staff in different locations. There had naturally been lively and frequent connections to various offices, schools, and other units at the home university, but not so much among the Gateways themselves. The change was sudden and likely permanent: on March 24, 2020, we had a first weekly meeting of the entire staff in the network as well as some other key officers in the Office of the Vice President via Zoom. We would—and I dare to say will—continue these Tuesday team meetings with very few exceptions. The meetings have not only been a great opportunity for exchange and thus learning from each other, but have also served to consider and plan joint activities.

Already in late March and early April 2020, we started talking about collaborative Gateway virtual events. Our colleagues in the Asia Gateways planned a joint webinar on venture capitalism, featuring several IU alumni in their region as well as IU faculty. We decided to create a webinar series with the IU Mexico Gateway devoted to "Art in the Time of Corona." Over the course of 6 weeks in May and June, we hosted a session each week featuring IU faculty and alumni, as well as representatives from our partner universities and other institutions in all our Gateway regions, discussing specific aspects in the arts, art administration, government support of the arts, and more. The series was a great success: we welcomed about 500 attendees and created many new international connections for our IU faculty participants. This first virtual event series also turned out to be a crash course on how to (somewhat) professionally run webinars: it seemed as if every week, we would encounter a new unforeseen challenge—from individual snafus to a significant earthquake at the webinar host's location a mere 5 minutes before we went live! We also learned one of the first positive lessons of the pandemic: it was so much easier to gather an outstanding panel of global experts for a virtual event than for an in-person presentation. Especially during the beginning of the pandemic, invited speakers seemed eager and curious to join our sessions, sometimes even at rather inconvenient times of the day (or night) because of vast time differences between our participant locations. Presenter and also audience eagerness to join virtual events should decrease over the course of the next year. Many of us eventually experienced "Zoom fatigue," a result of spending seemingly whole days on videoconferencing platforms. Yet, creating virtual events proved to be easier and less expensive than our traditional public outreach events. Such events also left a far smaller environmental footprint and were more accessible to a potentially global audience rather than to a mere local group of attendees.

The IU Global Gateways thus spent much of the year 2020 and the entire first half of 2021 organizing virtual programming. In addition to the abovementioned webinars that were addressed to an internal IU audience of students, faculty, staff, and alumni as well as our colleagues and friends around the world, we also produced programs specifically designed to continue to offer IU students a learning experience with international perspectives during a time when international travel had become impossible. At Indiana University, the internationalization of higher education has a long tradition, going back to the oldest recorded faculty-initiated study abroad programs, called Summer Tramps, first established in 1879. Over the two centuries of its existence, the university has created a myriad of diverse programs and ways for its students to study abroad, leading to IU Bloomington in recent years regularly ranking in the top spots among US colleges in overall number of students studying abroad, according to the annual Open Doors reports released by the Institute of

International Education.[1] Study abroad is, of course, only one expression of internationalization. Incoming international students, visiting faculty from around the globe, and the promotion of global teaching and learning across the entire curriculum are, among others, additional pieces of modern internationalization strategies. They are summarized in what has been coined *Internationalization at Home*, and one of the key benefits of all these forms of global engagement is that they are accessible to all students at a university, independent of their financial or time resources. In times when social justice and equity are rightfully demanded in all areas of society, these forms of offering students an international education have become more important than ever. The COVID-19 pandemic instantly put a pause on global travel for scholars and students alike. This upended plans for millions of students in the middle of programs in foreign countries or those who intended to start their studies in 2020. It also created significant budgetary difficulties at thousands of colleges and universities around the world since international student enrollment had become a major source of revenue in recent decades. And finally, the travel restrictions also had very negative effects on internationalization on campuses as from almost one day to the next many of the global perspectives of fellow students and faculty disappeared or were much less accessible. This is one of the areas where the IU Global Gateway Network together with the international partnerships team tried to have a meaningful impact. As an example, through our *Global Connections*[2] program, we have been able to help connect faculty members across the IU campuses with people, organizations, and opportunities across the world. We reached out to experts from foreign universities, NGOs, or governments to give guest lectures or participate in panel discussions; we connected classes to peer classes overseas; we developed flexible research-based exchanges and convened graduate-level reading groups bringing IU students in a particular discipline together with their counterparts across the world. Faculty were offered an easy way to reach out to us by filling out an online request form with their ideas and needs. We then decided which Gateway or other team member would follow up with the professor and develop the programming.

Another example of the programs that were designed and started before the pandemic but have taken off and gained so much momentum in that past 18 months is IU's *Global Classroom* program.[3] This initiative takes a class already being taught at any IU campus and pairs it with a parallel course taught at a foreign (often partner) university. Faculty continue to teach their respective courses independently, but will collaborate with their counterparts to design a project that requires students from both universities to work together and thus add international insights and perspectives and the opportunity to connect across borders to their classrooms. IU supports faculty by finding a suitable partner, offering preparatory workshops, instructional technology support, cross-cultural learning outcomes assessment support, as well as a fellowship grant. Programs like *Global Classroom* or even completely integrated

[1] https://www.iie.org/Research-and-Insights/Open-Doors

[2] https://global.iu.edu/resources/faculty/global-connections.html

[3] https://global.iu.edu/education/internationalization/classroom/index.html

and jointly taught courses between partner universities are prime examples of *virtual mobility* or *virtual exchange* options students have been able to access in recent years and the only options relatively widely available during the pandemic. They have become an important part of *Internationalization at Home* efforts, and for obvious reasons, they are less costly and more accessible than traditional mobility experiences. Virtual exchange programs are not an innovation brought on by the pandemic but accelerated by it. This development is amplified by higher education and international education funding agencies recognizing the need for such programs and encouraging HEIs to collaborate with partners around the world to create virtual mobility opportunities for students. In Germany, for example, the German Academic Exchange Service (DAAD) launched a new program for *International Virtual Academic Collaboration (IVAC)*[4] in June 2020.

## 3 Virtual Engagement: Takeaways

Over a year of organizing and hosting virtual events and other forms of international engagement has taught us a lot! Most importantly, it has been wonderful and also maybe a bit surprising to see how quickly the academic community around the world was able to adapt and embrace new formats of work and collaboration. Within weeks, Zoom meetings and webinars were the new normal, all participants tried to educate themselves about the features and limitations of the virtual meeting platform their institution used, and it became clear to most of us that this new form of working would bring benefits as well as challenges. For sure, this technology adaption process has not been easy—especially for faculty who now in addition to planning course curricula also had to figure out and then manage a whole new way of teaching. In many cases, professors had to be ready to teach in-person and virtually, in a *hybrid model*. For students it has been difficult to sit through entire days of Zoom classes without having any in-person exchange with other young people. And then, of course, we quickly had to come to the realization that access was once again one of the major problems: for a lot of people in higher education communities around the world, access to technology and a stable internet connection have been paramount obstacles to education and research during the pandemic.

In my own experience at the IU Europe Gateway, access to technology was thankfully never an issue. And access to another key resource—people—only expanded over the course of the pandemic as we have been able to reach out and connect with partners across the entire European continent much more often and better than before. Since attending our events did not involve potentially long and expensive travel, scholars and other experts from anywhere in Europe were now able to participate, offer their insights, and connect with peers from other institutions.

[4] https://www.daad.de/en/information-services-for-higher-education-institutions/further-information-on-daad-programmes/ivac/

For us, moving academic events such as panel discussions and lectures to the virtual space has led to more diversity in the range of speakers.

As mentioned earlier, one of the biggest advantages of virtual versus in-person events is certainly that they can reach a much bigger and geographically more diverse audience. However, this comes at a price. Not surprisingly, an audience at computer or mobile device screens is much harder to engage than people sitting in the same room with no or few distractions from the event at hand. There has been a fairly steep learning curve on best practices for structuring a webinar, what audience engagement tools to use, and other important aspects related to organizing virtual events. For the post-pandemic future, we imagine that our event programming will most likely be a mix of in-person and virtual events, as well as hybrid events that combine the in-person advantages of deeper engagement and networking with the outreach to a broader audience via streaming options.

While certain parts of our programming at the IU Europe Gateway—for example, public-facing panel discussions or lectures or guest speaker engagements for IU study courses—were relatively easy to adapt to virtual settings, one of our main pre-pandemic activities, hosting academic workshops and conferences, proved much more difficult to sustain. Most of our workshops would typically assemble 15 to 25 scholars from the United States and Europe for a couple of days at our Gateway to discuss their current research on a common topic or work on a joint book project. One could think that such a small group is able to work on such matters in a virtual space. Unfortunately, these small academic gatherings have been quite difficult to successfully transfer into an online setting. The biggest challenge is indeed screen fatigue. No matter how engagingly a virtual workshop is structured, there is a limit to how much time one can spend mostly watching and listening to others on a computer screen. We have found that limit to be around 4 hours per day. So, while our in-person workshops would meet for full workdays of around 9 hours, with several breaks and usually a joint dinner that offered more time to continue the academic conversations and go a bit off topic to develop new ideas, the virtual versions needed to be much shorter and hence stretched across multiple days. This was also necessary to accommodate participants across multiple time zones. The workshops were also missing those valuable periods of socializing and creating a bond that goes beyond a common academic interest. Many scholars also confirmed that the intensity and atmosphere of working together was simply not what they knew before. While the few virtual workshops we helped to organize were surely much less expensive and also did not leave the carbon footprint of in-person events requiring multiple international flights, they also did not reap the same benefits.

Most participants of virtual mobility programs for students would probably argue the same. Such programs are important to increase access to international experiences in general, and they have been more or less the only possibility to participate in international exchange since March 2020. Yet, they also show great disadvantages compared to an in-person experience in another country. A virtual international exchange experience—even if designed well and offering potential for intercultural learning—will never be able to replace the endless small and big opportunities for such growth that come along with a semester abroad or an internship in another country. From pre-departure preparation, followed by traveling—for many, especially U.S. American students, the first time—abroad, to the experience of living in a new place, being among a minority of foreigners rather than the majority of natives, speaking one or several foreign languages all day long, and the reverse culture shock of coming back home, physical mobility is so much more than hearing others' perspectives. Communicating about academic topics with scholars and students abroad can often be life-changing. Even the students who participate in the very brief short-term, faculty-led study abroad programs that we facilitate at the IU Europe Gateway, eat *Currywurst*, a local specialty in Berlin, walk across the tiny bronze *Stolpersteine* ("stumbling stones") in the Berlin sidewalks remembering victims of the Holocaust, visit local museums, and encounter locals (friendly and not)—all probably not life-changing moments but certainly creating a personal connection to a once foreign place. This is why we all cannot wait to make such moments, and, of course, much more that comes with international students' physical mobility, possible again. However, virtual exchange and mobility should and will continue to play an important role: they will offer access to international learning opportunities for students who would otherwise not be able to benefit from such, they will be part of new blended programs that combine virtual and physical components, and they will also continue to improve and mature over time.

## 4 Partnerships During the Pandemic

Many of our virtual initiatives, those for students as well as for faculty and for the general public, were developed in close collaboration with one or several university partners. Over the years and decades, Indiana University has built an extensive network of institutional partnerships with HEIs across Europe, ranging from school-level partnerships to university-wide that cover multiple disciplines and campuses. During the past two decades—and very much consistent with the general trend in the field—the focus has been much more on developing a limited number of high-quality and intensive international partnerships rather than further growing the quantity. Many institutions refer to these relationships as strategic partnerships. I have heard from many colleagues that the COVID-19 pandemic, as a period with extremely limited student and faculty mobility, has offered yet more opportunity to reevaluate partnerships, joint programs, and other parameters of collaborative work. At Indiana University, we noticed that a small number of our existing partnerships have become much more intense over the course of the past two years. In a time of crisis, we were strengthening the most reliable relationships. After a few weeks of crisis management "at home" and, of course, in consultation with peer institutions on the state and national level, we soon also sought out the conversation and exchange with our closest partners abroad. In pre-pandemic times, meetings between the leadership of partner institutions almost always happened face-to-face during visits to campus or during networking conferences such as the annual NAFSA, AEIA, or—specifically for Europe—EAIE events. Even on a working level, I remember very few virtual meetings with fellow administrators. Plans were usually developed during in-person meetings and then followed up by email. This has changed dramatically since the spring of 2020. I have regularly been meeting virtually with colleagues at our close partner institutions, and we enjoy more frequent engagement that also has become less formal. The result of this increased interaction has been the development of a myriad of joint (virtual) projects: we took campus initiatives like our annual poster competition for the United Nations Sustainable Development Goals[5] to a group of international partners, sharing the idea and further developing the initiative by adding a joint *Global Partners Research Forum* where the winners from all partnering institutions would present their research posters, share ideas, and build new networks. We created virtual knowledge communities to brainstorm and share best practices with each other—on ways to cope with the ongoing crisis as well as on other pressing questions, like education for sustainable development. Our teams organized joint webinar series featuring scholars from participating universities and addressing all members of the partner institutions. We are currently designing and planning virtual exchange opportunities, as explained above, for our students with a few very close partner institutions. All these initiatives have in common a vast increase in the number of beneficiaries to our partnerships. In the past, international partnerships offered opportunities to a fairly small number of students and faculty, mostly those selected for a study exchange or faculty exchange program. Most members of the university would not even know with which institutions we are aligning ourselves. The recently established programs are once again much more accessible and will lead to many more individual connections than we had ever imagined.

The majority of joint initiatives, and certainly those which require a high level of alignment and sometimes compromise, have been planned and executed with a single partner institution. Others involved several universities or the early stages of a partner network. The development of university networks and multilateral international partnerships can be observed globally, especially in Europe with, for example, the European universities' alliances[6] but also elsewhere, as with Universitas21.[7] It started well before the pandemic and now continues and picks up speed. These networks are likely to play a more important role in the European higher education landscape of the future, offering students extensive and easily accessible study mobility options across the network at all levels, leading to new research networks and initiatives, and—last but not least—to a high level of communication and collaboration between university leadership. In times of limited mobility, such networks are also likely to be more successful in the implementation of virtual mobility options for students and faculty.

[5] https://global.iu.edu/education/internationalization/sdg/index.html

[6] https://ec.europa.eu/education/education-in-the-eu/european-education-area/european-universities-initiative_en

[7] https://universitas21.com/

While the pandemic has been a challenging time to maintain and grow *all* partnerships, I have experienced it overall as a productive time for building and fostering strategic partnerships. Here too, joint creativity was called for and led to innovations that will likely be carried into post-pandemic practice.

## 5 Outlook

A year and a half into the COVID-19 crisis, during the summer of 2021 when these reflections are written, yet another surge of COVID-19 is raging through the United States and most of Europe. What everyone hoped to be a summer of returning to a more normal life due to widespread availability of COVID vaccines—at least on these two continents—has once again turned into something else. Plans of returning to regular campus life and in-person teaching are being reconsidered at many universities. Our own plans for the first three research workshops at the IU Europe Gateway in late 2021 are reevaluated on a regular basis. While the majority of scholars in the United States and Europe seems to be already vaccinated against COVID-19 or is waiting to do so, recent reports of breakthrough cases, virus transmission by vaccinated people, and also the seemingly never-ending appearance of new virus variants are keeping the level of uncertainty extremely high. Countries around the world continue to change travel regulations depending on COVID incidences at home and in destination countries. Nobody can predict with certainty when we will return to a place where one can somewhat reliably plan travel three months in advance. We will consequently continue to plan and postpone in-person activities at our Gateway as long as necessary while hoping that this will not last much longer. Once we arrive at the "new normal"—when decisions about travel and virtual versus in-person engagement are made by choice depending on goals, costs, and benefits rather than safety concerns and government regulations—it will be interesting to see where this leads us in international higher education and me specifically at the IU Europe Gateway.

Most of the aforementioned innovations either existed before or would have been possible without the pandemic. Yet, the almost simultaneous onset of a global crisis that changed the way we live and work for a very long time has led to an incredible amount of creativity and innovation in many industries, including international higher education and research. I am convinced that many of the new initiatives and programs are here to stay, as they also address other pressing issues of our time, like climate change and questions of access and equity. Very likely, we will eventually see a mix of old and "new": at the Indiana University Europe Gateway, we are already planning virtual, in-person, and hybrid workshops and public outreach events. The choice will depend on many factors like the type of event and corresponding benefits a virtual or physical setting have, the audience, the prospective budget, and more. Our new virtual international engagement programs will continue to be an easier and more sustainable way to bring global perspectives to an Indiana classroom. In these areas, our portfolio of who and how we can serve and support will be considerably larger than in 2019. Physical student mobility should and will return but will be supplemented by virtual mobility programs, and in some cases, merged into blended mobility programs. Professional travel in our field of international education administrators will pick up again but will likely not return to pre-pandemic levels, as we all have learned that collaboration is possible and sometimes even advancing more quickly if meetings are organized as video calls. Individuals and institutions will review their travel decisions and policies, and assess whether it is indeed necessary to travel to a meeting or if it can be replaced by other solutions.

Like many office workers around the world, we will not return to our offices full-time but will likely find a new balance between working from home and in the office. After many months of working far away from colleagues, many of us yearn for a return to a more collegial work environment. At the same time, we value the time saved by not having to commute to work five times a week and other benefits offered by a day of working from home.

For issues mentioned above and for many others, one of the important tasks in post-pandemic times will be to find the right balance between the ways we used to do our work and the creative new ways explored during the crisis. It will probably take some trial and error, some overstretching of resources and adjustments. I am convinced, though, that it will lead to progress.

As I reflect on the still ongoing pandemic, mourn the lives and livelihoods lost, remember the despair and exhaustion of so many people (frontline workers, parents, and many more), recognize the limitations to our life in this crisis, and shudder at the polarization and anger that has been growing, I also acknowledge and appreciate the creativity and progress that have come out of this catastrophe: from medical innovations that will help fight other diseases to better access to international education for students who cannot travel abroad. Despite the loss, we must keep sight of the silver lining.

**Andrea Adam Moore** is the Director of the Indiana University Europe Gateway Office. In her 20 years of experience in international higher education, she has worked for several institutions on both sides of the Atlantic, supporting universities in furthering their international bonds, fostering research collaboration, student mobility, and cultural exchange.

# The COVID-19 Pandemic as a Catalyst for Digital Entrepreneurship Education: Reflections on a Rapid Transformation of an Educational Ecosystem

**Christine K. Volkmann and Marc Grünhagen**

**Abstract** This chapter explores the implications of the COVID-19 crisis on entrepreneurship education at higher education institutions. Different challenges for university management, students and entrepreneurship instructors will be considered from a stakeholder-based, holistic perspective on transforming entrepreneurship towards digital education in the crisis. This view allows integrating a range of education management challenges that ultimately impact on the interaction between students and lecturers in digital entrepreneurship teaching. In addressing these challenges, the chapter also highlights possible approaches and remedies suggested in entrepreneurship literature and from university examples (e.g. structured professional development and institutionalization of student support in online entrepreneurship education; use of balanced synchronous/asynchronous as well as on-site/online components; adding crisis and resilience management to the entrepreneurship teaching agenda). Beyond the technological dimension of the digital transition of entrepreneurship education, the chapter also reflects on some managerial and psychological aspects and issues that came with the COVID-19 crisis for entrepreneurship students and start-up founders alike and derives ideas for future research.

**Keywords** Educational ecosystem · Entrepreneurship education · COVID-19 · Digital transition

## 1 Introduction

The advent and scientific discovery of the severe acute respiratory syndrome coronavirus 2 (SARS-CoV2; Zhu et al., 2020) and the following global COVID-19 pandemic have led to an unprecedented and massive change for all societies

---

C. K. Volkmann (✉) · M. Grünhagen
Chair of Entrepreneurship and Economic Development & UNESCO-Chair in Entrepreneurship and Intercultural Management, Schumpeter School of Business and Economics, University of Wuppertal, Wuppertal, Germany
e-mail: volkmann@wiwi.uni-wuppertal.de; gruenhagen@wiwi.uni-wuppertal.de



D. B. Audretsch, I. A. M. Kunadt (eds.), *The COVID-19 Crisis and Entrepreneurship*, International Studies in Entrepreneurship 54,
https://doi.org/10.1007/978-3-031-04655-1_18

worldwide (Garcia-Morales et al., 2021). Beyond the tragedy unfolding in countries' health systems, social distancing and other control measures imposed to keep the virus in check have put pressure on societies and people in many domains of daily life, including the education of young people at schools and higher education institutions (HEIs). According to UNESCO reporting, many universities and other HEIs either closed their premises completely or at least abandoned face-to-face classroom teaching at the beginning of the pandemic in spring 2020 and beyond (Marinoni et al., 2020). In Europe, apparently almost all HEIs in an EU survey moved to remote teaching as an immediate reaction to the pandemic (EU, 2021).

For university-level entrepreneurship education, the strategic and operational implications of the unfolding COVID-19 pandemic point in at least two directions: First, the need for an immediate transformation of entrepreneurship education programmes and training offers for university start-ups into digitalized and online formats within a few weeks between semesters (Ratten, 2020; Ribeiro et al., 2020). Second, there have been and still are massive impacts on new venture founders and start-ups in the centre of university entrepreneurship education and transfer. For start-ups (and many others), the COVID-19 pandemic represents a "black swan event" as "a surprising, unpredictable event of great significance and severe consequences that dramatically changes the political and economic environment" (Kuckertz et al., 2020, 1). While the crisis is surely putting burdens on many other firms and households, start-ups may suffer beyond the traditional liabilities of newness and smallness they face even in normal times (ibid.; Meahjohn & Persad, 2020). Correspondingly, entrepreneurship educators also face such a black swan event posed by the pandemic. Entrepreneurship education may subsequently have to appreciate such crisis impacts in teaching entrepreneurial management to put a stronger emphasis, e.g. on the adaptability and resilience of ventures and their business models.

Of course, the sudden move towards emergency remote teaching (EU, 2021) with education and instruction material being widely unprepared for teaching online and assisting start-ups with concepts for crisis management means that "we will all have to forgive in many ways" in this pandemic (as the German Secretary of Health coined it in 2020). However, beyond inevitable shortcomings and mistakes in the hasty transition towards digital entrepreneurship education at HEIs, there may also be chances and opportunities encapsulated in this digital transition of entrepreneurship teaching triggered by the coronavirus (Garcia-Morales et al., 2021; Liguori & Winkler, 2020). This may be both in terms of integrating new talent related to digital teaching and bringing novel concepts for learning into the education system including entrepreneurship education (Garcia-Morales et al., 2021).

Considering the need for a balanced perspective on solving admitted problems in the emergent digital transmission of entrepreneurship education in the short term, and the potential to enrich and further improve the delivery of entrepreneurship in HEIs prompted by the pandemic in the long term, the remainder of this chapter is organized as follows. The second section puts the transition and change of entrepreneurship education in the overall context of the crisis challenge faced within tertiary education at universities and other HEIs. Appreciating this organizational context will be critical for a successful long-term transition since university-level entrepreneurship education will be embedded in, and at least partly dependent on, the institutional infrastructures and resource provision of university organizations. The third section puts a lens on the particularities of entrepreneurship education as a field of predominantly practical and hands-on interactive learning. In addition to a short description of the distinct characteristics of our field, this part also considers different stakeholders in entrepreneurship education that need to be on board for moving entrepreneurship education digital. The fourth section reflects on and discusses potential preliminary solutions that have been found and employed by HEIs in their entrepreneurship education as a reaction to the crisis or that have been suggested in the literature. In the final section of the chapter, we will highlight selected future opportunities for the further development of entrepreneurship education and share some suggestions for future research.

## 2 The COVID-19 Crisis as a Challenge for Higher Education Institutions

Generally in the socio-economic domain, a crisis jeopardizes the smooth functioning of organizational entities and their performance for their stakeholders (Williams et al., 2017). In comparison to other crises such as hurricane Katrina in 2005 or the financial crisis in 2008, the COVID-19 pandemic hit people and organizations both globally (unlike a regional hurricane or flood) *and* suddenly (unlike an economic crisis unfolding over a longer period) at the same time (Kuckertz et al., 2020). To weather (and survive) a crisis of such magnitude involves substantial crisis preparation (ibid.), essentially requiring to prepare an organization for the unknown future event. The very nature of such an acute crisis implies that the impediments interrupting organizational functions are not clear ex ante, calling for organizations to develop a sense of principal structural uncertainty in a chaotic future organizational environment, and increase their systemic adaptability and agility for rapid organizational change (Pinkwart, 1992). In particular, the COVID-19 pandemic led to sometimes drastic social distancing, hygiene and lockdown measures taken in many countries within a very short time period. The turbulences that came with a crisis event like this disturb structures, routines and capabilities of education organizations and businesses, including start-ups, alike (Williams et al., 2017). For HEIs, this disruption as a sudden break of organizational operations (Garcia-Morales et al., 2021) represented an interruption of established, well-known models of knowledge transmission (Carolan et al., 2020; Mishra et al., 2020) posing a range of inter-related challenges to be tackled, for example:

- Initial *absence of necessary technological infrastructure, platforms and appropriate solid servers* for virtual education (EU, 2021)
- Problems with *technical operations and Internet connections* in online education (World Bank, 2020)

- Initial lack of *capabilities for online teaching* of lecturers, instructors and coaches (Garcia-Morales et al., 2021)
- Lack of appropriate *technical equipment for student participation* in online teaching via computers, laptops or smartphones

Correspondingly, at the pedagogical level, lecturers (and students) as communities of practice in tertiary education (Ratten, 2020) faced the urgent need to adapt the learning process in many ways. In particular, this involved rethinking the competences required by students in virtual instead of in-person learning (Jensen, 2019), further developing digital methods for learning including the provision of online learning tools and support systems (Krishnamurthy, 2020), as well as adapting methods for assessing students' learning outcomes in the end. From the perspective of university management, the overall aim in the crisis within the pillar of teaching continues to be maintaining the quality in a situation of rapid digital transformation (Garcia-Morales et al., 2021). The organizational quality assurance of HEIs is underpinned by a broad range of institutional knowledge sources, technological and other infrastructure for teaching and different sorts of resources such as personnel and funding.

Overall, available empirical data regarding HEIs support provided to students and lecturers during the preliminary climax of the crisis in 2020/2021 is very limited (EU, 2021). Measures included, for example, centralized helpdesks, webinars and tutorials (such as model courses via Moodle) for instructors to design online and blended learning experiences, the provision of (additional) hard- and software (e.g. campus licences for Zoom; Microsoft Teams, Blackboard, etc.), web design facilities, student loans for technical equipment, etc. (Gatti et al., 2020). Additional support instruments for students have been offering additional tutorials, options for asynchronous learning and adjustments in grading systems (ibid.). Globally, the opportunities within education systems and for HEIs have been very heterogeneous, based on different resources, facilities and know-how pools specific to the digital transformation of teaching at the outset of the crisis. In particular, the emergency responses of HEIs were found to be very diverse in an initial study of higher education intra-period digital pedagogy responses in a survey of 20 countries (Crawford et al., 2020). Measures ranged from almost no response at all to complete social distancing or closure concepts with a corresponding transition to complete remote teaching (ibid.). With regard to entrepreneurship education as a distinct field of teaching, of course many of the above challenges in general higher education are very similar. Beyond this, there may also be additional issues that came about during the pandemic, both for entrepreneurship education and university spin-offs as a specific domain of science transfer within the entrepreneurial university. The process of addressing these challenges and issues to keep up with entrepreneurship after the advent and throughout the course of the crisis unfolded in many ways at the individual level of universities and other HEIs in different countries. And this has been presumably with heterogeneous levels of know-how, resource and technical infrastructure support provided in the university organizations where the rapid transformation of entrepreneurship training and transfer took place. Some initial thoughts on this rather abrupt need for change within institutionalized university entrepreneurship will be addressed in the next section.

## 3 Entrepreneurship Education Going Digital Fast: Crisis Challenges for Stakeholders in Entrepreneurship Teaching

The entrepreneurial university embraces a range of strategic aspects, with teaching entrepreneurship and supporting regional new venture formation and spin-offs among them (Rothaermel et al., 2009). Preliminary discussion on the impacts of the COVID-19 pandemic on entrepreneurship in the higher education sector hint at different, often interrelated, challenges alongside the three missions in teaching, research and transfer within contemporary university organizations (e.g. Kawamorita et al., 2020). The focus of this chapter will be on entrepreneurship education within the core teaching pillar of HEIs. In following this perspective, we will, however, also briefly address potential COVID-19 challenges for university transfer regarding the support of start-up projects and spin-offs as an integral part of practical entrepreneurship education.

The genuine thrust of entrepreneurship education to develop students' entrepreneurial mindsets and support the creative development of venturing projects and university start-ups in the realm of teaching *for* entrepreneurship (Kirby, 2004) brings about the most specific crisis challenges for teaching our field: how to reconfigure education programmes (e.g. via distance learning) in the COVID-19 emergency (Secondo et al., 2021) for a discipline like entrepreneurship education which:

- Requires hands-on entrepreneurship in real-life examples (e.g. student business modelling projects or start-up internships) in immersive training (Ratten, 2020)
- Functions most effectively via action-based and highly interactive learning (Ribeiro et al., 2020)
- Needs concrete practical experiences for reflection beyond theoretical concepts of entrepreneurial management (Laferriere et al., 2019; Ribeiro et al., 2020)?

Typical examples of this general approach of experiential learning recommended widely in the literature (e.g. Fayolle & Gailly, 2008; Mahmood et al., 2020; Pittaway & Cope, 2007; Rae et al., 2009) are field visits to start-ups, team-based business plan competitions, building campus start-ups or hackathons. All such activity formats may be impeded or impossible to be offered face-to-face throughout different phases of the COVID-19 pandemic due to social distancing requirements and bans of public in-person meetings with larger groups of people (Liguori et al., 2021; Liguori & Winkler, 2020; Ribeiro et al., 2020).

To structure the potential implications of crisis challenges for entrepreneurship education beyond specific impacts on individual entrepreneurship course formats,

Ratten and Jones (2021) have suggested to consider *entrepreneurship education as a holistic process, including to take an entrepreneurial stakeholder perspective*. Such a perspective allows appreciating the different actors involved in curricular and extracurricular entrepreneurship education and relying on a range of institutional settings and teaching resources in university organizations as entrepreneurial education at HEIs evolves. Through this holistic lens of entrepreneurship education embedded in university organizations, the following strategic dimensions may be relevant (adapted from EU, 2015):

- Education *management* and *networking*: resource allocation to entrepreneurship education, in particular personnel, curricular integration, quality assurance of entrepreneurship offers, external networking and co-operation
- *Students and lecturers* in entrepreneurship education: involvement of student target groups and types of experts in teaching and mentoring
- *Design* of core entrepreneurship course offers: learning objectives and competences, structure of (extra-)curricular programme offers, entrepreneurship concepts and topics, teaching and learning methods, learning media, course infrastructure and scheduling and forms of feedback and evaluation

## 3.1 Crisis Challenges for Education Management and Networking

The most challenging problems for entrepreneurship education in the pandemic are predominantly related to the core issues of redesigning course offers and entrepreneurship programmes to meet and confirm to public health regulations during the pandemic. However, approaches and attempts to tackle such immediate operational challenges will be related to and take place within the overall crisis management of HEIs developing and executing emergency plans to take ad hoc centralized campus-wide measures. These initiatives taken by university rectorates come about both to combat the spread of the virus on campus and orchestrate alternative digital infrastructures for running their core business via remote teaching across many disciplines and faculties (EU, 2021). And for same disciplines with characteristic on-site practical learning components (e.g. medicine, experimental natural sciences, arts, design, sports and exercise science), the challenges posed by social distancing and campus lockdowns may have been even more severe.

In our field, a principal challenge or restriction for educators and coaches at entrepreneurship chairs or centres has hence been to adjust to such centralized approaches, for example, in terms of digital platforms, software and other technology offered university-wide (e.g. departments or entire universities to use Moodle or Blackboard as course platforms and Zoom or Microsoft Teams as videoconferencing tools). Likely, at most HEIs, the shift to online teaching has been performed with a pre-crisis base of personnel and technical resources at least in the beginning of the crisis in spring 2020. In this regard, the congruence of competences of existing teaching faculty with the requirements for teaching online has likely constituted a problem depending on the overall status of digital education at one's home university (Liguori et al., 2021; also see the section on student learning and lecturers below). From a university management perspective, the issue of maintaining the quality and breadth of course offers has been troublesome, particularly for less institutionalized extracurricular offers such as entrepreneurship fairs, hackathons, competitions or entrepreneurship weeks which are often less institutionalized and integrated in HEIs anyway (EU, 2015). Very often, such extracurricular offers may have simply been cancelled during the crisis since they would have involved public in-person meetings with externals and larger groups of university members.

In principle, entrepreneurship education benefits tremendously from integrating externals, in particular practitioners such as start-up founders, entrepreneurs, coaches, business angels and other investors, in the teaching process; and many HEIs employ instruments such as team-teaching with entrepreneurs, entrepreneurs in residence, guest lectures, etc. in their entrepreneurship education (EU, 2015). Therefore, external networking and co-operation within the university region and beyond is a constant network and stakeholder management issue around entrepreneurship education (Bischoff et al., 2018). In face of the COVID-19 crisis, there is a pressing need to transform these teaching and mentoring networks, which often have evolved over many years in a university region at the level of personal relationships (e.g. at Johannes Kepler University Linz, Austria; Grünhagen, 2017a), into digital entrepreneurial ecosystems around entrepreneurship teaching and transfer.

A particular issue relating to this external network nexus of entrepreneurship education is the involvement of start-up founders and entrepreneurs in our discipline, both entrepreneurs from the university region (or beyond) and founders of university spin-offs related to start-up support and transfer activities on campus. The process of founding, establishing and growing start-ups has been put at risk in many different aspects for entrepreneurs against the background of pre-existing liabilities of newness and smallness (Kuckertz et al., 2020). In particular, start-ups had to adapt and pivot their business models to the demands of the pandemic (Ratten, 2020a). For these attempts to make current and new start-up projects more resilient and robust also requires changes within individual entrepreneurship education around consulting and coaching for academic start-up founders and teams at university. Moving forward and assisting these concrete start-up projects may be particularly hampered as the process of start-up counselling banks specifically on collaborative hands-on start-up management work (e.g. around business modelling in design thinking) and trustful in-person cooperation between start-up teams and members of university start-up or entrepreneurship centres which is difficult to replicate online to full extent (cf. Ribeiro et al., 2020). Overall, transforming entrepreneurship education from an in-person offline to a remote online experience challenges all stakeholders involved in this experience in many ways, be it at the level of individual start-up coaching or in the context of classroom group teaching in entrepreneurship.

### 3.2 Crisis Challenges for Students and Lecturers in Entrepreneurship Education

The most salient stakeholder of entrepreneurship education is obviously the group of participating *students* in entrepreneurship classes or *founders* as mentees in start-up coaching and counselling. This stakeholder group has been faced by an abrupt shift to remote communication with instructors and coaches. Early articles report concerns over a potential cognitive overload at the receiving side of students in digital higher education (Ribeiro et al., 2020) and perceived weaknesses and limitations of digital platforms and educational technology tools in creating an acceptable learning experience (Secondo et al., 2021). Correspondingly, there is a demand for "keeping the pulse" on students' mental health (OECD, 2020) and providing individual and tutorial assistance to students to help adapting to a technology-based digital learning environment (EU, 2021). Similarly, around the COVID-19 challenge, the support of academic entrepreneurs and start-up founders from university requires more attention to the psychological and emotional level. Recently, Aly et al. (2021, 1) stressed the need to appreciate "the daunting emotional challenges confronting entrepreneurs as they traverse the entrepreneurial journey" which intensified further during the COVID crisis. Towards this end, the authors suggest concepts and tools in entrepreneurship education to build and strengthen the emotional skill and competence set beyond traditional entrepreneurship training (ibid.; cf. generally Ribeiro et al., 2020). In addition to the psychological challenges in the shift towards online education, also technical and operational issues are discussed in recent (entrepreneurship) education literature (EU, 2021; Kawamorita et al., 2020; Garcia-Morales et al., 2021; OECD, 2020). For example, typical problems have been Internet connection issues, access to devices and platforms, initial server capacity for large-scale online learning facilities and a lack of asynchronous course offers. Such issues constitute not merely technical problems for the attention of university IT operations, but also impact upon the learning process of students in entrepreneurship education which has to maintain quality also in a scenario of online education (Ratten, 2020) with limited technology resources at some universities.

At the other end of interaction between students and their instructors, *lecturers* and coaches, who offer courses and training in general entrepreneurship or hands-on start-up management, face corresponding challenges to switch to and navigate through a new digital environment of teaching online during the COVID crisis (Liguori & Winkler, 2020). Lecturers and instructors raised concerns particularly with regard to the ability to provide an adequate virtual learning experience for students in the new environment in a study reported by Liguori et al. (2021) during the crisis. This related to both problems in relation to the availability of appropriate technology for teaching online at university and teaching personnel not being familiar with digital tools to teach online. A potential lack of capabilities and university resources to use the full range of digital technology in the toolbox of entrepreneurship education is critical especially in view of demands for a varied and diversified use of media technology as well as asynchronous and live formats (generally OECD (2020)) and Ribeiro et al. (2020)) for the context of entrepreneurship). In essence, entrepreneurship educators have to adapt to a large extent to the individual environment of their university institution in terms of what kind of teaching technologies are available, but also personally concerning sources of know-how and advice to further develop their competences for online teaching (see Section 4 for possible approaches in this regard). Generally, the path towards digital entrepreneurship education ecosystems will surely be different for lecturers and students alike in HEIs across the globe as their ICT resource base for, orientation towards and actual utilization of digital technologies and online platforms is at different levels of acquaintance in response to the COVID crisis (cf. Crawford et al., 2020).

### *3.3 Problem Issues in the Design of Online Entrepreneurship Course Offers*

Closely related to the crisis problems faced by entrepreneurship students and lecturers is the challenge for reconfiguring and redesigning entrepreneurship courses and other formats in response to the pandemic and the digital shift it has caused. In the beginning, the sheer speed of required conformity to ad hoc health regulation and lockdown measures introduced at outset of the pandemic—and continued changes of the regulatory framework as the pandemic unfolded across the world—created temporary challenges in itself during spring 2020 as regards what and how to teach. Sometimes, education institutions and faculty made emergency moves within weeks to shift lectures to the virtual domain, e.g. in life lectures and seminars via Zoom or other videoconferencing tools (EU, 2021; Garcia-Morales et al., 2021; Ratten, 2020). Appreciating the speed of such reactions and changes made to the ways in which entrepreneurship curricula have been delivered, considerations about implications for learning objectives and didactical methods perhaps come only second or have been a rather unintended or implicit consequence of emergent changes at the level of technology and media use in entrepreneurship teaching. However, at least in the medium and surely in the long term, essential elements of the learning situation and environment at different levels need to be fitted in a congruent strategic approach (cf. Secondo et al., 2021). In particular, this involves redesigning course material and content suitable for digital education to be shared and communicated on stable web-based education platforms, which both has been an emergent challenge as the crisis unfolded (Kawamorita et al., 2020). This ultimately didactical rather than technical task needs not to be neglected as the immediate teething problems of technology implementation and IT capacity management for fully fledged online education have been resolved by HEIs. Beyond this challenge, there are also future opportunities for entrepreneurship education inherent in the large experiment of going digital with contents and teaching tools in the entrepreneurship education community, e.g. in terms of greater digital outreach including new target groups and entrepreneurship programmes as well as novel ways of delivering entrepreneurship experiences to students (see the next section).

Further, in the design of entrepreneurship offers and formats, two aspects appear to be particularly critical—first, the requirement for digital inclusion and second, the retention of students participating in extracurricular entrepreneurship offers where there are only few curricular offers (as often is the case for non-business students at HEIs where entrepreneurship is still a fairly young discipline; EU, 2015). With regard to the former, platforms and technologies employed must be accessible for all groups of entrepreneurship students at HEIs, which has been a problem that came up in the pandemic (Kawamorita et al., 2020). The latter necessitates entrepreneurship chairs and centres at HEIs not only to be occupied with accredited curricular offers during the pandemic but also to reconsider extracurricular entrepreneurship education activities and events that have been cancelled or at least downsized in pandemic lockdown periods. Often, such extracurricular formats have specific experiential and practical transdisciplinary teamwork aspects for students to work on real-life start-up projects with externals, which are particularly suitable in teaching *for* or *through* entrepreneurship (Ribeiro et al., 2020).

Finally, typical challenges in student interaction and feedback that arose in the pandemic have been needs to rethink course scheduling to allow hybrid or blended teaching and learning via asynchronous offers even for students in different time zones, e.g. small group in-person seminars and large audience online lectures or flipped classroom concepts (EU, 2021). Often, HEIs also had to reconsider course evaluation due to the difficulties and hardships for students caused by lockdown regulations and reportedly numerous European HEIs adjusted their grading policies (ibid.) or deadlines for the submission of students' coursework. Addressing all the above issues across the management and design of entrepreneurship education experiences in the "new normal" throughout and beyond the crisis surely sets a difficult challenge for higher education organizations as well as university managers, lecturers and coaches responsible for entrepreneurship teaching and start-up support in university transfer. However, the pandemic has also revealed that numerous HEIs embraced the change inflicted by the coronavirus with a diversity of experimental responses and novel concepts (Liguori & Winkler, 2020). These approaches, even though they may not contain final answers as to how to move entrepreneurship education into a more digital future, surely comprise interesting lessons learnt and opportunities for educational innovation (Ratten, 2020). And Liguori and Winkler (2020, 349) assess the COVID-19 crisis as a *sobering event for entrepreneurship education* and one essential aspect of this is that:

> [W]e teach students to adapt to market conditions, to remain agile, and to innovate, so this is a great challenge for us to practice what we preach.

# 4 Reflecting on Immediate Approaches for Transforming Entrepreneurship Education in Crisis Mode

Universities and other HEIs have tried and implemented a wide range of ad hoc changes in their teaching to adapt to the challenges set by the COVID-19 pandemic, and most approaches involved the use of digital technologies for distant online learning (Crawford et al., 2020). As the pandemic is still unfolding and seems far from over in autumn 2021 with many HEIs not back to traditional offline on-campus education, the pedagogical evaluation of these approaches in terms of effective teaching and student learning has yet to be completed. Nonetheless, it seems still valuable to reflect on selected approaches and measures taken in higher education to hold up and keep running entrepreneurship education in the "new normal" of the COVID pandemic. Given that in this dynamic situation many problems around tertiary teaching have been addressed by rather ad hoc measures and abrupt changes towards digital education, it is a good idea for HEIs to distinguish strategically between emergency remote teaching and online teaching (EU, 2021). The former merely means to shift existing teaching material and methodology for on-site education to the virtual area without any adjustments (e.g. pre-recorded, or live broadcasted lectures), while the latter appreciates curricula and methods to be adapted to the online context (ibid.). When reflecting on what has happened in entrepreneurship education in 2020 and 2021, we will come across approaches in both strands alike—ad hoc emergency measures to meet immediate challenges and keep teaching operations running and more strategic future ideas towards integrated digital entrepreneurship modules or programmes at universities. The aim of this reflection is to highlight some of these measures and approaches for entrepreneurship educators and university entrepreneurship managers and to do so in an integrated discussion, taking up the holistic stakeholder perspective on entrepreneurship education from above. Correspondingly, the remainder of this section is structured also around the same inter-related dimensions of entrepreneurship education: *entrepreneurship education management and networking, students and lecturers in entrepreneurship education and design of entrepreneurship course offers.*

## *4.1 Crisis Approaches in Entrepreneurship Education Management and Networking*

The starting point of education management is to support teaching and learning across many different disciplines in HEIs, including entrepreneurship education. The shift towards digital education in the COVID crisis is essentially based on the assumption that "[t]he adoption of digital technologies in EE [entrepreneurship education] can drive relevant changes in the students' experiences in terms of online collaboration, online engagement, and teamwork satisfaction" (Secondo et al., 2021, 1). In particular, the digital approach can serve the interaction between participating students and stakeholders involved in the entrepreneurship education process (e.g. lecturers, university coaches and training instructors, start-up founders in practical exercises, guest speakers from the community offering start-up support). This could be augmented further by integrating global virtual entrepreneurship networking platforms like "Startup Compete" of the Global Entrepreneurship Network which allows start-up founders and advisors to work together on new entrepreneurial opportunities and business concepts. Education management will have to actively support this regional network of stakeholders and additional international network relations in the virtual space in many ways including the institutionalization of student counselling in the online world, the professional development of entrepreneurship lecturers towards online education (see Subsection 4.2) and the provision of adequate technologies and organizational facilities for online teaching (this will be discussed further in Subsection 4.3 on aspects of the design of digital entrepreneurship education offers backed by technology).

As education management in crisis mode evolved and continues to develop during the COVID pandemic, an important institutional approach is to adopt a quality assurance strategy with regard to a blended and online delivery of study programmes and to preserve academic standards in online education (Aucejo et al., 2020; EU, 2021). This should entail the documentation of important adjustments in models for teaching and learning during the digital shift to allow an evaluation and further redesign of teaching methods and student learning objectives for online learning also beyond the pandemic (ibid.; Gatti et al., 2020). Such a further development of digital education in entrepreneurship will take time and has to be managed carefully during the further path of the pandemic allowing for flexibility and manoeuvring space for students and lecturers. We still have to understand what a shift to more blended or even complete online entrepreneurship education means, in particular for student learning during the crisis and beyond. Towards this end, it has been suggested as a crisis measure to increase the flexibility of university policies in the organization of study programmes, including adjustments in student course loads and assignments (EU, 2021). In addition to such regulatory institutional measures, effective learning and students mastering the transition to online education in the crisis have been a particular concern calling for instant measures in tandem with supporting lecturers at the operational level of entrepreneurship education.

### 4.2 Addressing Crisis Issues of Students and Lecturers in Online Entrepreneurship Education

Typical educational concerns about *students* in tertiary education centre around the potential implications of isolation as campus life halted and exchange as well as on-site collaboration and group work with fellow students became more difficult. In addition, adverse effects of isolation, frustration or anxiety have also been discussed around the use of remote online technologies in education, especially for larger audiences such as in MOOCs—massive open online courses (EU, 2021; Secondo et al., 2021). To address these issues, Chirikov et al. (2020) have recommended to provide additional resources and access for student health services. Also, user-friendly guidance and accessible counselling to assist with digital learning to be offered by universities have been suggested (EU, 2021). In particular, at-risk students may benefit from dedicated tutors and tailored work programmes (ibid.). Such mentors and adapted study schedules may also be useful for the particular case of student start-up founders to allow for an easier balance of student studies and entrepreneurial business work as a student start-up founder (as has been implemented already in normal times at the Erasmus University of Rotterdam in the Netherlands to support entrepreneurship; Grünhagen, 2017b). In addition, not only the overall workload in studies have been reported as a problem source but also possible cognitive overloads in students' reception of digital educational content (e.g. videoconference lectures or online workshops). Several solutions have been suggested and implemented by universities for this. Ribeiro et al. (2020) point at mixing synchronous and asynchronous learning options, group live activities in online sessions and offering specific tutorials for student learning in digital entrepreneurship education. Principally, it has been recommended to balance digital with screen-free learning activities (OECD, 2020). This balancing may be organized both via in-person meetings in small workgroups and contact time with course instructors as the pandemic situation allows and individually in one's study room. For studying at home during the crisis, helping students with resources or loans for ergonomic hard- and software equipment have been suggested (EU, 2021) to improve the study work of students in distance learning.

An essential approach to enhance the digital learning process in entrepreneurship or any other university education is to assist *lecturers* and other instructors involved in entrepreneurship training in managing the change towards digital teaching on their side of the equation. For this, it seems important to appreciate that often, e.g. at European (public) universities, engagement in and commitment to oftentimes novel digital teaching methods and material may come with opportunity costs with regard to available time to pursue academic research and transfer goals (EU, 2015); this may be also for allocating time to craft elaborate interactive online and blended teaching formats in entrepreneurship education. This requires university management to reconsider the incentive structures for teaching in the context of the overall university mission.

An important leverage to encourage lecturers to design and adopt suitable course material and methods for online teaching will be to make the tradition from well-known on-site concepts as smooth as possible. For the management of the current crisis and its digital transition in HEIs, it has been suggested to support teaching staff in preparing contents and enhancing the toolbox of teaching methods to online (EU, 2021) as well as to provide lecturers themselves with ample opportunities for digital learning (OECD, 2020). Some of these support instruments and opportunities for faculty will have been set up and done ad hoc at the individual academic or work group level in crisis mode. However, preferably this should be organized in extensive and structured professional training in online and hybrid teaching (EU, 2021) and considered as opportunities for the future professional development of entrepreneurship and other educators at HEIs (Liguori et al., 2021). Ultimately, the further transition towards more digital entrepreneurship education in the future will be a journey of lifelong learning for lecturers. Beyond individual learning and further development, HEIs offering entrepreneurship education may also consider the group of lecturers and other course instructors both from other disciplines and outside the university as a community of entrepreneurship practice with plenty of scope to share ideas and teaching resources (Ratten, 2020). With regard to this, it may also be a good idea to rethink the established one-person teaching model in classes and support frontline lecturers to be embedded in multidisciplinary team-teaching (EU, 2021). For example, this could involve experts in digital technologies and teaching methods, entrepreneurs alongside entrepreneurship lecturers to team up together in entrepreneurship courses.

### *4.3 Approaches for Designing Digital Entrepreneurship Course Formats During the Crisis*

With an elaborate support infrastructure to resolve teething problems and challenges for student and lecturer stakeholders in entrepreneurship education throughout the pandemic, digital technologies may enhance the collaboration between students and lecturers as well as other stakeholders in online courses, in the context of project sessions and in student mentoring (Secondo et al., 2021). While the success of digital technologies in the collaborative learning of groups of students will also depend on team acquaintance and instructor support (ibid.), the provision of adequate online platforms, hardware and software will be key for HEIs to navigate the digitalization of their teaching portfolio in entrepreneurship and other fields. During emergent crisis measures, HEIs may often have employed university-wide centralized solutions like Zoom or other videoconferencing and communication tools in order to enable a quick response to the COVID crisis (EU, 2021). In the medium and long term, more tailored and customized tools for different disciplines and fields of university teaching will be required. While we will not suggest specific technologies or software tools in this chapter, it will be interesting to reflect on some rather more organizational aspects of university management to provide platforms and technologies for online entrepreneurship teaching to keep up with the COVID crisis.

To approach the provision of technology for online education during the pandemic in a way that allowed a timely and fast reaction as well as an effective university-wide way forwards in the organization of the digital shift with all faculties and disciplines on board, it has been suggested:

- To consider existing platforms and extend their use
- To partner with private platform providers in a quick infrastructure response
- To collaborate in IT service sharing with other institutions and companies (OECD, 2020)

Further into the future, Gatti et al. (2020) suggest investing in effective online learning and teaching tools in an overall IT strategy. Ideally for the strategy of individual HEIs, one tailored platform may be used to access all teaching and learning resources and avoid patchwork (EU, 2021). Though the current pandemic crisis is a surely difficult phase, now may be a good time to start the process of furnishing HEIs with further digital technologies based on a thorough evaluation of the concurrent, almost global, experimentation phase within digital higher education and the lessons learnt from these ad hoc attempts to move online with entrepreneurship education.

In terms of blended and online learning in entrepreneurship education, Chen et al. (2021) identified three principal areas of technology use in their review of applied educational technologies entrepreneurship training. First, social media such as Facebook is used for student communication and feedback in curricular entrepreneurship courses and extracurricular activities. Second, entrepreneurship educators employ serious games for practical and experiential team and individual learning (Takemoto & Oe, 2021) in the need to simulate real entrepreneurial examples in the virtual domain in the pandemic (Ratten, 2020). Third, the integration of MOOCs like Coursera, Udemy and Udacity in entrepreneurship education broadens the access to prepared digital contents, cases and concepts in start-up and tech entrepreneurship. How these digital tools and platforms are used in individual entrepreneurship education will depend on the characteristics of individual entrepreneurship programmes at each HEI. Certainly, the choice of platforms and technologies to facilitate digital entrepreneurship education and the provision of a support infrastructure for entrepreneurship lecturers and students to work with these technologies will have to be considered against the background of the final learning experience of participants and the objectives of the entrepreneurship programme from the viewpoint of entrepreneurship centres and chairs at universities. The most critical aspect during the COVID-19 pandemic is the organizational turn from existing entrepreneurship course formats and material for on-site offline teaching towards novel online tools and concepts. We conclude this section reflecting on a short example of dynamic changes of entrepreneurship offers at a European public university, the *CLab@Salento* at the University of Salerno, Italy, documented in detail in the literature in Secondo et al. (2021). This main example is augmented by insights from a further hands-on entrepreneurship course, the *Ideenschmiede* (Idea Forge) at the start-up centre of University of Wuppertal, Germany (the home university of the authors of this chapter).

**An Example of Shifting to Digital Entrepreneurship Education: CLab@Salento** The example of the *CLab@Salento* is one of Italy's so-called Contamination Labs (in the sense of familiarizing students with real live entrepreneurial and business practice in this case). The CLab has been funded by the University of Salento in Southern Italy's Apulia region and the Italian government (see Secondo et al. (2021)) as the main source of this case example). Though surely many interesting examples of novel digital entrepreneurship courses from HEIs could have been presented, the CLab@Salento case and the additional example of the Idea Forge have been selected as short illustrations because they are course programmes specifically geared towards developing students' entrepreneurial mindsets in formats creating and working on concrete business ideas and start-up projects. In both programmes, former on-site concepts had to be shifted rapidly to a complete online format.

At Salento's CLab, the generations of students prior to the corona outbreak traditionally worked on-site on idea generation, in business games or pitching their ideas and participating in idea challenges with companies. The CLab approach involves four distinct phases of inspiration and engagement (1), experimentation and development (2), idea concretization and pitching (3) and final business planning (4). A similar approach has been taken alongside a multistep design thinking process in the *Idea Forge* at University of Wuppertal. The aim of both the CLab format and the Idea Forge is to arrive at executable business ideas (in the example of Wuppertal extended to further consulting and coaching of individual start-up teams in the start-up centre). All these activities for students and together with regional stakeholders from start-ups, companies and institutions involved in start-up support had to be moved online at Salerno (and Wuppertal) and to be reconfigured following the lockdown of Italian universities and similar measures in Germany in spring 2020. In the CLab at Salerno, in particular Moodle and Microsoft Teams as teaching technologies have been used to customize and support entrepreneurial learning and education activities (ibid.). The most immediate requirement for entrepreneurship instructors in the CLab has been to redesign the programme and serve course contents to still function as an experiential entrepreneurial learning format. Typically, the programme runs over a period of 6 months with 5-hour contact time per week which had to be transformed to online as the crisis started.

The first phase of the programme—Inspiring and Engaging—and particularly the second phase, Experimenting and Developing, have been reshuffled to online by providing student information about the available digital technologies to be used including means of exchange and communication. This has been backed by support offers to familiarize participants with these digital tools and mastering their functions. Further, guidelines have been developed to navigate and enable collaborative learning around the activities in the initial phases of the programme. To prompt and stimulate the exploration of ideas, videos, website material and papers have been provided and circulated together with tutor support to structure the group discussions (e.g. around IoT, digital trends and the circular economy as idea sources). In particular, using both synchronous and asynchronous communication has been promoted to keep up discussion and collaboration. Further, Secundo et al. (ibid.) note that the function of entrepreneurship instructors changed into an even more prominent role as supporters of student teams exploring different potential entrepreneurial opportunities. In a further step (phase three), an online elevator pitch has been set up, including an elaborate process of training, coaching and pitch preparation before final pitching and feedback. The core pitch has been recorded by students at home and then uploaded to Google Drive for communication and sharing. Students could use posters and prototypes of product and service ideas in their videos. The final evaluation of pitch presentations and further coursework has been adapted (see ibid. for details). Correspondingly, a similar teaching and learning process has been employed in the final step (phase four) of business plan preparation and presentation of the entrepreneurial ideas that students developed in the prior phases of the CLab programme.

There are many more interesting aspects to this example presented in the original source. The most striking aspect appears to be that the entrepreneurship programme has been redesigned and performed in its novel online format by a straightforward use of existing standard technologies and tools. In the Idea Forge at Wuppertal, Zoom and particularly Miro have been used as software tools in course teaching. Miro offers the potential to design and structure an entire five-step design thinking process in a collaborative, virtual mind map experiences. The software enables students to add aspects to the Miro board and make changes, also allowing individual breakout sessions to portion and guide discussions in student teams and other ad hoc groups around the problem solutions and business ideas of student teams in different phases of the design thinking process. The approach to utilize existing technology and software suites to adapt to entrepreneurship teaching (backed by existing social media tools like Facebook or WhatsApp) may be interesting especially for HEIs which cannot afford to put substantial resources and investments in procuring sophisticated high-end technology platforms and software for all teaching disciplines.

## 5 Future Chances for Entrepreneurship Education and Requirements for Future Research Beyond the Current Pandemic

Before wrapping up the chapter, in the final section, some particularly fruitful ideas and avenues for the future will be highlighted. These ideas originate from the above discussion in the literature and the contemporary commitment of entrepreneurship educators and education researchers to continue the supply of quality entrepreneurship education also in a digital online domain in the crisis and beyond. With entrepreneurship education in the COVID-19 pandemic mainly obliged with adapting to online teaching technologies and corresponding university management tasks around our field (including the discussion in this chapter), little has been said as regards the re-conceptualization and further development of what we teach, i.e. the content of start-up and entrepreneurial management as well as entrepreneurship policy. A suggestion with much future potential for both education and research in entrepreneurship comes from Ratten (2020), proposing to appreciate and integrate much more concepts from crisis management and business resilience in entrepreneurship education in the face of crises such as the current pandemic. This seems particularly promising given a presumed lack of knowledge and studies on crisis management and new business resilience (Kuckertz et al., 2020). This path may help start-up founders from both universities and beyond in navigating the entrepreneurial venturing process.

A key ingredient in this thrust is to appreciate the fact that uncertain new venturing may run into turbulences and crises, both rooting from external shocks like natural disasters and originating from more individual survival challenges around founders. This requires taking the emotional and psychological site of entrepreneurship on board more strongly in the context of turbulent entrepreneurial crises. For example, Aly et al. (2021, 12) stress the need to combine the stream of discussion on "emotional challenges and hazards limiting and deterring entrepreneurs" with existing instruments of entrepreneurship policy which predominantly address economic considerations such as resource and know-how shortages of start-ups and their founders; and such entrepreneurship policy instruments only rarely address the psycho-emotional aspects relevant throughout individual start-up endeavours. Towards this end, "emotional intelligence skills and the health of entrepreneurs" (ibid.), which is particularly challenged in times of crisis, should gain space on the entrepreneurship education agenda. These elements of novel content in entrepreneurship education may even be connected to other current and future trends such as the debate on climate change, which in itself may encapsulate future "crisis moments" for society. Certainly, digital entrepreneurship teaching formats enhancing the outreach to interested participant audiences and students especially from non-business disciplines may be fuelled by contents relating to the above trends such as sustainable, social or green entrepreneurship.

Finally, in addition to reconsidering the menu of contents of entrepreneurship education in light of the COVID crisis and beyond, the crisis will also constitute a very sensible opportunity to thoroughly evaluate all the experimental, ad hoc approaches that currently evolve in online entrepreneurship training. This may be done in both qualitative and quantitative future research in entrepreneurship education. This opportunity has emerged around the need of entrepreneurship in higher education to go digital fast over the last 18 months and which will hold many interesting lessons for the future. We should take this as a chance to further improve the field of entrepreneurship education towards the digital sphere (blending it with effective in-person on-site entrepreneurship formats) as well as towards the young generation of digital natives as the prime audience of university education for young adults.

## References

Aly, M., Audretsch, D. B., & Grimm, H. (2021). Emotional skills for entrepreneurial success: The promise of entrepreneurship education and policy. *The Journal of Technology Transfer, 46*(5), 1611–1629. https://doi.org/10.1007/s10961-021-09866-1

Aucejo, E. M., et al. (2020). The impact of COVID-19 on student experiences and expectations: Evidence from a survey. *Journal of Public Economics, 191*, 104271. https://doi.org/10.1016/j.jpubeco.2020.104271

Bischoff, K., Volkmann, C. K., & Audretsch, D. B. (2018). Stakeholder collaboration in entrepreneurship education – An analysis of the entrepreneurial ecosystems of European higher educational institutions. *Journal of Technology Transfer, 43*(1), 20–46.

Carolan, C., et al. (2020). Covid 19: Disruptive impacts and transformative opportunities in undergraduate nurse education. *Nurse Education Practice, 46*, 102807. https://doi.org/10.1016/j.nepr.2020.102807

Chen, L., et al. (2021). Online and blended entrepreneurship education: A systematic review of applied educational technologies. *Entrepreneurship Education, 4*, 191–232.

Chirikov, I., et al. (2020). *Undergraduate and graduate students' mental health during the COVID-19 pandemic*. Berkeley Center for Studies in Higher Education. Retrieved August 25, 2021, from https://escholarship.org/uc/item/80k5d5hw

Crawford, J., et al. (2020). COVID-19: 20 countries' higher education intra-period digital pedagogy responses. *Journal of Applied Learning & Teaching, 3*(1), 9–28.

EU. (2015). *Supporting the entrepreneurial potential of higher education*. EU Commission Report.

EU (2021). *The impact of covid-19 on higher education: a review of emerging evidence*, Luxembourg.

Fayolle, A., & Gailly, B. (2008). From craft to science: Teaching models and learning processes in entrepreneurship education. *Journal of European Industrial Training, 32*(7), 569–593.

Garcia-Morales, V. J., et al. (2021). The transformation of higher education after the covid disruption: Emerging challenges in an online learning scenario. *Frontiers in Psychology, 12*(6), 616059. https://doi.org/10.3389/fpsyg.2021.616059

Gatti, T., et al. (2020). *Practices at Coimbra Group universities in response to the COVID-19: A collective reflection on the present and future of higher education in Europe*. Retrieved August 25, 2021, from https://www.coimbra-group.eu/wpcontent/uploads/Final-Report-Practices-at-CG-Universities-in-response-to-the-COVID-19.pdf

Grünhagen, M. (2017a). Johannes Kepler University Linz: Inspiring teaching and a support network for academic entrepreneurs. In C. K. Volkmann & D. B. Audretsch (Eds.), *Entrepreneurship education at universities - learning from twenty European cases* (pp. 515–536). Springer.

Grünhagen, M. (2017b). Erasmus University Rotterdam: Building the Erasmus Centre for entrepreneurship and advancing corporate entrepreneurship. In C. K. Volkmann & D. B. Audretsch (Eds.), *Entrepreneurship education at universities - learning from twenty European cases* (pp. 623–654). Springer.

Jensen, T. (2019). *Higher education in the digital era: The current state of transformation around the world*. International Association of Universities (IAU). Retrieved August 25, 2021, from https://www.iau-aiu.net/IMG/pdf/technology_report_2019.pdf

Kawamorita, H., et al. (2020). Entrepreneurial universities in times of crisis: The case of the covid-19 pandemic. *Journal of Entrepreneurship, Business and Economics, 8*(1), 77–88.

Kirby, D. A. (2004). Entrepreneurship education: Can business schools meet the challenge? *Education & Training, 46*(8/9), 510–519.

Krishnamurthy, S. (2020). The future of business education: A commentary in the shadow of the covid-19 pandemic. *Journal of Business Research, 117*(1), 1–5. https://doi.org/10.1016/j.jbusres.2020.05.034

Kuckertz, A., et al. (2020). Startups in times of crisis – A rapid response to the COVID-19 pandemic. *Journal of Business Venturing Insights, 13*, e00169. https://doi.org/10.1016/j.jbvi.2020.e00169

Laferriere, R., et al. (2019). Addressing cognitive challenges in applying design thinking for opportunity discovery: Reflections from a design thinking teaching team. *The Journal of Design, Economics, and Innovation, 5*(4), 383–386.

Liguori, E., & Winkler, C. (2020). From offline to online: Challenges and opportunities for entrepreneurship education following the COVID-19 pandemic. *Entrepreneurship Education and Pedagogy, 3*(4), 346–351.

Liguori, E., et al. (2021). Covid-19 and necessity-based online entrepreneurship education at US community colleges. *Journal of Small Business and Enterprise Development. preprint.*
Mahmood, N., et al. (2020). Bottom-up framework for experiential and project-based four-year BS entrepreneurship program: An intrapreneurial conceptualization. *Journal of Entrepreneurship Education, 23*(5), 112–129.
Marinoni, G., et al. (2020). *Global survey report the impact of COVID-19 on higher education around the world.* International Association of Universities. Retrieved 20 August 2021, from https://www.iauaiu.net/IMG/pdf/iau_covid19_and_he_survey_report_final_may_2020.pdf
Meahjohn, I., & Persad, P. (2020). The impact of covid-19 on entrepreneurship globally. *Journal of Economics and Business, 3*(3), 1165–1173.
Mishra, L., et al. (2020). Online teaching-learning in higher education during lockdown period of covid-19 pandemic. *International Journal of Educational Research Open, 1*, 100012. https://doi.org/10.1016/j.ijedro.2020.100012
OECD (2020). *Education responses to covid-19: Embracing digital learning and online collaboration. OECD Policy Responses to the Coronavirus (covid-19).* Paris. https://doi.org/10.1787/d75eb0e8-en.
Pinkwart, A. (1992). *Chaos und Unternehmenskrise*. Springer.
Pittaway, L., & Cope, J. (2007). Simulating entrepreneurial learning: Integrating experiential and collaborative approaches to learning. *Management Learning, 38*(2), 211–233.
Rae, D., et al. (2009). Creating an enterprise culture in a university: The role of an entrepreneurial learning team. *Industry and Higher Education, 23*(3), 183–197.
Ratten, V. (2020). The coronavirus (covid-19) and the entrepreneurship community. *Journal of Enterprising Communities, 14*(5), 753–764.
Ratten, V. (2020a). The coronavirus (covid-19) and entrepreneurship: Cultural, lifestyle and societal changes. *Journal of Entrepreneurship in Emerging Economies, 13*(4), 747–761. https://doi.org/10.1108/JEEE-06-2020-0163
Ratten, V., & Jones, P. (2021). Entrepreneurship and management education: Exploring trends and gaps. *The International Journal of Management Education, 19*(1) preprint.
Ribeiro, A. T., et al. (2020). Entrepreneurship education going remote: A response to Covid-19 restrictions. *Journal of Entrepreneurship Education, 23*(2), 1–9.
Rothaermel, F. T., et al. (2009). University entrepreneurship: A taxonomy of the literature. *Industrial and Corporate Change., 16*, 691–791.
Secondo, G., et al. (2021). Threat or opportunity? A case study of digital-enabled redesign of entrepreneurship education in the COVID-19 emergency. *Technology Forecasting and Social Change, 166*, 120565. https://doi.org/10.1016/j.techfore.2020.120565
Takemoto, T., & Oe, H. (2021). Entrepreneurship education at universities: Challenges and future perspectives on online game implementation. *Entrepreneurship Education, 4*, 19–27.
Williams, T. A., et al. (2017). Organizational response to adversity: Fusing crisis management and resilience research streams. *Academy of Management Annuals, 11*, 733–769.
World Bank (2020). *Tertiary education and COVID-19: Impact and mitigation strategies in Europe and Central Asia, World Bank.* Retrieved on 25 August 2021, from http://documents1.worldbank.org/curated/en/783451590702592897/COVID-19-Impacton-Tertiary-Education-in-Europe-and-Central-Asia.pdf
Zhu, N., et al. (2020). A novel coronavirus from patients with pneumonia in China, 2019. *New England Journal of Medicine, 382*, 8.

**Christine K. Volkmann** is a professor of economics and holds the UNESCO Chair of Entrepreneurship and Intercultural Management at the Schumpeter School of Business and Economics at the University of Wuppertal. Her research, teaching, and transfer activities are based on the UN's Sustainable Development Goals and promote sustainable and responsible entrepreneurial thinking and acting.

**Marc Grünhagen**, Ph.D., is a researcher in entrepreneurship at the Schumpeter School of Business and Economics, University of Wuppertal, Germany. Marc's research interests are in entrepreneurship policy and university entrepreneurship. He teaches entrepreneurial management and economics. Before joining academia, Marc has worked as an investment manager of a venture capital fund.

# Index





D. B. Audretsch, I. A. M. Kunadt (eds.), *The COVID-19 Crisis and Entrepreneurship*, International Studies in Entrepreneurship 54,
https://doi.org/10.1007/978-3-031-04655-1